W9-BZT-057

FÊTE ACCOMPLI!

THE ULTIMATE GUIDE TO CREATIVE ENTERTAINING

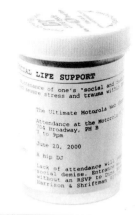
...CIAL LIFE SUPPORT

...fficience of one's "social and...
...n severe stress and trauma with...

The Ultimate Motorola Web...

Attendance at the Motorola...
164 Broadway, PH B
7 to 9pm

June 20, 2000

A hip DJ

Lack of attendance wil...
social demise. Entranc...
without an RSVP to Din...
Harrison & Shriftman

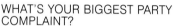

dear lara,
Thank you so mu...
be a part of such a l...
it was truely an...
that exuded such clas...
"good energy." ☺ i ha...
... and what can...
my watch!! it is so be...

Thank you Lara ...

hope to see y...
all my lov...

WHAT'S YOUR BIGGEST PARTY COMPLAINT?

- DAVID COPPERFIELD: "SMOKERS. AT A PARTY IT'S HARD TO GET AWAY FROM SMOKE. I HATE THE SMELL OF IT AND I HATE LEAVING A PARTY AND HAVING MY CLOTHES SMELL LIKE THEY WERE USED TO MOP DOWN THE BAR AT LOTUS."

- DUCHESS OF YORK: "WAITING IN LINE FOR COATS, FOOD, LAVATORIES, . . . WAITING IN LINE FOR ANYTHING."

- LARA FLYNN BOYLE: "GROUND THAT IS UNKIND TO STILETTOS."

- MICHAEL KORS: "VIP ROOMS THAT ARE FILLED WITH NON-VIPS."

Jennifer Aniston
Brad Pitt
Cameron Diaz
Ben Affleck
Julia Roberts
Hugh Grant

FÊTE ACCOMPLI!

THE ULTIMATE GUIDE TO CREATIVE ENTERTAINING

WRITTEN AND LIVED BY
LARA SHRIFTMAN & ELIZABETH HARRISON
AND KAREN ROBINOVITZ

CLARKSON POTTER/PUBLISHERS
NEW YORK

COPYRIGHT © 2004 BY
LARA SHRIFTMAN, ELIZABETH
HARRISON, AND KAREN ROBINOVITZ

ALL RIGHTS RESERVED. NO PART OF
THIS BOOK MAY BE REPRODUCED OR
TRANSMITTED IN ANY FORM OR BY ANY
MEANS, ELECTRONIC OR MECHANICAL,
INCLUDING PHOTOCOPYING,
RECORDING, OR BY ANY INFORMATION
STORAGE AND RETRIEVAL SYSTEM,
WITHOUT PERMISSION IN WRITING
FROM THE PUBLISHER.

PUBLISHED BY CLARKSON POTTER/
PUBLISHERS, NEW YORK, NEW YORK.
MEMBER OF THE CROWN PUBLISHING
GROUP, A DIVISION OF RANDOM
HOUSE, INC.
WWW.CROWNPUBLISHING.COM

CLARKSON N. POTTER IS A
TRADEMARK AND POTTER AND
COLOPHON ARE REGISTERED
TRADEMARKS OF RANDOM
HOUSE, INC.

PRINTED IN THE UNITED STATES
OF AMERICA

LIBRARY OF CONGRESS CATALOGING-
IN-PUBLICATION DATA
HARRISON, ELIZABETH.
    FÊTE ACCOMPLI! : THE ULTIMATE
GUIDE TO CREATIVE ENTERTAINING /
ELIZABETH HARRISON, LARA
SHRIFTMAN, AND KAREN ROBINOVITZ.
1. ENTERTAINING. 2. COOKERY.
3. MENUS. I. SHRIFTMAN, LARA.
II. ROBINOVITZ, KAREN. III. TITLE.
TX731.H35   2004
642'4—DC22   2003020794

ISBN 1-4000-4748-X

10 9 8 7 6 5 4 3 2

FIRST EDITION

ACKNOWLEDGMENTS

Special thanks to Marysarah Quinn, the creative director at Clarkson Potter, for being so helpful, supportive, and inspirational and for always being there throughout this entire project. We couldn't have done it without you; you're a goddess. And thanks to Christy Fletcher, our book agent at Fletcher and Parry.

Thanks to all of the New York, L.A., and Miami Harrison & Shriftman staff, especially: Kim Pappas (for working so hard, and for being so dedicated, brilliant, and helpful), Vanessa Poskanzer (for your undying support and love), Eliane Henri, Erika Koopman, Gretchen Braun, Jamie Scott, Kate McCusker, Dabney Mercer, Ashley Kraines, Jenelle Chinn (for always being so great), Jordana Zakim (for all of your research), and interns Jamie Alter, Jane Oster, Kourtney Kachler, Frederick Sykes, Meredith Frisco, Samantha Rosenberg, and Teresa Harris.

Thanks to Elana Posner for your support and inspiration forever, as well as your help with the visuals. We couldn't have done it without you. You saved our lives and our photo shoots!

Thanks to Paul Costello, photographer extraordinaire. (You styled everything immaculately and gave us so much of your valuable time and energy. We appreciate you—beyond!) And thanks to our other genius photographers, Patrick McMullan (for your great tips and your continual support and friendship), Cesare Bonazza (the Barbie party was so much fun), Devon Jarvis, Sara Jaye Weiss, and Seth Browarnik. Thanks to WireImage photographers Amy Graves, Denise Truscello, Donato Sardella, and Lester Cohen, and especially Jeff Vespa for setting up all the great shots at our events and always being so amazing to work with.

Thanks to Adam Keen; Adam Nelson; Amy Larocca from *New York Magazine,* for that "Sales and Bargains" inspiration; Ann Jones; Anne Slowey, for the five-year plan; Ari Howoritz; Barton G.; BBT; Ben Leventhal; Bertille Glass at Master Foods; Cary Richardson of Cary's Cooks; Cary Songy; Christine and John Gachot; David Copperfield; Edmundo Macais; Eric Buterbaugh, for his beautiful flowers and beautiful tips; Erin Hosler; George Wayne, for introducing LS to CF; Geyer Kosisnski, Grif Frost; Hugh Crickmore; Ian, Rita, Sophia, and Ava Schrager; Jason Binn; Jaques Wizman; Jay Penske; Jeanie Pyun; Jennifer DeFilippi at Random House; J. T. McKay; Jeffrey Chodorow; Joe Dance; Jonathan Shriftman, for being the best brother and inspiration ever; Keith Robbins; Kristin Von Augtrop; LFB, for all the toasts, tips, support, and love; Laura Palese at Random House; Lyle Kula; Maggie Goudsmit; Marco Macioni; Mary Alice Haney; Mary Parent; Michael Davis, for always being so supportive; Michael Michele; Michael Robertson; Olivier Cheng; Jenny Glasgow and Heidi Van Evenhoven from Olivier Cheng Catering & Events; Peter Morton; Rachel Zalis, for putting up with the Blackberry 24/7 and being a great friend; Richie Notar; June Fujise; Jessica Issacs, Nobu's amazing pastry chef; Erica Matsunaga; Joanne Takahashi from Nobu; Robin Maguire, for the best tips and all of your samples; Sam Firer; Sara Ruffin; Sarita Tabarez; Shelley Zalis; Karen Brown and the staff at OTX Research; Stephannie Barba; Steve Carson at La Conversation; Stephen Dorff; Steven Hall; Tammy Blake and Tina Constable at Random House; Tamara Beckwith; and Taylor Stein.

Special thanks to all of our amazing parents for always entertaining us.

CONCEPTS

LOCATIONS

INVITATIONS

PRODUCTION

BEVERAGES

FOOD

DESSERTS

ETIQUETTE

RESOURCES

CONTENTS

INTRODUCTION 8

ONE: GETTING STARTED
READY, SET, PLAN! 12

TWO: WHERE'S THE PARTY?
LOCATION, LOCATION, LOCATION 22

THREE: YOU'RE INVITED!
DON'T FORGET TO RSVP! 36

FOUR: PARTY PRODUCTION
SET THE STAGE 60

FIVE: WE'LL DRINK TO THAT
QUENCH YOUR THIRST IN STYLE 86

SIX: FOOD, GLORIOUS FOOD
EAT IT! JUST EAT IT! 110

SEVEN: SWEET TOOTH
DIET, SHMIET! 126

EIGHT: OH, BEHAVE!
MIND YOUR MANNERS 140

NINE: ANALYZE THIS!
CASE STUDIES TO STUDY 160

TEN: EAT, DRINK & BE MERRY
RECIPES GALORE 204

EVENT BUDGET TEMPLATE
CALCULATE THE COST OF YOUR ULTIMATE PARTY 248

ELEVEN: OUR YELLOW PAGES
ALL THE CONTACTS YOU EVER WANTED BUT WERE AFRAID
TO ASK FOR 250

INDEX 269

INTRODUCTION

THE SCENE: A swanky party. White roses are in full bloom. Champagne's a-flowing. Lighting is sultry. Hors d'oeuvres—the type that involve some sort of puff pastry situation and pungent cheeses—are passed by beautiful servers wearing fashionably tailored tuxes. Conversations about this season's hot new boot and the stock market fly. And everyone in the room is trying not to stare at the stunning, six-foot-tall brunette, clad in nothing but sheer organza.

It's lavish. It's posh. It's—er—expensive.

It's the exclusive type of gathering you read about in magazines. In the tony social world of celebrities, where the well-heeled and attractively employed (and married) sip '82 Lafite on a Gulfstream V private jet, entertaining is a full-time job, something that takes months of planning. Sometimes years. It involves having a serious party planner and, more important, a serious budget.

We should know. We have been passionate about entertaining for as long as we can remember. Among the three of us, we have more than fifty years of professional experience entertaining millions of people, whether we were throwing film premieres, fashion shows, store openings, product launch parties, record release bashes, A-list celebrity soirees, or charity balls, or crashing the gatherings our parents hosted when we were little kids.

Elizabeth Harrison and Lara Shriftman met through a fashion editor friend, hit it off, and decided to start their own business. In 1995 they opened Harrison & Shriftman, a public relations, special events, and marketing firm. Elizabeth's graphic designer friend named the company and her aunt created the logo. Lara's printer printed the letterhead for free. And with a $5,000 loan from Lara's parents, they were set. They began by working out of Lara's apartment, but that didn't last long because Elizabeth couldn't deal with the fact that there was only one phone line and Lara got two hundred calls a day.

So Lara found a penthouse office on Madison Avenue for only $500 per month (a steal in New York City). At the onset, they had one major client: Gucci Timepieces. Soon their reputation grew, as did their retainer client list and events department. Their events have been featured in the pages of every national magazine (*W, Vogue, Harper's Bazaar, InStyle, Elle, New York*) and on television shows like *E! Entertainment News, Entertainment Tonight,* and *Access Hollywood.*

The demand for their services became so great that they opened offices in Los Angeles and Miami, and now they're known for organizing the most glamorous affairs, such as film premieres for big blockbusters like *Charlie's Angels* and *Bridget Jones's Diary*; charity balls for AMFAR; fashion shows for Oscar de la Renta and Celine; store openings for Jimmy Choo, Hogan, Roberto Cavalli, and Michael Kors; product launches for Mercedes-Benz, Motorola, Van Cleef & Arpels, and Cartier; and big bashes for hotel openings and celebrities like Puff Daddy, Jay-Z, and Matt Damon.

At one of their events, Lara and Elizabeth met

Karen Robinovitz, a writer who often covers posh parties for publications like the *New York Times* "Sunday Styles" section, *Elle, Harper's Bazaar, InStyle,* and *Marie Claire.* Karen has always been obsessed with parties. In the sixth grade, she invited a gaggle of girls over for a slumber party, where she asked her mother to make steak tartare and Brie pizzas instead of ordering in pizza and grilling up burgers. Then, her father piled all the girls into a minivan and took them to see *The Rocky Horror Picture Show.* Karen even provided each guest with a backpack full of goodies (toilet paper, rice, flashlights) and instructions for when and how to use them.

It's no surprise that she now makes a living by observing the most marvelous affairs—and by taking notes on every minute detail, from the center-pieces and napkin rings to the lighting, music, food, and of course what everyone's wearing. From New York to Paris, one aspect of Karen's job as a reporter involves simply going to parties. She has picked up so many tips along the way that she herself has become an entertaining pro.

After working the party circuit for so many years, we were constantly being asked questions about how to make a party special. Our friends wanted to know what they should do for their birthday bashes; where they could find good paper for invitations (and what the invitations should say); how to plan a menu; how to figure out the amount of alcohol and food necessary to satiate a crowd of five, ten, fifty, or five hundred; the secrets to protecting their precious furniture from wine stains; what kind of music to play during cocktail hour; and all sorts of random questions.

It occurred to us that there is real value in teaching people how to throw parties. Parties are the sin-gle best way to meet new people, connect with old friends, celebrate a monumental occasion, promote an aspect of your business, and just have fun. And that is why we decided to write this book, which serves as a guide to giving your friends, family, and colleagues a good time and provides instructions for creative entertaining in style. Because we've organized countless parties and been invited to more than we can begin to count, we have Rolodexes full of contacts, drawers and drawers of ideas, and more information, insider secrets, and chic tips than we know what to do with.

Hollywood premieres and socialite soirees aside, entertaining—the act of amusing others and throwing a good party—does not require the bank account of an heiress. Nor does it require hiring a well-connected circle of professional planners and serving food with names you can't even pro-nounce. You don't have to be the wife of a big shot, a New York City fashion publicist, or Madonna. Anyone can be the perfect host(ess) and make an impact with the kind of party people will remember forever. And, as far as we're concerned, there's always a reason to celebrate: birthdays, anniver-saries, premieres of your favorite TV show, Bastille Day, the full moon, even just because it's Wednesday.

Like a tour guide, we will walk you through every step of party production. The chapters are organ-ized in the same order we follow when we throw parties of our own. We will begin by showing you the importance of creating a concept, which is the focal point of the party and the mood it evokes. Before you start inviting anyone to your party, you have to figure out what kind of party you want and then work from there. For instance, do you want to have a sit-down dinner for fifty, a manicure-pedicure party for your best friend who's having a baby, a wild night of dancing until 5 A.M., or a hangover brunch to heal your friends after a night of debauchery?

It is the concept that dictates the location, invitations, décor, drinks, food, music, and little extras that make the party special. Without knowing what kind of party you're throwing and what it's for, it's impossible to create the perfect ambiance, menu choices, and sound track. Chapter One focuses solely on concepts: how to create one, ideas for theme parties, and making (and sticking to) a budget you can afford.

Once you have settled on your concept, we will show you how to find a location for your party, whether it's in your living room, at a nearby nightclub, on a patch of sand at the local beach, or in a little Indian restaurant in an off-the-beaten-path neighborhood. We'll teach you our secret (and efficient) negotiating skills to use when you're setting up shop in a restaurant, club, rented mansion, chartered yacht, hotel suite, bowling alley, or anywhere outside of your own home.

In Chapter Three, we delve into everything you need to know about who to invite and how to invite them. Remember, a party is only as good as the guests. Everyone we've interviewed about parties has said the same thing: It's all about the people.

Once your guest list is settled, you can think about invitations. These are the first impression of your party. So it's important to make them sharp, as they will set the mood for what guests can expect from your event. There are three basic types of invitations: classic, funky, and kitschy-gimmicky. We will show you the art of custom ordering, buying off the rack, and designing at home, with computer tricks that will make it look like you've spent thousands on stationery. After all, creating a chic invitation doesn't have to mean charging up a storm at Cartier. We'll teach you calligraphy tricks, the inside scoop on what your invitation should say, and inventive alternatives for sending fun invitations that double as gifts. Our invitation chapter covers layouts, fonts, how to make your envelopes stand out in a crowd, and post office rules to live by. In addition, we will showcase save-the-date and response cards and show you samples of our own invitations, which are like little pieces of party décor in a package.

As a host, your job is to be the party's producer. In Chapter Four, we show you how to create the overall vibe of your party and how to make it reflect the concept. Production involves designing the space; creating the décor; thinking about flowers, lighting, music, gift bags, and cheap tricks—the extra-special touches and sophisticated strategies that make your party stand out. Our ideas cover the bases from classic, traditional options to wacky, innovative ones. Whether you keep the feel of the party all white and clean with nothing more than white flowers and white candles for decoration or you go all out to transform a space into a bubblegum-pink fantasy land, producing a party means paying keen attention to every detail. But don't fret. It's not as difficult as it may sound. We will break everything into easy steps. Quench your thirst with a bevy of beverages in Chapter Five. Drinks are always a pivotal point of any party. They're conversation stimulants ("So, have you tried that pineapple punch?"). Plus, they give guests a reason to linger longer. That said, our ode to beverages features an easy-to-follow chart to help you figure out how much alcohol to buy for each guest. We'll go over all of the necessary ingredients for a home bar, tools of the trade, and we'll give you the lowdown on service, from hiring bartenders and/or cocktail waitresses to offering bottle service at tables or a do-it-yourself bar.

People always go to parties hungry, so even if you're having a simple cocktail party with just wine and champagne, you need to have a little something for everyone to nibble, which can range from high (caviar, anyone?) to low (please pass the P B & J doughnut sandwiches!). We stuffed the food chapter with the kind of yummy tips multistar executive chefs swear by, sophisticated serving options, and information about landmark establishments around the country that deliver gourmet goods to your doorstep. When you finish the food chapter, we'll cure your sugar cravings by feeding you simple dessert how-to's, such as making grocery-store purchases appear chic, and building cakes out of layers of doughnuts, Twinkies, and candy.

Just when you think you're finished with all of the party planning, however, there's still one more important factor to think about: etiquette. What good is being a perfect host (or a guest) if you don't know how to behave? Chapter Eight educates you on the basics of good party behavior—for hosts and for guests. This chapter will also give you the skinny on introducing people to one another in a way that isn't awkward, on dealing with friends who might have had too much to drink, and on writing the perfect thank-you note.

Then to show you how to string everything together, we provide an entire chapter of case studies, a scrapbook of some of our best parties. Each case study illustrates one party from beginning to end, detailing everything we bought, made, and mixed to come up with a tasty drink menu; delicious food choices that fed into our concepts; the kind of music we played to set the right mood; and the cheap tricks that made it complete. It is the ultimate shopping list for any party, with a clear instruction sheet from A to Z that includes how we created a concept, found a location, came up with the perfect invitations, and embellished the décor. You may want to use this chapter as a resource for ideas or as a template for a party just like one of ours.

The recipe chapter shares more than fifty of our favorite drink and food recipes, which we've gathered over the years while frequenting restaurants, interviewing caterers, and having tastings before events we've planned.

In the very last section of the book, we organized a list of all the resources you'd ever need. We call it "Our Yellow Pages." It's a compilation of all of the vendors we swear by, which many a party lover would kill for.

Parties are the focal point of each of our lives, professionally and personally. We put our life's work—and love—into this book. The ideas we share are amazing for parties of any size or occasion. Some of our thoughts are sophisticated and elegant, while others are offbeat and out-of-the-box. No matter what style you follow, you are sure to have fun.

Let the party begin!

CHAPTER ONE
GETTING STARTED
READY, SET, PLAN!

GETTING STARTED
READY, SET, PLAN!

So, you want to throw a party?

There are invitations, guest lists, and menus to think about. You have to find a location, pick the perfect outfit, and you still have to take care of the décor, lighting, sound system, and something else . . . something else . . . but . . . you can't remember! It's easy to get carried away, stressing over every minor detail of what goes into making a party special. There are so many things that can get overlooked, like having enough toilet paper or making sure you have enough ice. So before you freak out, call it quits, and seek solace in retail therapy (new shoes!), take a deep breath and remember this: The first step to throwing a fabulous affair is recognizing that you're able.

This chapter will help you organize your party, so it doesn't become daunting. So before you plan away, you should ask yourself these basic questions.

1. WHAT IS YOUR PARTY FOR?

Is it someone's birthday, anniversary, or bridal shower? Is it a holiday (Halloween, Christmas, Kwanzaa, New Year's, Memorial Day, Purim, to name a few), the sad time of year when your favorite sitcom is having its season finale, or a work event? Although it may seem obvious, figuring out what your party is for gives it a focus, which will enable you to organize everything.

PARIS HILTON, ALEX VON FURSTENBERG, NICKY HILTON, RENA SINDI, AND ANH DUONG AT CHRIS HEINZ'S AND LARA SHRIFTMAN'S BIRTHDAY AT SUITE 16. PHOTO COURTESY OF PATRICK McMULLAN/PMc.

2. WHAT KIND OF PARTY DO YOU WANT?

A lunch, a friendly afternoon of tea, a sophisticated cocktail party, a casual dinner for fifty, a swinging singles bash for hundreds, manicures and martinis with fifteen friends? The reason behind your party might dictate the type of party you have. Think about it. A crazy, swinging night of dancing until 5:00 A.M. might not be the way to go if you're celebrating your recent promotion—with your boss . . . and your boss's boss.

3. HOW MANY GUESTS ARE YOU INVITING?

This sets the tone for the kind of event you're having. A small intimate dinner for ten is totally different from dessert and dancing for five hundred (or even fifty). The number of guests will also help you narrow down locations for your event because you may not be able to accommodate thirty people in your home. It will also help you figure out what kind of party you can afford, given your budget. Just remember: A dinner for twenty and cocktails for two hundred can wind up costing the same amount of money.

4. WHAT TIME WILL YOUR PARTY BEGIN?

Will your event be an afternoon affair with lunch, or an evening cocktail party? Dinner bells sound at 7:00 P.M., 8:00 P.M., or even 9:00 P.M. You can have a two-tiered affair that begins with an 8:00 P.M. sit-down dinner for sixty and dancing for two hundred more guests after 10:00 P.M., a crazy late-night soiree that goes from 10:00 on, or an after-hours, 4:00 A.M. breakfast feast with sugar cereal, an omelet bar, and pancakes galore. The time of the party directly affects the kind of party you're having. For instance, if you're having a family affair and your grandma needs to be in bed by 9:00 P.M., you might want to plan a daytime lunch or tea rather than dinner.

CHIC TIP YOU NEVER WANT YOUR PARTY TO BE TOO LONG (SIX HOURS IS USUALLY PUSHING IT). IT'S BETTER FOR YOUR GUESTS TO LEAVE WANTING MORE THAN TO LINGER ON AND GET BORED.

5. WHAT IS YOUR BUDGET?

Be realistic and map out how much you want to spend on your event. Decide what you can afford, make a list of every element involved in your party, and allot a certain amount of money for each area, depending on what you want and what you don't. Once you tally your total budget number, figure out what is most important to you. Is your invitation everything or is it all about a really expensive, decadent birthday cake? There's no right answer. The only rule you need to follow is this: Whatever is the most important aspect of your party (to you), make sure you have the funds to cover it. The worst thing that can happen is sending out a fantastic invitation, making the décor perfect, and then coming up short in the food department (for an elegant dinner!) because you ran out of money. We'll go into detail about budgets later in this chapter and we give you a master template on pages 248–49.

6. WHERE IS YOUR SOIREE?

At home, a swanky lounge, a new boîte? Do you want to track down an empty warehouse, set up cocktail tables and plush seating in a park or on a beach, or do something more unusual, say, at a gallery, a museum, or a movie theater? We will give you a list of great location ideas in Chapter Two.

7. ARE YOU SENDING A CASUAL OR FORMAL INVITATION?

Is it an e-mail, fax, phone call, or something that requires more ceremony and perhaps some calligraphy? You have to tell each guest you're having a party, right? So you need to let them know the details of your party somehow, but it's up to you to decide if you want to order custom stationery, make invitations at home, or buy something already packaged from a stationery store. An invitation sets the tone of the party because, if done well, when your guests receive it, it will give them an idea of what kind of party you're having: something formal, something casual, something wild. It's a clear indication of what vibe your entire party will evoke. We will cover more of this in Chapter Three.

8. WHAT KIND OF PRODUCTION IS INVOLVED?

Think décor, lighting, music, gift bags, the extra touches that make your party stand out, and valet parking (even if it's your friend's brother manning the keys). Will you be reorganizing your home, renting furniture, searching for accessories like candles, lights, and tabletop accoutrements? Are you arranging flowers or hiring someone to do it for you? Will you be designing place cards for seating assignments? These sorts of things need to fit into your budget and the general feel of your party. Later we will go into more details about décor, which include design, lighting, and music.

9. WHAT ARE YOU DRINKING?

Are you setting up a bar at home, creating a martini salon, sticking to an ethnic theme, serving wine and champagne only, or going nonalcoholic? The drinks have to mirror your concept and fit into your budget. For instance, at a lunch party, you might want to offer only water, iced tea, lemonade, wine, coffee, and tea. If you're having a martini and cigar night, you'll need to invest in vodka, gin, and vermouth. If it's the Super Bowl, stock up on beer—and decide if you want to serve bottles or cans, exotic imports or American classics. Once you plan a drink menu, you need to think about how you want the drinks to be served. Do you want to hire a bartender and/or cocktail waitresses? Or is everything do-it-yourself, with bottles of alcohol and mixers on tables and at the bar, so each person can mix and match his or her own potions? See Chapter Five for more information.

10. WHAT KIND OF FOOD ARE YOU SERVING?

Like the bar menu, the food has to fit into your budget and reflect your concept. That may mean hors d'oeuvres, five decadent courses, a buffet, just desserts, birthday cake only, or even glamorously presented fast food. You also need to think about a waitstaff—or rather, decide whether or not you want one—as well as how you want to serve your food. There are two main serving options: placed (the food is placed on tables or presented in a buffet) and passed (servers pass through the crowd with trays of finger food). We cover more on this in Chapter Six.

11. HOW DO YOU PLAN TO MAKE YOUR PARTY EXTRA SPECIAL?

Enhance your concept with something as simple as sparklers on a birthday cake (and blasting the *Star Wars* theme when the cake makes its debut) or providing Polaroid or disposable cameras (in chic glass cylinders) at each table.

You may want to hire entertainment—a palm reader or even a Tupperware Lady—to entertain your guests over cocktails. Or you could just invite a surprise guest, such as your town's mayor, a celebrity lookalike, or someone famous, to pop in and stir things up.

A concept is born

Once you answer these questions, your concept should be ready to go. If it's not, don't worry; go back to question one: What is your party for? We've had parties for the most professional reasons—to launch products; celebrate the opening of a new store; invite trendsetters to sample the menu of a hot, new restaurant—and for the most ridiculous reasons: to see friends we haven't hung out with in a few months and paint pottery on a Sunday afternoon. If you can't think of a reason to party, then have a party for that . . . and call it a no-reason-at-all ball. The thing is, there are countless reasons to have a party aside from the tried-and-true staples, like birthdays, showers, bachelorette parties, and traditional holidays like Halloween, Christmas, Kwanzaa, New Year's, Valentine's Day, St. Patrick's Day, Memorial Day, July 4, Bastille Day, Labor Day, Jewish New Year, Passover, and Easter. But why not do something different, like celebrate your half-birthday or one of those esoteric holidays, like Secretaries' Day (pad and pencil, mandatory), All Saints' Day (dress as a saint—or a sinner), or Mardi Gras (buy everyone the kind of colorful plastic beads that people go crazy for on the streets of New Orleans during Mardi Gras festivities). Find any reason at all to bring people together and throw a party.

One winter, we were at a restaurant known for its diverse wine list. We had no idea which bottle to pick. The menu was as overwhelming as a tax return. Because we didn't know as much about wine as we would have liked, we thought, *Why not have a wine-tasting party?* And a new party concept was born. We asked our friend Lyle, a wine consultant, to give a wine-tasting lesson to a group of thirty in the groovy loft where one of our friends lived. And we went from there, blending everything—from the invitation to the gift we gave our guests on their way out—with our concept. We sent invitations that looked like they had been stained by a glass of Merlot (a computer-savvy friend designed it for us). Before the party, Lyle gave us a list of the wines we would taste and he described the flavor of each, so we could decorate the table with things that would complement each wine: We placed chips of smoked wood near the woodsy wine, dried gooseberries near the wine that boasted a gooseberry taste, and glass cylinders with apples near the fruity wine from Australia. We served light appetizers that enhanced the flavor of each wine and by midnight, we were so loopy that we decided to order in pizza. To keep up our sophisticated, "adult" concept, we cut the slices into bite-size pieces and served them on sleek chrome trays with toothpicks. And when the guests left, we sent each of them off with a bottle of aspirin to help prevent any hangovers.

Having a clear idea of what your party is for will lead you to a concept and enable you to narrow the focus for each and every aspect of your party. It helps you figure out how you want to follow through with your ideas and make the magic happen.

THERE ARE 365 REASONS TO HAVE A PARTY, ONE FOR EACH DAY OF THE YEAR. THESE ARE SOME OF OUR FAVORITE EXCUSES TO PARTY

- An anniversary
- The six-month mark since you quit smoking or stopped a bad Diet Coke habit
- The first day of fall
- Super Bowl Sunday
- Your all-time-favorite film is on television
- It's spring and you can finally stop bulking up with chunky sweaters
- You want to get rid of the clothes you no longer wear. Instruct each guest to bring their old frocks, then gossip and swap. One girl's trash is another girl's treasure.
- Gandhi's birthday (October 2)
- The winter equinox
- A full moon (howling optional)
- Mercury's in retrograde
- The Academy Awards
- Your favorite TV show is starting after a summer hiatus
- You want to learn something new, like sewing, cooking, cake decorating, yoga, or painting pottery
- You just quit your job after years of dreaming of having the guts to
- You got a promotion at work
- It's Wednesday
- *Hola,* it's Cinco de Mayo
- You're newly single
- To break in the new barbecue
- Your favorite band just released a new album (call it a record-release bash)
- Because you have nothing else to do

One year, Lara wanted to have a huge blowout birthday party with her friend Tamara, and we wanted an over-the-top, outrageously sassy concept. We thought of a decorative theme, a recurring motif that matches the concept and runs throughout the course of the party. A theme is a fun way to tie your party together. It gives the event a point of view and makes for excellent conversation. The theme should show up on invitations and tabletops, in the aesthetic of the space, in the drink and food selections and music, and everywhere in between.

For Lara's bash, our theme was Barbie and Ken. We invited sixty people for a sit-down dinner and then three hundred more for dancing and cocktails. We sent out a bubblegum-pink invitation with a big image of Barbie on the front.

Before the party, everyone became obsessed with what kind of getup they were going to wear. And at the party, which was held at a chic restaurant in Los Angeles, everything was pink and girlie: Pink helium balloons covered the ceiling like deliciously puffy clouds, the tablecloths and napkins were a vibrant pink, Barbie bracelets doubled as napkin rings, and pink paper menus waited at each place setting. Everyone dressed as their favorite Barbie (Marilyn Barbie, bad-girl Barbie, Hawaiian Barbie, and loads of Kens) and everywhere you turned, there were dollhouse accessories, Barbie-doll centerpieces, and flower arrangements with Barbie dolls glued to the vases. It was a dreamy fantasy world with ice sculptures lit up with pink lights, and Barbie lollipops for everyone. We had the best time getting innovative about décor ideas and drink menus, and finding candy in shades of pink (we even special-ordered M&Ms in pink), all of which were extensions of Barbie life. For tips on re-creating this party, check out the complete case study, beginning on page 166.

Think of a concept and theme as an experience you want to give your guests and turn anything you like—sports, fondue, tree decorating before Christmas, Arabian nights, glam rock music, mobsters, 1930s Paris—into a party. You can take people to an exotic country by basing the concept and theme on China, Japan, Tibet, India, or Italy, by serving food indigenous to that area, and by creating an ambiance to match. And you can give your guests more than one experience in a night by blending more than one concept or theme, such as having a pottery painting and cooking party or a manicure and movie night.

Some of our favorite concepts and themes include going western (bust out the ole cowboy boots and call your night a hoedown); toga times (make sexy togas with sheets or wear designer Grecian-inspired frocks with a homemade crown of hand-picked leaves in your hair—just don't rent *Animal House* for pointers!); getting naughty with a leather-and-lace or red-light-district theme (think bordello décor and burlesque dancers); and buying or renting an at-home karaoke machine (or renting out a karaoke bar) and Barry Manilow the night away. You can invite people to dress as their favorite celebrity, superhero, glam rock-and-roll star, or cartoon character—and make everything about the party represent that world. Try having an "era party," for which you pick a decade (twenties, fifties, seventies, eighties), dress the part, and design the space (and music playlist) to represent it, as if your affair were a time capsule.

WHAT DO YOU LOOK FOR WHEN YOU GO TO A PARTY?

- DAVID COPPERFIELD: "TO RELAX AND KICK BACK AND HAVE A GOOD TIME. UNLESS IT'S AN INDUSTRY THING, I'M LOOKING FOR SOME DOWNTIME WITH FRIENDS."

- DUCHESS OF YORK: "SPACE TO SIT WITHOUT DISCO MUSIC IN YOUR EARS SO YOU CAN SPEAK."

- LARA FLYNN BOYLE: "I NEVER LOOK; JUST LISTEN FOR LAUGHTER."

- MICHAEL KORS: "TO LAUGH, GOSSIP, AND MEET SOMEONE NEW WHO IS INTRIGUING."

- DONALD TRUMP: "A GREAT TIME AND, ABOVE ALL, GREAT PEOPLE."

- AERIN LAUDER: "TO SEE GOOD FRIENDS."

HERE ARE SOME OF THE BEST IDEAS WE'VE DREAMED UP OVER THE YEARS

- **A FASHION "FAUX PAS-TY"**
No matter what the occasion, make sure your guests know that they should arrive wearing their biggest fashion flubs—any outdated, tacky, or ill-fitting ensemble. We did this once for *Glamour* magazine because in every issue, the back-page article, called "Glamour Dont's," featured women wearing outfits that were all wrong, along with black bars over their eyes in order to disguise their identities. The whole theme was based on "Dont's." We served things we'd normally never be caught dead eating, like squeeze cheese. We dared to put carnations on the table in plastic cups. The only "do" was the gift bag, which included the best mascara, hand lotion, lip balm, hair products, and a T-shirt.

- **OLD-SCHOOL SLUMBER PARTY**
You can take everyone back to sixth grade with an old-fashioned slumber party. For one slumber party we asked everyone to bring sleeping bags. We gave each person a warm, snuggly blanket, along with junk food like peanut butter and Fluff sandwiches. We chatted, tried out facial masks, and spent the night watching chick flicks.

- **COLOR PARTIES**
Choose one color—red, white, black, blue, green, orange, pink—and make sure it's every-where: the invitation, tabletop accessories, candles, lightbulbs, drinks, and food. Don't admit any guest who isn't decked in the hue of the moment. If you live in a modern, all-white house, a white party might suit you perfectly. That way, you won't risk any red-wine stains on the sofa.

■ VENETIAN MASKED BALL
Take cues from old Italy, where masks were a part of upper-class nightlife. Ask each guest to show up in evening attire and a mask. This works really well for grand extravaganzas, ballroom affairs where large bands play and a long table laden with hors d'oeuvres seems to stretch for a mile.

■ HIGH ROLLER
Head to Las Vegas for an evening of poker, blackjack, and craps with a gaggle of friends. Check into a hotel and transform your room into a chic lounge with candles, floor pillows, and flowers. Or you can turn any venue into a gambling zone, where proceeds go to charities or winning chips are only redeemable for gimmicky prizes. At the Dunhill store opening on Madison Avenue, we hosted a night of gambling, complete with genuine casino tables. At the end of the night, everyone cashed their chips in for clothes. And at Hugo Boss's store opening, we did something similar with models as dealers and the proceeds going to charity.

■ TARZAN AND JANE
Go into the wild jungle by transforming your venue into a tropical paradise with trees (blow-up versions or large, life-size drawings pinned to the walls), plants, faux animals, and Astroturf flooring. Use giant rocks and tree stumps as chairs and ask your guests to show up wearing Tarzanesque attire: leopard print one-shouldered getups, unitards, and sarongs; accessories made of plastic bones; fig-leaf bikinis and the kind of outfits that are reminiscent of Wilma Flintstone.

■ HEAVEN AND HELL
Make one part of the room represent heaven. Think white, angelic décor, filled with candles, serene music, and light appetizers. Transform the other part of the party into hell. Add alcoholic drinks, hard-rock music, and chocolate-covered everything, and start sinning.

■ MARRAKECH EXPRESS
Blast Middle Eastern music, bring in belly dancers, drape tapestries from the ceiling, serve hummus, get a set of tabla drums, hand out finger cymbals, and transport your crowd to Morocco.

■ THE BABY ZONE
Find your inner child. Serve drinks in baby bottles. Hand out candy pacifiers. Decorate the room with mini everything. Wear footsy pj's. Cry if you want to.

■ PAJAMA PARTIES
Madonna and Hugh Hefner made these sexy soirees famous. No one enters the party unless they're wearing pajamas. It doesn't matter if they're silk and lace or flannel.

CHIC TIP
When you're having a theme party that requires your guests to dress up, it should last all night. Otherwise, someone will wind up dressing up as "bad girl Barbie who fell off the wagon" and get stuck trying to get into a restaurant, looking like a fool, a few hours later.

PARTY-POOPING PREVENTION

When you know what kind of party you want to throw, kick it up a notch with creative tactics that give your concept a boost of brio. Instead of our traditional Christmas holiday lunch, we wanted to give our employees the gift of rest and relaxation. So we had a beauty party at the BuffSpa at Bergdorf Goodman. Everyone got manicures and pedicures. Some girls got their hair done. And servers passed healthy drinks like iced green tea and fresh fruit juices along with champagne and spa lunches.

You can do something like this in your favorite nail spot or at home. Add some extras like makeup artists to teach your guests how to make their eyes smoky and their lips look bee-stung. Whether your beauty party is for five friends or one hundred, this tactic is sure to take the fun of your party one step further. Some other groovy ideas include:

- COCKTAILS AND CANDY

  Serve yummy candy-flavored cocktails with gummy bears, licorice-stick straws, caramels, and Jolly Ranchers. Fill cocktail glasses with all sorts of confectionery delights and use cocktail candy (also called colored sugar) around the rims of the glasses. Serve the drinks on trays that are covered with the kind of candy that's in the drink. Give your drinks deliciously creative names and give your crowd a sugar fix.

- BOWLING EXTRAVAGANZAS

  Rent a bowling alley (or at least a few lanes) and serve hot dogs, burgers, French fries, and beer. Take the concept one step farther with glow-in-the-dark bowling. Talk to the manager of the alley and arrange to bowl in the dark with glowing balls and pins and disco blasting in the background. Give each person a pair of socks (if someone forgets, there's nothing worse than going barefoot in rented bowling shoes) as a gift.

- ROLLER-SKATING PARTIES

  Rent a roller rink or find a large nightclub with a hardwood floor that's good for four wheeling, and do your best Xanadu. Leg warmers are optional.

- A DETOX DAY

  Host a spa party, serve guests healthy elixirs, herbal teas, and wheatgrass shots to cleanse their systems and pamper them to perfection. Serve carb-free vegan fare. Hire a reflexologist, a roaming masseuse, or a reiki master to ease tension. This is excellent for intimate groups, bridal and baby showers, a birthday, or for bachelorettes who abhor strip-club parties and loud, smoky bars. And if you can't afford going to a spa, make one at home.

- BEACHY KEEN

  Why not host a seafood feast with a Hamptons-style clambake on the beach instead of a run-of-the-mill picnic?

- ROAST SOMEONE

  Every year at the Friars' Club, the renowned private club for comedians, members roast someone famous. Roasting is when you lovingly make fun of the guest of honor, mocking his or her quirky habits, past mistakes, and biggest blunders.

- GETTING CRAFTY

  Invite people for an afternoon of arts and crafts. Get candle-making kits; buy dried flowers, Styrofoam balls, glue, and flower pots so you can all create topiaries; paint; draw; or design mosaic mirrors with chunks of old pottery. Embrace your inner Martha Stewart.

- STARRY NIGHTS

  Invite people to an astrology party. Send out invitations along with horoscopes, hire an astrologer to read your guests' charts, and use glow-in-the-dark star stickers to decorate the room. Have a psychic, a mentalist, and a tea-leaf, tarot-card, or palm reader on hand. Give your guests a deck of tarot cards (and instructions for how to use them) and a journal so they can take notes on their readings.

■ VEHICULAR MADNESS

Host a party at a car dealership, museum, or, better yet, a car wash, where you drive through the washing track to get to the valet. If you can arrange it, allow your guests to test-drive cars. Dress servers in motorcross gear. Rent car-related video games. Screen scenes from famous car races on a wall. Your guests' spirits will go from zero to sixty in no time.

■ GIRLS' NIGHT OUT

Everything should be about bonding with your friends. Do whatever it is that you and your girlfriends love. It could be a dinner at home, a knitting circle, a night of chick flicks or romantic comedies, or renting out a V.I.P. area of a club and dancing all night long.

Girls Night!

WE SIMPLY MUST GET TOGETHER WHILE OUR GUYS DO WHATEVER IT IS THEY DO ON BOYS NIGHT.

WHEN: AT   O'CLOCK

WHERE:

ACTIVITIES WILL INCLUDE, BUT NOT BE LIMITED TO:
1.) GENERAL CAROUSING
2.) BOISTEROUS MERRYMAKING
3.) CONSIDERABLE SNICKERING
4.) SHAMELESS FLIRTING
5.) LEERING
6.) HIGHLY INTELLECTUAL DISCUSSIONS, NATURALLY

CALL ME UP AND LET ME KNOW IF YOU CAN COME!

PHONE:

MONEY TALKS $$$

Before you go any farther with your planning, make sure you can pay for everything. Do some math and make yourself a budget. Without a realistic budget, it's easy to overspend. The last thing you want to do is spend so much on one thing that you have no money left for everything else. Let's say you have $1,000 to work with. You have to think about how much each element of the party, such as invitations, décor, drinks, and food, is going to cost. It seems easy, but there are many hidden expenses that are easy to overlook, such as printing or photocopying your invitations if you're not doing them at home on your computer; stamps, which may add up if you're throwing a big party; tipping the servers if you choose to hire a wait-staff; bags of ice for the bar; extra toilet paper for the bathroom; and cleanup supplies or service.

The point is, if you don't clearly map out how much money you want to allot for each and every detail of your party, you will wind up in accounting hell. It's necessary to decide what's important to you. You might not care about the invitation and want to put more energy (and money) toward the food. If you're not a big foodie, maybe the bar—and having experienced bartenders—is where you want to go all out. Even if you're inviting only twenty guests, you might hate stuffing envelopes and want to pay someone to do the job for you. Asking an assistant at your office to do it for ten dollars is an expense.

On page 248, you'll find our budget template where we have listed every major and minor detail you might need to consider when you're hosting a party.

IT'S NOT ALWAYS WHAT YOUR INVITATION LOOKS LIKE THAT MATTERS, BUT WHAT IT SAYS. SO BE CREATIVE WITH YOUR WORD CHOICE AND COMPOSE SOMETHING SASSY IF THE OCCASION PERMITS. COURTESY OF STUDIO Z MENDOCINO, WWW.STUDIO-Z.COM.

CHAPTER TWO
WHERE'S THE PARTY?
LOCATION, LOCATION, LOCATION

WHERE'S THE PARTY?
LOCATION, LOCATION, LOCATION

In the film industry, there are people who are hired strictly to scout locations, which is just an insider way of saying, "find the right place to shoot certain scenes." These scouts spend hundreds of hours searching for a place with the perfect vista, ambiance, attitude, and historical accuracy. Without that, the film can flop. And the same goes for parties. When you're figuring out where your party should be, you have to start seeing yourself as a location scout. Explore as many places as possible in order to decide which one you want and how you can get the best bang for your buck. Check out airport hangars, fields of wild mustard, castle ruins, stark white spaces that you can morph into anything, and every possible spot you can come up with, even your very own home.

This chapter is all about the importance of locations, whether you're having a party at home or renting a space. If you don't want people living it up in your home—or if you don't have a home that will do—we will show you how to take your party outside and transform the great outdoors into party central. We will give you details on having a party at a restaurant or nightclub (and tell you how best to order food and drinks), as well as negotiating tips for securing a party space, and a list of unexpected venues. The location sets the mood, creates the ambiance, and enhances the entire

LOCATION IS EVERYTHING, WHICH IS WHY WE FOUND THIS AMAZING PRIVATE HOME, A VERITABLE MECCA FOR MODERN DESIGN, FOR THE SIMS ONLINE LAUNCH PARTY. PHOTO COURTESY OF LESTER COHEN/WIREIMAGE.COM.

affair. Finding the right spot requires time and energy and asking yourself some important questions. For example, are you throwing a dinner party and, if so, do you want it at home (whether you have a dining-room table, a roof deck on top of your building, or just a floor) or at a restaurant? And if you want it at a restaurant, do you want a new, trendy place, a classic landmark watering hole, something ironic and funny like McDonald's, or an Indian dive that serves the most sumptuous naan on earth? The right spot should always enhance your concept.

Expressing your dark side with a gothic, vampire theme? Head to an old, or even abandoned, church or synagogue. If your theme relates to Japan, consider having your party in a Japanese garden, at an authentic Japanese restaurant, or in the middle of your living room, decorated with bamboo mats, floor pillows, kimono fabrics, and tables low enough for dining on the floor. The secret to locations is learning how to make the most of them.

HOME, CHIC HOME
It doesn't matter if you have a sprawling, modern loft or a 400-square-foot dump with a bathtub in the kitchen. The fact is, there's no place like home. The key to making your home party special is simple: Just work with what you've got. Only a futon? Open it up and let people lounge on the bed. Throw pillows on the floor and—voilà!—you have

WHAT IS YOUR BEST PARTY TIP?

- DESIGNER DIANE VON FURSTENBERG SAYS, "MIXING PEOPLE. MAKE SURE THE PEOPLE WILL HAVE THE OPPORTUNITY OF MEETING PEOPLE THEY DON'T KNOW. MAKE SURE THAT YOU HAVE A GOOD TIME. IF AS A HOST YOU CAN BEHAVE LIKE A GUEST . . . IT IS A GREAT PARTY."
- ACTRESS LARA FLYNN BOYLE'S RECIPE FOR THE PERFECT PARTY IS SIMPLE, "BELUGA AND FIVE MEN TO EVERY WOMAN."
- ENTERTAINER DAVID COPPERFIELD SAYS, "INVITE EVERYONE YOU REALLY HATE, EVERYONE YOU REALLY LOVE, THEN SLIP OUT AND WATCH WHO GETS ALONG WITH WHOM. IT'S A GOOD WAY TO FIGURE OUT IF YOUR TASTE IN PEOPLE IS ASKEW OR ON THE MONEY."
- DESIGNER MICHAEL KORS SWEARS, "BEAUTIFUL PEOPLE ARE MORE IMPORTANT THAN A BEAUTIFUL ROOM."
- DONALD TRUMP'S RECIPE FOR A GOOD GUEST LIST IS: "HAVE LOTS OF BEAUTIFUL WOMEN AND GREAT MUSIC. MY BIGGEST PARTY COMPLAINT IS BORING PEOPLE WHO DON'T KNOW WHEN IT'S TIME TO GO HOME."
- MUSICAN RUSSELL SIMMONS SAYS EVERY PARTY SHOULD HAVE "LOTS OF SOCIAL ACTIVISTS, SUPERMODELS, AND KID CAPRI AS THE DEEJAY."
- JOAN RIVERS INSISTS, "THE PARTY SHOULD HAVE A 'PURPOSE'—BE GIVEN IN HONOR OF SOMEONE OR SOME EVENT. THIS REALLY CHANGES THE ATMOSPHERE."
- MELISSA RIVERS ADVISES, "RELAX AND HAVE A GOOD TIME."
- AERIN LAUDER SAYS, "INVITE GOOD FRIENDS."
- BOBBI BROWN RECOMMENDS, "WHEN YOU'RE GIVING A PARTY, KEEP THINGS SIMPLE AND DO AS MUCH AS YOU CAN AHEAD OF TIME—AND REMEMBER TO HAVE A GOOD TIME AT YOUR OWN PARTY."
- HUGH JACKMAN'S STRATEGY IS SIMPLE: "GIVE GUESTS A SHOT OF ALCOHOL AS THEY ENTER THE DOOR."

yourself a plush little haven of comfort. If your space is as small as a dorm room, keep the guest list tight, make use of every countertop and windowsill, dim the lights, spark up dozens of candles, and suddenly, you'll have a cozy, intimate setting that's far from cramped. If you're living large with a dining-room table for twelve, organize a sit-down dinner and invite more people after hours to dance on chairs, make their own sundaes, and watch movies until 4:00 A.M. If you're just moving in to new digs? Make your concept a move-in party and invite your friends over for pizza and wall painting. No matter what type of party you're putting together, having it at home is the best way to invite people into your world and make them feel welcome. Home sweet home is an intimate, personal, warm environment—as long as it's neat. Before transforming your crib into party heaven, remember to clean and prepare your home for impending action.

MR. CLEAN

Get rid of the dust bunnies, loose change, and those bills that have been lying on the kitchen table for weeks. It's time to make friends with some Windex. Protect your furniture, so it doesn't get ruined from the wear and tear of party action. Spray Scotchguard (it's still available at most hardware stores) on the sofa so you won't have to stress over cocktail mishaps. Roll up the rugs if you don't want anything to happen to them. Put plastic underneath all tablecloths; this prevents liquid from seeping through the cloth and staining the table (you should expect at least one big spill for every party). And don't worry about candle wax, which is likely to get on the floor, the tabletops, and expensive table linens. To remove it at the end of the party, just rub it down with ice, which hardens the wax so that you can peel it right off. You have to do more than just clean your home, however. You have to party-proof it.

PARTY-PROOFING YOUR HOME

Once your place is spotless, put away your personal items (no one needs to see your birth control pills) and breakables. Lock your bedroom door if you don't want anyone to hang out on your six-hundred-thread-count sheets. And while you're at it, do something with Fido (not everyone will love your one-hundred-pound pooch or your twelve-pound Yorkie). If you don't want people to smoke indoors, place a sign on the door that reads SMOKE OUTSIDE! and let your staffers in on the no-smoking policy. That way, they can tell an unknowing guest to put out his or her cigarette. If, however, you don't mind smoking in your home, you might want to create a smoking area, with ashtrays and perhaps a SMOKING LOUNGE sign by an open window. Put waste baskets in all of the bathrooms and supply paper napkins so no one has to use your expensive towels after washing their hands.

Make sure that there are no stray electrical cords. You don't want anyone wiping out or twisting an ankle. Buy or rent a coat rack or clear out the hallway closet in order to store your guests' coats in an organized fashion. A smart way to handle coat organization is to put a name tag (written before guests arrive) on each hanger. As you're running around, getting things together, do a sound check to ensure that your stereo or CD player works. If it's out of order, rent or borrow one for your party. Speaking of sound, you should really warn your neighbors that you're having a party and invite them, whether you like them or not. Otherwise, they might call the men in blue. And finally, contact your local insurance carrier in order to get insurance. It's possible to purchase a policy for a specific event, and we cannot stress the importance of this enough. If a guest gets hurt you'll be liable, and you could be looking at a lawsuit.

Party-proofing requires more than just making your home a safe place for a party. It involves refining your space to make it crowd friendly. Start by moving your furniture around so that there's space for your guests to walk around comfortably. Get rid of cumbersome objects: Store them in closets, under your bed, in a room you're not using for the party, or in an attic. If you're friends with your neighbors, ask them if you can stash some of your things, like the piles of books that are on the floor, your laptop computer, or a chair that takes up too much room, at their places. While you're rearranging, place two to three chairs in every corner to provide a cozy conversation nook for guests to talk in private. If you don't have furniture—or enough of it—you don't have to go on a shopping spree. It's possible to rent anything these days.

RENT IT

Yes, everything's for rent: sound systems, movie screens, smoke machines, mechanical bulls, bright-red seventies-style sofas shaped like Marilyn Monroe's lips. You name it. If you're not sure whether to rent or buy, just ask yourself if the things you need are worth the investment and worth owning permanently. Renting tables, chairs, patio furniture, sofas, and tents is a good idea because not only will renting save you money, but it will also save you the trouble of storing large items at home.

We suggest you check out everything you rent before party time to make sure it's exactly what you want. It's important to score comfortable chairs and things that match your environment and concept. You should also know that the convenient world of renting doesn't start and end at just the big things. If you don't have enough silverware, coffee mugs, glass pitchers, and speakers, befriend the Yellow Pages. The phone book is full of rental services that offer pickup or delivery of table linens, glasses, plates, and more. Most places will even allow you to return things that are dirty, like the dishes that are covered with crusty tomato sauce (thank God because, come on, who really wants to spend time scrubbing?).

WHAT ELSE IS FOR RENT?

Plenty of things that most people never imagined.

- HOT TUBS
- DANCE FLOORS
- TELEVISIONS AND FILM SCREENS
- ABOVEGROUND SWIMMING POOLS
- VOLLEYBALL NETS AND BALLS
- COSTUMES
- MATTRESSES
- PROFESSIONAL BAR TOOLS
- SUSHI BARS
- OYSTER PLATTERS
- MULTI-TIER SERVING TRAYS
- COOLERS
- BARBECUES
- COCKTAIL TABLES
- BEANBAG CHAIRS
- SHOT GLASSES

AT YOUR SERVICE

You've bought, rented, and organized your location into shape. Now you have to ask yourself this: Can you do everything on your own, running around to make sure each guest's glass and plate is always full, or do you want some help? No matter how small (or large) our parties, we always hire servers. There is something so civilized and sophisticated about having someone pass refills and tidy up as the party progresses. Working with professional butlers and the kind of companies that provide an upscale waitstaff can be costly, so if you don't want to blow your budget here, don't fret.

ENTER PLAN B, OUR RELIABLE STRATEGIES FOR GETTING GOOD HELP ON THE CHEAP.

- Hiring an intern from your office

- Finding a student in need of cash (post a query on the website of a local school)

- Asking your favorite waiters at the restaurant you always go to

- Begging someone's younger sibling—and his or her friends—to do the job for a quick twenty dollars each

- Offering someone an opportunity to trade services if you can give them something that will benefit their career (or their wardrobe) in some way

- Contacting a catering or bartending school near you and working with someone in training

- Scouring a local modeling agency or art school and hiring hungry-for-work students who are capable of mixing drinks and serving food. You can probably get away with paying them just half of what a professional company would charge. Beautiful staffers add to the chic factor of your décor. (In Los Angeles, there is actually a company called Beautiful Bartenders! We use them all the time.)

When you hire servers, make sure they are well put together and wearing some kind of matching ensemble. It could be as simple as all black or jeans with a crisp, white T-shirt. You can either ask the staff to wear their own duds or give them something to wear that goes with your concept. Your servers should be well informed about exactly what they're serving. If they're tending bar, give them a few trial runs to make the drinks on your menu. They also should be knowledgeable about the ingredients of the food and each drink; you never know who's allergic to what, and the last thing you want is to deal with a guest's violent allergic reaction to tarragon. And they should even know how something tastes. If they can say, "This French cabernet savignon is robust and fruity with slight hints of oak and tobacco. It will go well with your lamb," everyone will be impressed.

You should also explain to your staff how you want things to be served. Let them know if you want them to mingle with a tray full of shrimp or if you want them to simply place trays in certain areas, clearing and refilling as needed. The key to good service is making your crowd feel like they're being taken care of, as if they were at a fine restaurant. The same service rules apply to parties that are not at home or in a restaurant, but outside, say, in the park or on a beach.

HEY! BUSTER! DO YOU WANT TO TAKE THIS OUTSIDE?

Whether you don't want people packed in your house or you're craving some fresh air, it may be time to stop and smell the roses. Literally. Try having your party in a garden, a lush park, or in the desert. Settle in by a lake, near a swimming pool, in a sandbox, on a rooftop, at a farm, or on a random plot of grass (with the proper permission, of course). Having parties outside is refreshing, festive, and relaxing all at once. So invite people to be one with nature, take a ride in a rowboat, pick strawberries, soak up some sun, barbecue on the deck, plant flowers, have a bonfire beach party, or sing in the rain. Just remember to wear sunblock (keep a supply for your forgetful friends); borrow, rent, or buy an outdoor sound system (even if it's an old battery-operated boom box); invest in those anti-mosquito candles (or break open mint leaves near the food and drinks; the oil is a natural bug repellant); and get a permit! When the men in blue

show up, you won't want to worry about whether or not your party is legal.

A paramount issue when having a party outside is making the environment as comfortable as your home. There may not be any furniture (save for a picnic table, if you're lucky), let alone a kitchen. So you have to transport your food and drinks in containers—coolers, hot pots, foil, Tupperware—to keep it fresh. You will most likely need to bring some furnishings from home, rent furniture, or get creative with whatever resources you have. Turn bales of straw, covered in blankets, into seats. Place pillows on tree stumps or use them as tables. Make sand castles or use the sand to build groovy, seventies-style lounge chairs. Like a Hollywood set designer who creates elaborate locations on film, you need to roll up your sleeves, get dirty, and start building to give your outdoor space that extra je ne sais quoi.

CREATE A CANOPY

THINK OF IT AS AN ADULT FORT. BENEATH YOUR CANOPY, YOU CAN SCATTER PILLOWS, BEANBAG CHAIRS, AND BLANKETS ON THE GROUND SO LOUNGERS CAN RELAX, OR GO WITH A TRADITIONAL PICNIC TABLE. IT'S EASY TO MAKE.

1. Get four tall bamboo poles from a plant shop, garden center, or flower market.

2. Stand them upright by plowing them either into the sand or into a large sand-filled bucket.

3. Drape a lightweight piece of fabric over the poles, letting it sway in the middle for dramatic effect.

4. Tie the fabric to the top of the poles or secure with a staple gun so it does not fly away.

5. Chill out with a cocktail.

DINING OUT

Lack of a swank home or backyard should never deter you from having a party. And if you think "I just don't want to have a party at home" is a good excuse to not host an event, you're mistaken! Just take your show on the road—to a local restaurant, bar, club, or bowling alley. This way, you won't have to stress about ruining your brand-new white sofa, bringing in food, and cleaning up after. Besides, finding the right site is fun. Whether you're exploring a new place that just opened (everyone likes being the first to try a new restaurant, bar, or club), returning to a classic watering hole that's always reliable, or looking for someplace offbeat, it's important to comparison shop. Check out at least five to ten spots before you make a solid commitment to one. It's like dating: Who gets married after one date? You need to make sure that the location you wind up with meets your needs: the right mood and size for your concept, an agreeable manager or owner, and food and drinks you and your guests will like. You also need to negotiate in order to get the best bang for your buck. Every place will offer you a slightly different deal—and feel.

WHEN YOU BEGIN LOCATION SCOUTING, CONSIDER THE FOLLOWING:

- Look for new spots. Check the paper for grand openings of hot new spots.

- Avoid a place that everyone has been to a hundred times unless it's a classic.

- Throw your event on an "off night," when the venue is not busy. You won't be able to secure prime party real estate at the most popular place in town on a Saturday night without big money.

- Find a spot that isn't doing well and confidently say, "I'll fill your space for the night. I'll bring in people who have never been here and those who haven't been here in ages. We'll spend money here and in return, I want the place to myself." Before you know it, you'll be the promoter/entrepreneur you always knew you could be—and you'll get a better deal.

- Offer to do your party during a restaurant's "last seating," which is the very last hour you can possibly get in and still eat, in order to negotiate a discount on price or get into a trendy boîte you may have a hard time locking down otherwise.

- Choose an out-of-the-way, inexpensive, offbeat restaurant in a notoriously unhip neighborhood. Once you have a successful party there, it will become hip.

As you narrow down your search, you need to know how to negotiate for what you want. If you don't take a proactive approach to your hunt for the perfect place, you might wind up feeling seriously disappointed. So think of location scouting as a giant interview process. You are out to hire the best candidate for the job. Meet with the owners and managers. Take along a notebook or a clipboard. Take notes (you'll look like a professional who's been doing this all your life). Go armed with a list of questions. You certainly don't want any surprises on the big day, so be sure to cover all of your bases, including what you'll be charged for and exactly what your deal includes. Remember, if you don't ask, you don't get.

HERE'S OUR LIST OF POINTS TO DISCUSS WHEN NEGOTIATING VENUE FEES.

- Is the venue private? If so, is there a private room?

- Is there a room rental fee? There often is and people like to spring such things at the end of the night. You don't want to pay one. Be upfront about it so there are no post-party surprises.

- Is there a minimum guarantee? A minimum guarantee means that you have to guarantee that a certain number of people will attend the party and if someone doesn't show, you have to pay for that person's place regardless. Everyone always has one flaky friend who's a no-show. Who wants to pay more for no reason? Not you. If it's part of the venue's policy, see if you can get out of it.

- Can you have a preset menu, especially if you're having a brunch, lunch, or dinner of eight or more?

- Restaurants are famous for charging a small fortune for birthday cakes. So bring in one of your own. (Hello, Pillsbury box mixes or one of those Baskin-Robbins ice-cream cakes.) Just find out if there's a plating fee (it's usually one to four dollars per slice, but see if you can get out of that charge while you're on a negotiating roll).

- See if coffee and tea are included in the deal. Negotiate espresso and cappuccino so that they're not separate fees.

- Find out exactly how many waiters they will provide. If what they provide is not enough, ask how much it will cost to hire more. It's important to have enough servers for your party so everything runs smoothly (one for every six people is ideal).

- Are the deejay, valet, coat check, hostess, and security included? Look the restaurateur in the eye and say, "I am bringing in good business and a good crowd. These things should be included in the price." If you act like you're powerful, you will come across as such.

- If there's no deejay, can you bring your own? Wait. Is there even a sound system? If not, can you rent and install one? If so, will they allow you to provide your own eclectic mix of CDs instead of depending on the restaurant's playlist?

- Find out how they charge for drinks. Is it per drink/per hour/per person, or is it based on consumption? (See page 31 later in the chapter for more details.)

- If you're bringing your own wine, watch out. The restaurant will probably charge you a corkage fee. Try to get out of it. Just promise to order lots of other types of drinks and ensure the owner or manager that you'll be bringing in new potential customers and spending money on other things.

- Does the restaurant provide décor (flowers, centerpieces, table linens, and such) and if not, can you bring your own table accoutrements? You may not need any if the restaurant has enough character on its own.

- If the restaurant works with a particular florist, see if you can work out a deal with that person if flowers are your thing. By using the florist the restaurant works with, you may be able to save the cost of delivery fees because your flower shipment will come with whatever arrangements the restaurant is expecting. If the restaurant tries to charge you a delivery fee, ask if you can waive it. Using the florist the restaurant has an established relationship with may also enable you to get more for your money because the restaurant probably has affordable set rates with the florist.

- Will the restaurant provide special menus for your party? Menus are a nice touch for sit-down meals. People like to see a list of things they're eating or choosing from. Place them at each person's seat or on the buffet table, though we prefer to have them at each table setting. It's more tasteful. If the restaurant won't provide special menus, don't fret. You can create them at home on the computer. Print the menus on nice paper, arrive early, and place one on each setting. You can print two, three, or four on a page and cut them to size.

■ Can you supply your own doorperson? It's always nice to have a friendly face greeting your guests.

■ Finally, ask if tax and tip are included in the final price.

ORDERING AROUND

Once you get the basic negotiation topics out of the way, get into the finer points, like food and drinks. As a host(ess), it's your job to order for everyone. No matter what kind of party you're throwing, there's a lot of pressure to come up with choices that will please each guest's palate. (FYI: Hosting a lunch or brunch at a restaurant is about 25 to 50 percent less costly than a dinner party.) Everyone has different tastes. One's a vegan. Another eats only fish. So-and-so is a ravenous carnivore. And half the women at your party are completely carb-a-phobic.

When it comes to food, it's simple to satisfy every picky eater and drinker in the crowd when you have cocktail parties with appetizers or small dishes. Just offer a bit of meat, some vegetables, and snacks like peanuts or pretzels. But at a sit-down dinner, when you're not having a buffet, it's a whole different animal. If you allow people to order whatever they want off the menu, your bill could wind up as big as your phone number! What you need is a system that makes everyone happy. The answer? Offering a selection of three or four entrées with some side dishes (at a price you agree upon beforehand) or presenting food family style, served on big platters for all to share.

At a dinner party for twenty-five people we hosted at Giorgio's, an Italian restaurant in Los Angeles, for a celebrity friend's twenty-ninth birthday, we came up with the best food plan. It was part pre-setting the menu and part family style. We secured a private room and sat at one long table. As soon as everyone took their seats, waiters passed clams in white wine sauce. It was a small portion, only four clams per plate. As we all finished, a waiter politely asked each guest if he or she wanted seconds. Then, the waiter gave each person one piece of bruschetta (and asked each guest if he or she wanted more after). Next, there were three kinds of ravioli (lobster, mushroom, spinach and goat cheese) and gnocchi, served with a choice of two sauces (marinara and pesto). The servers first doled out two pieces of lobster ravioli. As we cleared our plates, we were each served two pieces of the mushroom ravioli. And so it continued, along with the gnocchi. We followed up the pasta dish by making sure each person was given a plated salad. Then the entrées came! Each guest received a plate with lobster tail, spinach, and potatoes (there was pasta for those who disliked seafood). And along the center of the table stood plates of three types of fish—white fish, halibut, and salmon—so guests could take whatever they wanted. For dessert, each person was given one small piece of apple pie and a small piece of tiramisù. Preordering the food in this way allowed us to offer a huge selection of food. Although the portions of each were small, the guests had the chance to try all of the restaurant's specialties.

THERE'S AN ART TO ORDERING PARTY MEALS AT A RESTAURANT.

- Always have something on the table for pre-meal picking: vegetable platters, hummus, olives, chips, breadsticks, white-bean dip. The trick is to have something cold that won't spoil if left untouched for an hour or more.

- Offer a selection of warm, fresh bread. Make sure butter and dipping oils are on the table.

- Order a basic salad with walnuts and a cheese for each person, placed before or after people arrive. Make sure the dressing is on the side.

- Offer a selection of chicken, fish, and/or pasta vegetarian dishes. If it's family style, this usually calls for placing large dishes in the center of the table so your guests can serve themselves. You can also have a waiter pass platters of each dish and serve guests a bit of whatever they want. If you preset the menu, a waiter will typically ask each guest what he or she wants in advance and dole out individual plates.

- Make sure there is a selection of at least three side dishes, placed or passed.

- Get a dessert platter instead of individual orders. That way, each person can taste a bit of warm chocolate soufflé, banana tart, cheesecake, or tapioca pudding. Offer a plate of cookies and petit fours for each group of four; it's very Le Cirque, the famous four-star New York City restaurant.

DRINK MENU

After making the food arrangements, your next order of business in planning a restaurant party involves the drink menu. You can have an open bar all night, which will typically run you five to fifteen dollars per person, per hour. If you go with the open bar, find out if the deal includes top shelf (the best brands of alcohol) or well (generic brands of liquor). As always, negotiate this in advance. As an alternative, offer an open bar for a set amount of time then change to a cash bar. Or set up your bar so that you pay for drinks upon consumption, which means that you'll get a bill at the end of the night for the total. This is, perhaps, the most expensive way to go because you can't control what people will order (some drinks are more costly than others) and how much they'll drink (some people go crazy when the alcohol is free). If you want to keep your bill down, arrange the bar so that certain kinds of (pricey) liquor are off limits. So what if your open bar isn't as open as your guests think it is!

You can also keep costs down by preordering red and white wine only or serving wine in addition to preselected mixed drinks served from pitchers (sangria is always a fruitful choice) set at each table. Another cheap but chic solution is to forgo splurging on bottles of champagne and buy just enough to give each person one glass of champagne. Then you can have a champagne toast at some point during the party.

If possible, avoid bottled water, which costs at least eight dollars per bottle in a restaurant and adds up after your guests have poured through ten to twenty bottles. Why waste your money on something that's available for free? To make the water selection seem more appealing, keep ice water in pitchers on the table and flavor each one with lemon, lime, sliced cucumber, watermelon wedges, or other flavorizers (our favorite: fresh basil and mint).

Finally, make sure your drink list includes non-alchoholic options (you never know who's not drinking). Make sure you provide decaf coffee in addition to espresso and cappuccino. Flavored coffees are also a delicious addition.

GETTING CLUBBY

When you want to have a cocktail party, a bachelorette party, a girls' or guys' night out, or an opportunity to celebrate your newfound singlehood, get your evening going at a bar or nightclub, where life is all about letting the alcohol flow. Throwing a party at a bar is usually cheaper than doing it at a restaurant. Bars come with a built-in staff, cushy seating, flattering lighting schemes, and a deejay and/or live band.

AFTER HUNTING DOWN THE RIGHT BOÎTE, THERE ARE SOME THINGS YOU NEED TO GO OVER WITH THE MANAGER OR OWNER IN ORDER TO GET THE BEST POSSIBLE DEAL.

■ Negotiate the bar setup. You don't need to rent the whole club or offer a full open bar all night, which can be pricey. In addition to the aforementioned choices, you can set up an open bar with a price limit and after that dollar amount is reached, the party shifts to a cash bar; people will then pay for their own drinks. You can offer one drink that gets passed (Cosmopolitans are a favorite) all night, while everything else is cash bar. You can also go with the "bottle service" plan, which is very South of France. Bottle service is when you, the host, pick your favorite brand(s) of liquor. Place selected bottles in buckets of ice at each table (or at some tables), along with containers of ice, mixers, a lineup of glasses, and lemon and lime. This way, everyone can make their own cocktails. You can also do any combination of the above.

■ Reserve tables if the place is not exclusively yours. Make snappy signs that read RESERVED! A-LIST F.O.E.S (FRIENDS OF ELIZABETH) ONLY!

■ Nightclubs are notorious for ripping people off, so it's important to make sure the club's doorman is aware of your party—and has a copy of your list—so your guests don't have to pay an admission fee.

■ Arrange for your guests to get a special hand stamp or cute bracelet to let them in and out of the club for the night. Try a Hello Kitty number and give it to the club's doorman to handle, or provide your own gatekeeper (even if it's just a burly friend), if need be.

STRICTLY BUSINESS

Once you've picked a place, squared away your requests, and negotiated the food and drink menu, you should get a contract. It's a business-savvy way to ensure you don't get taken for a ride. And having a contract will give you the backup you need so you don't wind up paying for things you didn't get or ask for.

CHIC TIP

Make sure that "extra chairs" are part of the deal. If people come by after a dinner, you always want to make them feel welcome by giving them a place to sit.

After you sign on the dotted line, everything will be set. We always recommend getting to the party at least forty-five minutes early in order to give the scene a once-over and make sure everything is perfect.

THE COUNTDOWN

TO GIVE YOU AN IDEA OF HOW TO PLAN, FOLLOW THIS SAMPLE TIME LINE TO A DINNER PARTY.

4 WEEKS BEFORE
- SET THE BUDGET
- PICK A DATE
- BOOK A VENUE
- MAKE A GUEST LIST

3 WEEKS BEFORE
- MEET WITH THE VENUE'S STAFF AND CHOOSE A TABLE OR PRIVATE ROOM FOR YOUR GROUP
- PICK AN AREA OF THE SPACE FOR THE COCKTAIL HOUR OR HORS D'OEUVRES
- SELECT A DRINK AND FOOD MENU
- DESIGN AND CREATE THE INVITATIONS

2 WEEKS BEFORE
- SEND THE INVITATIONS
- PLAN THE DÉCOR AND BUY, RENT, OR BORROW WHAT YOU NEED

1 WEEK BEFORE
- ORDER THE CAKE IF YOU'RE HAVING A SPECIAL CAKE MADE
- ASK GUESTS TO PREPARE SHORT TOASTS IF IT'S A SPECIAL OCCASION
- BUY THE FLOWER ARRANGEMENTS

2 DAYS BEFORE
- CONFIRM THE MENU
- CONFIRM THE GUEST LIST

1 DAY BEFORE
- GET THE FLOWERS AND CAKE TO THE SPACE
- PREPARE THE TABLE AND SPACE DÉCOR
- INTRODUCE YOURSELF TO THE STAFF OF THE VENUE (IF IT'S AT HOME, MEET WITH THE STAFF AT YOUR PLACE) AND DISCUSS HOW YOU WANT THE EVENT TO BE HANDLED

PARTY PLACES

YOUR HOME, A BAR, A GREAT RESTAURANT, THE PARK, AND THE BEACH ARE ALWAYS PERFECT PARTY REFUGES. BUT THERE ARE PLENTY OF OTHER HOT SPOTS THAT ARE ATTENTION-GRABBING AND UNIQUE.

- **A DINER**
  Preset a menu of french fries with melted cheese, turkey clubs cut into finger sandwiches, milk shakes, cherry soda, and chocolate pudding. It's all so fifties. The party for Alexandra von Furstenberg's eighteenth and Marie-Chantal of Greece's twenty-first birthdays was at Big City Diner, which became the hottest place in Manhattan afterward.

- **THE BOARDWALK OR A THEME PARK**
  Meet up for a cotton candy buffet and a mean round of Skee-Ball.

- **AN ART GALLERY**
  Discuss what the artist was trying to say over white wine and goat cheese crostinis. It's a hip way to introduce people to each other and take in some culture. Hire a caterer, pack sandwiches, or order in food.

- **A BEAUTY SALON**
  After salon hours throw a beauty party, where you and your friends indulge in pedicures, blowouts, eyebrow waxes, and makeup.

- **A BOAT**
  Charter a yacht (very Steven Spielberg) and head for St. Barth's. Or on a more affordable scale, call a local yacht club or boating dock. Boats are usually available for rent for the day.

- **MOM AND DAD'S HOUSE**
  It's always better than your own.

■ A HOTEL SUITE

Upscale suites are usually quite lavish, complete with sofas, fantastic room service, CD players, the softest pillows, and enough space to mingle with fifteen friends (or even more in some cases). Two words: pillow fight!

■ A HOTEL BALLROOM

Perfect for big, lavish, dramatic bashes like your Venetian ball.

■ A MOTEL

You can set up different themes and décors in different rooms.

■ THE AIRPORT RUNWAY

Head for a private airport, where you can set up a tent, a bar, tables, and a lounge among ritzy GVs. Fireworks not recommended.

■ THE COUNTRY CLUB, DARLING

Invite people to indulge in a proper cup of tea, a lavish brunch with a huge omelet bar, a fancy dinner, or a charming cocktail party. Country clubs are great because the waitstaff is extremely experienced with handling large crowds and catering to their every whim.

■ ANOTHER STATE

Parties can be like mini vacations. Whether your guests take a train, bus, rental car, or plane, road trips are always fun.

■ POOLSIDE

Bring flip-flops, serve drinks in hollowed-out pineapples, consider hiring a masseuse, and hand out misters filled with Evian water. If you don't have a pool, see if you can host a party at a friend's house where there is a pool, or at the neighborhood pool.

■ A MOUNTAINTOP

Get into country living. Your guests can hike their way up to the party and be taken home by a driver, a chairlift, or a sleigh (that is if it's winter and it's a ski resort). Yodeling should be verboten.

■ A SLEEK PHOTO STUDIO

Photo studios are usually large, open, bright spaces that make excellent canvases to decorate. There are also party homes—mansions, farms, townhouses—that are available strictly for parties. They usually come equipped with kitchens and the kind of décor you'd kill for.

■ A MOVIE THEATER

They're often available for rent. Supply brown paper bags filled with treats and send microwave popcorn as an invite. If you see *The Rocky Horror Picture Show,* make sure you instruct everyone on what to do and say throughout the film.

■ A CLOTHING STORE—AFTER HOURS— WHERE EVERYONE EATS, DRINKS, AND SHOPS

Harrison & Shriftman have hosted shopping and launch parties at Scoop, Sergio Rossi, Dunhill, Hugo Boss, Cartier, Louis Vuitton, and Express. Be warned: Alcohol and shopping can be a very dangerous mix.

■ A FURNITURE OR ANTIQUES STORE FOR BUILT-IN DÉCOR

Invite guests to come in period costumes.

■ YO, ADRIAN!

Check out a boxing gym. Who needs décor when you have a ring, heavy bags, and manly equipment? There's a grubby-chic vibe at a gym. Screen *Rocky,* if possible.

- AN OFFICE SPACE

  Sure, it's all about faxing, filing, and grunt work during the day, but after dark, put a velvet rope in front of the conference room, add a disco ball, candles, and booze. Get your boss a little more than tipsy and—presto!—Studio 54 (sort of).

- THE ROOF DECK OF YOUR APARTMENT BUILDING, A HOTEL, OR A RESTAURANT

  Make sure it's legal and safe. Throw down a collage of plastic mats and floor pillows and you're set.

- A PARKING LOT

  Meet up hours before a concert for a high-school-style tailgate party—with coolers, hibachi grills, and picnic blankets.

- A GO-CART RACE TRACK OR MINIATURE GOLF COURSE

  Having a party at a place that offers an activity keeps people busy and excited. Also, these places are so unexpected for adults that they're sure to loosen everyone up.

- A VIDEO ARCADE

  The vibe may be cheesy, but that's part of the fun. Provide tokens or quarters in specially designed cups. Serve beer. Bring in a cake and a buffet table and let the games begin.

- A CANDY OR TOY STORE

  Everyone can be a kid again. Bust out the Twister. Give people oak tag and paint. Serve the kind of drinks and food everyone loved as children: Hawaiian Punch, macaroni and cheese, ice-cream sandwiches, and frozen hot chocolate.

- AN ARTS-AND-CRAFTS STUDIO

  You can throw down paint, clay, and a cold one.

- BY THE LAKE

  Rent rowboats and hire a guitar player to lead sing-alongs.

PLAY IT COOL

This affair is just as much for you as it is for your friends—or the guest of honor—and you want to have fun! Showing up and being ready early will let you take care of things to your satisfaction before your guests arrive. That way, you won't waste your energy righting all the wrongs throughout the party. When you arrive early, it's smart to meet the staff—doormen, security, bartenders, waiters, manager—so they know who you are. Buddy up to them. Smile. Wink. Charming others is the best way to assure V.I.P. treatment—and it's all about the V.I.P. treatment. Once you have them in the palm of your hand, double-check that there are enough servers for your party. If the tip wasn't included in the price of your party, figure out the gratuity in advance and put the tips in little envelopes and give them out at the end of the meal. Also, you want to make sure that no one hands you a bill at the end of the night. It's tacky. Give a credit card in advance or deal with the bill in private. Follow up with receipts (you should keep them, just in case) the day after.

The only way you'll be able to relax and have a great time is if things are in order. So the most important thing you can bring to your party is a checklist to keep things organized before your crowd trickles in. Menus on each plate? Check. Candles for the birthday cake? Check. Extra seating cards, table cards, pens? Check, check, check. Table décor? Check. Flowers? Check. The correct wine? Check. Disposable cameras? Check. You should do this no matter where your party is.

CHAPTER THREE
YOU'RE INVITED!
DON'T FORGET TO RSVP!

YOU'RE INVITED!
DON'T FORGET TO RSVP!

A party begins with the invitation. It sets the tone for the entire event. And unless you're putting together a last-minute party (and informing everyone via e-mail or the telephone), everything about your invitation—the color, font, and how it's designed, printed, stamped, and delivered—should reflect the concept of your party. Stop seeing an invitation as just a sheet of information and start viewing it as an extension of your party. No matter what type of party you're having, the invitation will give your guests a clear indication of what they can expect, be it a healthy spa lunch or a wild night of dancing.

This chapter reveals the A to Z of creating the perfect invitation. We will walk you through the steps in creating the perfect guest list and introduce the basic types of invitations, which we broke down into three categories: classic and traditional, funky and fun, and kitschy and gimmicky. We will teach you how to produce each type of invitation, whether you're custom-ordering something from an up-scale paperie, finding the right prepacked product, or getting crafty and doing it yourself. We'll show you the art of navigating stationery stores; give you clues as to what to look for; educate you on fonts, layouts, calligraphy, and befriending your printer; and share savvy computer tactics that will make it look as if you splurged at Cartier.

We will go into detail about what invitations

INVITE THE BEST! CAMERON DIAZ, LUCY LIU, AND DREW BARRYMORE AT THE ROLLING STONES POST-CONCERT PARTY. PHOTO COURTESY OF DENISE TRUSCELLO/WIREIMAGE.COM.

should say, from something traditional to something sassy. We'll introduce you to the extended family of the invitation, which includes save-the-date and response cards as well as how to provide directions and maps to your party destination. We will cover envelopes, from the address to the stamp, because they provide the first impression of your party. So we'll show you how to give your guests a good one. From there, our "Going Postal!" section will reveal surprising postal secrets the government never shares and delivery tips you can count on.

After you create and send the invitations, we will tell you how to handle post-mailing follow-up so you won't have to worry about no-shows. By the time you're finished with this chapter, everyone will RSVP to your events.

GUESS WHO'S COMING TO DINNER
Who are you inviting to your party? Before you think of invitations, you have to get your guest list in order. Of all the parties we've had, the best ones have had nothing to do with limitless budgets, months of careful planning, and five-star food, but rather the people. The right mix is everything. We go to parties to mingle, meet new people, and see old friends, so inspire everyone by creating a well-thought-out guest list. It doesn't matter if you're having a party of five or a party of five thousand—just think about whipping up the perfect personality cocktail.

IF YOU DON'T WANT TO SUFFER FROM EMPTY-CHAIR SYNDROME, FOLLOW THESE BASIC POINTS:

1. Analyze your list. There are probably two groups of people: the crew you ideally hope will show up and a troop of those who are "sure things." If you are having a job-oriented party and you really want someone from a specific firm—we'll call it X—to show up, invite five people from X, in the hopes that someone will RSVP.

2. For every twenty people, add five to your list. Yes, for every twenty people you invite, chances are, three to five won't be able to attend.

3. Factor in "plus-ones," which are guests of guests.

4. Consider the time of your party. If it will linger for more than two hours, there will probably be two turnovers throughout the event. That means, a group of people will arrive, hang out for a while, and leave, while other people may show up later.

5. Send invitations to your ideal guests, the A-listers. Keep a pile of B-list invitations on hand and send them out as you start finding out who, of the A-listers, is not coming to your party.

BEFORE YOU START YOUR LIST, KEEP ONE THING IN MIND: OVER-INVITE. YOU CAN'T COUNT ON EVERYONE YOU INVITE TO ATTEND.

There are other things to think about when you want your guest list to shine. Make sure there's an even mix of boys and girls—and don't invite the girl who slept with your friend's husband (and nearly broke them up), even if she's hilarious, cool, and beautiful. (Actually, especially if she's hilarious, cool, and beautiful!) Invite people who do different things for a living. Crowd diversity is key to a lively scene. And be brash! Invite someone you just met or barely know. Ask a friend to invite someone you've never met. And invite people who invited you to their events (it's good karma). Your guest list should be deliberate—and tight so you don't overcrowd the room (that's a surefire way to "lose" guests).

CHIC TIP

If you're having a two-part party—dinner, then cocktails and dancing—invite a whole new crowd for the second half of the evening. Bringing in new blood is a clever way to breed new bonds and energy.

- Invite a crew of cool young people to pop by after dinner; they won't mind not eating with you. Our celebrity photographer friend Patrick McMullan calls them "toothpick guests."

- If a friend calls you in a panic and says, "I have five friends in from out of town. Can I bring them to your party," don't feel obligated to say yes. If you can't accommodate that many extra people, invite them for the early-bird special, the cocktail hour before dinner bells ring, or after dinner, for dessert.

SURPRISE GUESTS

Have a trick up your sleeve. A friend's friend was having a dinner party, and it was deader than a slab of tofu. The hostess was an anxious wreck. So she pulled the trump card and called a neighbor with whom she was friendly, begging him to stop by. The neighbor in question? Paul Newman! He dropped in for only five minutes, but by the time he left, the party was hopping. You may not know Paul—or a major celebrity—but it's always smart to have at least one scene maker (a magician friend, a drag queen, the town mayor, a guy who just came back from a safari in Africa and has pictures to share, the head of a wonderful charity, the local news anchor, some kind of business mogul, someone in the circus who will come by on stilts, or any small-town star who knows how to raise an eyebrow or two) on your list, or on hand to pump things up. At a sit-down dinner party we organized for the sixty-year anniversary of *Glamour* magazine, we arranged to have Matt Damon and Ben Affleck show up. They were our surprise celebrity guests and they made the dinner. People still talk about it.

WARNINGS

Once you've tallied your RSVPs, you can bet that some people who accepted won't show. You will have cancellations for no reason at all. Someone may need to jet off on a last-minute business trip. Another person may be sick. On average, there are roughly five no-shows for every twenty people who planned to attend a party. That is why, when we're having a party for twenty people, we like to confirm that twenty-five will come. And if the party is for fifty people, we always make sure we have sixty "definites." The reason? Aside from the no-shows, some guests will arrive late; others may pop in with an unexpected friend on their arms; three people might leave early. When it comes to the number of people you're inviting, more is more. It's always better to be safe than sorry.

INVITATIONS: THE CLASSIC ROUTE

You're a traditional kind of gal with country-club-perfect manners. Big budget or not, small party or large, your invitation must remain simple and elegant. With this kind of invitation, you don't need much to make your point. No flash, glitter, or gimmicks are necessary. When you're taking the classic route, less is always more, especially when you have quality paper; a simple, clean design; and immaculate lettering.

The basic formula requires a traditional color palette, such as a white or off-white card with navy, black, silver, gold, chocolate brown, even the signature Tiffany blue ink. As far as paper is concerned, thicker is always better, though it does cost more. Classic invitations are typically 4x6 or 5x7 inches in size. And the font, curvy and artful or crisp modern block lettering, should be flawless and consistent from the greeting to the return address. The layout, which is the placement of the lettering, should be flush to the left or centered. Your envelopes must, must, *must* match. Whether you custom-order your stationery from a highbrow store or make something at home that looks like it came straight off Fifth Avenue, what makes a classic invitation classic is that it's sophisticated and timeless, just like your party.

Sandra Bernhard, Tamara Beckwith, Zoe Cassavetes, Lisa Eisner, Shalom Harlow
Stephanie Haymes, Kate Hudson, Julianne Moore, Winona Ryder

invite you to celebrate the ten year anniversary of

Tracey Ross

Friday, the sixth of October
nine o'clock in the evening

Cicada
617 South Olive Street, Los Angeles

D.J. Samantha Ronson
RSVP Harrison & Shriftman 310.271.6411

A CLASSIC INVITATION FOR TRACEY ROSS'S TEN-YEAR ANNIVERSARY PARTY. EVERYTHING IS CENTERED, SIMPLE, AND CHIC. SPELLING OUT THE DATE THIS WAY IS ALSO A VERY FORMAL. INVITATION FROM CARTIER.

DO YOUR HOMEWORK

Visit a posh stationery store like Tiffany, Cartier, or Crane's, or an exclusive paperie or invitation store to scope out the scene and see what's out there. Any upscale stationery boutique will have portfolios of sample invitations to give you ideas. Most places will even send or lend you samples to consider at home. Looking at a wide selection of invitations, even the ones that are way out of your price range, will inspire you and help you figure out what you want. But before you go any farther, there are a few things you should know. A potentially snooty salesperson might ask you about thermography, engraving, motifs. So educate yourself before you begin your pursuit of class. Below is a list of important terms that are sure to come in handy.

- **CARD STOCK** is the thickness and weight of the paper: sixty-five-pound, eighty-five-pound, and one-hundred-pound.

- For an **ENGRAVED INVITATION,** the wording is etched in reverse onto a copper plate, which is then stamped onto the invitation, creating a raised impression (the paper is actually raised and ink is applied to the raised surface).

- When **THERMOGRAPHY** is used, the printing appears to be raised. The effect is created by a powder, which is then melted over the flat, printed ink.

- **MONOGRAMMING** is having your initials or name engraved.

- **MOTIFS** are cute little images (a martini glass, a duck, an engagement ring) that can be printed on your cards.

- **BORDERS** are the lines that mark the perimeter of the card. For classic invitations, use the same color as the lettering.

MADE TO ORDER

If you're custom-ordering, we warn you: It can be an overwhelming process. There are hundreds of fonts and styles of invitations to choose from. If you don't know what you're doing, it might get stressful. Your best bet is to visit a good store, ask for guidance, and see examples of invitations. If you don't have time to do the research, order a catalog and call customer service. Someone will be able to walk you through the process on the phone.

CHIC TIP

While you're at it, think about getting save-the-date cards and thank-you notes that match your invitation. It's stylish to stay consistent with the paper, color scheme, and invitation theme.

Order extra invitations and envelopes in case you add people at the last minute or have to send second invitations to those who, for some reason, never received the original.

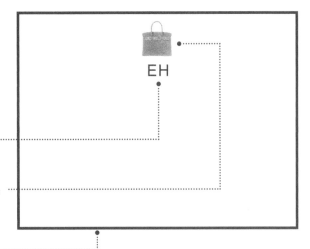

A CLASSIC CARD FROM PREPPYCARDS.COM. YOU CAN USE YOUR INITIALS, YOUR FIRST NAME, YOUR FIRST AND LAST NAME, BORDERS, NO BORDERS, BRIGHT COLORS, MATTE COLORS, OR ANY KIND OF MOTIF.

THE ULTIMATE CHECKLIST FOR CUSTOM ORDERING CLASSIC INVITATIONS

DON'T FORGET TO:

■ PICK THE RIGHT PAPER. Determine whether you want the paper to have a matte or glossy finish. We like matte because it is understated and elegant.

■ Figure out if you want the words to be FLUSH to the LEFT or CENTERED.

■ CHOOSE A COLOR SCHEME. White or off-white with navy, black, silver, gold, chocolate brown, and Tiffany turquoise are the most traditional.

■ Decide if you want ENGRAVING or EMBOSSING and MONOGRAMS or MOTIFS.

■ SIZE THINGS UP. Do you want to go with an invitation that's 4x6 inches or 5x7 inches?

■ FIND A FONT YOU LIKE.

■ Ask yourself if you want to use ALL CAPITAL LETTERS, all LOWER CASE, or a mix of both.

■ LAY OUT YOUR DESIGN by placing the text vertically or horizontally on the card. Whatever you decide, make sure the envelope is oriented the same way.

■ CHOOSE MATCHING ENVELOPES. They can be lined with tissue paper, which should match the ink color.

■ Consider PRINTING THE ENVELOPES WITH RETURN ADDRESSES on the back flap. It is the most polished way to custom-order an invitation, though it is more costly.

■ PROOFREAD the invitation copy and addresses. Sign the proof and have the person who's printing the invitations sign the proof, too, so you're in cahoots. Ask a friend to proof the invitations also. How many times have you overlooked mistakes when you're a little too close to a project?

■ KEEP A COPY of the bill and put a deposit of half down. Get a delivery date in writing.

IN THE BOX

So, you're not going the custom-ordering route. Don't fret. You can pull off the classic look by buying in-the-box invitations (prepackaged stationery) without losing an ounce of cachet (okay, maybe an ounce, but who's counting). Just look for "imprintables," which are cards or invitations and matching envelopes, made so that you can print them on your computer at home.

You can also find chic white or off-white watermarked paper and, if your penmanship is flawlessly sophisticated, hand-write the invitations. Use a calligraphy pen, which is guaranteed to glamorize anyone's handwriting. Some of the most eye-catching invitations are scripted with hand calligraphy.

CLASSIC INVITATIONS, RIGHT OUT OF THE BOX, FROM SMYTHSON OF BOND STREET AND CARTIER.

SCRIPT

Calligraphy comes from the Greek word *kalligraphia,* which means "beautiful writing," and it's the stuff that amazing invitations are made of. Calligraphy can be expensive and time consuming (it costs anywhere from one to five dollars per line per invitation and requires over a month to complete), so you might want to consider it just for the envelopes. You can also hire someone to write one invitation with calligraphy and have the rest offset printed at a copy store, or save the calligraphy just for each person's name, which makes the invitation more special.

There are many different types of calligraphy, ranging from formal to casual. Pick one that suits your invitation and your party. If you're inspired, take a calligraphy class through a local art store, school, or university. Then let it casually slip out at your party that you were responsible for the fine handwriting on the invite. (They'll wonder how you did it all.) If you're inviting ten or more people and you don't want to risk hand cramps, you can get away with creating one invitation and taking the rest to a copy store to have them offset printed.

Every year, for *Vanity Fair*'s famous Oscar party, the magazine's editor-in-chief, Graydon Carter, sends a lucky group of celebrities, filmmakers, and high-profile personalities the most fabulous invitation (below). It's on one-hundred-pound ivory parchment paper that is laid out horizontally; each guest's name is written by hand in calligraphy, while the rest of the lettering is printed. It's the most coveted invitation in town, not just because of the stellar crowd, but because the invitation itself is so beautiful.

Spencerian Script

Traditional Copperplate

Swingline Script

Pointed Pen Variation

Flourished Copperplate

Italic Script

SIX STYLES OF CALLIGRAPHY THAT RANGE FROM SOCIAL SCRIPT TO FORMAL, DESIGNED BY ARTIST ERICA MCPHEE, CALLIGRAPHER AND DESIGN ARTIST AND OWNER OF PAPER WHITE STUDIOS. PICK SOMETHING THAT MATCHES THE KIND OF EVENT YOU'RE HAVING.

CHIC TIP

You can always download a calligraphy font from the Internet and run your invitations through your printer at home. No matter which option you choose, your guests will certainly be impressed. The following font is called Lucida.

Lucida Font
abcdefghijklmnopqrstuvwxyz
ABCDEFGHIJKLM
NOPQRSTUVWXYZ
1234567890

KNOCK IT OFF!

You have a Z-list budget and an A-list personality. Don't demolish your bank account for the invitations. Rip off the classic formula and make it look as if you've spent a fortune. If clothing designers can knock off the greats, why can't you? Pay a little visit to the most expensive stationery place near you and pick something that you'd love if money were no object. At home, scan your computer for a font that matches the sample typefaces you liked. If your computer doesn't have what you're looking for, you can surf the Internet and download something new. There also are dozens of programs, full of interesting fonts of all shapes and sizes.

Start with high-quality white or ivory paper and matching, preferably lined, envelopes from a paper or even office supply store. Be sure to get something thick enough to look impressive, but thin enough to slide through your printer. Start typing. Play with font styles and sizes to find one that works for you. Experiment by bolding certain words like "birthday party" and italicizing "RSVP." Try different spacing formats. Print out a few options on sample paper to choose from.

Once you settle on your font, size, and design, it's time to settle on a layout. Print a version with the text set flush to the left and print another mock-up with the text centered. Once you decide which works for you, decide if you want the cards to be viewed horizontally or vertically, although the envelopes you bought might dictate that for you. Print out the invites and then cut the paper to the classic size, which is either 4x6 or 5x7. In order to save money, get crafty with your computer and print two to four invitations on each sheet and then cut them. This way, you won't have to buy as much paper. If you're technically challenged, print one invitation and take your paper to a copy store, where someone can copy up to four invitations on each piece of paper and cut them to size for you. This is called a "paste up."

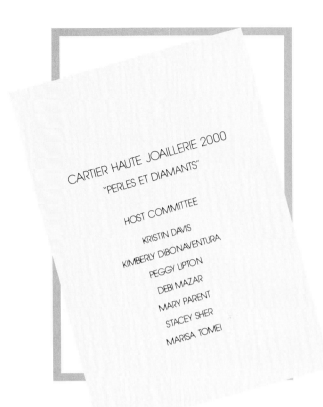

A CLASSIC INVITATION FROM CARTIER. VELLUM IS THE PERFECT ACCENT TO AN INVITATION. HERE WE PRINTED THE NAMES OF THE HOST COMMITTEE AND ENCLOSED IT.

THIS IS A VERY TRADITIONAL INVITATION: THICK CARD STOCK WITH ALL CAPS PERFECTLY CENTERED.

CLASSIC FONT STYLES & MOTIFS

FÊTE ACCOMPLI!

44

CLASSIC COMPUTER GENERATED FONT EXAMPLES

Palatino 12 plain	The quick brown fox jumps over a lazy dog
Palatino 12 bold	**The quick brown fox jumps over a lazy dog**
PALATINO 16 SMALL CAPS	THE QUICK BROWN FOX JUMPS OVER A LAZY DOG
PALATINO 14 ALL CAPS	THE QUICK BROWN FOX JUMPS OVER A LAZY DOG
Palatino 14 italic	*The quick brown fox jumps over a lazy dog*
Helvetica 16 plain	The quick brown fox jumps over a lazy dog
Helvetica 16 bold	**The quick brown fox jumps over a lazy dog**
Helvetica 16 italic	*The quick brown fox jumps over a lazy dog*
HELVETICA 16 SMALL CAPS	THE QUICK BROWN FOX JUMPS OVER A LAZY DOG
HELVETICA 14 ALL CAPS	THE QUICK BROWN FOX JUMPS OVER A LAZY DOG
Times 16 plain	The quick brown fox jumps over a lazy dog
Times 16 bold	**The quick brown fox jumps over a lazy dog**
Times 16 italic	*The quick brown fox jumps over a lazy dog*
TIMES 16 SMALL CAPS	THE QUICK BROWN FOX JUMPS OVER A LAZY DOG
TIMES 14 ALL CAPS	THE QUICK BROWN FOX JUMPS OVER A LAZY DOG

ENGRAVED STYLES

Mr. and Mrs. Peter Hollis Simpson	NO. AE195 ROYAL SCRIPT
Mr. and Mrs. Montgomery McKeon	NO. AE214 SLOOP SCRIPT
Mr. and Mrs. Spencer William Thurston	NO. AE203 SHADED ANTIQUE ROMAN
Mr. and Mrs. Thomas James Rousseau	NO. AE482 OXFORD SCRIPT
Mr. and Mrs. Stephen Ignatius Allen	NO. AE210 SAINT JAMES
Mr. and Mrs. Franklin Myles Kramer	NO. AE053 CAVALIER SCRIPT
MR. AND MRS. CARLOS GUSTAVO CORTÉZ	NO. AE198 SERLIO ROMAN
Mr. and Mrs. Jean-Paul Moreau	NO. AE300 DORIC TEXT
Mr. and Mrs. Anthony Louis Marlow	NO. AE196 ROOK SCRIPT
Mr. and Mrs. Nicholas David Benedict	NO. AE030 BERNHARD FASHION

SMYTHSON OF BOND STREET
EST. 1887

AMERICAN ENGRAVED LETTERHEAD LAYOUTS
BRITISH LAYOUTS AND FURTHER ENGRAVED LETTERING STYLES AVAILABLE ON REQUEST

Hugo B. Forster	*40 Portland Place London W1N 3DY*
KRISTIN CARMICHAEL	820 FIFTH AVENUE APARTMENT 7D NEW YORK, NY 10021
Camilla May Albright	*120 East Westminster Lake Forest, Illinois 60045*
MR. AND MRS. JOHNNY STORM	2000 VAUGHAN ROAD BLOOMFIELD HILLS MICHIGAN 48304
CASPIAN PRICE DAVENPORT	6 PLACE SAINT GERMAIN 75007 PARIS

SMYTHSON OF BOND STREET EST. 1887

HOUSE ENGRAVED MOTIF DIES

YOU CAN'T REALLY COMPARE SMYTHSON'S, TIFFANY'S, OR CARTIER'S CALLIGRAPHY TO THE STANDARD FONTS OR MOTIFS IN ANY COMPUTER, BUT YOU CAN FIND SOMETHING SIMILAR THAT DOES THE TRICK. BOTTOM LEFT AND RIGHT: THESE LETTERING STYLES ARE THE PROPERTY OF SMYTHSON OF BOND STREET AND THEY RESERVE THE COPYRIGHT.

CLASSIC . . . WITH A TWIST!

You may belong to the country club, but you'd never be caught dead wearing a twinset and pearls. Sure, you're sophisticated, but you have an edge. Sound familiar?

THEN AN INVITATION THAT'S CLASSIC WITH A TWIST IS YOUR ANSWER.

- Send out a 5x7 matte or glossy white card with bright orange, hot pink, lime green, or aqua lettering—or do the reverse and send a colored card with white writing.

- Use classic block lettering, all flush to the left.

- Stay simple with the font size. You're making enough of a statement with the color contrast. You don't need to do any other fancy stuff.

- You can print the type in different shades of one color, which is called Pantone shading. It is not as expensive as using multiple colors but it looks rich.

- Keep the envelope twisty as well. Either use a white envelope with type in the same color ink as the invitation inside or do the opposite, with a colored envelope that matches the invitation's text color and the address and return address written in white ink.

STEPHEN DORFF AND LARA SHRIFTMAN INVITE YOU TO CELEBRATE HARTWELL'S BIRTHDAY. WEDNESDAY, SEPTEMBER 12, 2000 TEN P.M. TO ONE A.M. MORGAN'S BAR 237 MADISON AVENUE NEW YORK CITY RSVP 917 351 8684

·········· ALL CAPITAL LETTERS

ORANGE PRINTING ON A WHITE CARD ADDS SPUNK

·········· THE COPY IS FLUSH LEFT

YOU'RE INVITED!

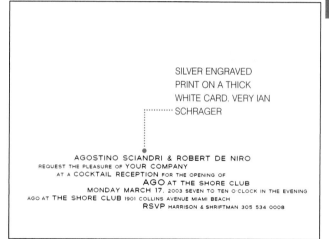

SILVER ENGRAVED PRINT ON A THICK WHITE CARD. VERY IAN SCHRAGER

AGOSTINO SCIANDRI & ROBERT DE NIRO
REQUEST THE PLEASURE OF YOUR COMPANY
AT A COCKTAIL RECEPTION FOR THE OPENING OF
AGO AT THE SHORE CLUB
MONDAY MARCH 17, 2003 SEVEN TO TEN O'CLOCK IN THE EVENING
AGO AT THE SHORE CLUB 1901 COLLINS AVENUE MIAMI BEACH
RSVP HARRISON & SHRIFTMAN 305 534 0008

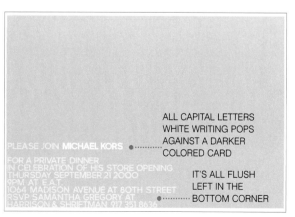

PLEASE JOIN MICHAEL KORS
FOR A PRIVATE DINNER
IN CELEBRATION OF HIS STORE OPENING
THURSDAY SEPTEMBER 21 2000
9PM AT E.A.T.
1064 MADISON AVENUE AT 80TH STREET
RSVP SAMANTHA GREGORY AT
HARRISON & SHRIFTMAN 917 351 8684

ALL CAPITAL LETTERS WHITE WRITING POPS AGAINST A DARKER COLORED CARD

IT'S ALL FLUSH LEFT IN THE BOTTOM CORNER

Hugh M. Hefner & Christie Hefner invite you to celebrate Playboy's 50th Anniversary

Thursday, December 4, 2003 9pm-1am / 11pm Tribute

The New York State Armory Lexington Avenue at 26th Street

This invitation admits two Non-transferable / Photo ID Required Dress to Kill

RSVP to Harrison & Shriftman 917 351 8684 No cameras allowed

LEFT: CLASSIC INVITATIONS GET A GROOVY EDGE USING AN EMBOSSED LOGO, SETTING THE PRINT FLUSH RIGHT, AND CHOOSING CHIC CARDSTOCK. WHAT BETTER WAY TO HEAR ABOUT PLAYBOY'S 50TH ANNIVERSARY BASH?

COME ON, GET FUNKY

If classic with a twist is still too stuffy for your taste, forget the standard card and go for something big and buxom or extra-petite. (Just note: Small and large envelopes may require more postage.) Blow off clean, simple fonts in favor of dramatic cursive, bubble letters, and kooky calligraphy.

You can even abandon paper altogether. We've printed or written invitations on nylon, spandex, leather, and lace. It doesn't matter what the medium is: glass, Plexiglas, Lucite, or a cocktail napkin—we've used 'em all for fun little cocktail parties.

At a party for the opening of the Los Angeles Hugo Boss store, we printed the invitation on red paper with black ink. We framed the card in a magnet, which guests could stick on their refrigerators as a reminder. For landmark birthdays, like twenty-one, thirty, and fifty, send invitations printed on the back of baby photos.

A SOPHISTICATED INVITATION, PRINTED ON LEATHER, WAS A MASCULINE TOUCH FOR THE OPENING OF DUNHILL, A LUXURY LIFESTYLE BRAND FOR MEN. YOU CAN PRINT ON ANY KIND OF FABRIC OR ATTACH A CARD TO MATERIAL USING GLUE, INDUSTRIAL STAPLES OR LEATHER OR RIBBON TIES THROUGH HOLE PUNCHES. STILL LIFE: DEVON JARVIS.

CHIC TIP

You may feel you need help with your invitations. If you have a large budget, call a graphic design company.

COMPUTER GENERATED FUN FONT EXAMPLES

zapf chancery	The quick brown fox jumps over a lazy dog
Elephant	**The quiek brown fox jumps over a lazy dog**
Kidprint	The quick brown fox jumps over a lazy dog
Party LET	The quick brown fox jumps over a lazy dog
Spumoni LP	**The quick brown fox jumps over a lazy dog**
Giddyup	The quick brown fox jumps over a lazy dog
Gadget	**The quick brown fox jumps over a lazy dog**
NYX	THE QUICK BROWN FOX JUMPS OVER A LAZY DOG
CUTOUT	THE QUICK BROWN FOX JUMPS OVER A LAZY DOG
Comic Sans MS	The quick brown fox jumps over a lazy dog
Jokerman LET	The quick brown fox jumps over a lazy dog
Bickley Script LET	The quick brown fox jumps over a lazy dog
Khaki Two	The quick brown fox jumps over a lazy dog
Greymantle MVB	The quick brown fox jumps over a lazy dog
MOJO	**THE QUICK BROWN FOX JUMPS OVER A LAZY DOG**
OUCH	THE QUICK BROWN FOX JUMPS OVER A LAZY DOG
XBO Futura Extra BoldOblique	**The quick brown fox jumps over a lazy dog**
Impact	**The quick brown fox jumps over a lazy dog**
Textile	*The quick brown fox jumps over a lazy dog*
Humana Serif ITC TT-Light	The quick brown fox jumps over a lazy dog

FUN FONTS YOU CAN FIND ON YOUR COMPUTER.
(THE SENTENCE USED AS A SAMPLE CONTAINS EVERY LETTER OF THE ALPHABET.)

OUT OF THE BOX

A stationery store can be your best resource for creating a funky invitation. Hunt for sassy imprintable or fill-in-the-blank creations with bubblegum colors, fanciful writing, inspirational quotes, or wild images that match the theme of your bash. There are hundreds of companies that make great products that you can personalize with stickers or ribbons. In Chapter Eleven, you will find a list of our favorite resources for such invitations.

But you don't even have to use cards that were designed specifically for invitations. Why not use simple notepad paper, embellished with a groovy design, or print something on long, rectangular slips of velum? For a Puff Daddy party, we had one day to print the invitations. So we bought blank white response cards that were 3x5 inches. We took them to a photocopy store and had them printed with the basics: time, date, and location of the party. We closed the envelopes with a fabulous gold wax seal. The whole thing cost less than $50 for 500 invitations. It may have been a simple, inexpensive job, but it let everyone know a funky evening awaited.

HANDS-ON

Got a few hours to kill? Some of the best invitations can be created by revisiting your sixth-grade arts-and-crafts projects. Here are some crafty tips.

- Can't splurge on fabulous paper? Take plain sheets of white paper and soak them in tea or red wine. It will stain the paper and give it a thicker, antiquated (hence expensive) appearance.
- Make gatefolds. Take a rectangular piece of paper and fold the edges inward to meet in the middle, creating flaps that, when opened, reveal a center panel with the invitation text. Take this trick one step farther by gluing a card with the details of your party on the center of a larger, rectangular piece of paper. Then create gate-like flaps by folding over the excess paper and sealing it with a sticker, wax, or label.
- Put retro photo corners to use. Stick the corners to a piece of paper and insert your card. This adds weight to the invitation, giving the impression of heavy card stock.
- Punch a hole—or many—in the top of the invite and weave it to a background piece of paper with ribbons, string, or yarn.
- Use a sewing machine to make decorative zigzag stitches or to attach two pieces of paper together.
- Glue pressed, dried flowers to paper.
- Use vintage postcards, or make your own by copying an image onto simple ecru notepaper.
- Make a collage using color copies of maga-

dance

as though no one is watching you,

love

as though you have never been hurt before,

sing

as though no one can hear you,

live

as though heaven is on earth. -souza

MAKE UP YOUR OWN QUOTE, SOMETHING THAT REPRESENTS YOUR PARTY AND YOUR PERSONALITY, AND SEND THAT. GREETING CARD COURTESY OF QUOTABLE CARDS, DESIGNED BY GILLIAN SIMON.

zine cutouts, your favorite photos, or even old junk (ticket stubs, wine labels). For a friend's bachelorette party, the invitation was a collage made up of pictures of all of her ex-boyfriends.

- Make liberal use of transparent vellum paper. You can print on vellum and attach it to a piece of colored or patterned paper or print on the paper and cover it with vellum, to give the invitation a rich, layered effect. Vellum comes in every color imaginable.

GIMMICK-A-GO-GO

If you abhor tradition and want to do something utterly unique, gimmicky and kitschy invitations may be right up your alley. Start thinking of your invitation as a gift, a pre-party present for your guests. Everyone will remember your invitation when you send something unique: a great book (even if you made it), a T-shirt, a journal, a toy, a poster. This works well for theme parties when you send a gimmick that matches your concept.

Your guests may even immortalize the invitation by displaying it. For a dinner party in Manhattan for *Hamptons* magazine, we turned a large conch seashell, calligraphied with the time and date of our party, into an invitation. Each shell came in a beautiful shiny white box tied with an ocean blue ribbon. Half of our friends still have the shell on display on their coffee tables. Anything can become a kitschy souvenir: a feather, a mask, a package of lemon candy with a note that says, "You're a lemon if you don't come."

Don't be afraid of being a little corny. For a dinner party at a restaurant or bar, send a box of matches inscribed with the words, "Come light it up for so-and-so's birthday." For a Christmas party, why not send a snow globe with an invite that reads, "Shake things up this holiday season." We actually did this for the premiere of a TNT Christmas film called *A Christmas Carol*. And at Old Navy, you can actually buy snow globes made

with your own photos. The ideas are endless, whether you print the invitation on a gimmicky item or you send a simple white card tweaked with some kind of trinket.

TO LAUNCH SIMS ONLINE, EVERYONE RECEIVED A CUTE T-SHIRT. THE INVITATION IS PRINTED ON THE BACK. WE SENT IT IN A WHITE, GLOSSY MAILING TUBE. WARNING: COSTLY! THE SIMS™ PARTY INVITATION COURTESY OF ELECTRONIC ARTS, INC. STILL LIFE: DEVON JARVIS.

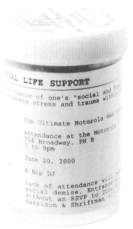

THE RX FOR FUN: A PILL BOTTLE, LABELED WITH THE INFORMATION FOR A MOTOROLA PARTY. TO DO IT YOURSELF, BUY EMPTY PILL BOTTLES, MAKE LABELS THAT RESEMBLE A PRESCRIPTION (WITH A 100-MG DOSE OF YOUR PARTY STATISTICS), AND FILL IT WITH CANDY. THEY'LL TAKE TWO AND RSVP IN THE MORNING. STILL LIFE: DEVON JARVIS.

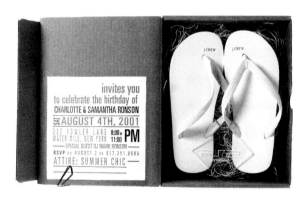

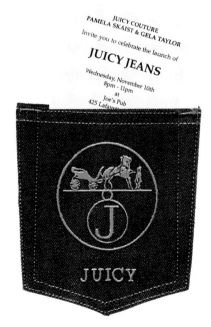

CLOCKWISE FROM TOP LEFT: SNUGGLY SOCKS AND A CARD WITH AN IMAGE OF A SNOWFLAKE WAS A WARM WAY TO INVITE GUESTS TO OUR EXPRESS APRÉS SKI SUITE DURING THE 2002 SUNDANCE FILM FESTIVAL. COURTESY OF PAM SEIDMAN, EXPRESS DIRECTOR OF PUBLIC RELATIONS AND COMMUNICATIONS. WE SENT A SWEET INVITATION FOR THE *LEGALLY BLONDE* PREMIERE: PINK JELLY BEANS, LIPGLOSS, A FAUX PINK-JEWELED RING, AND A PINK-AND-WHITE CARD. FOR JUICY COUTURE'S JEAN-LINE LAUNCH, WE SENT THE INVITATION IN THE POCKET FROM A PAIR OF THEIR JEANS. TO PICKPOCKET THE IDEA, HEAD TO THE SALVATION ARMY, A THRIFT STORE, OR A GARMENT MANUFACTURER TO GET BACK POCKETS FROM JEANS. PRINT AN INVITATION AND SLIP IT INSIDE. EMBROIDER THE DENIM IF YOU HAVE THE TIME. FOR A BEACH PARTY, J. CREW FLIP-FLOPS IN A SAND-COLORED BOX. TO SEND SOMETHING LIKE IT, FIND CHEAP FLIP FLOPS AND TIE THE INVITATION TO THE STRAP. THROW IN SOME SUNTAN LOTION. ALL PHOTOS, STILL LIFE: DEVON JARVIS.

INVITATION INNOVATION

THE MORE ORIGINAL THE INVITATION, THE MORE LIKELY YOUR GUESTS WILL WANT TO COME TO YOUR PARTY—AND REMEMBER IT.

- A view finder. Look inside to get the scoop.

- An empty watch box with a card that reads, "It's time for lunch." We did this for a Gucci Timepiece party. When our guests arrived, we actually gave each a watch!

- A pair of flip-flops printed with the invitation—the better to have a pedicure, my dear. Also, try it for a beach party.

- A CD. Jay-Z once sent nothing but a shiny silver CD in the mail. Printed on the case were the words "Play me." The disc contained a rap song with all of the details for his record release party.

JAY Z, DAMON DASH & ROC-A-FELLA RECORDS INVITE YOU TO CELEBRATE THE RELEASE OF THE DYNASTY SKATE TO THE SOUNDS OF DJ MARK RONSON TUESDAY NOVEMBER 7TH 9PM RSVP CHRISTMAN 310 271 6411

SEND A CD, THE COVER OF WHICH IS YOUR INVITATION. BUY DISCS AT A VINTAGE OR USED MUSIC STORE TO SAVE MONEY OR BURN A MIX OF YOUR OWN. CUT A PIECE OF PAPER (PRINTED WITH THE WHO, WHAT, WHEN, WHERE, AND WHY OF YOUR EVENT) TO SIZE, INSERT IT IN THE CASE, AND PUMP UP THE VOLUME. PARTY INVITATION COURTESY OF ELECTRONICS ARTS, INC.; STILL LIFE: DEVON JARVIS.

- Bags and containers from fast-food places. For a gourmet dinner party, we printed invitations on Burger King bags and then served lobster pizza and steak tartare. We love mixing things up!

- Fortune cookies with the invitation inside. Arrange this through your local Chinese restaurant. You can deliver them in white paper take-out boxes.

- An inexpensive fork, knife, and spoon wrapped in a cloth napkin. Use a marker to write the time, date, and necessary information on the napkin. You can also send the silverware with a "napkin ring," made of a long strip of paper that unravels to reveal the time, date, and place of your party.

FORK • KNIFE • SPOON • FORK • KNIFE • SPOON • FORK • KNIFE • SPOON • FORK

DINNER FOR ....

DINNER DATE ....

DINNER PLACE ....

DINNER TIME ....

DINNER HOST .... RSVP ....

TIE A RIBBON AROUND A NAPKIN-WRAPPED FORK AND ATTACH IT TO THE CARD (OR USE AN INVITATION LIKE THIS ONE FROM SOOLIP, A PAPERIE IN LOS ANGELES, TO WRAP THE UTENSILS).

COACH

REED KRAKOFF, EXECUTIVE CREATIVE DIRECTOR FOR COACH SAYS,

"THERE IS A FORTUNE COOKIE BAG IN YOUR FUTURE."

TUESDAY, OCTOBER 17, 2000 DINNER AT EIGHT O'CLOCK IN THE EVENING

TRADER VIC'S THE BEVERLY HILTON 9876 WILSHIRE BOULEVARD

RSVP TO HARRISON & CHRISTMAN 310 271 6411

CONFUCIUS SAY: GET A FORTUNE COOKIE, PUT IT IN A WHITE PAPER CHINESE TAKE-OUT BOX, SEAL IT WITH A LABEL YOU CAN PRINT OUT AT HOME, AND DELIVER IT IN A BROWN PAPER SHOPPING BAG AS IF IT'S LO MEIN TO GO. STILL LIFE: DEVON JARVIS.

- An iconic game piece. Say you're inviting people for a night of old-school games (Monopoly, backgammon, Twister, checkers, Connect Four). Score points by sending out a hint of what the evening will bring, such as Monopoly pieces, play money, or dominoes.

- Dice, chips, or cards from a nice deck. Perfect for a gambling party.

A DECK OF CARDS WAS THE INVITATION FOR A GAMBLING SOIREE HOSTED BY HUGO BOSS. TO DO THIS AT HOME, STICK A LABEL ON ANY DIME STORE DECK. JOKER'S WILD! STILL LIFE: DEVON JARVIS.

- Cocktail mix or candy that blends with the theme of your bash.

- A little something your guests will eat up, like baked goods, special candy bars with a picture of you on the wrapper, or something exotic from a candy store. For the opening of the first Jimmy Choo U.S. boutique, we sent everyone a chocolate high-heeled shoe. And for a cookbook launch party, we hand-delivered bottles of lemonade and cookies to our guests in the middle of the day.

FOR A BOBBI BROWN AFFAIR WE SENT AN EMPTY LIP GLOSS PALETTE FOR GUESTS TO INDULGE AT THE BOBBI BROWN BEAUTY SUITE AT THE FOUR SEASONS HOTEL TO GLAM UP FOR THE GRAMMYS. GUESTS FILLED THE PALETTE AT THE PARTY. DO THE SAME WITH ANY PRODUCT—NAIL POLISH, SHAMPOO BOTTLES, LIPSTICKS—AND ATTACH A CARD OR LABEL TO THE ITEM. STILL LIFE: DEVON JARVIS.

- Makeup! You can send a flavored lip gloss for a beauty party. For a Clinique party, we sent a pink suede box filled with pastel glosses.

- Socks. For a CAA Motorola party at the Sundance Film Festival one year, we sent invitations along with J. Crew cashmere socks that were sure to keep our guests cozy for the night.

- Key chains. For a Mercedes-Benz launch, the invitation included a road map and a Mercedes-Benz key chain.

- Jigsaw puzzles. You can make your own puzzle by printing the invitation on thick card stock and then cutting it into jigsaw-puzzle pieces, which your guests will have to reassemble in order to decipher.

- Magnet cards. Slide a flat magnet in photo corners on one side of a card and print the invitation on the other. Presto! Magnet card!

THE ENVELOPE, PLEASE . . .

Once you finish the invitation, you need a place to put it: an envelope, packet, or container of some sort. Now we'll show you the art of sealing things up in style.

After putting time and energy into your invitation, you don't want to overlook the envelope. In fact, it's probably the most important part of the invitation because if it's not eye-catching, it will wind up in the garbage. Find envelopes that are brightly colored or use stickers, wax seals, or fabulous fonts that scream, "Open me!" Marc Friedland, president of Creative Intelligence, Inc., who has designed invitations for the likes of Tom Hanks, Steven Spielberg, Oprah Winfrey, Brad Pitt, and Jennifer Aniston, recommends dressing up envelopes with vintage stamps for a bohemian look. He also warns against putting glitter or sand in the envelope, lest your guests hate you for creating a mess.

Do keep in mind that the envelopes should match the look of your invitation and the theme of your party. Our *Glamour* "Don't" party paid homage to the back page of the magazine, where there are always examples of what not to wear. So we created an envelope that epitomized everything you shouldn't do. We used a hideous cheap fluorescent green envelope. We wrote "S.W.A.K." (as in "Sealed with a kiss") on the back flap as well as "Invitation Enclosed" on the front. We used awful return address stickers, the cheap kind you buy

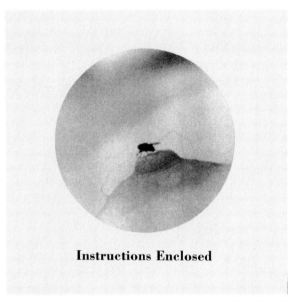

Instructions Enclosed

THE ARTIST'S WAY: ADD A VISUAL GRAPHIC TO THE FRONT OF THE ENVELOPE AND SAVE THE BACK FOR THE GUEST'S ADDRESS AND RETURN ADDRESS. © 2003 BY SEAN LENNON. USED BY PERMISSION.

when you're watching an infomercial at three A.M. Everything about the envelope matched the theme of the party. And everyone tore it open!

You can either custom-order your envelopes or embellish them yourself.

HERE ARE SOME ENVELOPE ENHANCEMENT TIPS

- Ask a friend who has great handwriting to write the addresses—with a calligraphy pen, of course—or hire an art student to do it for a small fee.
- If that doesn't work, run the envelopes through your printer. Use the same font as the one on the invitation. Your printer manual should have explicit instructions for accomplishing this seemingly daunting task. (Please say you didn't toss the manual during a frantic episode of spring cleaning!)
- Not on good terms with your printer? Instead of printing on the envelopes, print out all of your

JUICY LABEL FOR YOGA INVITE: WE MAILED A MINI MAT IN A TUBE WITH AN EYE-POPPINGLY BLUE LABEL THAT INCLUDED ALL OF THE PARTY'S ELABORATE SPONSORS. IT MADE THE PACKAGE STAND OUT.

CURVACEOUS, OVERSIZED (EVEN COLORFUL) SCRIPT MAKES AN ENVELOPE STAND OUT. THIS IS THE WORK OF BERNARD MAISNER OF BERNARD MAISNER CALLIGRAPHY & FINE STATIONERY IN NEW YORK. HE'S A FAMOUS CALLIGRAPHER IN SWANKY SOCIETY CIRCLES.

guests' mailing addresses on clear Avery labels. There are white labels and clear ones. Clear is much more chic. When printing on them, keep the font consistent with that of the invitation. And place the label smack in the middle of the envelope. Consider using a mix of all capital letters for the name and lowercase letters for the address. Use a fancy script for the guest's name. Avery labels are our secret weapon. We use them for everything from sealing gatefold invitations to addressing envelopes.

- Get big labels for big envelopes. And, like the envelope itself, the look of the label should match the invitation. If you're doing something classic, keep the label basic with the same font as you used for the invitation. If you're doing something funky, play with the font and font size. You can even scan an image on the labels to give them some oomph. (Most computers have label printout programs and instructions; make sure to match the type of labels you buy with the program your computer has.) See the Barbie case study for a visual.
- Get an embosser, stickers, wax seals, or colorful ink stamps to embellish cheap white

envelopes. While you're at it, invest in an envelope sealer or glue stick from an art supply store. Paper cuts on the tongue are the worst!

- Use a decorative peel-off stamp and place it neatly in the corner. The post office has holiday, birthday, and graphic stamps to choose from. Pick one that matches the style of your invitation. For an Old Hollywood party, we used Cary Grant stamps.
- Write the return address on the back flap. Always spell out words like "Street" instead of using abbreviations. Return address labels can be tacky, so if you can't write neatly, forget doing a return address altogether. Mark the back flap with a monogrammed stamp or an antique-inspired wax seal to further personalize the envelope.
- Try printing the return address on one envelope and take the rest to a printer to get them copied.
- Write "Personal" on the front.
- Forget tradition. Try going for something unusual, like mailing tubes, boxes, or padded metallic or vellum see-through envelopes.
- Avoid sending postcard invitations because they too easily wind up in the trash bin.
- Don't print "Invitation Enclosed" across the front. We can guarantee it won't wind up with the intended receiver.

THE WRITE STUFF

As soon as you make a commitment to the kind of invitation you want to deliver, you have to come up with something to say. Your wording has to be clear and concise; otherwise who knows where and when people will show up! You can be as formal and earnest or as devilishly clever as you'd like, as long as you cover the basics, like what the party is for and who the host is. There may be a cohost or a committee of hosts; either way, list all of the names involved, as people often go to parties to support their friends and colleagues. You also need the date, time, place, and address.

- While it's always smart to include "RSVP," it's not necessary unless you need to know how many people are coming so you can prepare.
- Specifying attire is optional—unless, of course, attire is an intrinsic part of the party (i.e., black tie, masquerade, hats are a must).
- If the invitation is for a guest and a friend of the guest, or a "plus one," as it is often called, you might want to include that in the beginning. For example, "You and a guest are invited to . . ."
- You may want to include a line that says, "This invitation is nontransferrable," if you don't want random people at your party.
- For a cocktail party, where you have exclusive use of a club only from, say, 9:00 to 11:00 P.M., write "9:00 P.M. sharp" on the invite to prevent people from showing up at 10:30 P.M. and having only thirty minutes before the general public crashes the room. Be specific.
- The invitation for Lara's birthday dinner one year read "Dinner, cocktails, and dancing at 8:00 P.M." The problem was that it was a two-tiered party: Fifty guests were invited for a sit-down dinner at 8:00 P.M., followed by drinks and dancing for two hundred from 10:00 P.M. on. Some of the dinner guests didn't show up until 9:00 P.M. and there was very little time for them to eat. Seating arrangements had to be changed. (Luckily, Lara was armed with extra pens, place cards, and a friend who helped her move chairs around.) If the invitation had said, "Dinner, 8:00 on the dot," things would have run more smoothly. Luckily, in all mistakes come lessons! We learned that it's wise to be specific about the time things start (and end) if timing is an issue.

OM, SWEET OM. FOR GOOD KARMA, WE PRINTED A FUNKY INVITATION ON A PIECE OF AN ACTUAL YOGA MAT TO LAUNCH JUICY COUTURE'S YOGA LINE. NAMASTE.

FÊTE ACCOMPLI!

BIRTHDAY PIECE LXX

Come to a party celebrating Yoko's Birthday
at Mr. Chow on February 18th 2003 9pm NYC.
Clothing optional. Chanel No. 5 optional.
Bring your heart and high heels; sunglasses optional.
Guests will be expected to wear the sky on their sleeves.
Clouds optional.

2003 spring

R.S.V.P. Harrison & Shriftman 917 351 8680

NO NEED TO BE BORING, BE CRAFTY WITH YOUR WORDS.
© 2003 BY SEAN LENNON. USED BY PERMISSION.

PAMELA SKAIST-LEVY & GELA NASH-TAYLOR CO-FOUNDERS JUICY COUTURE and KIM FRANCE EDITOR-IN-CHIEF LUCKY MAGAZINE

INVITE YOU TO CELEBRATE THE LAUNCH OF

Down Dog Couture
by Juicy

THURSDAY FEBRUARY 27TH 11AM TO 4PM

Revitalize your wardrobe with a
complimentary Down Dog Couture yoga ensemble
and a pair of Ugg boots

Renew your body with healthy snacks from Whole Foods
herbal teas from Coffee Bean & Tea Leaf
and vitamins from Country Life

Replenish your spirit in a yoga session with Anna Getty
and receive a foot massage by a soothing reflexologist
then get a naughty tarot reading from Dori Midnight
and leave with your own dirty deck

For good karma, make an appointment

DJ Kidada Nash on the iPod

RSVP with your shoe size to Harrison & Shriftman 310 271 6411
(This invitation admits one and is non-transferable.)

namaste

CHIC TIP

Enclose a personal note in the envelope when you're sending an invitation to someone really special.

For classic invitations, spell out dates (i.e., "twentieth of September") and years (i.e., "two thousand and four"). The copy should be straightforward and formal. Consider using phrases like "[Insert name] requests your presence on the eighteenth of April at nine o' clock in the evening." If you're not sending something that meets the classic formula, you don't have to be so stuffy. Put a little personality into what you write.

HERE ARE SOME EXAMPLES

A BIRTHDAY
At this point in time, direct all of your attention to [name of person].
Stop talking and thinking of anything else.
Drop everything you're doing.
It turns out that [insert name] is turning [insert age]. Be prepared to tell her you love her, that everyone loves her, that she's wearing the hottest outfit you've ever seen, that she should be Madonna's godchild, that you want her to be your godmother, and that she is the nicest, smartest, most spectacular person in the universe. [Add details of time and place here.]

A BIRTHDAY PARTY FOR AN ARTY TYPE
Come to a party celebrating [the name of the person]'s birthday at [the place] on [the date]. Clothing optional. Chanel No. 5 optional. Bring your heart and high heels; sunglasses optional. Guests will be expected to wear the sky on their sleeves. Clouds optional.

NO NEED TO BE BORING. **BE CRAFTY WITH YOUR WORDS.**
© *GLAMOUR*, CONDÉ NAST PUBLICATIONS, INC.

A LADIES' LUNCH
Yes, Bippy, darling, the time has come for another of our lavish lunches. Be a dear and have James bring the car around on [the date and time] and meet the ladies at the Colonial Diner. Oh, but please, don't make a mention of this to that Buffy Deardale. As of yesterday, she is no longer a member of our club.

A GIRLS' NIGHT OUT
If you don't have something nice to say, sit next to me. Gather for a night of gossip, cavorting, and all-around bad behavior.

A COCKTAILS AND DESSERT PARTY
Wear something yummy and get your sugar high over cocktails and candy for Karen's 3-0!

A DINNER PARTY
Let's all be civilized (somewhat, anyway) and sit down for a proper meal at my place. Bibs, a must.

AN OSCAR-NIGHT PARTY
Come watch the Oscars and make fun of bad dresses, guess who's wearing Versace, and bet on the winners. The envelope, please . . .

THE EXTENDED INVITATION FAMILY

Save-the-date, response, and direction cards (or maps) are close cousins to the invitation. They are not necessary, but, like a supportive family member, they often make your life easier. No matter what the size of your party, these cards are great anxiety inhibitors in that they let you alert your guests to the date of your party. They give you a tangible indication of who is coming and they alleviate your fear that no one will find your event.

PUT IT IN YOUR FILOFAX (OR PALM)

Before sending the invitations, consider sending save-the-date cards, which are cards that let people know you have big plans and you want them in on the action. A month or two before your event, pop a save-the-date card in the mail, so your guests know to keep their calendars clear for your party. Save-the-date cards can be anything: a formal card, an e-mail, a well-designed fax. The key to sending a sharp save-the-date card is making sure it matches the invitation's concept, style, and color scheme. These cards—even if they're in the form of an e-mail—always get people excited, giving them something to look forward to. For a huge roller-skating party we threw to launch Skechers Four Wheelers, a modern version of the seventies' sneaker-skate, we sent each of our guests one hot-pink wheel, printed with the date of our party. Who's not going to immediately block off the date after getting something like that? Of course, the main thing a save-the-date card requires is—well—the date, as well as the occasion for the party and the name of the host. If you want to add time and place, that's fine, but it's not necessary.

SEND SASSY SAVE-THE-DATE CARDS, LIKE THIS ONE (TOP) DESIGNED BY ROBIN MAGUIRE, A DIVISION OF THE CHATSWORTH COLLECTION. THE CARD FOR JIMMY CHOO'S SUPPER IN SOUTHAMPTON FEATURED A SIMPLE CLASSIC SCRIPT ON A WHITE 3X5 CARD WITH EMERALD GREEN WRITING (CENTER).

please

SAVE

the

of

for

invitation to follow

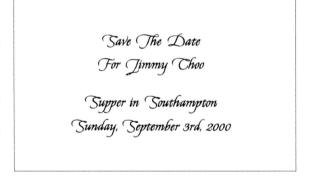

Save The Date
For Jimmy Choo

Supper in Southampton
Sunday, September 3rd, 2000

TAG THIS DATE!
WHO...
WHAT...
WHERE...
WHEN...

USE DIFFERENT PHRASES LIKE "CHECK THIS DATE," "HOLD THIS DATE," OR "PUT IT IN YOUR PALM." PUNCH A HOLE IN THE CARD AND EMBELLISH IT WITH A RIBBON OR LEATHER CORD OR PRINT IT ON A BOOKMARK. CARD FROM EDITIONS LIMITED, A DIVSION OF THE CHATSWORTH COLLECTION.

HEY, ARE YOU COMING OR NOT?

Response cards let guests tell you if they're accepting or declining your invitation. Response cards belong in the envelope with the actual invitation, and you should provide an addressed return envelope for them. Stamps are optional, but are always a nice touch. Response cards are typically 3x5 inches; they always match the invitation in font, ink, card stock, border, and motif and they should include a deadline by which to respond. Response cards are only necessary for formal affairs. Here are some examples.

THE TRADITIONAL RESPONSE CARD

Example 1
RSVP (optional line)
The favor of a reply is requested before the eighth of December
M_____
Will _____ attend

Example 2
RSVP by February first (or Reply requested by . . .)
_____ will attend
_____ will not attend

Example 3:
M_____
_____ accept with pleasure
_____ decline with regret
Please respond by the second of April.

Your language, however, can be a bit more feisty. Here's an example.
_____ will spend the night with you.
_____ won't spend the night with you (and will live to regret it)!

If it's a charity, add a line like: Please accept my donation of _____

You might want to include food options and have someone check off what they want to eat, i.e., the striped bass or the Cornish hen.

RSVP
before the twenty-seventh of March

M _____

will _____ *attend*

____ *Poulet Cordon Bleu*   ____ *Tournedos Auberge*
____ *Truite Florentine*

_____

REGRETFULLY DECLINES

TO DO WHAT

YOU ASK.

Reply requested by January thirty-first

_____ *will attend*

_____ *will not attend*

Please accept my donation of $ _____

ASK YOUR GUESTS TO TELL YOU IF THEY'RE COMING OR NOT. INCLUDING MENU CHOICES MAY MAKE YOUR CATERER'S (OR YOUR) LIFE EASIER (TOP, CARD BY CRANE'S). AN RSVP CARD DOESN'T HAVE TO BE TRADITIONAL (CENTER, CARD BY STUDIO MEN-Z MENDOCINO). IF YOU'RE HOSTING A CHARITY BENEFIT, MANY GUESTS SEND DONATIONS WHETHER THEY'RE ATTENDING OR NOT. SO MAKE SURE THERE'S A LINE THAT SAYS, "PLEASE ACCEPT MY DONATION OF . . ." (BOTTOM, CARD BY CRANE'S).

CHIC TIP

Instead of sending response cards, include on the invitation an RSVP number that has a scripted voice-mail message, repeating the details (time, date, place, dress code) of your party so you don't have to call anyone back.

TURN RIGHT AT BRANDYWINE DRIVE

No matter where your party is—at an out-of-the-way house up a long and winding road, at a restaurant in a neighborhood that's often tricky to navigate, on a plot of sand on the beach, or a hundred yards to the left of a famous landmark—sending directions will save you hours of jockeying phone calls from guests who have no clue how to get to your party. Sure, people can find directions on a map or online, but sending them is always wise. In addition to traditionally written directions, we like to give our guests maps that are clear but cleverly designed. You can include this with the actual invitation or send it just days before the party. You can mail it, deliver it, fax it, or e-mail it. Just be sure to include the name, date, and time of the party so it doesn't accidentally wind up in the trash. Also, make sure you offer directions from the north, south, east, and west.

GOING POSTAL!

You have your invitations (and all of the accoutrements) printed, sealed, and ready for delivery. All you have to do now is send them. The post office is a tricky place. How many times have you sent out mail that didn't reach its destination on time? And how many more times has something been returned to you because you used the wrong stamp? Every savvy entertainer should understand the ways of our mail system. Here are some tips and vital facts.

- Weigh the invitation to make sure you have the right postage amount. For a very high-profile fashion show we produced, we didn't weigh our invitations . . . and they all came back to us.

- Mail an invitation to yourself. This will give you an indication of how long it takes to arrive.

- Avoid metering. It looks bad and should be reserved for business mailings only.

- Sending off a load of three hundred invites or ten boxes filled with something gimmicky? The post office has pickup service for a flat fee of about $10.25.

- The deadline for dropping something at a post office so that it will go out the same day is approximately 6 P.M. on weekdays and 4 P.M. on Saturday; however, local times may vary.

- Check the size of the envelope. A standard letter cannot exceed 6⅛ inches in height, 11½ in length, and ¼ in thickness or be heavier than 1 ounce.

- Sending something intracity (you live in Omaha, you're mailing something to a friend in Omaha) should take two days at the most.

- Mailing something to another city takes three to five days.

- It takes about a week—and more money—to send air mail to another country. Surface mail? Allow a month.

- Christmas is the busiest time for the post office, so allow at least one week for your mail to arrive.

- Mail invitations no more than two to three weeks in advance. Otherwise, you'll be at what we call a high cancellation risk. People don't always know their schedules very far in advance. And when too much time elapses between your invitation and the actual party date, half your guest list may forget about your party. A save-the-date will be your best bet if you're dying to let people know about your party a month (or longer) in advance.

THE FINAL COUNTDOWN

You may have sent out your invitations long ago, but your job isn't over yet, my friend. Unfortunately, a lot of people are not responsible RSVPers; sometimes a piece of mail never winds up in the right mailbox; and one of your guests might have moved without your realizing it, so it's important to call whomever you haven't heard from to see if they received your invitation and if they're coming to the party. We always organize this process by typing up a list, alphabetized by first name (it's often easier to remember first names), and checking off who's attending and who's not. Having this in chart form will make it easy to stay on top of your guest list. Twenty-four hours before P-Day (party day) call each guest to confirm that they're coming to your event. You never know when a friend might get so caught up with work that he or she completely forgets about your party. Or scan your invitation into the computer and send a mass e-mail to

your guests (blind CC everyone; you must protect each person's privacy). Once you've taken care of this, roll out the red carpet and let the good times begin.

THE KEY POINTS

The reason there are different types of invitations is that there are different types of parties. If you're having a classic affair, a formal dinner, or a lavish cocktail party where dancing on the tables is a no-no and wearing jeans is not an option, your invitation should follow suit and evoke a traditional feeling with classic paper, hues, lettering, and formats. If you want to do something different, your invitation can be artful, unusual, even quirky. Invitations should be fun, not stressful, so don't drive yourself crazy trying to make them perfect. Just give yourself enough time to make them complete. Use a checklist so you don't miss a beat. Do your research. Shop around to get ideas. Always over-invite—and print extra invitations in case you add people to your guest list at the last minute. Have extra envelopes on hand. Remember the postal regulations. And after delivery, follow up with a phone call.

CHAPTER FOUR
PARTY PRODUCTION
SET THE STAGE

PARTY PRODUCTION
SET THE STAGE

You are not just the host of your party. You are its producer, the head honcho in charge of turning a vision into a reality. This may mean coordinating and setting things up yourself and/or hiring the right people to make the magic happen for you. Either way, your job is to figure out everything you need for a smash hit, one that projects your personal style. Production details are endless, from décor, lighting, and music to gift bags and tricks that make your party extra special. There is so much to think about. For example, do you have a place for your guests' coats? Are you equipped with the appropriate number of plates and serving trays? If your party is outside, do you have an emergency plan if it rains—either a rain date or a tent that you can have set up? Did you devise a lighting scheme and music playlist? It's important to stay organized.

Begin by making lists of everything you *want* and then figure out everything you *need*. The key to any production is that you must stay within your budget. We always recommend doing a run-though, which is a fancy way of saying set it up and see how it all works beforehand (even if it's at home) just to ensure you're set. And while you're dotting your i's and crossing your t's, talk the plan through with a friend to make sure you haven't forgotten something. In order to keep production

CHIC LIGHTING INSPIRED BY THE DELANO HOTEL IN MIAMI BEACH. USE A LARGE SQUARE SILVER TRAY AND ARRANGE AN ASSORTMENT OF WHITE PILLAR CANDLES ON IT (THESE ARE FROM CRATE & BARREL) TO BEAUTIFY ANY TABLE SETTING. © CESARE BONAZZA.

a manageable task, this chapter will be divided into subsections elaborating on specific topics: décor, flowers, lighting, music, gift bags, and fabulous fixes that give your party panache. A producer's job isn't always easy. But, then, nothing worthwhile is.

GET IN THE MOOD

Devise a friendly, inviting environment that shows off your sense of style and meshes with your theme and concept. This leads us to your first official role as producer: interior designer. Your job: to craft the ambiance. At the onset, take the time to envision your party. Think of the space and how you can transform it. Ask yourself what is the space's personality; what does it convey? Is it a mecca of modernist hip, a symbol of rustic country warmth, a luscious Latino escape, an elegant picture of tradition, a retro flashback, a playful pop playground, a Zen garden of tranquillity, a sexy New Orleans–inspired bordello, or a combination of different schemes?

Begin by contemplating the type of party you're having. Will there be a meal? If the answer is yes and you're sticking to formal traditions, it's best to have a table (or many tables, depending on the party's size) and chairs—and enough room to squeeze in a few last-minute guests. Whether you're having a party at home or not, these things are all rentable, as are tablewares of all kinds. If you're hiring caterers, they will go through everything you need from chairs and tables to flatware and serving trays with you—and provide their own for a fee. Say you're having a party that is informal. Be creative and turn the dining area into a Japanese lounge, where your guests eat on the floor (plump up those pillows), or invite people to sit on the living room furniture and eat with plates on their laps; that makes for a laid-back aura that we always appreciate. Turn a long rectangular dining table so it's horizontal and use it for the buffet.

The décor, if done well, will tap into your guests' emotions, give them something they want or need, and take them to a delightful place, whether it's a romantic Parisian park on the roof of your apartment building or a shagalicious seventies palace in your transformed dingy garage. At the parties to launch the Express store in Los Angeles, Miami, and New York, our design concept was denim. The concept was simple, but we took ample time thinking about each element of the event and how we could incorporate denim into it. We covered the furniture and the bar counters in different washes of denim. Coasters, placemats, and napkins were denim. Denim-wearing servers passed cookies, shaped like blue jeans with blue sprinkles, on trays, also swathed in denim. The drinks were denim blue. The "red carpet" was denim. Gobos (lights) of blue denim lit up the floor. There was a denim bar, where guests brought in their old jeans for charity and walked away with a new pair from Express. Everything was denim, right down to miniskirts in the (denim) gift bags. The guests thought it was jean-ius.

You can do the same thing with any material—bubble wrap, aluminum foil, cellophane, silk, satin, leather, plastic—or any concept. Ethnic themes are particularly easy: Do your research on a favorite country and fill the space with décor items, as well as wine, food, and music, that are indigenous to that culture. See the Indian dinner case study, page 188, for inspiration. The point of décor is that it represents the party's character. At a party for

Love Heals, the Alison Gertz Foundation for AIDS Education, at which the Go-Go's performed, we painted round white paper lanterns to look like beach balls. We strung them from trees and put them all over the ground, along with red and white beach balls, to give the party a feeling of fun. For another Love Heals event, the theme was Argentina. To create a sense of dramatic, spicy flair, we got inspired by flamenco-style dresses and took cheap glass vases, covered them with black lace, and filled them with blood-red roses.

For a wintergarden theme, you could mix snowy white table runners with winter-appropriate flowers, foliage, and fruits. Mix warm and cool colors, adding hints of soothing gold, rust, and chocolate, be it fabrics, votives, or decorative items.

No matter where your party is, decorate accordingly. If you're setting up shop in a field, cover straw bales with fabric to make sofas. Make a patchwork of wool blankets and overstuffed pillows on the ground. Serve water out of old-fashioned jugs and pitchers. Bring a picnic table for the buffet. Get an old truck and offer hayrides, play country music and hire a square-dance caller. Use galvanized tubs to make fire pits at night. There are no limits to what you can do. For Lara's birthday party, she transformed the tennis court at Rachel Hunter's house into a luxurious lounge and a dance floor. Mini tents, filled with pillows, lounge furniture, and candles, were placed around the court to create private cabanas where guests mingled.

Each of the case studies in Chapter Nine elaborates on a particular décor. Regardless of the type of atmosphere you manufacture—a formal black-and-white ball with white satin tablecloths, sleek silverware, white roses in full bloom, and white candles and crystal chandeliers flickering throughout or a loco Mexican fiesta with cacti centerpieces, piñatas, and sombreros as chip baskets—you should always keep one thing in mind: comfort.

CREATIVE LOAFING

The most important thing to keep in mind when you're designing your party's décor is to make sure there is enough room for at least half of your guests to sit and for all of them to move around comfortably. That may mean removing some furniture from the space or bringing in furniture. You can buy, borrow, or rent beanbag chairs, folding chairs, futons, chaise lounges, and even mattresses. Move the bed from your bedroom to the common area of your party, be it poolside or in the living room, or rent a California king.

We always construct some sort of lounge area so people can get cozy while they converse. To do this, cluster together chairs, stools, ottomans, floor pillows or cushions, love seats, sofas, low tables, and seating of any kind so that small groups can gather.

CHIC TIP SET UP A FEW LOUNGE CLUSTERS NEAR EACH OTHER SO THAT PEOPLE IN CLUSTER ONE CAN SWIVEL AND CHAT WITH THOSE AT CLUSTER TWO, AND SO ON.

You can do this kind of rearranging anywhere, even at a restaurant, where you can remove tables, push chairs together into groups, and bring in furnishings of your own. At the Hard Rock Hotel & Casino in Las Vegas, we organized a pre–Rolling Stones concert dinner party followed by a post-concert bash at Simon. While the guests were at the concert stadium, we arranged to move the restaurant tables out and replace them with cushy sofas and lounge seating.

CHIC TIP BRING INDOOR FURNITURE OUTSIDE AND VICE VERSA. THERE'S NOTHING LIKE A HAMMOCK IN THE MIDDLE OF A LIVING ROOM OR A LEATHER SOFA BY THE POOL.

WELL FURNISHED
REARRANGE YOUR FURNITURE AND GET INTO THE COMFORT ZONE.

- Line the furniture around the perimeter of the room and leave the central space open or line the furniture around a few open areas, which may wind up doubling as dance floors.

- Remove every stitch of furniture from a venue and lay down low-pile carpeting, pillows, beanbags, cushions, and blankets. Very Playboy Mansion.

- Lean full-length or larger-than-life mirrors against walls or even trees to give the illusion of more open space.

- Hang fabric across a room or a space from one tree or pole to another to divide the area.

- Get exotic with fabric. Place it on the floor, drape it over chairs, and pin it to the corners of a room and to the center of the ceiling to create a sexy cavern-like look.

- Add some cush to the floor with a patchwork of area rugs in suede, faux suede, sheepskin, faux grass, and even bathmats (which are great for outdoor parties). Or go mod with sisal, black Astroturf, or slabs of cork. Get self-adhering carpet savers to hold small area rugs or fabric in place.

- Build a wood, Plexiglas, or linoleum dance floor over the pool, tennis court, or open plot of grass in the yard. This calls for an expert and a hefty budget. We built a dance floor out of canvas at Mr. Chow's restaurant in New York City for Yoko Ono's seventieth birthday. Canvas seemed appropriate for her: She's an artist and her pieces were on exhibition throughout the space.

YOUR GUESTS WILL GET COZY, LOUNGING ON PLUSH SOFAS SET UP IN CLUSTERS. USE INDOOR FURNITURE OUTSIDE, PILE PILLOWS IN CLUSTERS, AND FACE CHAIRS TOWARD EACH OTHER. PHOTOS COURTESY OF AMY GRAVES/WIREIMAGE.COM.

- Hire a construction worker to build levels into an open space and turn each one into a lounge with a different décor theme.

- Paint the room red for a dose of instant sultriness.

- Rent a velvet rope to make your party feel exclusive. (It's called a stanchion.)

- Set up a bar in the corner near the tables where your guests are eating, so people can get up and mingle over drinks throughout the course of the meal.

Once you have the general scheme of your furniture layout, start looking at the details. Here is our guide to tricking out the tables to perfection.

TABLE TIME

It's party time. Do you know how to set a table, what side of the plate the fork should rest on, and where the proper location for the wineglass is? In the etiquette chapter, "Oh, Behave!" we give you a specific diagram. But now we're focusing on embellishments, the real art of tabletop design. Like the rest of décor, tabletop accents can be minimal yet still sophisticated (an autumn theme with long-stem leaves on the plates, a potpourri of fall fruit in glass cylinders at the center of each table, and napkin rings made of strands of dried gooseberries) or playful and fun (trays decorated with dominoes, faux-money name cards, and candy, silly string, retro toys, and party hats).

Have fun with your tabletops and remember it's the little things, like having a bowl of goldfish on the table when you're serving a casual seafood dinner, that make a difference. Even at a formal dinner, you can add some fun by giving guests disposable cameras tied with ribbon and labeled with the date of your party. Put salt and pepper in stylish little dishes with mother-of-pearl spoons.

Instead of traditional napkin rings, use bangle bracelets, oversized safety pins, or inexpensive beaded bracelets that spell out each guest's name. At a luncheon to benefit the American Ballet Theater, underwritten by Celine and hosted by Iman, David Bowie, Blaine Trump, and Michael Kors, napkins were elegantly tied with a Celine bracelet, a gift for each guest, and plates rested on leather placemats.

You can go crazy and spend lavishly on tablecloths, napkins, napkin rings, vases, and such. But you can also make do with what you have. Your plates do not have to match. In fact, it gives a party character when they don't. Clean old alcohol bottles, wrap them with fabric or ribbon, and use them as vases or pitchers. Use strips of fabric or wrapping paper as table runners, tablecloths, or placemats. Or keep things simple with an all-white scheme, which is the easiest, cheapest, and chicest choice to pull off. Think white plates, serving trays, and napkins tied with white ribbon, bud vases with single white roses or white tulips, orchids, white votive candles, and a waitstaff dressed in head-to-toe white.

The ideas are never-ending. You can buy, say, picture frames and incorporate them into the décor. At a dinner we planned for Coach at Asia de Cuba, a trendy boîte in Los Angeles, Coach picture frames holding the menus were at each setting; the guests took them home as gifts at the end of the night. Or you can make something on your own. For buffets, wrap sets of silverware in napkins and place them in glass cylinders, which make cool-looking and functional centerpieces. For beach parties, use empty shells for shrimp cocktail sauce. Graffiti a large piece of hemp cloth and use it as a tablecloth. Sometimes the best ideas are the easiest and oftentimes they're the most unlikely. Just don't forget the main attraction of the table: the centerpiece.

AT THE CHARLES WORTHINGTON SALON COUTURE RESULTS LAUNCH EVENT FOR BEAUTY EDITORS, EVERYTHING WAS BEAUTY-INSPIRED, RIGHT DOWN TO THE CENTERPIECE—LUSCIOUS ROSE PETALS IN SIMPLE WHITE PORCELAIN DISHES. PHOTO BY SARA JAYE.

EASY CENTERPIECES WE LOVE

- Sea glass, seashells, and starfish, placed on the table or in glass containers.

- A large square silver tray, holding white candles of varying sizes. If you don't have great trays, fill bowls with sand and insert tall white candles to create a similarly sexy effect. Or just place a row of white pillar candles down the center of the table. It's so elegant, you won't even need flowers.

- Something that captures the beauty of nature, like peacock feathers in vases. Ostrich eggs, pebbles, banana leaves, pinecones, and cinnamon sticks are also good centerpiece embellishments.

- Float gardenias in water. It's simple and elegant. Add food coloring to the water for drama.

- For an autumn party, place candles in carved or painted pumpkins and add seasonal foliage.

- Glass hurricane lamps filled with pastel-colored Jordan almonds and pillar candles are perfect for parties in April, May, and June.

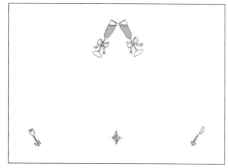

CHIC TIP YOU NEVER WANT TO BUILD A CENTERPIECE THAT'S TOO TALL. IT PREVENTS GUESTS FROM SEEING ONE ANOTHER ACROSS THE TABLE.

PLACE CARDS

Place cards are another vital element of the tabletop landscape. Even for parties as small as six, assigning seats is a smart way to introduce new people to each other, mix up conversations, and alleviate the guests' anxiety over where they should sit.

BOXED PLACE CARDS WITH KITSCHY GRAPHICS FROM ROBIN MAGUIRE, A DIVISION OF THE CHATSWORTH COLLECTION.

WHAT'S IN A NAME?

For formal parties, we always recommend that place cards resemble your invitations. Use the same paper, font, motifs, and style to keep things consistent. Just as with your invitations, you can individualize place cards by hiring a calligrapher, running them through your computer, or handwriting them with a great pen (we like Sharpie's calligraphy pen and the Pentel signing pen).

GET PLAYFUL WITH YOUR PLACE CARDS

- Write each person's name on an object that blends with the theme of your party. For example, write each name on a pretty rock for a Japanese, Indian, or Zen-themed party; use water guns, labeled with each guest's name, for a mobster-theme night. Or find fabulous paper and attach it to something that goes with your theme, such as dolls or game pieces.

- Scribble names on plates with chocolate sauce for dessert parties.

- Buy inexpensive director chairs and have them monogrammed with your guests' names. This is great for movie nights, and the chairs make great party gifts.

- Find die-cut place cards and tie them with ribbon or string to water or wine glasses.

- Pin or tie a ribbon to the back of each chair and attach the place card. Add a flower for extra flair.

- Make collage-style cards using letters cut out from magazines.

- Place a photograph of each guest in a frame.

- Personalize each guest's place card. Write a note to your guest, such as "I sat you next to [insert name] because . . ." or "Talk to [insert name]; she's cute!"

CONTAINERS CUSTOMIZED WITH SWAROVSKI CRYSTALS AND FILLED WITH YVES PIAGET GARDEN ROSES EN MASSE, SURROUNDED BY VOTIVE CANDLES. TO KNOCK IT OFF, GET OUT THE GLUE GUN AND RHINESTONES TO WHIP UP YOUR OWN AND ADD COLORFUL LINENS TO COMPLEMENT THE TROPICAL FLAVOR OF THE FLOWERS. COURTESY OF ERIC BUTERBAUGH, ERIC BUTERBAUGH FLOWER DESIGNS.

WRAP THE INSIDE OF A VASE WITH FABRIC, RIBBON, LEAVES, OR ANYTHING TO SET THE MOOD. THEN SCATTER FLOWERS AROUND THE TABLE. TO KEEP THE FABRIC DRY, USE OASIS, WHICH YOU CAN GET AT ANY FLOWER STORE. COURTESY OF ERIC BUTERBAUGH, ERIC BUTERBAUGH FLOWER DESIGNS.

FLOWER POWER

Flowers can be very simple and inexpensive. You don't need to be a master arranger—or even know your peonies from your poinsettias. Just be aware of what you like and what looks good. Sometimes simple sprigs of ivy in a glass on a table is all it takes. Flower arrangements can be elaborately crafted productions that cost a fortune—why not bring in trees and large plants to line the perimeter of your venue—or as easy and affordable as scattered petals, a bunch of tulips from the grocery store, calla lilies in bud vases, roses from 1-800-flowers.com, or one white orchid in a pretty pot, spray-painted to match your venue.

Flowers, like any aspect of your décor, should match the vibe and concept of your party. If you're doing something seasonal, like a feast for the fall, find flowers to match, like bright-orange honeysuckle combined with glass cylinders filled with olives or plums, which are both in season during that time of year. For the summer, use sunflowers along with shells and sand.

If you're going with an Asian scheme, you may want to find cherry blossoms or lotus flowers. You could even plant white roses or tulips in lovely Japanese teapots. Fill vases or champagne buckets with sand or rocks and add bamboo to enhance the Asian flavor. At Aerin Lauder's island-style beach party, guys were given fresh floral leis and girls received flowers to wear in their hair. No matter what type of flowers you use, add a sooth-

ing glow to the arrangements by surrounding the containers with candles of varying sizes.

When it comes to arranging, we learned a few important tricks from Eric Buterbaugh. Before you buy the flowers, visualize how you want them to look in the end. Otherwise, you might overbuy or wind up without the proper supplies. According to Eric, the thing most people overlook is the supplies. It takes more than a vase and some blooms to make an astonishing arrangement. It's all about the equipment. You might need oasis, a moldable clay-like substance that absorbs water and fits inside containers so you can stick flower stems in it; chicken wire to hold the oasis together; green floral tape; and frogs, the heavy spiked metal discs that hold flowers in place.

Buterbaugh also recommends cutting flower stems as soon as you get home. Then put them in water at room temperature for three hours before creating arrangements. This makes the flowers

FOR A BALINESE DINNER PARTY, ERIC BUTERBAUGH FILLED A THAI WOODEN BOWL WITH SPHERES OF MARIGOLDS, CHRYSANTHE-MUMS, AND SEASHELLS. GET EXOTIC WOODEN BOWLS AND ARRANGE SOMETHING LIKE IT, COMPLETE WITH VOTIVE CANDLES AND SINGLE FLOWERS STREWN ABOUT. COURTESY OF ERIC BUTERBAUGH, ERIC BUTERBAUGH FLOWER DESIGNS.

stronger. Also, feed your flowers. Buy Crystal Clear from the flower market or put two to three spoons of sugar and a cup of bleach in a gallon of water. The bleach kills bacteria so the water stays clean and the sugar feeds the flowers to make them last longer. And ice cubes will be your new best friend. If you have orchids, put ice in the container weekly to keep them fresh.

Once you've decided on your arrangements, figure out where you want to place them. While flowers obviously complement dinner tables, there are plenty of other spots where they do a party justice, including the entrance, cocktail tables, the bar,

HERE ARE SOME FAST AND FLAWLESS
FLOWER FIXES YOU CAN DO ANYWHERE.

- Place pretty petals in clear glasses of any kind.
- Place a single flower in the fold of each napkin.
- Tie a ribbon around the back of each chair and place a flower in the middle of the bow.
- Buy bouquets of cheap roses from a supermarket and hedge them at home. To hedge, remove all thorns, leaves, and baby's breath, and cut the stems to one uniform length. Pack the flowers tightly together and put them in a low round or square vase, which you can embellish by tying with ribbon that matches the flowers. This works just as well with calla lilies, daisies, tulips, even branches and pussy willows.
- Tie together three separate bunches of roses—each bundle a different shade of pink or a different color all together—with a ribbon and place them in one vase for a grand arrangement that sits near the entrance of the party.
- Purchase clamps from a hardware store and nail them into the wall. Insert single bud vases in the clamps and add one long-stem rose—the kind that comes with a plastic water container attached to the stem—in each clamp. Create a flower wall with rows and columns of floral clamps.
- Use fresh herbs—rosemary and basil, for example—instead of flowers. Place them in glass containers on the tables. They're aromatic and earthy.
- Place different types of wildflowers on each table to paint the room with vibrant colors.
- Put one flower from the centerpiece arrangement at the top of each person's plate.
- Decorate vases with fabric; surround vases with candles; turn wine bottles, fish bowls, glass cylinders, or chic boxes into vases. Decorate your candle holders to match.
- If you have a nearby flower mart, visit it at the end of the day, when vendors lower their prices.
- Use flat rocks or marbles in glass vases for a decorative element.
- Place a simple vase of brightly colored flowers on a wooden tray. Scatter the same flowers on the tray and add votive candles for an exotic look.

serving tables of any kind, the place card or gift bag table, window ledges, mantels, powder rooms, and any other place that needs a bit of decoration.

If flowers are important to you, make them the focal point of your décor. Visit an upscale flower shop to get arrangement ideas. But remember, flowers are not must-haves. We have thrown many great events without a single petal.

LET THERE BE LIGHT!

Once you've handled the furniture, general décor, tabletops, and flowers, the next level of design is the lighting, which can make or break any party—and will dramatically affect the way everyone looks. As Donna Summer sings, dim all the lights, sweet darlin', and dance the night away.

Regardless of the type of party you're throwing, lighting is essential. The right lighting will make your room, drinks, food, and guests look more beautiful. Whether you hire an expert to wire your space or buy a bunch of votive candles from your local housewares store, lighting creates the ambiance, from serene (candles and dimmers) to rock 'n' roll (rent strobe lights and mirrored disco balls).

Think about the type of party you're having and the statement you want to make when you're planning a lighting design. For something flashy or promotional, we often get gobos. These are thin patterned discs like stencils that are placed over lights to create images on the floor, wall, ceiling, or any other surface. At the launch for Wet by Beefeater at the Delano Hotel in Miami, Florida, we installed flaming-red gobos that projected the word "Beefeater" in the pool. If the party involves entertainment of any kind—a band, a dance performance, a fashion show—the lighting must highlight the act. It's always important to consider the venue in question. For instance, stores are not known for subtle lighting, so when we hold events in boutiques, we typically soften the lighting or even bring in an entire new lighting scheme.

INTERIOR LIGHTING

Day or night, for parties of five or parties of five hundred, you never want your room to be too bright. The only exception to this is the entrance; it should always be well lit. To keep the rest of your party space on the dark side:

- Head to a hardware store or a place like Target or Wal-Mart for DIMMERS, which you can connect to any lamp.

- Pick up amber and GOLD LIGHTBULBS, which add warmth to a space; pink and red bulbs for a theatrical element; and blue and green bulbs to add a cool hue to the room.

- Look for EDISON BULBS, which have exposed filaments; they look chicer than your average, run-of-the-mill bulb.

- NIGHTLIGHTS are really sexy lighting for a party. They are an inexpensive alternative to lighting.

- Add romance and highlight your guests' best features by UPLIGHTING a room, which is done by using halogen bulbs in floor lights (lights that are set into the floor) and pointing them against the wall.

- At a local lighting store, find GLASS FILTERS for any lamp; these illuminate the space in a lovely, ambient way.

- Bentley Meeker, who has done the lighting designs for many Harrison & Shriftman parties as well as the weddings of Liza Minnelli and Catherine Zeta-Jones, recommends replacing the bulbs in recessed lights with narrow spots to CREATE POOLS OF LIGHT.

- Bring on the CANDLES—the easiest and cheapest way to get in the mood. Just don't use too many—no more than three to six candles per three hundred square feet of space—because they give off more light than you'd expect.

- Place varying sizes of votives, white pillar candles on trays, wax creations in shapes or colors that evoke the theme of your party, or FLOATING CANDLES in containers of water everywhere—up the stairs, in a fireplace, on the floor around the perimeter of the party space, on tables and window ledges.

- If you have double-hung windows, CENTER ONE WHITE CANDLE IN A SMALL GLASS on the bottom sill and the middle sash for a clean, modern aesthetic.

- Use CANDLES OF DIFFERENT HEIGHTS to add dimension to your tables; this also adds depth to the room.

- Use TEA LIGHTS to spell something out, perhaps a message to your guests. Find letter candles and do the same with them. Get candles in shapes or with cutouts in order to flicker images against the walls.

- Introduce SWEET SCENTS in the atmosphere with a few aromatic candles.

- Use CANDLE-MAKING KITS and create your own in vintage wineglasses of varying sizes.

INSTEAD OF USING FLOWERS, BUY WHITE VOTIVE CANDLES AND LINE THEM UP AND DOWN THE TABLE, SPACED TWO INCHES APART. AT THE END OF THE LINE, USE A CANDELABRA TO ADD GOTHIC DRAMA. © CESARE BONAZZA, AT THE DELANO HOTEL IN MIAMI BEACH.

GET A ROUND SILVER TRAY (THIS IS FROM CALVIN KLEIN) AND SET UP WHITE VOTIVE CANDLES, ARRANGED CONCENTRICALLY FROM THE OUTSIDE IN FOR A CHIC AND SIMPLE CENTERPIECE OR ENTRANCEWAY EMBELLISHMENT. © CESARE BONAZZA.

CANDLES SERVE A DUAL PURPOSE: THEY'RE AS MUCH A PART OF THE ACTUAL LIGHTING DESIGN AS THEY ARE THE DÉCOR. Add them to any centerpiece, or make them the focus of the centerpiece, as there are so many styles that are decorative, highly embellished, and colorful. Our resource guide is full of places to find our favorite wicks.

When it comes to candles, however, take proper precautions to keep the party safe. Make sure all candles are placed in suitable holders that do not easily tip over. Make sure the flames are not near curtains, furniture, and foliage. They should also be out of reach of children and pets. And when the party's over, make sure you have extinguished all of them.

Another lighting trick is to use spotlights to highlight certain areas of the room, such as the buffet table, dance floor, cozy corner lounge, or guest of honor's seat. You can also light up plants, banisters, and columns with strands of white Christmas lights. Less is more if you're sticking with an elegant décor, but go crazy with lighting if you want to add some funk. You can get Day-Glo groovy with glow-in-the-dark stickers on the ceiling, plates, tables, and napkins. Give your guests glow-in-the-dark toys such as yo-yos, glow sticks, bangles, rings, even shoelaces. Play glow-in-the-dark tic-tac-toe. Plug in the lava lamp. Darken the room, turn on the black light, and give everyone white T-shirts so that they glow, too.

While these lighting ideas work well inside, you can incorporate them outside, as well. Christmas lights look smashing on trees, as do disco balls. Rig moving spotlights or flash them on trees. There are other things that work well outside, too.

EXTERIOR LIGHTING

Make sure the venue and the address of your party are well lit. Use a spotlight to save your guests from driving in circles in search of a good time.

We also like to create paths with candles, tiki torches, and lanterns for outdoor parties, especially when we're building a bonfire, another source of light. The path of light works well up a driveway, along a walkway to the beach, around a pool, or leading to the restrooms. Make use of lumis, which are sand-filled paper bags containing candles. Hang flashlights, crystal chandeliers, paper Chinese lanterns, or Moroccan fixtures from the trees. Bring out the candles and use them as you would indoors—up stairs, on tables, around the party's perimeter, floating in water. Set off fireworks at midnight or at the end of the meal to signify a new phase of the night. Get heat lamps if the weather is chilly. And take floor lamps outside to make nature feel as lounge-y and as cozy as your home.

Regardless of where the party is—inside or out—pick any one of these options or use a combination. Any lighting store will offer ideas.

TURN A PATIO INTO A SULTRY OUTDOOR CLUB, COMPLETE WITH SEXY WHITE CHRISTMAS LIGHTS WRAPPED AROUND TREES, LANTERNS HANGING FROM BRANCHES, AND HURRICANE CANDLES ON TABLETOPS AND THE FLOOR, WHICH ARE ENCASED IN GLASS SO THEY WON'T BLOW AWAY. PHOTO BY NIKOLAS KOENIG.

SOUND FACTORY

Music is vital to any party. Tunes, like lighting, are an intrinsic part of the décor, and can make or break an event. We've been to parties where the food and drinks were below average, but the music was so good, we had the best time. At a dinner party for a friend's birthday, our goal was to keep the evening high-energy and wild. So we blasted classic seventies and eighties tunes all night, and everyone got up, Jimmy Choos and all, to dance on the tables. The food, drinks, and lighting may have been perfect, but the party was all about the music.

We've also been to many events at which bad music choices killed the harmony of the night. At the V.I.P. post–Bruce Springsteen–concert fête at the Hard Rock Hotel & Casino in Las Vegas, we hired a rock 'n' roll deejay . . . who played hip-hop all night. Not that there's anything wrong with hip-hop, but it wasn't right for our gathering. But all fiascos offer valuable lessons: We learned to discuss playlists with deejays before all parties.

But before you figure out what to play, you have to figure out how you want to play it. It doesn't have to be complicated. You can keep things simple and handle the sound yourself. Just get a few killer compilation CDs—storebought (see page 252 of "Our Yellow Pages" for more details) or homemade—and use your own stereo. Just make sure, in advance, that your equipment works well and you know how to use the shuffle and random functions that keep the music going.

If you don't have decent sound gear, borrow from a friend, rent it, or get high-tech with an at-home deejay computer program that shuffles and mixes songs as well as Janet Jackson's producer. If you're hiring a deejay, get a demo mix before you sign a contract. It's also wise to ask to drop in on a party where the deejay is spinning to make sure you like his or her work. And if the party is outside, you'll need a generator, heavy-duty extension cords, or battery-operated equipment.

If you don't want to handle the music yourself, hire, beg, or bribe someone to do it for you. While a well-known deejay may set you back $5,000, there are amateurs out there, up-and-comers aching to get their start, who will do the job at an affordable price. Talk to deejays you like at local bars and clubs. Ask your friends if they know any music-obsessed, tech-keen people who could work your party. If you can find a deejay class, reach out to the students, who would probably be so happy to get some experience that they'd do your party for free.

You can also hire live performers: a groovy band, a cool folk singer you discovered at the coffee shop (hey, that's how Jewel got her start), dancers, harpists, pianists, violinists, or students at music schools who are available at very low cost.

IT RUNS IN THE FAMILY. BROTHER AND SISTER DEEJAY-DYNAMO DUO MARK AND SAMANTHA RONSON IN ALL THEIR SPINNING GLORY. PHOTO BY JEFF VESPA/WIREIMAGE.COM.

CHIC TIP

Always do a sound check before the party starts to make sure everything is in order. Find a decibel level that's right for you. At a cocktail or dinner party, for instance, the music should be loud enough to be noticed, but not so loud that your guests have to scream in order to converse.

JOHN TAYLOR OF DURAN DURAN
ON PARTY MUSIC
DURAN DURAN IS ONE OF OUR FAVORITE BANDS. THEIR GREATEST HITS ARE A GREAT CD FOR ANY TYPE OF PARTY.

FOR A GOOD PARTY I NEED TO RELAX AND NOT WORRY ABOUT THE SOUNDS. LITTLE PREPARATION IS NECESSARY. I RECOMMEND:

- SOMETHING JAMAICAN—MY FAVORITE IS *STUDIO ONE ROCKERS* (SOUL JAZZ RECORDS). IT CUTS A FIERCE SWATHE THROUGH THE LAST FORTY YEARS OF JAMAICAN MUSIC: SKA, REGGAE, AND EARLY DANCEHALL. A HISTORY LESSON.
- SOMETHING INDISPUTABILY FUNKY—WITH JAMES BROWN'S *STAR TIME* COLLECTION (POLYGRAM RECORDS), THE *JAMES BROWN'S FUNKY PEOPLE* CDS ARE ALSO FOOLPROOF. YOUR GUESTS WILL ASSUME YOU ARE A FUNKY MUTHAFUCKA.
- I FEEL THE SAME WAY ABOUT CHIC, ALTHOUGH THEIR FUNK IS COOL, NOT SWEATY. TRY *THE BEST OF CHIC VOLUME 2* (RHINO). EVERY TRACK HAS THAT FAMILIAR CHIC VIBE WHICH IS AN UPLIGHT TO ANY GET-TOGETHER.
- SOMETHING GRUNGY AND ENGLISH—I REALLY LIKE CD NUMBER ONE OF A RECENT TWO-CD ROUGH TRADE COMPILATION, *POST PUNK 01* (ROUGH TRADE/MUTE).
- SOMETHING FOR THE WIFE—IN MY CASE, SOMETHING SMOOTH AND SEXY. WE LIKE THE HOTEL COSTES'S CDS, MIXED BY STÉPHANE POMPOUGNAC, ESPECIALLY *QUATRE*. MIND YOU, WE LIKE EVERYTHING ABOUT THE HOTEL COSTES: THEIR CANDLES, THEIR CHOCOLATE CAKE, THEIR ACCENTS. PROBABLY BECAUSE OF THE NAUGHTY BUSINESS WE LIKE TO GET UP TO IN THEIR ROOMS.
- SOME TECHNO WITH EDGE—*MUZIK MAGAZINE* GAVE AWAY AN AMAZING COLLECTION TITLED *ELECTROCLASH 19 TRACK MIX* BY MISS KITTEN (MUZIK). IT'S THE BEST ELECTROCLASH ALBUM UNDER GOD'S SUN.
- AS RECOMPENSE I SUGGEST CHECKING OUT MIXMAG.NET. THEY WILL SEND YOU SAMPLES OF THE HOTTEST BRITISH DANCE FLOOR TUNES EVERY MONTH.

If you're having a cocktail or dinner party, create a musically mellow mood with something lounge-y and chill or beautiful and classic, not overpowering. These options can range from Beethoven to jazz, Frank Sinatra to Marvin Gaye. If you expect to entertain a funky crowd, add flavor to the music repertoire with music that sparks conversation: a brand-new band from London, a Latin import, some exotic world-music group, or a compilation mixed by a famous Parisian deejay. If you're having a dance party, it's always best to pick music that your guests are familiar with. When people hear tunes they like to sing along with, they will be inspired to hit the dance floor.

THE VINYL COUNTDOWN! DJ RUKUS AND LENNY KRAVITZ AT SETAI'S "ART LOVES MUSIC" EVENT AT THE SKYBAR AT THE SHORE CLUB HOTEL IN MIAMI. PHOTO BY SETH BROWARNIK/RED EYE PRODUCTIONS.

HERE ARE SOME SUGGESTIONS FOR MUSIC WE LIKE FOR VARIOUS TYPES OF PARTIES.

EASYGOING BREAKFAST, BRUNCH, OR LUNCH

Keep music in the background so people don't have to yell to have a conversation. The sound should be unassuming but cool enough to ease your guests into a pleasant mood. Try soul or gospel, or choose Nina Simone, Chet Baker, Miles Davis, Getz & Gilberto, Diana Krall, India Arie, Van Morrison, Dido, Indigo Girls, and anything from the classical section of the music store.

DISCO BRUNCH

Pair pancakes with Abba and turn on the Bee Gees, Donna Summer, and the Village People. Your model is Studio 54 in its heyday, a fun, happy, playful mix of seventies hits. Order one of those greatest disco dance hits soundtracks so often advertised on television.

AFTERNOON TEA

Consider hiring a harpist or pianist or roaming violinist—or all three of them. If that's not up your alley, get airy with Enya, soothing with Ravi Shankar's sitar, and peaceful with the type of new age music you'd hear during your yoga class or at a boutique that sells incense and crystals.

CLASSIC COCKTAIL PARTY

Get suave with Cole Porter, Billie Holiday, Philip Glass, opera arias, Elton John, Burt Bacharach, or any selections from the aforementioned Afternoon Tea and Easygoing Breakfast, Brunch, or Lunch parties.

FUN COCKTAIL PARTY

If the scene is hip and urban, the music should be sexy, sultry, and lounge-y. Think Sade, British funk, Roy Ayers, Ray Charles, big funk bands like Groove Collective or Luscious Jackson, downbeat R&B, *Buena Vista Social Club,* and Brazilian or Afro Cubano CDs (see the "world music" section of any music store). You could even bring in a gospel singer, bongo players, or Indian tabla drummers; hire some percussionists; or find a band that takes recognizable pop hits and transforms them to campy "elevator music."

LATE-NIGHT COCKTAIL PARTY

Turn it up a notch with hip-hop, light rap, and classic rock 'n' roll à la the Beatles, David Bowie, Bruce Springsteen, Lenny Kravitz, the Doobie Brothers, Warren Zevon, and the Rolling Stones. Have fun and shock your guests with something crazy. Consider playing hard rock and hiring burlesque dancers for entertainment. If you're having a cocktail or dinner party that transitions into a late-night bash with dancing—or wild behavior of any sort—start the evening off with something slow and sultry and then ease into more upbeat music to change the energy of the soiree.

FORMAL DINNER PARTY

Refer to Easygoing Breakfast, Brunch, or Lunch; Afternoon Tea; and Classic Cocktail Party for ideas.

Or, offer a bolt from the blue, like Moroccan music and belly dancers or a mariachi band between courses. Wow your guests from time to time.

FUN DINNER PARTY

Think sexy, soulful sounds, as well as R&B, reggae, jazz–hip-hop–fusion, salsa; and anything Latin. Many great hotels offer compilations of sultry sounds, which you can find online. They're perfect for lounging all night long.

BEACH OR POOLSIDE PICNIC

Keep it light and fun with salsa reggae; Peter Tosh, Maxi Priest, Black Uhuru, Steel Pulse, and any member of the Marley family will do. Hire a samba or salsa band if your budget permits or bring in djimbe drummers and African dancers.

CASUAL OUTDOOR DINNER

Go for classic songs and singers that everyone loves. Think James Taylor, Simon and Garfunkel, Cat Stevens—or hire an acoustic guitarist. If the theme permits, you could also play country.

FORMAL OUTDOOR DINNER

Classical music is always lovely, but to add a bit of a twist, offer swing music at the end of the evening—and perhaps bring in professional dancers to give lessons to your guests.

BILLY BOB THORNTON'S MUSIC PICKS
ACADEMY AWARD WINNING ACTOR/WRITER/ DIRECTOR/PRODUCER AND MUSIC GURU BILLY BOB THORNTON OFFERS UP HIS BEST PARTY MUSIC.

EASYGOING BREAKFAST, BRUNCH, OR LUNCH
GEORGE WINSTON/AUTUMN
JAMES TAYLOR/THE BEST OF JAMES TAYLOR

DISCO BRUNCH
DONNA SUMMER/ ON THE RADIO

CLASSIC COCKTAIL PARTY
EDGAR VARÉSE

LATE-NIGHT COCKTAIL PARTY
TOM WAITS

FUN DINNER PARTY
COMMANDER CODIE

BEACH OR POOLSIDE PICNIC
THE BEATLES

CASUAL OUTDOOR DINNER
NORAH JONES
THE ALLMAN BROTHERS
A CD MOST PEOPLE DON'T KNOW, JJ CALE. IT'S SPOOKY SULTRY MUSIC.

COOL COMPILATIONS

Whatever kind of party you're having, there is a compilation CD that will work with your concept, from quiet dinner-party music to mood-mellowing jazz, to hits from the fifties, sixties, seventies, and eighties. Buy a few, put them in your CD player, and hit the random button. Here are some of our favorites, which you can find online and at most music stores.

- **CAFÉ DEL MAR**, an exotic blend of sensual, smooth funk and jazz, by a combination of artists such as Bent, Groove Armanda, Dusty Springfield, and Fila Bazilia, which reflects the Balearic spirit of Ibiza. Madonna has said it's one of her favorites. Bliss out to it.

- **HOTEL COSTES #5**, mixed by Stéphane Pompougnac, a French deejay who spins at Le Costes, one of the most exclusive hotels in Paris. It's a collection of smooth, mellow funk so hip, you'll need a martini just to listen to it.

- **THE STANDARD: ROOM SERVICE**, a chill concoction, mixed by deejay Nasir, who plays parties at The Standard, a hotel/celebrity magnet in Los Angeles owned by André Balazs.

- **FUTURE LOUNGE 03**, smooth sounds that unify Latin, deep house, Brazilian, and light techno. Great for chilling out.

- **LA MUSIQUE DE PARIS DERNIÈRE**, an upbeat, somewhat campy synthesis of Malik ("Shaft"); funky remakes of classic tunes like "The Beat Goes On," "Can't Take My Eyes Off of You," and "Rock Around the Clock;" and a few songs in French.

- **MAXIM'S DE PARIS**, a beautiful blend of classical piano, soft techno, and funk, often played at Maxim's, the venerable nightclub/restaurant in Paris.

CHIC TIP THERE IS A COMPILATION CD FOR EVERY MUSIC GENRE—OPERA, CLASSICAL, BALLET, JAZZ, REGGAE, AND SO ON. IF YOU'RE NOT COMPLETELY "DOWN" WITH THE MUSIC SCENE, CONSULT WITH A SALESPERSON AT YOUR LOCAL STORE OR SHOP WITH A FRIEND WHO'S VERY SAVVY ON THE TOPIC.

RUSSELL SIMMONS'S MUSIC TIPS

WHAT IS YOUR FAVORITE COCKTAIL PARTY MUSIC? "DELPHONICS."

WHAT IS YOUR FAVORITE DINNER PARTY MUSIC? "PUBLIC ENEMY (*IT TAKES A NATION OF MILLIONS TO HOLD US BACK*), 50 CENT, ICE CUBE, RUN-D.M.C. (*RAISING HELL*)."

WHAT IS YOUR FAVORITE LATE-NIGHT PARTY MUSIC? "SAME AS DINNER PARTY MUSIC."

PUFF DADDY'S SOUND RULES

- MY FAVORITE COCKTAIL MUSIC WOULD BE SOMETHING DEEP AND INTROSPECTIVE LIKE MILES DAVIS OR JOHN COLTRANE, SEGUEING INTO SOMETHING MORE ENERGETIC TO GET THE MOMENTUM RIGHT.

- DINNER MUSIC MUST BE LIGHT YET MELODIC AND FULL OF SUBSTANCE, SO FOR DINNER I'D BE MORE APT TO LISTEN TO MARVIN GAYE OR STEVIE WONDER.

- LATE-NIGHT PARTY MUSIC IS ENERGETIC THAT YOU CAN DANCE TO. AT THIS POINT IN THE EVENING, YOU THROW OUT ALL THE EXTRA SEXINESS AND GET FOCUSED ON YOUR PARTY, AND YOU NEED TO KEEP IT ENERGETIC BECAUSE WE WILL NEVER STOP! ANYTHING BAD BOY WILL DO . . . WE INVENTED PARTY MUSIC!

MOVIE MADNESS

SOUNDTRACKS FROM FILMS ARE NOTHING MORE THAN GREAT COMPILATIONS. BELOW ARE SOME OF THE SOUNDTRACKS WE LOVE THE MOST.

- REALITY BITES, a mix of Seattle grunge rock that's great for casual gatherings at home.

- MOULIN ROUGE, a playful mix of pop hits, performed by Nicole Kidman and Ewan McGregor in a fun, whimsical way. Add to cocktails and dinners.

- FAST TIMES AT RIDGEMONT HIGH, a light-hearted time capsule of rock circa 1983. It's upbeat and good for taking musical trips down memory lane. We love it for cocktails, dinners, playful beach parties, and eighties theme nights. If you like this, you'll also love the soundtrack from *Valley Girl*.

- PRETTY IN PINK, a medley of eighties soft punk that your girlfriends are sure to love. Perfect for girls-only nights and eighties theme bashes.

- SATURDAY NIGHT FEVER, an amalgam of classic disco hits (Bee Gees and more) that will keep you staying alive when you want everyone to boogie.

- CARLITO'S WAY, a simmering concoction of seventies tunes that are a bit more obscure than those in *Saturday Night Fever*.

- VIRGIN SUICIDES, a seductive, synthesizer-heavy soundtrack from Air, a hot French techno-jazz band. Excellent for cocktails, dinner, and post-party chitchat.

- LEGALLY BLONDE, a loud, upbeat "chick disc," with songs from Mya and Lisa Loeb that will make everyone cheery. Fun in the afternoon, on the beach, or outside on a breezy night.

- ALMOST FAMOUS, an old-school rock 'n' roll combination of Elton John, Led Zeppelin, The Who, and Rod Stewart. Blast it late at night.

- BRIDGET JONES'S DIARY, a fierce fusion of feel-good rock and disco from Chaka Khan, Sheryl Crow, Robbie Williams, Diana Ross, and Marvin Gaye. Play it for morning brunches when you want to amp up the energy or late into the night, when you don't want things to simmer down.

- JACKIE BROWN, an eclectic mishmash of soul, rap, and country. Great for cocktails; as a general rule, so is any soundtrack from a Quentin Tarantino film.

- CRUEL INTENTIONS, a playground of some of the greatest hits of the nineties, featuring everything from ballads and hard rock to British rock and alternative tunes from the likes of Fatboy Slim, Aimee Mann, Counting Crows, and The Verve.

- FRIDA, a sample of Mexican folk music that recalls the full life of the painter Frida Kahlo. We love it for southwestern-style parties and even classic dinners, because it's sexy and rich without being intrusive.

GIVE YOUR GUESTS AN ELEMENT OF SURPRISE AND MUSICALLY MIX THINGS UP. HERE ARE SOME IDEAS:

- If you're having a party at home or someplace where there are many rooms, play different music in different areas to create different vibes. Make one room a disco, another a sixties lounge, and another a haven of classical melodies.

- Ask a musically sophisticated, technologically advanced friend to burn you a CD, mixing music in fresh combinations, like techno and opera and country and rap.

- Throw people for a loop and play something totally unexpected, such as hip-hop at a twenties flapper party.

- Blare show tunes if they fit with your party theme—or if your guests have a great sense of humor.

- Bring on the karaoke. After a drink or two, there's nothing like performing Barry Manilow's "Mandy."

- Rent an old-fashioned jukebox, so people can pick their own tunes.

- Stack CDs by your stereo with a note that says, "Play deejay," along with instructions for using your system. Give everyone the chance to get involved with the music selection.

- Hand everyone sparklers, turn off all the lights, and blast the theme from *Star Wars* when the guest of honor enters the room. Or play the tune when you bring out a birthday cake.

- Burn a CD, name it after your party, and give copies to your guests as a parting gift.

 CHIC TIP MAKE SURE YOU HAVE ROOM TO HOUSE THE BAND'S EQUIPMENT AND CONSIDER SETTING UP A STAGE AREA, EVEN IF THAT MEANS COVERING THE POOL OR TENNIS COURT OR MOVING SOFAS OUT OF THE ROOM FOR THE NIGHT.

GOING LIVE

Live performers add excitement to a party. They offer your guests a free show, a private concert. At the Versace boutique opening on Madison Avenue, Elton John performed. He played only a few songs, but that was all that was needed to get things in gear. And at the opening of the flagship Hugo Boss store on Fifth Avenue, we went with a more gimmicky approach to live music. We hired the "Dan Band," which is led by a goatee-sporting guy's guy who sings—and acts out—strictly female pop hits from the seventies, eighties, nineties, and the present, like "Gloria," "Oh Mickey," and "Love Is a Battlefield."

A performer can really alter the attitude and energy of the entire party. At one conservative Hamptons bash for Mercedes-Benz Formula One, we hired rapper Wyclef Jean to perform. His wild stage antics were something the crowd wasn't quite used to seeing, but Wyclef Jean's performance loosened everyone up and gave people something to talk about.

LIVE ENTERTAINMENT ADDS PIZZAZZ AND GLAMOUR AND WILL ENSURE THAT PEOPLE ARE TALKING ABOUT YOUR EVENT LONG AFTER IT'S OVER.

TRY ANY OF THE FOLLOWING IDEAS:

- If you're having an ethnic-theme party, stick with musicians that reflect the culture. Get a sitar player for an Indian-themed dinner, flamenco dancers for a Spanish affair, and a Brazilian calypso band to transport your guests to Rio for the evening.

- You don't have to get someone famous. The band you like at your favorite bar will certainly do.

- Design the space to match the music. At a Watermill Center party in the Hamptons sponsored by Giorgio Armani, Philip Glass performed under the stars on a beautiful night. Rows of candles lit the walkway to the Armani chairs, which were set up in rows like at the symphony. And at a Bottega Venetta store opening, Duncan Sheik performed while the crowd got comfortable on overstuffed floor pillows that provided a mellow ambiance for the earthy singer's mini concert.

- Find a fun disco cover band, a kitschy Neil Diamond impersonator, or someone who sticks strictly to Dolly Parton hits.

- Hire entertainers to perform with the music, such as swing, tango, or salsa dancers; break-dancers; drummers; acrobats; or celebrity musician lookalikes. A comedian could introduce the music and play emcee.

- Find classical musicians, even if they come from the local high school or university.

- Hire an a cappella group.

- Go Motown with a band that features a horn section and great back-up singers.

- Research independent music managers on the Internet and find one who works locally. These people usually represent up-and-comers who are eager for exposure, or old-timers who are looking to make a comeback. Either might play on the cheap—or even at no charge.

GIFTED

Gift bags are fixtures on the high-profile party circuit: store openings, film premieres, charity benefits, and such. While they're not imperative, they're a nice touch. They let your guests take a piece of the party home, something to remember it—and you—by. Harrison & Shriftman bags are always filled with fun stuff, from beauty products and gift certificates to candy, food, and clothing.

You don't have to be a principal at a public relations company to produce a great gift bag. Gift bags don't even have to be expensive to be good. At a slumber party, say, you can give guests something as simple as a toothbrush and toothpaste—or something as extravagant as monogrammed pajamas if you can afford it. When it comes to favors, it's the thought that counts.

The key is to think about things that either your guests want or are new. Like everything else we mention, party gifts work best when they further the concept, theme, or personality of your event. For example, if you're having a beach-themed event, give people the gift of sun lotion or flip-flops or even a towel. Just remember to make the gifts unisex or have one bag for women and one for men.

If you're having a charity event, companies are often willing to give their product at no charge. Some of the items we like to include in gift bags are chocolate truffles in a beautifully wrapped box, mints, incense, perfume, gift certificates, candy bars with customized wrappers, T-shirts with an iron-on with the name of the party and the date, scented candles, lip gloss or lip balm, slippers, and journals.

 CHIC TIP GIVE A LIVE GOLDFISH IN A BAG. THE PARTY THEN LIVES ON EVERY TIME EACH GUEST SEES THE FISH.

Once you know what gift you're giving, ask yourself how you want to present it. Do you want to use a bag and if so, what kind? A brown paper lunch bag, a glossy or graphic bag from a stationery store, a Ziploc? The bag could even be part of the gift. At parties for Cartier, Coach, and *Glamour,* we gave canvas totes filled with loot. We still spot people carrying those bags to this day. You may forgo the bag concept and put the bounty in a plastic pail, a lovely box, or a pouch made of tissue paper that is tied shut with a ribbon. You can also place the gift at each table setting or have someone hand it out to guests as they leave at the end of the party.

CHIC TIP

Make sure you have someone hand out the gift bags or watch the gift bag table, usually placed by the exit of the party. This prevents guests from pilfering three, four, or ten (we know people who've been thrown out of parties for gift bag theft). And have ten extra bags for every one hundred people at your party. It's better to have too many than not enough.

The Standard
Downtown LA

If you liked playing in this room tonight,
don't make it just a one night stand.
Come again.....

For your next stay, book a
"WOW!" Room and we will give you the "Cheap" price.

Have fun,
André Balazs

STICK A CUTE, PERSONAL NOTE IN THE GIFT BAGS (OR WITH YOUR INVITATIONS). COURTESY OF ANDRÉ BALAZS, THE STANDARD, DOWNTOWN LOS ANGELES.

The book-launch party for *Maneater* by Gigi Grazer, which was held at the home of CAA's Bryan Lourde, was hosted by Ron Meyer, head of Universal Studios; Jim Wyatt, head of William Morris; Rita Wilson; and Steve Martin. The gift bag was so good, consisting of all the elements of the book, such as La Perla underwear, gummy bears, and so on, that when Penny Marshall and Cindy Williams (Laverne and Shirley) left, there were no more and we had to give them posters. And for *Legally Blonde 2: Red, White, and Blonde,* the gift bag included a limited "Elle Woods" edition of Barbie, made just for the film.

CHEAP TRICKS

We can't close the production chapter without mentioning what we call cheap tricks. In the land of happy revelry, a great party is all about the extra touches: the cigars you imported for your modern-day Havana Club, the sparklers you planted on the cake instead of candles, the umbrellas you had on hand for each guest at the end of the night if the weather called for possible showers. We call them cheap tricks (even if some of them are rather pricey) and they elevate any party from drab to fab. If you are hosting a simple affair, add one cheap trick. That is all it takes to make the party special. If you're keeping things traditional, consider throwing your guests for a loop with one zany trick, say, funky place cards affixed to individual handcuffs. Here are some other tips that may inspire you.

- Get hand-held WALKIE-TALKIES (Motorola Talkabouts are the best) to communicate with your staff during the party.

- People love photos. Put DISPOSABLE CAMERAS OR DIGITAL CAMERAS on the tables so everyone can document the night. E-mail the photos or develop the photos later and send them out with a thank-you card. Rent an OLD-FASHIONED PHOTO BOOTH and let guests take fun shots of themselves. Hire a photographer to take Polaroids; frame the pictures in paper frames designed specifically for your party, and hand them out. Or have a disc made with photos from your party and send them to your guests after the fact.

- Provide a GUEST BOOK or a SCRAPBOOK for guests to sign in and write messages. Keep a Polaroid camera and tape nearby so they can stick photos of themselves in the book.

- Create a SPECIAL MEMENTO for your guest of honor. At Kidada Jones's twenty-seventh birthday party, catered by Jerry's Deli in Los Angeles, we created a glitter-enhanced "kissing board." We gave Kidada a Polaroid camera and instructed her to get photos of each guy at the party kissing her. We then taped the pictures to the board and gave it to her as a gift at the end of the night. She loved it. And it got everyone out of their shells.

- Hire a MAKEUP ARTIST or a HENNA TATTOO ARTIST to doll people up. Or bring in entertainment that adds something spicy to the night: CARICATURE ARTISTS, PSYCHICS, MAGICIANS, FACE PAINTERS, OR TAROT CARD READERS.

- DO SOMETHING CRAZY that no one would expect. At a joint fortieth birthday party for two Fortune 500 moguls, the bartenders were naked!

- Give away SHAWLS or something warm if you're having a party outside. At a beach clambake hosted by Lara and Elizabeth Saltzman, the guests were given CASHMERE SWEATERS after dark, when it typically gets chilly by the ocean. You can do this with SWEATSHIRTS, LONG-SLEEVED T-SHIRTS, or WRAPS. If your budget allows, have them embroidered or stenciled with the date of your soiree.

Hello
my name is

Ivana B. Taken

Hello
my name is

Jail Bait

Hello
my name is

Prima Donna

CHEEKY PARTY TAGS (LIKE THESE FROM SMART ALEX) ARE GREAT ICE BREAKERS. MAKE UP YOUR OWN TO GO WITH YOUR PARTY.

PLEASE BE SURE TO BRING PHOTO I.D.

ENTRANCE PASS

Event Name
Venue
Sunday, January 1, 1900
11:30 PM ARRIVAL

PLUM SYKES

Admit
1

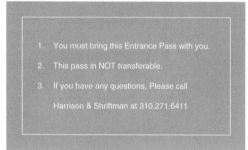

1. You must bring this Entrance Pass with you.

2. This pass in NOT transferable.

3. If you have any questions, Please call

   Harrison & Shriftman at 310.271.6411

January 20–February 18

Aquarius

You have an inventive mind and are inclined to be progressive. You lie a great deal.

You are inclined to be careless and impractical. You depress people.

Even your dog hates you.

CUSTOMIZE COASTERS BY PRINTING LABELS AND STICKING THEM ON TOP. DO IT WITH SUGAR PACKETS, JARS, BOTTLES, AND MATCHBOOKS, TOO. SMART ALEX HOROSCOPE COASTERS STIMULATE FLIRTY CONVERSATIONS ("HEY, WHAT'S YOUR SIGN?").

TO KEEP YOUR PARTY TIGHT, SEND EACH GUEST AN ENTRANCE PASS WITH HIS OR HER NAME PRINTED ON IT. TELL THEM TO BRING A PICTURE ID TO GET IN. CHEAP TRICK: GIVE GUESTS A CONFIRMATION NUMBER WHEN THEY RSVP SO YOU CAN CHECK THEM—WITH PHOTO IDS—AT THE DOOR.

- To break the ice at one party, we gave everyone CHEEKY PARTY NAME TAGS that said, Hello, my name is . . . Hoover Upright, Miss Behave, Ice Queen, Lucy Goosey, Ivana B. Taken, Jail Bait, and Anita Mann.

- To add cachet, mail or hand out PERSONALIZED PARKING PASSES as guests arrive.

- MONOGRAM NAPKINS, towelettes in the bathroom, ashtrays, matchbooks. Your guests will take them home as tokens.

- Don't forget to provide SOMETHING YOUR MALE GUESTS WILL APPRECIATE: shoe shine kits, gift certificates for a massage or a deluxe shave, or fancy cigars. At a Dunhill store opening, the theme was CIGARS and GAMBLING. For cheap tricks, we hired a tarot card reader who specialized in reading financial fortunes, we set up A SCOTCH BAR with tasting stations, and we also brought in a Cuban ex-pat to hand-roll cigars.

- Wind the party down by SCREENING A FILM against a wall, a white sheet, or a rented screen. You can buy a cheap projector or rent one. Or make the film part of the décor by screening it on mute. Pick a flick that goes with the theme of your bash. If you can't think of one, James Bond classics and black-and-white Fellini masterpieces make excellent backdrops.

- Rent a SMOKE MACHINE and put it in high gear when people are burning up the dance floor or being mellow with martinis.

- Hire PROFESSIONAL DANCERS to get a dance party started. And have these experts give lessons, whether it's disco, swing, ballroom, or tango.

18th Annual George Christy Luncheon
Saturday, September 7, 2002
Print Room

FOUR SEASONS HOTEL
Toronto

Wine Selections:
Pouilly Fumé, "Villa Paulus," Masson-Blondelet
Cabernet Sauvignon, Ironstone Vineyards, California

Luncheon Menu

Attack of the Heirloom Tomatoes
in honour of Mr. Ivan Fecan
----- § ----

George Christy's Traditional Chicken Pot Pie
With Fresh Vegetables
in honour of Mr. Garth Drabinsky
----- § ----

Mad, Bad and Dangerous to Know
in honour of Mr. Klaus Tenter
----- § -----

A Rendezvous of Petits Fours
----- § -----

Demi Tasse

- At a party at the Delano Hotel in Miami that we threw for Aquarian friends born in late January through February, we hired an ASTROLOGER and labeled the tables after different signs of the zodiac. We set up TELESCOPES for guests to view the stars; we placed astrology coasters on the tables; and we gave guests an astrology book and g-strings decorated with star signs.

- Use PAPER TABLECLOTHS and offer CRAYONS so your guests can decorate them.

- For sporting events, hire CHEERLEADERS or a marching band from a local high school.

- TRANSPORT YOUR GUESTS to and from the scene of the party. If the parking area is a bit of a walk from the party venue, have someone drive the guests to and from IN AN SUV OR CLUB CAR. We once produced a surprise party for some friends who were celebrating an anniversary. Accompanied by a marching band, guests showed up at the couple's house, put them on a school bus, and rode with them to the party's venue.

- Have guests at a dinner party CHANGE TABLES FOR EACH COURSE, so people can chat with new groups throughout the night.

MENUS ARE AS MUCH A PART OF THE DÉCOR AS THEY ARE CENTERPIECES. PRINT THEM OUT ON GREAT PAPER AND LABEL THEM WITH THE NAME AND DATE OF YOUR PARTY, THEN PLACE ONE AT EACH SETTING. NAME THE DISHES AFTER YOUR FRIENDS—OR THE CONCEPT OF YOUR EVENT—LIKE GEORGE CHRISTY DID AT HIS LUNCH AT THE FOUR SEASONS DURING THE TORONTO FILM FESTIVAL.

- On the night of a big lottery drawing, give all your guests LOTTO TICKETS.

- Buy PERSONALIZED MINTS from a company that takes custom orders or make your own by pasting homemade labels on craft store tins.

GAMING

GAMES ARE A GOOD WAY TO GET PEOPLE TO INTER-
ACT AND BE PLAYFUL. HERE ARE SOME OF OUR
FAVORITES.

- RENT A POOL OR PING-PONG TABLE, OR RETRO
  VIDEO GAMES, SUCH AS PAC-MAN AND CENTIPEDE.

- BRING BACK CHILDHOOD GAMES, LIKE MUSICAL
  CHAIRS, LIMBO, PIN THE TAIL ON THE DONKEY,
  CHARADES, AND A PIÑATA.

- PLAY "FORTY QUESTIONS," WHERE EACH GUEST
  WRITES A FAMOUS NAME ON A SLIP OF PAPER AND
  DROPS IT INTO A HAT. NEXT, EACH GUEST PICKS
  ONE OUT AND, WITHOUT READING IT, STICKS THE
  PAPER TO HIS FOREHEAD, SO EVERYONE ELSE
  SEES THE NAME. THEY GET TO ASK THE CROWD UP
  TO FORTY YES OR NO QUESTIONS TO FIGURE OUT
  WHO THE PERSON IS (I.E., "AM I A MAN? AM I DEAD?
  AM I A MUSICIAN? AM I A MOVIE STAR?").

- PLAY CLUE, CHESS, CHECKERS, BACKGAMMON,
  GIN RUMMY, DOMINOES, POKER, TIC-TAC-TOE, DICE,
  CARDS, JACKS, DARTS, MONOPOLY, TRIVIAL
  PURSUIT, PICTIONARY, OR "SIX DEGREES OF KEVIN
  BACON."

- SET UP SONY PLAYSTATION®2 OR XBOX ON BIG-
  SCREEN TELEVISIONS—ALL OF WHICH YOU CAN
  RENT.

- GET A GAME BOOK FOR MORE IDEAS; SEE PAGE
  253 OF "OUR YELLOW PAGES."

 CHIC TIP USE A TWISTER MAT AS A TABLECLOTH IF THE
THEME OF YOUR PARTY IS GAMES.

BE A PLAYER. MAKE GAMES, EVEN THE KIND FROM THE SIXTH
GRADE, PART OF THE FUN. PICTURED HERE ARE CARDS FROM
(TOP) "50 OF THE FINEST ADULT PARTY GAMES" AND (BOTTOM)
"50 OF THE FINEST AFTER DINNER GAMES." COURTESY OF THE
LAGOON GROUP, WWW.THELAGOONGROUP.COM.

Hide and Streak

THIS IS A VERSION OF THE TRADITIONAL
CHILDREN'S GAME – ONLY TO BE PLAYED BY
CONSENTING ADULTS!

HOW TO PLAY

YOU WILL NEED:
FOUR OR MORE PLAYERS
HIDING PLACES
AROUND THE HOME
OR GARDEN

Just like in the children's game, one
player goes off and hides somewhere
in the house, and then everyone else
goes to look for them. Whoever finds
the hidden player first, becomes the
next person who has to hide and be
discovered by the others.

But here comes the "adult" element: the finder is allowed
to nominate one of the other players,
and this person will have to remove
an item of clothing. And so the
game continues.

Obviously there is a question
of attitude here. Players can be
either fair-minded, into equal
opportunities and generally
magnanimous – in which case they
will make sure that everyone undresses

101

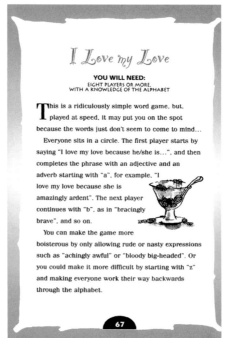

I Love my Love

YOU WILL NEED:
EIGHT PLAYERS OR MORE,
WITH A KNOWLEDGE OF THE ALPHABET

This is a ridiculously simple word game, but,
played at speed, it may put you on the spot
because the words just don't seem to come to mind...

Everyone sits in a circle. The first player starts by
saying "I love my love because he/she is...", and then
completes the phrase with an adjective and an
adverb starting with "a", for example, "I
love my love because she is
amazingly ardent". The next player
continues with "b", as in "bracingly
brave", and so on.

You can make the game more
boisterous by only allowing rude or nasty expressions
such as "achingly awful" or "bloody big-headed". Or
you could make it more difficult by starting with "z"
and making everyone work their way backwards
through the alphabet.

67

DON'T FORGET ABOUT THE BATHROOM

When planning a party, people always forget about the bathroom. One of the worst things that can happen at any event is if you don't have enough restrooms. If you have only one and there are more than fifty people invited, consider renting some high-quality portable toilets. And whether you rent a venue or entertain at home, all restrooms must be clean and inviting.

- Stock up on extra rolls of toilet paper and place them in a basket by the toilet. Running out of T.P. mid-party is a real pain in the . . .

- Get a wonderfully scented liquid hand soap. It's more sanitary than having all of your guests share one bar; we like Bath & Bodyworks' cucumber melon.

- Provide individual, disposable towels.

- Light scented candles or incense, or place aromatic room sprays on the counter.

- Create a beauty bar. Fill baskets or bowls with hair gel, hand cream, mouthwash in a labeled pump jar, along with mini paper cups and perfume. Tampons can also be kept separately under the sink, as all women instinctively look there first.

- Set out a bowl of individually wrapped lollipops, gum, candy, and mints, all of which can be labeled with the name and date of your party.

- Whatever flowers you use in the main space of the party should also be in the restroom—even if it's just a single bloom.

- Float gardenias, rose petals, or rose buds, along with candles, in the bathtub, to give the room a romantic aura.

- Change the lightbulbs to pink or amber bulbs; they are more flattering than the usual 100-watt numbers.

- Post women's and men's room signs on the doors if there are separate restrooms. And hang pictures, photos, and other decorations that evoke your concept in the stalls.

- Keep extra garbage bags on hand and make sure you—or a helper—take out the trash periodically, so it doesn't overflow.

- Get an attendant to help out if you have the funds.

 **CHIC TIP** KEEP A PLUMBER'S NUMBER HANDY IN CASE OF AN EMERGENCY.

LIGHTS, CAMERA, ACTION

Think about your party's décor right from the beginning. Factor in furniture, tabletops, flowers, lighting, music, and a few tricks to make the event stand out. Hire your staffers and entertainment well in advance, so you're not stressing out at the last minute. And remember that less is more. It's better to make a few fabulous touches stand out than to overcrowd a space and overextend your budget with every creative idea you have. Make the mood magical, comfortable, sexy, soothing, fabulous, and fun. It's all about fun, after all.

CHAPTER FIVE
WE'LL DRINK TO THAT
QUENCH YOUR THIRST IN STYLE

WE'LL DRINK TO THAT
QUENCH YOUR THIRST IN STYLE

You've come up with a concept, scouted locations, invited, and decorated. The next task is to determine what you'll be serving your guests. Start with the drinks, since great libations can jump-start any event. Like everything else, they should mirror your party concept. For instance, if you're having a Mexican fiesta, invest in tequila and transform your bar into Margaritaville. If you're gearing up for an Asian theme, go to a Japanese market to stock up on sake and Kirin beer. At Karen's thirtieth birthday party, our concept was cocktails and candy. We're all huge candy lovers, so we used this theme to save money on food and keep the octane (and flavor) quotient at an all-time high. We placed gummy bears, Sprees, mini Hershey bars, Swedish Fish, and licorice in cocktail glasses and glass jars on each table. For the drinks, we created a sweet menu of candy-flavored martinis, which we called "Karentinis." There was a yummy gummy-bear martini, with gummy bears in lieu of olives. Bartenders mixed watermelon martinis, made with watermelon juice and served with watermelon Jolly Ranchers. And we served chocolate martinis, enhanced with Godiva liqueur and a chunk of milk chocolate. Candy embellished each serving tray and tabletop. Guests used licorice as straws and frozen gumdrops in place of ice cubes. Those sweet treats made the party, as all good drinks do.

Drinks, even the nonalcoholic ones, should never be an afterthought. Savvy hosts are knowledgeable about bartending tools of the trade. They can tell you how many bottles of wine to get for a party of twenty (they can also open wine suavely, without leaving a trace of cork inside the bottle). They know a highball glass from a tumbler and a madras from a mai-tai. They're resourceful when it comes to mixing special drinks and they always have a bar trick (or two) up their sleeves. That is why this chapter will include information on all of the bar basics, like how to shop for alcohol, how to calculate how many bottles you need for parties of any size, the types of glasses and tools you need, and valuable service tips. We will also give you a list of the ingredients that make a home bar potent, and a 101 on wine, champagne, beer, tequila, apéritifs, cordials, cognac, and sake. For your drinking pleasure, we'll introduce you to wacky alternatives for going bottoms up; and provide drink menus for cocktail, dinner, late-night, brunch, lunch, and tea parties. In closing, the chapter ends as all good meals do—with coffee and tea.

Clink-clink.

THESE DRINKS AND JEAN COASTERS ARE FROM OUR EXPRESS DENIM LAUNCH PARTY. COLOR YOUR THIRST WITH MARTINIS, MADE BLUE WITH A DASH OF BLUE CURAÇAO. RIM THE GLASS WITH MATCHING COCKTAIL CANDY AND THROW IN LITECUBES TO ADD INSTANT DÉCOR. MAKE FABRIC COASTERS FOR AN EXTRA KICK. PHOTO BY PAUL COSTELLO.

LET'S DRINK TO THAT

WHAT'S YOUR FAVORITE PARTY DRINK?

- DAVID COPPERFIELD: "SAMBUCA. OR, DEPENDING ON MY MOOD, EVIAN. STRAIGHT UP, THANK YOU."

- DUCHESS OF YORK: "PINK CHAMPAGNE."

- LARA FLYNN BOYLE: "SHIRLEY TEMPLE WITH A SPLASH OF RED BULL."

- MICHAEL KORS: "VODKA."

- DONALD TRUMP: "I DON'T DRINK ALCOHOL. MY SIGNATURE DRINK IS A DIET PEPSI OR COKE."

- AERIN LAUDER: "SANGRIA."

- BOBBI BROWN: "MARTINIS."

TOP DRINKS

HERE ARE THE TOP DRINKS THAT ALMOST EVERY GIRL LOVES AND EVERY GUY SHOULD KNOW HOW TO MAKE.

- COSMOPOLITAN
- MARTINI (THE CLASSIC FORMULA OR VARIATIONS, LIKE THE DIRTY MARTINI, THE APPLETINI, AND SO FORTH)
- SCREWDRIVER
- MARGARITA
- SEX ON THE BEACH
- KIR ROYALE
- BELLINI

BASIC BAR REQUISITES AT HOME

If you're having a party at a bar or restaurant, someone on staff will figure out how much alcohol you'll need to order, based on your budget. The same goes for when you hire a caterer. But if you're having a party at home or at a venue where you're providing the drinks, you'll have to be a smart shopper. Navigating through liquor stores can be a nightmare. There's so much to choose from that, unless you know exactly what you're looking for, it's easy to wind up overbuying or overlooking something important.

First, you have to determine your budget, figure out what you want to serve, and then create a drink menu and list all the ingredients—alcohol, mixers, and garnishes—you'll need. Then figure out how much alcohol you have to buy, which, of course, will depend on the number of guests you're entertaining and the length of the party. You will need considerably less alcohol for a party that goes from 6:00 P.M. to 8:00 P.M. than for something that lasts for four, five, even six hours. The average person consumes one drink per hour. But you can't simply multiply the number of drinks by the number of people you're entertaining and then divide to find the total number of bottles you'd need. You have to factor in the mixers, the ice, the fact that some of your guests may be heavy drinkers, and the size of your glasses, all of which make for a tricky equation—the kind your high-school math teacher probably never prepared you for. Following is a general guide that will help you calculate the drink numbers. Remember that the actual amounts will vary depending on what you want to serve—whether it is only wine, champagne, and vodka cocktails, or a simple selection of beer—and how strong you're making the drinks.

USE THIS CHART TO FIGURE OUT HOW MUCH ALCOHOL YOU NEED

BOTTLES OF WINE FOR DINNER

NO. OF GUESTS	4	6	8	10	12	20	50	100
750 milliliter	2	2+	3+	4	5	8	20	40
1.5 liter	1	1+	2	2	2+	4	10	20

DRINKS PER BOTTLE (MIXED DRINKS)

BOTTLE	1	2	4	6	8	10	12
750 milliliter	16	33	67	101	135	169	203
1 liter	22	45	90	135	180	225	270
1.5 liter	39	78	157	236	315	394	474

DRINKS PER BOTTLE (WINE AND CHAMPAGNE)

BOTTLE	1	2	4	6	8	10	12
750 milliliter	5	10	20	30	40	50	60
1.5 liter	10	20	40	60	81	101	121

FACTORS SUCH AS THE SIZE OF YOUR GLASSES WILL AFFECT THESE NUMBERS.

FOR 6 GUESTS

LUNCH
10 wine/cocktails
10 glasses wine
6 liqueurs

COCKTAILS
12 cocktails
12 glasses of wine
for first 2 hours
9 drinks per hour
thereafter

DINNER
12 cocktails or wine
12 glasses of wine
with dinner
6 liqueurs
6 drinks per hour
after dinner

FOR 10 GUESTS

15 cocktails/wine
15 glasses wine with
lunch
10 liqueurs

20 cocktails
20 glasses of wine
for first 2 hours
15 drinks per hour
thereafter

20 cocktails or wine
20 glasses of wine
with dinner
10 liqueurs
10 drinks after dinner

WINNING WINE TIPS

- FOR A THREE-HOUR EVENT, PLAN ON TWO OR THREE GLASSES OF WINE PER GUEST.

- FOR BRUNCH, BUY MORE CHAMPAGNE THAN WINE.

- BUY EQUAL AMOUNTS OF RED AND WHITE WINE.

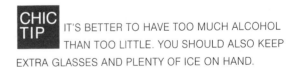 **CHIC TIP** IT'S BETTER TO HAVE TOO MUCH ALCOHOL THAN TOO LITTLE. YOU SHOULD ALSO KEEP EXTRA GLASSES AND PLENTY OF ICE ON HAND.

SPECIAL THANKS TO BARTON INCORPORATED FOR USE OF "MR. BOSTON OFFICIAL BARTENDER'S AND PARTY GUIDE" AND ITS TIPS FOR HOW MANY DRINKS TO PLAN.

WE'LL DRINK TO THAT

CHAMPAGNE

MARTINI

RED WINE

CORDIAL

HIGHBALL

WHITE WINE

LOWBALL

SHOT

SHELF LIFE

There's a specific glass for every kind of drink. While you don't need to own each and every one, it's wise to educate yourself on what's available.

GLASSES YOU SHOULD GET TO KNOW. PHOTO BY PAUL COSTELLO.

HERE'S A LIST OF BARWARE BASICS.

COLLINS

SHOT

HIGHBALL

OLD-FASHIONED

BEER MUG

BEER PILSNER

IRISH COFFEE GLASS

RED WINE

WHITE WINE

SHERRY GLASS

CHAMPAGNE FLUTE

BRANDY SNIFTER

MARTINI

GLASS CLASS

DON'T BREAK THE BANK TRYING TO STOCK THE BAR WITH PERFECT STEMWARE AND SNIFTERS. BE CREATIVE!

- BUY GLASSES AT VINTAGE STORES, FLEA MARKETS, OR TAG SALES. BE QUIRKY AND LOOK FOR RETRO, MISMATCHED, GROOVY STYLES.

- BUY INEXPENSIVE GLASSES AT DISCOUNT STORES.

- USE BEER GLASSES FOR MIXED DRINKS AND WINE GLASSES FOR COCKTAILS IF NEED BE.

- OFFER SMALL PORTIONS OF MIXED DRINKS IN SHOT GLASSES—AND CALL THEM COCKTAIL SHOOTERS.

- RENT GLASSES. THE BEAUTY IS THIS: YOU GET THEM CLEAN AND CAN RETURN THEM DIRTY.

 CHIC TIP SERVE MIXERS IN PITCHERS, CARAFES, OR GLASS CYLINDERS. NOT ONLY DO THESE LOOK GOOD, BUT THEY WILL MASK THE FACT THAT YOU BOUGHT B-LIST BRANDS.

FÊTE ACCOMPLI!

BAR ACCOUTREMENTS

What good is having a bar if you don't have the right tools to open the bottles, stir things up, and shake cocktails to perfection? Below are the tools of the trade that will make you look—and feel—like a professional bartender.

- Can and bottle openers

- Easy-to-use corkscrew

- Glass-stirring rod or long spoon

- Strainer

- Tall heavy-duty mixing glass or shaker

- Sharp knife for cutting and peeling fruits

- Wooden muddler for mashing herbs or fruit

- Large pitcher

- Blender

- Measuring spoons

- Jigger measure with half- and quarter-ounce measures

- Ice bucket

- Ice tongs

- Punch bowl and cups

- Assortment of straws, swizzle sticks, coasters, cocktail napkins, and toothpicks

- One recipe book of cocktail basics. Nothing is more humiliating than not knowing how to make a guest's favorite drink, even if it's something as obscure as a Slimy Lizard.

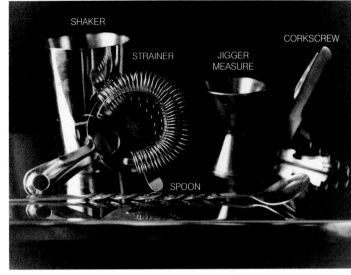

THE TOOLS OF THE TRADE—SHAKERS, BOTTLE OPENERS, JIGGERS, AND SUCH—WILL BE YOUR BAR SAVIORS. THIS SET IS FROM CRATE & BARREL. PHOTO BY PAUL COSTELLO.

SERVICE WITH A SMILE

Once you're well equipped with the basic bar must-haves, it's time to think about how you want to serve your drinks. Presentation is everything. That said, there are essentially two options for getting drinks into your guests' hands: Do it yourself or hire servers. If your budget does not permit you to go on a hiring spree, there are many ways to maximize self-service and make it seem upscale and sophisticated.

- PLACE DRINKS BUFFET STYLE on cocktail tables, coffee tables, or countertops. By mixing drinks in advance and leaving them out for anyone to take, your guests won't get thirsty and you won't have to worry about playing bartender. This works best with wine, bottled beer, and non-carbonated mixed drinks. Keep the ice on the side.

- SET UP MINIBARS near your seating arrangements, so people can help themselves. Offer the things you'd expect to find in a hotel room:

a refrigerated selection of mini bottles of alcohol, various mixers, and prepackaged snacks like nuts and pretzels.

- SAY BONJOUR TO BOTTLE SERVICE. Chill a bottle of vodka over ice and surround it with cocktail glasses and small containers of mixers, such as orange juice, cranberry juice, and tonic, so people can help themselves. This also works with wine, champagne, and pitchers of premade drinks.

SETTING UP TABLES WITH BOTTLE SERVICE IS VERY V.I.P. CLUB CHIC. PHOTO BY PAUL COSTELLO.

BEST SHOTS! MAKE A SHOT BUFFET WITH SHOT GLASSES PLANTED IN A BOWL OF ICE. THIS ONE IS FROM PETROSSIAN (IT'S ALSO A GREAT GIFT). PHOTO BY PAUL COSTELLO.

- CREATE A SHOT COOLER by placing shot glasses in a large glass bowl filled with ice.

- MAKE THE ENTIRE BAR DO-IT-YOURSELF. Let your guests shake, shake, shake it up on their own. You can attractively print out drink recipes, so people know what they're doing or can learn to make something new.

- DON'T FORGET TO TIDY UP as the party progresses by removing half-filled and empty glasses. And always make sure you or a friend remembers to ask your guests if they'd like refills.

CHIC TIP WHEN ADDING MIXERS TO ALCOHOL, STIR IT UP FOR NO LESS THAN TEN SECONDS UNLESS THE DRINK IS CARBONATED, IN WHICH CASE YOU SHOULD STIR FOR ONLY FIVE SECONDS.

If you're doing your own bartending or even mixing drinks in advance, don't be intimidated. Find recipes from your favorite restaurant, a bartending guide book, or a magazine and practice making the drink at home, well before your party starts. Begin by learning the art of pouring. Get speed

FÊTE ACCOMPLI!

pourers, the kind of bottletops that are used in bars; any kitchen equipment store will have them. Then practice pouring: You'll want to start off by filling an empty alcohol bottle with water because it takes a while to perfect the art of pouring and no one likes wasting liquor.

If you hire servers, you'll have someone flitting about with trays of drinks, collecting empty glasses, and offering refills. To hire a bartender, ask a friend who knows his or her way around behind the bar, a student from a local bartending school, or splurge for a pro.

Make sure to offer guests drinks as soon as they arrive. This might mean pointing them in the direction of a table with drinks, having a pedestal that displays drinks near the door, or positioning a server there with a full tray of glasses. This makes people feel welcome. Plus, it gives them a chance to settle into the party without having to wonder where the bar is.

CHIC TIPS

- Never add ice to any drink. Instead, pour the drink into a glass already full of ice. This chills the alcohol evenly as the glass fills up.

- When serving vodka martinis, keep the cocktail glasses and bottles cool. Let them sit in the freezer for at least an hour before using. If you have to recycle a martini glass, just fill it with ice as you mix up the drink. Then spill out the ice before you pour.

- To frost a glass, bury it in ice until it turns white. For a salt- or sugar-rimmed glass, first moisten the rim with a slice of lemon or lime and then dip it into salt or sugar.

POUR STREAK

The proper pouring method is as follows: Hold the bottle at its neck and turn it over, pointing the bottle downward so the liquid flows into a glass. While the bottle is inverted, count to four. That pours out about 1.5 ounces; a martini usually has between 2 and 4 ounces of the primary alcohol per serving. When a recipe calls for a splash, that is a count of one. A dash is a quick count which you achieve by covering the spout with your thumb right after the liquid shoots out.

WELL STOCKED

If you're having a party at home, your first order of business is stocking your bar—and stocking it well. There is nothing worse than running out halfway through a party. It will send you into a tizzy and your guests will catch on that something's wrong. So start to think of your home bar as a collection you're building. Like decorating a new home, if you buy a bit here and a bit there, everything will be complete (and less nerve-racking) by the time your party rolls around.

You may not have a professional bar setup, but it doesn't matter. A desk, kitchen table, countertop, mobile trolley, even a pull-out shelf will do. We always keep a few bottles of wine, champagne (chilled in the refrigerator), and vodka (stored in the freezer) at home at all times because we never know when having one friend over for dinner will turn into an impromptu party. When it comes to alcohol, you rarely need every flavor under the sun. We've thrown parties where we've had nothing more than three spirits (vodka, tequila, and rum) and a bevy of mixers, and other parties where we've kept it even simpler and served only red and white wine and water. When you're planning something specific, however, it's wise to be prepared. So before you go into the liquor store, make a list of what you need.

HERE'S OUR OFFICIAL INDEX OF THE BEST CONSTITUENTS FOR YOUR HOME BAR

The number of bottles will differ depending on the size of your party and what you want to serve, but our guide is based on having A PARTY FOR TWENTY TO THIRTY GUESTS. (Use the guidelines we gave you earlier to figure out the amount of alcohol needed for larger or smaller groups.)

- 1 to 3 bottles of VODKA, including flavored ones. Vodka is always a safe bet because you can serve it on the rocks and it mixes with any kind of juice, soda, or tonic.

- 1 bottle of GIN for old-school martini lovers and tonic drinkers galore.

- 1 bottle of TEQUILA. It's the prime ingredient of a margarita—and a great shot.

- 1 bottle of RUM to make some mean mojitos or spice up sodas, fruit salads, and fruity flavored mixers.

- 1 bottle of WHISKEY, which is basically a broad category that includes bourbons and scotches.

- BEER, red and white WINE, and CHAMPAGNE are a given. Having all three on hand is best, but not a must. And if you're strapped for funds, it's okay to have only enough champagne for one glass per guest for a group toast.

- MIXERS, GARNISHES, and FLAVOR BOOSTERS to add punch to your cocktails. Straight alcohol does not a full bar make. For more details, see the next section.

CHIC TIP TRY TO HAVE YOUR ALCOHOL DELIVERED AND MAKE A DEAL WITH THE STORE THAT YOU CAN RETURN WHAT YOU DON'T USE.

MIX MASTER

A SAVVY HOST ALWAYS KNOWS HOW TO CUT THE STING OF ALCOHOL WITH JUICES, SODAS, AND OTHER FLAVORFUL BEVERAGES. SO LOAD UP ON THE FOLLOWING MIXERS TO MAKE YOUR BAR MORE FLAVORFUL.

- SODA: Tonic, Coke or Pepsi and diet versions, club soda, and fancy flavors, like vanilla-flavored cream soda.

- JUICES: orange juice (freshly squeezed or from the carton), cranberry, grapefruit, lemon, lime, fresh peach for extra-special Bellinis.

- FRUIT PURÉES: melon, watermelon, pear, raspberry, you name it. Display them in labeled containers so people can road-test them all.

- VEGETABLE JUICES: cucumber or tomato.

- HERB INFUSIONS: rosemary or cilantro, to make any cocktail novel.

COCKTAILS FOR FIFTY

REMEMBER THIS: FOR A COCKTAIL PARTY FOR FIFTY, YOU WILL NEED

- 6 QUARTS OF ALCOHOL OF WHATEVER TYPE YOU CHOOSE:
- 4 GALLONS OF JUICE MIXERS
- 25 LITERS (COMBINED) OF WATER, TONIC, AND SODA
- 20 BOTTLES OF WINE
- 1 BOTTLE OF VERMOUTH FOR MARTINIS
- AND 2 CASES OF BEER (OPTIONAL).

IN ADDITION, YOU'LL NEED

- 20 LIMES
- 20 LEMONS
- 10 ORANGES, SLICED FOR GARNISHES
- 10 JARS OF OLIVES
- AND 50 POUNDS OF CRUSHED ICE.

FÊTE ACCOMPLI!

"LITTLE SOMETHINGS"

A COCKTAIL IS ALWAYS SOMETHING WITH SOMETHING, PLUS A LITTLE SOMETHING. HERE ARE THE "LITTLE SOMETHINGS" THAT AMP UP YOUR TASTE BUDS.

- BITTERS—An herbal concoction used to desweeten cocktails, especially champagne cocktails.

- GRENADINE—A liqueur made from pomegranates. It'll add a dose of fruity deliciousness to any colorful cocktail. Mix with margaritas for a refreshing treat.

- COARSE SALT—Use it on the rim of glasses for margaritas, margarita shots, tequila shots. Or sprinkle it in the oyster of your hand (when you cross your forefinger and thumb, the bulge that pops up is the oyster) and take a lick of salt with a shot of tequila.

- TABASCO SAUCE—A few drops in a Bloody Mary pops the flavor and supposedly kills germs (that's why people in New Orleans use hot sauce on oysters).

- CINNAMON STICKS—They work with mulled concoctions, especially wine heated with spices and herbs to create a fireplace favorite.

- GROUND CINNAMON—Use it to flavor sugar when rimming glasses for holiday cocktails such as eggnog. Toss a pinch in a Cosmopolitan to give it an Indian flavor (call it a Tajmopolitan).

- GINGER, CHILES, AND PEPPERCORNS—good for heating things up. Ouch.

PREMADE MIXERS

When bartending at home, the best way to save yourself some time and energy so you won't have to stress during your party is to prepare ahead of time. You can buy premade drinks or mixes (Mr and Mrs T mixers, Margarita, Piña Colada, or Strawberry Daiquiri mixes, etc.), store them, and whip them out when needed. Or, mix up cocktails in advance, store them in pitchers, refrigerate, and bring them out when the event gets started. Just make extra, so you don't have to return to the kitchen to make more in the midst of the event.

GARNISHES

GARNISHES ARE ALL ABOUT STYLE AND FLAVOR. THESE ARE THE ONES TO GET.

- LEMON—Add a lemon twist to any vodka cocktail other than a martini. Keep sliced wedges in a glass by the bar at all times.

- LIME—Add to any gin cocktail other than a martini, unless someone orders one with a twist.

- OLIVES AND STUFFED OLIVES—A martini standard. Load up on them because martini lovers always appreciate extra olives in their drinks.

- ORANGES—Good for anything with Cointreau. Plus, the vitamin C cancels out the negative effects of alcohol.

- CELERY—Its crunchy texture, subtle flavor, and shape make it fun to eat and play with.

- PINEAPPLE—Adds a summery flair to any ole drink like rum and tonic and Screwdrivers.

- BANANAS—Throw a slice in with your chocolate martini.

- FRESH MINT—For juleps, mojitos, and even plain water, a fresh sprig of mint makes all the difference.

- SUGAR—It adds a big burst of sweetness to most cocktails, especially when you use it to rim the glass.

- MARASCHINO CHERRIES—Shirley Temple or Manhattan? Choose your poison. Also toss a cherry into anything it can float on for a sexy splash of red.

- WHIPPED CREAM—It'll froth up hot coffee cocktails to make them lighter and smoother.

CHIC TIP

No bartending license? No worries. With Rose's Cocktail Infusions, you don't need any skills aside from pouring and serving with a smile. Just add one of their flavors—Cranberry Twist, Sour Apple, or Blue Raspberry—to vodka, gin, even champagne, in a chilled, frosted glass and accessorize with a piece of fruit, candy, or a little umbrella.

LESS IS MORE

Stocking your bar doesn't have to be intimidating. When in doubt, it's always best to keep the menu simple. Too many choices mess up the mix. You certainly don't need every little thing we've mentioned. If you're having a simple party at home and you're not hiring a caterer, you don't need every kind of liquor, mixer, and garnish under the sun. Focus on one kind of alcohol, and provide perhaps three flavors or brands of vodka and tons of mixers to make a variety of drinks. Or do the reverse and invest in four different kinds of alcohol and keep only one kind of juice and soda on hand to mix things up. But in any minimalist drink menu, always remember one important rule: Have water, soda, and drinks for those who are aren't drinking alcohol. Here are some of our favorite options for a less-is-more bar, which can work for parties of any size, shape, or concept.

- Serve red and white wine only. It's sophisticated, chic, and easy.

- Serve wine and beer or wine and champagne only. Most people like one or the other.

- Offer champagne only.

- Serve wine and add one mixed drink. You can offer vodka or rum with a selection of mixers (i.e., cranberry, orange, or pineapple juice and tonic) or serve premade cocktails (i.e., Cosmopolitans, Screwdrivers, or even rum and Coke) from a pitcher. This is a good solution for those who don't have the confidence to be an on-demand bartender. And people will generally drink whatever is premade.

- Keep three basic spirits on hand (tequila, vodka, and rum) and as many mixers as you'd like. This will make the bartender's job easy and it won't overwhelm your guests with too many choices.

CHIC TIP

If you're serving a premade drink, make it special: Spice it up by serving it in a groovy glass, adding a cute straw, or throwing in a gourmet garnish.

Once you have an idea of the kind of offerings you want, you can focus on the specifics: the kind of wine you want, the type of champagne worth serving, the range of beers you'll offer. There are so many brands out there that it's virtually impossible to know each and every one. But we can help you map your way around. Below, our guide to wine, champagne, beer, and tequila, the Mexican creation that has a lot more to offer than worm myths.

WINE-O

Someone says, "You choose the wine," and you break out in hives. Red, white, rosé, Shiraz. Should you go with California, France, South Africa? Did you even know they made wine in South Africa? Wine lists are frightening when you don't know what you're doing. Forget all of the correct pronunciations, stuffy rules, and high price tags. The right wine is a matter of opinion. Everyone has different taste buds and appreciation. All you have to know is whether you want something crisp, smooth, bubbly, or bold. And, well, what those adjectives mean.

- CRISP. It's summery, grassy. Think green apples, tart fruits, and citrus flavors. It's always white. (Example: sauvignon blanc.)

- BUBBLY. Sparkling wine, which should not be confused with champagne, which is actually made from grapes that hail from the Champagne region of France. Bubbly wines are dramatic (popping corks, lots o' fizz), and although the flavor depends on the quality of wine you buy, they're usually fresh.

- **BOLD.** Rich, deep red wines that are full-bodied and complex. Dark fruits, figs, dates, raisins are the flavors that typify bold wines. (Cabernets and pinot noirs are bold.)

- **SMOOTH.** It's oaky and suggestive of vanilla. It would never make your mouth pucker. It's a casual wine, good for conversation while sitting on a patio, watching the sunset. Beaujolais is a light red that is also smooth, and chardonnay, the most commonly sipped substance in America, is a smooth white wine.

CHIC TIPS

- Do not confuse a fine rosé with a cheap white zinfandel. Rosés from Provence in France are incredibly luscious and perfect for a hot summer day. White zinfandel is good only for fraternity parties!

- People tend to over-chill whites; when they're too cold, the subtleties of their taste is lost. Pop a bottle in the refrigerator no more than an hour before drinking it. Wine served at 55 degrees is best. Red wines, on the other hand, should be at room temperature.

- All wines should be stored lying horizontally. This aerates the wine and moistens the cork, so that it's easy to remove. Don't be hard on yourself if you have trouble removing a cork. That just means the bottle must have been improperly stored.

A LITTLE EDUCATION

If you want to be a wine connoisseur, there are plenty of books and courses to help you. But here are a few important facts about wine that all hosts should be aware of. And remember, when you're navigating a wine store, ask questions. Wine salespeople are an educated breed.

There are fifty major white grapes grown in the world—just so you know—and the three most important are riesling, sauvignon blanc, and chardonnay. There are forty main red grapes in the world but the ones you should know include pinot noir, merlot, and cabernet sauvignon.

- Rosés are neither red nor white. They are pink and very European. The best ones come from Provence and from Tavel, in the southeast of France. They're best drunk young and are usually tart and fruity.

- French wines are listed by the region they come from; in other words, Bordeaux, Beaujolais, and Champagne are areas in France.

When it comes to buying wines, there are two things to understand. The first is that you should never buy a good bottle of wine in a liquor store that doesn't specialize in wine because more than likely, that wine has sat there for a long time, and its temperature has probably fluctuated, altering the natural flavors. So if you're going to spend over thirty dollars, go to a specialty wine boutique. The second rule is that you don't have to spend a lot of money to find a good bottle.

CHIC TIP IF YOU'RE SERVING MORE THAN ONE TYPE OF WINE THROUGHOUT THE MEAL, ONE FOR EACH COURSE, FOR EXAMPLE, ALWAYS SERVE THE LIGHT WINE FIRST AND THEN THE HEAVIER WINE. THAT MEANS WHITE WINES SHOULD BE SERVED BEFORE RED WINES.

OPENING ACT

To open a bottle of wine is a simple procedure, but many a good wine has been spilled and spoiled by a corkscrew mishap. Of course, before you plunge into a cork with something sharp, first remove the foil. Then slowly insert the pointy end of the corkscrew into the middle of the cork. Screw the worm downward, turning it about four times. You want to impale the cork without going through it, since completely puncturing it will leave chunks of cork inside the bottle. Then smoothly and firmly withdraw the cork. Once the bottle is open, you're ready to pour.

PROPER POURING TECHNIQUE

After opening a bottle of wine, hold the bottle firmly in your hand. If you're pouring white wine, use a towel as a buffer, since the natural body heat from your hand will alter the temperature of the wine. Don't ever let the bottle and the glass touch. Even a little. It's considered a pouring faux pas in the wine world, something only a novice would mistakingly do. You should also know how much wine to pour in a glass. Contrary to popular belief, a glass should never be filled to the rim. Instead, fill it half to three-quarters full. For instance, an 8-ounce glass should take about 5 ounces of wine. The reason: Air is good for wine. It allows the wine to "open up," as they say, which enables its flavors to pop. After pouring the glass, give the bottle a little upward twist as you pull it away, so the bottle's neck turns clockwise. This not only looks graceful, but also prevents the wine from dripping. Never cup a poured wineglass in your hand; body heat alters the flavor.

If you want the wine to open up, pour it into glasses. Simply opening a bottle to let it "breathe" won't much help the wine. Instead, pour it into a glass and let it sit, allowing air to reach a greater surface area of wine.

WHAT'S BETTER THAN A MINI UMBRELLA IN YOUR DRINK? ADRIEN BRODY AND NICK RHODES NEAR YOUR DRINK. FROM THE DURAN DURAN POST-CONCERT PARTY AT THE HARD ROCK HOTEL & CASINO IN LAS VEGAS. PHOTO COURTESY OF DENISE TRUSCELLO/ WIREIMAGE.COM.

BOTTOMS UP! MATCHBOX 20'S ROB THOMAS AND HIS WIFE, MARISOL, AT LARA AND LARA'S OLD HOLLYWOOD BIRTHDAY BASH. PHOTO BY JEFF VESPA/WIREIMAGE.COM.

CHIC TIP

Tag your guests' glasses with "wine charms." These bracelets attach to stems to act as markers so your guests can keep track of their glasses. You can buy them or make your own with beads on wire or pretty colored string. It will avoid the dilemma of whose glass is whose.

BUBBLY!

Bubbly is a vital part of many parties and you couldn't have Bellinis or mimosas without it. When it comes to champagne, you should be aware of certain brand names. Like fashion, champagne is all about the name on the label. There are six big brands you should know. Below, a breakdown.

- VEUVE CLICQUOT—A classic label that used to be obscure, but became chic after a huge marketing campaign in the 1990s. Now, it's served at most restaurants, at the opera, and at events everywhere. It's delicate and aromatic; but, like all things that become super-trendy, the quality isn't what it used to be.

- PERRIER-JOUET—With its beautiful Art Deco bottle decorated with flowers, this champagne looks fabulous on any cocktail table.

- MOËT & CHANDON—One of the most popular brands in the United States, Moët & Chandon is expensive and very well made; it's a bit stronger and muskier in flavor than Veuve Clicquot. Dom Perignon is the top champagne made by Moët & Chandon; it's the bottle they always order in movies when someone wants to celebrate or splurge.

- LOUIS ROEDERER—A posh, old-fashioned house that's known for its purist take on champagne, with a taste that is balanced and never musky. This company also makes Cristal, an exclusive champange originally created for the czar of Russia.

- KRUG—A flavorful number that's very expensive and very worth it.

- MUMM—It's cheap, cheap, cheap, but it will do the trick.

Now that you know brands, you should know that you don't have to stock the most expensive bottles in order to host a sophisticated gathering. If you are serving an inexpensive champagne, we recommend prepouring the bubbly in glasses before your guests arrive and leaving them out. That makes a chic impression and your guests won't even notice that they're not sipping Cristal. If you—or a server—are pouring the champagne, mask the brand name by wrapping a towel around the label. You'll fool everyone. Even yourself. If you don't have champagne glasses—and don't care to invest in them—offer individual mini bottles; we like to serve them with long straws.

CHIC TIP

It's better to buy the cheapest bottle of the best brand rather than the best bottle of a cheap brand for the same price. And if you can't splurge on dozens of bottles, get just one and have a champagne toast.

ONCE YOU HAVE CHAMPAGNE TO SERVE, YOU NEED TO KNOW HOW TO OPEN IT.

- WRAP THE CHILLED BOTTLE IN A TOWEL AND UNDO THE WIRE AROUND THE CORK.

- POINT THE BOTTLE AWAY FROM PEOPLE. THIS IS VITAL; YOU DON'T WANT TO SHOOT SOMEONE'S EYE OUT.

- HOLD THE CORK WITH ONE HAND AND GRASP THE BOTTLE WITH THE OTHER HAND BY THE INDENTATION NEAR THE NECK.

- TURN THE BOTTLE SLOWLY UNTIL THE CORK POPS.

CHAMPAGNE GLOSSARY

WHEN SHOPPING FOR CHAMPAGNE, THESE ARE THE WORDS TO LIVE BY.

- BRUT—A CHAMPAGNE STYLE THAT HAS LITTLE OR NO SUGAR AND IS THEREFORE DRY.
- CUVÉE—A BLEND OF MANY STILL WINES THAT ARE DESIGNED TO BECOME SPARKLING WINES.
- RESERVE—WINE FROM PREVIOUS VINTAGES, ADDED TO THE CUVÉE FOR CONSISTENT QUALITY AND STYLE.
- ROSÉ—CHAMPAGNE WITH A SLIGHTLY PINK TINT THAT COMES FROM EITHER THE ADDITION OF A SMALL AMOUNT OF RED WINE TO THE CUVÉE OR CONTACT WITH RED GRAPE SKINS.
- VINTAGE—THIS REFERS TO THE YEAR IN WHICH THE GRAPES WERE HARVESTED, AND IN THE RAREFIED WORLD OF CHAMPAGNE, A BOTTLING IS ONLY DECLARED VINTAGE IF IT CAME FROM AN EXCEPTIONAL YEAR.

There are plenty of ways to serve champagne, aside from the tried-and-true traditional method—in a glass on its own. Some of our favorite cocktails make use of champagne as a mixer, just one of the ingredients in the potion. Any champagne mixed with fruit purée is a crowd pleaser. And so are the Bellini and Kir Royale. For the recipes, see Chapter Ten, "Eat, Drink & Be Merry."

CHIC TIP THE HOTEL DU CAP, THE FIVE-STAR HOTEL WHERE ALL OF THE STARS STAY DURING THE CANNES FILM FESTIVAL, SERVES BELLINIS WITH LITTLE BOWLS OF PEANUTS AND ROUND CRACKERS.

BEER HERE!

Let's put an end to one prejudice about beer right now: It's not just for frat boys. Beer can be a sophisticated substance to imbibe. For an owner's box party at a football game, we provided some guy's-guy favorites—beer, chips, and junk food—but took the menu up a notch by serving gourmet imported beers, homemade chips with a selection of dips, and steak tartare instead of burgers. We hired astrologers, manicurists, and massage therapists to entertain the women, who wound up drinking more of the beer than the men!

HERE ARE EIGHT INTERESTING IMPORTS THAT ARE GUARANTEED TO IMPRESS.

- BODDINGTON'S—An English ale, it's richer and more full-bodied than, say, a Bud, but not as hard-core as a Guinness.
- DUVEL—A Belgian ale that's very strong, aggressive, and spicy. Not surprising that *duvel* means "devil."
- FOSTER'S "OIL CAN"—This Australian lager beer has a flavorful malty taste, but it's not as strong as Boddington's.
- FRANZISKANER WEISSBIER—A German unfiltered wheat beer with a complex but crisp flavor. Good for those who want to experiment.
- GUINNESS—The light, dry rendition of a classic stout, with a coffee-like flavor. It's velvety and creamy and easy to drink.
- LINDEMANS FRAMBOISE—Our favorite. This is a classy Belgian beer. With a sweet, tart, raspberry flavor, it's more like a wine cooler than a beer.
- SAPPORO—A Japanese beer, made mostly with rice, so it has body but it's not too heavy or rich. An excellent mate for sushi and seafood.

- STELLA ARTOIS—A light, crisp, fruity Belgian lager that hipsters like to order along with mussels and pomme frites.

CHIC TIPS

- Chill beer glasses before serving by placing them in the freezer for an hour.

- To pour, tilt the glass so the beer makes an entrance on a slant. Then straighten as the glass fills. This alleviates over-fizzing.

- Serve bottles of beer unless you're having a clambake. If you're clambaking, go for a keg—and make it chic by hiring a server to work the pump.

- Play quarters and beer-drinking games (check out "Our Yellow Pages" to find a book full of drinking games). They're still fun and crazy after all these years.

- Make a gimmicky beer cocktail by mixing one quart of beer with one-half pint of brandy, two eggs, and small amounts of cinnamon, cloves, and nutmeg to taste.

R&B CHANTEUSE MACY GRAY BETWEEN SIPS AT THE DURAN DURAN POST-CONCERT PARTY. PHOTO COURTESY OF DENISE TRUSCELLO/ WIREIMAGE.COM.

TEQUILA!

Tequila is one of the more exciting spirits. Although tequila is usually thought of as the type of drink that goes hand in hand with spring-break trips to Cancún, producing it is a refined art. High-quality tequila is a delicacy that can cost up to one thousand dollars a bottle. Tequila's top brand names are Cuervo, Patron, Chinaco, Don Julio, Porfidio, and Casa Noble. If you're going with a premium tequila, sip it slowly, as you would a fine wine. Otherwise, you'll miss the subtleties of the flavor.

To shop effectively for tequila, you must be able to decipher the labels. First of all, you should know the type of tequila you like. There are four.

- BLANCO, or white. This type is uncommon in the United States. It's young, no older than sixty days. Although tequila is drinkable right after fermentation, it can be harsh on the taste buds at this stage.

- ORO, or gold. It's the same thing as blanco but with additional coloring and flavoring that makes it look and taste aged.

- REPOSADO, or rested. This tequila is aged from two months up to one year in oak barrels, which makes the flavor woodsy and rich.

- AÑEJO, or aged or vintage. This type has been sitting around for at least one year and up to ten years. After four years, it is placed in a stainless-steel barrel to prevent evaporation and to avoid a too-woodsy flavor. This tequila is dark and delicious.

While you can serve tequila straight up (one glass should really last someone an hour), it is also a fantastic cocktail ingredient for—what else?—margaritas. See Chapter Ten for some of our favorite recipes for killer margaritas.

CHIC TIPS

- **MONOGRAM A FROZEN MARGARITA** by blending Chambord and honey and using a honey squeeze bottle to create the monogram on top of the frothy drink.

- **SERVE DIFFERENT KINDS OF MARGARITAS** in pitchers and offer cocktail glasses, pre-rimmed with salt. Also offer chips and salsa to complement the flavor.

- **USE COCKTAIL CANDY,** which is tangy flavored and brightly colored sugar, to rim the glasses.

- **OFFER A TEQUILA SAMPLER.** This is a platter of shot glasses with various types of tequilas. The Pink Taco, a Mexican boîte at the Hard Rock Hotel & Casino in Las Vegas that is frequented by Bruce Springsteen, the Rolling Stones, Oasis, and the Black Crowes, offers one.

- **SERVE DIFFERENT TYPES OF TEQUILAS** in test tubes. Call it an experiment.

- **GO FROZEN** and serve fruit-flavored margaritas, blended as if they were smoothies.

APÉRITIFS, ANYONE?

- **LILLET.** IT HAS A CITRUS EDGE. SERVE WITH A TWIST OF LEMON OR ORANGE.
- **RICARD.** IT TASTES LIKE CARAWAY SEEDS, THE SAME SEEDS FOUND IN RYE BREAD.
- **PERNOD.** IT'S A FRENCH SPIRIT WITH A STRONG LICORICE TASTE. AS A COCKTAIL, IT BLENDS WELL WITH ORANGE JUICE AND TONIC.
- **SHERRY.** IT'S SWEET, WOODSY, AND NUTTY.

In addition to vodka, gin, rum, tequila, wine, champagne, and beer, there are rare grapes that make luscious dessert wines, cognacs fit for kings, and all sorts of extras for the alcohol aficionado. So let's take a look at the more advanced alcoholic options.

BEYOND THE BASICS

For your more sophisticated pleasures consider apéritifs, cordials, and after-dinner digestifs like cognac. Whether you're organizing a proper dinner party with superb butler service or a casual evening of cocktails at home, these drinks are impressive. Consider them the aristocratic relatives of the basic bar.

Let's look at them in the order in which they're served at a meal. Apéritifs are "openers," the precursors to a meal that awaken the taste buds to the flavors to come. The traditional choices are Pernod or Lillet, but anything—champagne, a rosé, a special tequila import—can be an apéritif if you serve it before the food. Just keep the servings small, as apéritifs are not meant to be full drinks or thirst quenchers. When it comes to apéritifs, it's the thought that counts!

The same goes for cordials, which are generally sweet-flavored liquors and are often a wonderful accompaniment or finishing touch to a meal. They may not be a mandatory addition for a home bar, but they certainly add some pizzazz to the drink menu, even if you're simply adding Kahlúa to coffee or hot chocolate. If you are serving your guests a rich, Italian, garlic-heavy dish, offer Jägermeister or Sambuca, which are so licoricey and strong that they will kill the taste of the garlic between courses. If you're whipping up a fruit salad, try mixing orange juice with Campari, a cherry-flavored cordial, or Midori, a tropical melon-flavored potion, which will complement the sweetness and tartness of the fruit. If you think of cordials as if they were spices, and you take some

CARE FOR SOME CORDIALS?

- AMARETTO DI SARONNO. THIS SWEET AND NUTTY FLAVOR IS GREAT WITH WARM DRINKS, LIKE COFFEE, TEA, AND HOT COCOA, IN WINTER.
- BAILEY'S IRISH CREAM. THIS IS A MIXTURE OF WHISKEY AND CREAM AND, LIKE MANY CORDIALS, MIXES WELL WITH COFFEE.
- GRAND MARNIER. IT'S A RICH, SUGARY, AND FULL-BODIED ORANGE LIQUEUR. USE IT IN COSMOPOLITANS INSTEAD OF TRIPLE SEC.
- GODIVA. A CHOCOLATE-FLAVORED LIQUEUR THAT GIVES ANY DRINK A MOCHA FLAIR.

AFTER-DINNER DRINKS

- COGNAC. ALL COGNACS ARE BRANDIES BUT NOT ALL BRANDIES ARE COGNACS. THEY BOAST A FULL, FRUITY FLAVOR WITH NUTTY AND VANILLA UNDERTONES. BEST SERVED IN A TULIP-SHAPED GLASS IN ORDER TO TAKE IN THE FULL FLOWERY AROMA, THEY ARE AN EXPENSIVE TREAT.

- CALVADOS. KNOWN AS APPLE BRANDY, CALVADOS IS DISTILLED CIDER; IT PRODUCES A WARMING SENSATION ON THE PALATE.

- SINGLE-MALT SCOTCH. SMOOTH AND SMOKY, THESE ARE MEANT TO BE DRUNK ON THE ROCKS OR WITH A SPLASH OF WATER.

- GRAPPA. IT'S CONSIDERED "FIRE-WATER" BECAUSE IT'S ALMOST PURE ALCOHOL.

- PORT. NUTTY, SWEET, AND CREAMY, IT BLENDS FABULOUSLY WITH CHOCOLATE AND WITH CHEESE PLATTERS.

- SINGLE-BARREL BOURBON. THE CHARCOAL-SMOKE FLAVOR OF THIS LIQUOR COMES FROM BEING AGED IN BURNT BARRELS. LIKE SINGLE-MALT SCOTCH, IT'S MEANT TO BE SIPPED. (BAD BOURBON WILL HAVE A MEDICINAL TASTE.)

time to figure out which flavors will match the food you're serving, they will enable you to embellish any party.

If cordials are enhancers that bring out or mask various tastes, then after-dinner drinks, such as cognacs, port, and late-harvest wines, are digestives. Their full-bodied essence is said to settle the stomach. With a relaxing effect that lasts for hours (cigar not included), great for ending an ambitious meal, after-dinner drinks are weighty and dense and are the perfect thing to offer a crowd of people who are getting cozy on the sofa. Offer guests "flights" of spirits—a selection of one type such as single-malt scotches, cognacs, or grappa—in order to introduce them to unfamiliar flavors. Everyone loves trying something new.

KIEFER SUTHERLAND AND KELLY WYNN AT THE MARTINI, MOGUL, AND MEGA-STAR FILLED ROLLING STONES PRE-CONCERT DINNER AT SIMON. PHOTO COURTESY OF DENISE TRUSCELLO/WIREIMAGE.COM.

HEAD TO JAPAN FOR SAKE!

With an alcohol content of 4 percent to 21 percent, sake (pronounced *sah-keh*) is Japanese wine made of rice yeast, water, and an enzyme called koji. It is the drink that most people order at sushi bars, but it goes well with almost anything: seafood, lightly prepared vegetables, chicken lo mein from the take-out Chinese restaurant you love, or steak frites. There are over fourteen thousand kinds of sake on the market. But all you need to know is that there are two basic types of sake: Junmai, which is considered top-shelf because no distilled alcohol is involved (it's typically acidic in flavor); and Honjozo, which is mixed with distilled alcohol, so it's not as pure or tasty.

Within these two broad categories, there are a slew of other kinds. Futsu, or ordinary sake, is your run-of-the-mill type that typically retails for four to five dollars for a 750-milliliter bottle. Futsu sake is great when it's used as a mixer, as even the slightest splash will up the interest of any cocktail. Ginjo, or premium sake, is much smoother and more fragrant than Futsu. It's also, not surprisingly, more expensive, typically costing ten dollars and up for a 750 milliliter bottle. Then there is Daiginjo, or ultra-premium sake, which is more aromatic and flavorful than any of the above. It starts at about twenty dollars and can go up to one hundred dollars for a 750-milliliter bottle. We love Daiginjo because it's virtually hangover free!

The other important thing to note about sake is how to serve it. It can be served hot or cold. How do you know when to do which? The premium stuff is always served cold. If something is mediocre, it is often served warm because heating it up masks the below-par flavor. Sake is also best served in small, almost doll-size ceramic or glass cups. If you don't have a real sake set, use old shot glasses. But don't slug sake down. Like fine wine, sake is meant to be sipped slowly and enjoyed for its aroma and complex flavor. Unlike wine, however, vintage sake is no good. The fresher it is, the

better. Anything older than seven or eight months is considered D-list and should be avoided at all costs. And once you open a bottle of sake, it will keep only for about a week in the refrigerator.

SAKE IS A WONDERFUL ADDITION TO ANY COCKTAIL. IT TURNS A MARTINI INTO A SAKETINI, A MARGARITA INTO A SAKERITA, AND A COSMOPOLITAN INTO A SAKEPOLITAN. JUST ADD SOME TO A TRADITIONAL COCKTAIL RECIPE—OR CONCOCT SOMETHING NEW AND DIFFERENT. SEE CHAPTER TEN TO FIND RECIPES THAT WILL WORK SAKE INTO YOUR REPERTOIRE.

CHIC TIP

Put a shot of sake in a beer glass and knock it back. This is really fun to do in between courses. The first one done is the winner.

WACKY WAYS TO GO BOTTOMS UP

Now that we've schooled you in the ABC's of alcohol, it's time to get creative. Whether your party is classic or not, freshen things up by adding an extra dose of fun to the way you offer the drinks. Doing something a little out of the ordinary gives your guests something to "ooh" and "aah" about. Even at the most sophisticated parties we throw, we always like to add an element of surprise to loosen people up, create conversation, and make the event memorable. So here are some of our favorite alternative ways to go bottoms up.

- Get saucy with a CANDY-FLAVORED (AND CANDY-COLORED) MARTINI BAR everyone will remember. Make a raspberry martini with raspberry vodka, a splash of cranberry juice, and red gummy bears instead of olives. Then serve it on a tray covered with gummies. Mix a sour-apple martini with Berentzen apple liqueur, a splash of sour mix, a slice of apple, and green apple Jolly Ranchers or Pixie Stix as a garnish.

- Remember SNOW CONES, the icy treats that were the highlight of your childhood summer days? Well, bring them back infused with alcohol. They add a playful element to any bar menu.

- Have your guests bob for apples in a vat of champagne and call it "BUBBLING FOR APPLES." Warning: Do this at the end of the night when they won't care so much about their hair and makeup. Also, use waterproof mascara!

- RENT DAIQUIRI MACHINES. You can make strawberry and pineapple daiquiris or banana-mango piña coladas with flavored rum or you can make them sans alcohol.

- Have a SHOT SERVER whose sole job is to pass shots. And these don't have to be straight alcohol. You can also serve mixed drinks in shot glasses between courses of the meal or throughout the night.

- Offer SHOTS IN TEST TUBES resting in test-tube holders, or in campy shot glasses, the kind you find at highway rest stops.

- Serve SCREWDRIVER POPSICLES by freezing vodka and orange juice in Popsicle containers.

- Provide ONLY WHITE DRINKS. This is especially good if you don't want to risk staining the carpet.

- Splurge for an ICE SCULPTURE. Nothing is more fab. At a big Warhol opening at Morton's in Los Angeles, there was a dollar-sign ($) ice sculpture. It was so pop. So cool. So Warhol.

- GIVE YOUR DRINKS PERSONAL NAMES that your friends will "get."

TRADER VIC'S SCORPION BOWL. GET LONG STRAWS AND PEOPLE WILL SHARE. IT'S PART DÉCOR, PART COCKTAIL, AND FULL OF FUN. SCORPION BOWL, COURTESY OF TRADER VIC'S, MERV GRIFFIN'S BEVERLY HILLS HILTON HOTEL, BEVERLY HILLS, CA; PHOTO BY PAUL COSTELLO.

- HOT APPLE CIDER (with or without liquor), served with a cinnamon stick, is delish après-dinner or at an afternoon brunch.

- Serve FRUITY MIXED DRINKS IN FISH-BOWLS with multiple straws (community drinking!). Float a plastic alligator in the bowl. (See page 210 for Trader Vic's Scorpion Bowl.)

- Remember CRAZY STRAWS? If not, reacquaint yourself. Fast.

- Garnish martini glasses with LICORICE STICKS, which do double duty as stirrers and as straws when you bite off each end.

- Make the birthday girl or boy do the amount of **SHOTS FOR THE NUMBER OF YEARS** he or she is celebrating. When we threw a dinner party for a friend at Bond Street, he had to do twenty-one shots to commemorate his twenty-one years.

- Dazzle your crowd and **SET YOUR DRINKS ABLAZE.** Warm up a bottle of brandy, or some other high-octane drink, by heating it in a saucepan over a low flame. Hold the glass by its stem over a flame, as well, to warm that up, too. When the alcohol is good and hot, ignite it with a match. It'll flame up like a science experiment. Pour the flaming liquid into a glass for your crowd. Flames can get unruly, so use pot holders and have a box of baking soda nearby in case you need to extinguish an accident.

- **ADD LIQUOR TO COFFEE,** iced coffee, and ice-blended coffee drinks.

- Make **JELL-O SHOTS** and serve them elegantly; see page 213 for the recipe.

WATCH IT WIGGLE . . . SEE IT JIGGLE . . .
Jell-O shots are not just for frat parties anymore. At a beautiful party for an uptight socialite crowd, we spiced things up by serving colorful Jell-O shots in exquisite china on silver trays. We even offered sugar-free versions for the dieters in the crowd. There were plenty of people whose names began with "Prince" or "Princess," and the shots were a huge hit.

CHIC TIPS

- Use different flavors of Jell-O and alcohol to make funky drinks. For example, Lime Jell-O + Tequila = Margarit-O shots. Orange Jell-O + Vodka = Screwdrive-O shots. Strawberry Jell-O + rum = Daquir-O shots.

- Chill the Jell-O shots in cookie-cutter molds (hearts, stars, moons, animals) and offer them on trays to your guests as they enter the party. It's so much more fun than traditional champagne!

- Place your shots in mini muffin liners or on lovely china plates and leave them on tables or have someone pass them around.

JELL-O SHOTS GRADUATE FROM FRAT PARTY TO SOPHISTICATED COCKTAIL HOURS, ALL WITH THE RIGHT GLASS. PASS ON TRAYS. PHOTO BY JEFF VESPA/WIREIMAGE.COM.

CHIC COCKTAIL TIPS

- Print something that relates to your party on the coasters. At a film premiere party at the Sundance Film Festival, we printed coasters with the name of the film being screened. It's a great marketing and promotional tool.

- Use novelty ice cubes like "Litecubes" (plastic cubes that light up in an array of hues), chunks of frozen lime-shiso jelly, frozen hibiscus tea with star fruit in the center, ice dyed with a drop of food coloring, and sterilized crystals that have been in the freezer overnight before usage.

- Find drinks that you like from other countries . . . and knock them off. We like to add the limoncello, a classic Capri cocktail, to our menus.

WOULD YOU LIKE A DRINK MENU?

It doesn't matter if you're throwing a party for four or a party for five hundred. These drinks are some basic menu templates that please any crowd.

COCKTAIL PARTY

PLAN A
Keep it simple. Serve only wine.

PLAN B
Plan A, plus champagne (either enough bottles to serve everyone, mini bottles for all, or enough for one champagne toast for each guest).

PLAN C
Plan A or B, in addition to one specialty cocktail and/or a full bar. Vodka cocktails are the easiest.

DINNER
For a premeal cocktail hour menu, refer to the cocktail menu above.

DINNER PARTY
- Water on the table.

- Red and white wine.

- Optional: Add a specialty drink on the table in a pitcher or have it served by a waiter. If you're having a theme dinner, make sure the cocktail relates. For example, if it's a luau, make a Trader Vic's Scorpion Bowl. See Chapter Ten for recipes.

- Optional: Add a full bar.

- Coffee and tea.

FOR A LATE-NIGHT PARTY (9 P.M. ON)
Late-night parties are all about mixed drinks. This is where you can bring in the shots server, come up with potent concoctions on your own, offer bottle service, and get playful with vodka and gin-based drinks.

BREAKFAST AND/OR BRUNCH PARTIES
- Water, flat and sparkling.

- Orange juice; freshly squeezed is always a plus.

- Grapefruit juice as well, if possible. A mixture of orange and grapefruit juice makes a great combination.

- An assortment of coffee and tea.

- Sodas.

- One classic brunch cocktail, like a Bloody Mary, mimosa with fresh orange juice, or a Bellini.

- If you want to go all out, consider adding fresh, homemade juices, smoothies, elixirs, and mixtures with protein powder and tonics. Get a juicer, a blender, and a great book or recipes.

REGINA KING PICKS A FLAVOR OF ROSE'S COCKTAIL INFUSIONS FOR A TASTY TINI. PHOTO COURTESY OF JEFF VESPA/WIREIMAGE.COM

CHIC TIP

Add Emer'gen-C, a petite packet of energy-boosting powder, packed with 1,000 milligrams of vitamin C, to water for a quick pick-me-up. There are fourteen flavors.

LUNCHEONS

- Water, flat and sparkling.

- Homemade iced tea. Consider flavoring iced tea with fresh fruit purées or with whole strawberries, orange slices, and mint leaves. Peppermint extract (⅛ teaspoon per three tea bags used) and sugar (1 cup per three tea bags used) will yield the most refreshing drink. Tratorde Noti in Malibu mixes two blends of iced tea for extra flavor.

- Sodas.

- Wine or champagne are optional.

- Coffee and tea.

AFTERNOON TEA PARTY

Refer to our case study on page 176.

WATER WORLD

EVERYONE KNOWS YOU'RE SUPPOSED TO DRINK AT LEAST SIX TO EIGHT 8-OUNCE GLASSES OF WATER A DAY. SO PROVIDE YOUR GUESTS WITH A HEALTHY SUPPLY OF WATER. WHETHER YOU BUY BOTTLED WATER LIKE GLACEAU OR PERRIER OR RELY ON THE TAP, MIX PITCHERS OF COLD WATER WITH SOMETHING FLAVORFUL: FRESH LEMON OR LIME, CUCUMBER SLICES, MINT LEAVES, WATERMELON CHUNKS, BITS OF CANTALOUPE, CRUSHED CRANBERRIES, OR ANYTHING YOU FANCY. USE SLEEK PITCHERS AND CALL THEM "AGUA FRESCAS."

COFFEE, TEA, OR ME?

An event cannot function on alcohol alone. Coffee—regular and decaffeinated—is a must and, like the foundation in your makeup bag, it is not the place to skimp. The warmth of coffee and tea at the end of a meal is soothing to the stomach. A cup of either beverage allows conversation to continue and gives people a reason to sit back and relax while digesting. At the bare minimum, you need regular and decaf coffee for any party you host. But if you want to go crazy, try:

- GOING GOURMET. Butterscotch toffee, Irish cream, cinnamon hazelnut, chocolate, and vanilla are just some of the flavored coffees you can buy preground or as packaged beans. (See "Our Yellow Pages" for details.)

- CREATING YOUR OWN BLEND. Brew the coffee with vanilla or mocha powder. (See "Our Yellow Pages" for supplies.)

- OFFERING ESPRESSO SHOTS. Serve small portions of espresso in shot glasses or mini mugs.

- GETTING A CAPPUCCINO MACHINE. Who doesn't love a frothy coffee with steamed milk and thick foam? Add cinnamon sticks to the mix.

- WHIPPING UP COOL COFFEE CONCOCTIONS. Try an Americano, which is espresso mellowed with a bit of hot water; a café latte, which is espresso with steamed milk and foam; or café con leche, which is Cuban espresso poured over steamed milk and three spoonfuls of sugar.

SOMETIMES GREEN TEA IS BETTER THAN VODKA, ACCORDING TO KAREN ROBINOVITZ AND ROSE MCGOWAN, SHOWN HERE AT THE BRUCE SPRINGSTEEN PRE-CONCERT DINNER PARTY AT NOBU. PHOTO COURTESY OF DENISE TRUSCELLO/WIREIMAGE.COM.

In addition to offering coffee, provide your guests with a proper cup of tea. There is something restful about tea. It is a therapeutic beverage. It is healthy. It is also a calorie-free drink that always has less caffeine than coffee and often has no caffeine at all. (Black teas have the most caffeine, then come green, white, and oolongs, while herbals, fruit blends, and Rooibos are all caffeine-free.)

Serving tea also lets you get creative by mixing it with fresh fruit flavors, fresh herbs, and spices. So forget the simple iced tea with sugar that you grew up on. Add strawberries and oranges, mint sprigs, pineapple, honey, or cinnamon to make your concoction more fresh. Serve it up in wine glasses with a slice of fruit. Or mix it with lemonade, like they do at the Beverly Hills Hotel and the Ivy (also in Beverly Hills). If you have no time to play gourmet, blend different flavors of Snapple to make something new and tell everyone it's a family recipe.

CHIC TIPS

- Have regular milk, skim milk, even soy milk on hand.

- Pouring chilled coffee or tea over ice will give the drink a refreshing summer feeling.

- Add a touch of Mexican cinnamon and coconut flakes to spruce up a cup o' joe.

- Offer hot chocolate or vanilla for non-coffee-drinkers.

- Add some whipped cream to make plain old coffee sing.

DRINKS ARE AN ESSENTIAL PART OF ANY PARTY.

There are no absolute rules to serving drinks, as long as you make sure to have water and nonalcoholic choices in your repertoire. Be creative. Be playful. And do your research. Educate yourself on wine by talking to someone at a liquor store that specializes in wine. Find new recipes online. Read books. Scan cookbooks. Go to a bar before it gets crowded and pick the bartender's brain. Don't be scared to start mixing. You can always rely on pre-made drink mixes if you have to. Always get a little more than you need because, believe us, nothing is worse than running dry midway through a party. When the drinks are flowing, everything will be all right.

CHAPTER SIX
FOOD, GLORIOUS FOOD
EAT IT! JUST EAT IT!

FOOD, GLORIOUS FOOD
EAT IT! JUST EAT IT!

People go to parties with a ravenous appetite for more than just fun. And so, one of your primary duties as a host is to feed your guests. You don't necessarily have to provide a full meal, but you at least have to offer something to snack on. If your party is at home and you want to cook, go for it. We recommend preparing food in advance and freezing it if you have the time. For last-minute parties, don't make anything that takes longer than thirty minutes of your time.

If you aren't cooking, don't fret. That is what caterers, delivery services, restaurants, and delis are for. Especially if your party is not at home, there's no shame in bringing in premade food, only in serving it without a hint of style.

When it comes to food, think about how it will smell. David Bouley, one of New York City's most revered chefs, says, "Aromas and scents are an important element of any occasion. They stimulate the senses, set the mood, and build anticipation and excitement. Some of my favorite scents are the smell of sea grass from my Indonesian place mats, the aroma of ripe apples and other fruit, and the perfume of high-quality scented candles."

Scent aside, consider your theme when you're devising the menu. If you're working with a Mexican theme, think burritos, chips, and salsa. If it's Asian, add chopsticks, lo mein, sweet-and-sour sauce, and fried rice. If you want to spoil your guests with excess, create a theme like around-the-world-in-a-million-calories, and serve up deliciousness from around the globe.

For special affairs, sumptuous food is to be expected. It requires planning and research to come up with the right menu, one that complements your party and matches its theme, location, invitation, and décor.

For more casual get-togethers, there's no need to offer a five- or even three-course meal. Finger food, little nibbles, and even fast food are all completely acceptable. The trick is to keep things simple and provide light bites your guests will appreciate. Think about the people you're inviting, and what kind of food they enjoy. Do they appreciate hearty comfort food, perched on a sofa with a tray on their laps? Do they count each calorie and prefer to eat while they make their social rounds around the room? Or are they formal types with sophisticated tastes and a preference for tables and chairs? Are they at your party for fun or for work? Are they in a rush or do they have all night?

Your answers to these questions will help you design a menu. It could range from Kentucky Fried Chicken served with spicy sauce on fine white china for a New Orleans–style soiree in a haunted house, to caviar beggar's purses for a classic cocktail party at a swanky hotel suite, to breaded shrimp served in paper popcorn boxes for an outdoor movie night in the courtyard.

WHO NEEDS FANCY PLATTERS WHEN YOU HAVE OLD GAME-BOARDS. BUST OUT THE SORRY, CANDYLAND, MONOPOLY, AND CHECKERS FOR A SASSY WAY TO SERVE FOOD, ESPECIALLY CHEEKY MINI BITE-SIZE DELIGHTS. PHOTO COURTESY OF PAUL COSTELLO.

CHEF DAVID BOULEY ON PARTY MENUS

WHAT IS YOUR IDEAL MENU FOR LATE NIGHT?
"NO CARBS. SASHIMI, STEAMED VEGETABLES."

WHAT IS YOUR IDEAL MENU FOR BRUNCH?
"SALMON GRAVLAX POTATO ROSTI WITH OSETRA
CAVIAR AND CITRUS CRÈME FRAÎCHE. THIS IS A
DISH THAT EVERYONE LOVES. THE CRUNCH OF THE
POTATO WITH THE SALMON AND CAVIAR IS A PER-
FECT COMBINATION. IT IS GREAT FOR GROUPS
BECAUSE IT IS SO EASY TO MAKE AND HOLDS UP
REALLY WELL."

CAN YOU SHARE ANY OTHER TIPS/SECRETS?
"I ALWAYS USE THE FRESHEST SEASONAL
PRODUCTS."

The food can be as easy as pizza, pasta, and sandwiches, as gourmet as foie gras and seared scallops. There are no rules, no matter how large or small the party is. An amazing menu is often one that mixes the high (caviar, crème fraîche, escargots) with the low (spaghetti, scrambled eggs, burgers) and balances hot and cold food. It could also take your guests away to another place—to Little Italy, or the Caribbean—or down memory lane: to sixties suburbia or turn-of-the-century Paris.

This chapter will give you a lot of food for thought. You'll get an overview of the type of equipment you'll need and how to be creative with it. You'll learn about serving options, and foods you can place versus food you can pass, as well as what to serve for brunch, cocktail, dinner, and late-night parties. Plus, we offer ideas for ordering in food and tips from some of the country's best chefs, while Chapter Ten offers recipes for some of our favorite dishes. We provide a list of the most mouth-watering cookbooks in Chapter Eleven, and we cover breakfast, brunch, and tea parties in the case studies in Chapter Nine.

So, here's to good food. Over the mouth and through the gums, look out stomach . . . here it comes!

WELL EQUIPPED

Aside from the traditional pantry full of cookware—from pots and pans to mortars and pestles, measuring cups and cutting boards, knives, and what have you—a party host could need serving trays and platters, buffet plates, three-tiered plates, cheese plates, large bowls, serving spoons and forks, bread baskets, and more. As you plan your menu, always think about how you're presenting the food to your guests. It counts just as much as—and maybe even more than—the food itself.

The soul of a party, however, is not about exquisite china and delicate hand-blown glasses. It is about projecting your style, perhaps by using something traditional in a nontraditional way. Serve dinner or lunch in the bento boxes typically found in Japanese restaurants. Serve food airplane style, presenting the entire meal at once. Cookie plates and cake stands work well for sliced cheese and light bites. And believe it or not, so do random household accessories.

Remove that eight-by-ten-inch picture frame from the wall and use it as a tray to serve crudité. No bowl for chips? What about that sombrero or cowboy hat that's been hiding in the back of your closet? Just line it with napkins first. Don't have a place to put french fries? Wrap them in clean white paper and pass them out in cone-shaped birthday hats or in newspaper cones. No breadbaskets in sight? Revive old lunch boxes. Buy Chinese take-out boxes, which you can decorate, and then serve everything with lacquer chopsticks, Asian theme or not.

 CHIC TIP EVEN THE MOST HUMBLE KITCHEN ITEM CAN HAVE MULTIPLE USES. FOR EXAMPLE, ORDINARY PAPER BAGS CAN MAKE ANY CUT OF MEAT TENDER AND JUICY. JUST TAKE THE COOKED MEAT OUT OF THE OVEN, PLACE IT ON WAX PAPER IN A BROWN BAG, FOLD IT SHUT, AND LET IT SIT FOR FIVE MINUTES. THE STEAMED MEAT WILL GET PLUMP AND MOIST AND FALL RIGHT OFF THE BONE.

HERE ARE SOME OTHER SAVVY SERVING TIPS.

- Use faux plant leaves as cheese plates to match an autumn décor theme.

- Plant carrot and celery sticks in terra-cotta and ceramic flowerpots for garden parties.

- Type your menu, then make copies of it enlarged to eleven by seven inches at the copy store and use them as place mats. It's very French bistro.

- Pour sauces such as ketchup or soy sauce into baby bottles. You may need to enlarge the holes with scissors.

- Head to the hardware store for linoleum, ceramic, or vinyl tiles. They make cool serving trays. And pick up parquet slats for hors d'oeuvre trays and cutting boards.

- Aluminum or plastic pails, as well as champagne and ice buckets, are perfect for chips, pretzels, popcorn, even fried calamari and vegetable tempura.

- Borrow from your bar. Martini glasses and shot glasses are good for chilled soups, ceviche, shrimp cocktail, oyster shooters, bite-size eats to pick up with a toothpick, sauces, even sea salt and ground pepper.

LUCITE TRAYS ARE A MUST. YOU CAN BRAND YOUR PARTY BY BLOWING UP IMAGES AND PLACING THEM ON THE FLOOR OF THE TRAY. USE AN X-ACTO KNIFE TO CUT THE IMAGE TO MAKE IT FIT. THE EXPRESS LOGO HOLDS BURGERS AND BLTS. FROM OLIVIER CHENG CATERING & EVENTS. PHOTO BY PAUL COSTELLO.

SOUP IN ESPRESSO CUPS, GARNISHED WITH BITE-SIZE GRILLED CHEESE, COMPLEMENTED A TRAY THAT WAS MEANT TO RESEMBLE A RUBIX CUBE GAME (MADE FROM PIECES OF COLORED PLASTIC). A GOLDFISH IN A BOWL WITH RED GRAVEL IN THE BOTTOM FINISHES THE LOOK. FROM OLIVIER CHENG CATERING & EVENTS FOR A SIMS ONLINE PARTY. PHOTO BY PAUL COSTELLO.

FOOD, GLORIOUS FOOD

ADD DEPTH TO BUFFET TABLES BY PLACING THE FOOD ON DIF-
FERENT LEVELS USING BRICKS, BOOKS, FABRIC-COVERED BOXES
OR BLOCKS OF ICE. PHOTO BY PATRICK McMULLAN/PMc.

Once you have the food on its proper plate or tray, or in its bag or bucket, it needs to move from the kitchen to your guests. How are you going to serve it? Like drinks, food can be placed, passed, set up as a buffet, or done as a combination of all three.

A HELPING HAND

Whether the food is placed or passed, hiring servers frees you up to enjoy your party. But remember that too many servers can overcrowd any party or room. If you're looking to hire some-one on the cheap, talk to a waiter at a restaurant you often frequent or look into finding a cooking student who is trying to gain catering experience and may not charge much.

With or without servers, you can provide a meal that circumvents the standard appetizer–entrée–dessert trilogy by offering a myriad of appetizer-size portions, going family-style, or setting up a buffet. You could also serve a seated dinner, fol-lowed by a dessert buffet table.

For buffets, we like to set a table in the center of the room so guests have to circle it to see what's there. We often serve pasta in the pans in which it was cooked. And we like to place food platters on different levels, using shelving made of glass, con-crete, or giant rocks. No matter how you choose to set up your buffet, make sure there's a separate area, at the end of the table or perhaps on a cre-denza near the table or in the living room, for plates, silverware, and napkins.

Just remember that regardless of how and what you serve, you should still offer finger foods for your guests to nibble at. People like to snack at parties, whether or not a full meal is offered. And they like to help themselves.

So no matter what kind of party you have, always leave out food-filled bowls, dishes, platters, trays, or containers on tables, windowsills, and pedestals. The obvious choice is mixed nuts and pretzels, but we like to choose nibbles that match the general concept and style of our soirees. For example, try sweet bruschetta topped with berries for a picnic in the park or mini hot dogs and burg-ers for a bowling or Fourth of July party. Fill square trays—even brownie pans—with ice and then place atop the ice small shot glasses or seashells holding oysters Rockefeller, fluke ceviche, seared pepper tuna, or some other seafood delicacy. And just like that, you have a raw bar.

EASY, QUICK, AND CHEAP NIBBLES.

- EDAMAME. In Japan, these salt-covered soy beans are considered beer nuts. Buy them in bulk at the grocery store (they're in the frozen food department), boil them quickly, and salt them. Set them out in bowls, along with empty bowls for discarded shells.

- A SELECTION OF OLIVES. Offer imported Sicilian, French picholine, French black with herbs, French black with roasted garlic, or pitted kalamatas, along with napkins or side dishes for the pits.

- BREADSTICKS AND CHEESE STICKS. Serve in buckets or tall glasses.

- CRUDITÉS. Cut up carrots, peppers, squash, cucumber, celery, even okra, a sadly under-rated veggie. Hollow out a pepper to hold the dip. If you don't feel like doing the slicing, you can find precut vegetables at a grocery or gourmet store.

- MIXED DRIED FRUITS. You can buy great goodies like dried dates, figs, and apricots prepackaged from specialty stores like Hadley's Dried Fruits in Palm Springs, California.

- GOURMET CHEESE. Make small slices or cubes that can be picked up by hand or with a toothpick. Place the cheese in the middle of a platter and surround it with crackers and seed-less grapes, cherries, and apple slices.

CHEESE PLATTERS ARE NEVER CHEESY. PLACE FROMAGE NEATLY ON A TRAY EMBELLISHED WITH FRESH FRUIT AND A SERVING KNIFE. PHOTO COURTESY OF PAUL COSTELLO.

CHIC TIP
Red and green apples, stacked in glass cylinders or piled up on a silver platter, make sophisticated accessories.

POP CULTURE
POPCORN ISN'T THE MOST INNOVATIVE SNACK AT PARTIES, BUT IF YOU ADD A DASH OF THIS AND A DASH OF THAT, IT'LL BE A CROWD PLEASER.

- LATINO POPCORN. GET PAN-FRIED RUSSIAN DEHYDRATED SWEET CORN, WHICH YOU CAN FIND, BAGGED, IN MOST GROCERY STORES. PUT IT IN A BOWL WITH MOTE CORN (GIANT PERUVAN CORN), TOASTED PUMPKIN SEEDS, A BIT OF CHILE POWDER, AND KOSHER SALT, AND ADD TO PLAIN POPCORN POPPED IN VEGETABLE OIL.
- SWEET POPCORN. SEASON REGULAR POPCORN WITH CINNAMON AND SUGAR. SHAKE IT UP IN A BAG AND SERVE.
- SMART FOOD OR PIRATE'S BOOTY. KIDS OF ALL AGES LOVE 'EM. AVAILABLE IN THE SNACK AISLE AT MOST GROCERY STORES.

116

FÊTE ACCOMPLI!

DUNK VEGGIES AND CHIPS IN DELECTABLE DIPS YOU CAN BUY AT THE GROCERY STORE OR MAKE AT HOME.

- HUMMUS. Salty and protein-packed, this blend of chickpeas, tahini, garlic, and lemon can be made from scratch or bought from a supermarket or gourmet store. You can also add your own ingredients to prepared hummus, including roasted garlic, cayenne pepper, olives, and herbs, to make it special. Then serve with warm pita points and mini carrot sticks.

- A COMBINATION OF TRADITIONAL GREEK DIPS. Tabbouleh, which is made of tomato, spring onions, parsley, cracked wheat, olive oil, and lemon; tzatziki, a mixture of fresh yogurt, mint, cucumber, and garlic; and taramosalata, a creamy concoction of red caviar, lemon juice, olive oil, and onions, are delicious.

- GUACAMOLE AND SALSA. Everyone loves these Tex-Mex classics. See Chapter Ten for a wonderful guacamole recipe from Rosa Mexicano, a famous Mexican restaurant in Manhattan, plus a great artichoke dip from California Pizza Kitchen.

Light snacks work well with any kind of party and we often serve nothing more than them, especially at cocktail parties, where people focus more on drinking and mingling than they do on eating. Sometimes, however, we kick it up a notch and provide a well-edited menu of delicacies that everyone appreciates. In the next section, we go into more yummy details.

CHIC TIP COCKTAIL HOUR SHOULD BE JUST THAT: ONE HOUR.

COCKTAIL PARTY PROPS

Cocktail party food, passed or placed, doesn't have to be fancy. And there doesn't have to be a lot. The best kind of cocktail party food is the type that your guests can eat without the use of utensils. Finger foods, preferably foods that are not too juicy, and thence, too messy, are the smartest way to go. Not only are they easy for you to prepare and clean up after, but they're easier for your guests to eat while chatting it up with a drink in hand. We tend to offer at least three choices for guests to choose from because you never know who likes what. Always have at least one vegetarian choice.

Let the theme of your party and the time it will span be the guide to your menu. Is your party a simple work function from 6:00 P.M. to 8:00 P.M.? Will the fête be formal, from 8:00 P.M. to 10:00 P.M., with the best bubbly? Are your guests hobnobbing after midnight and potentially craving an assortment of munchies like fried chicken fingers and homemade chips and blue cheese? Or are you planning a cocktail hour before dinner is served? If so, stick to light fare like shrimp cocktail, just enough to whet your guests' appetites.

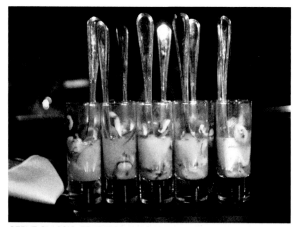

SERVE CLASSIC, TRADITIONAL FOOD IN A NONTRADITIONAL WAY. HERE, CEVICHE "VUELVE A LA VIDA" IS PRESENTED IN HIGHBALL GLASSES AT THE ART BASEL COCKTAIL PARTY HOSTED BY JORGE PÉREZ, MARISA TOMEI, AND TOMAS MAIER. CREATED BY CHEF MICHELLE BERNSTEIN. PHOTO BY SETH BROWARNIK/RED EYE PRODUCTIONS.

HERE ARE SOME IDEAS FOR A CLASSIC
COCKTAIL PARTY. SERVE ONE OR ALL.

- Boiled new potatoes topped with a dollop of sour cream and caviar.

- Smoked salmon. It's a mainstay, but be warned: It leaves your guests with bad breath.

- Anything on skewers: grilled vegetables, chicken, pork, beef, seafood.

- Any kind of layered phyllo-dough offering, whether filled with goat cheese, wild mushrooms, or spinach and pesto.

- Mini tartlet crusts called pastry shells, which can be filled with whatever you want: mozzarella and roasted tomato, caramelized onions and Brie, Cheddar cheese and bacon.

- Mini crab cakes.

- Mushrooms stuffed with crab meat.

- Prosciutto-wrapped melon.

- Tapenade, or olive paste, on toast points.

- Bowls of sun-dried tomatoes.

- Risotto with caviar.

CAVIAR, DARLING. DISH IT OUT WITH A MOTHER-OF-PEARL SPOON. AND REMEMBER THAT THE BEST THING TO DRINK WITH CAVIAR IS NOT CHAMPAGNE, BUT A CHILLED SHOT OF GOOD VODKA. PHOTO BY SETH BROWARNIK/RED EYE PRODUCTIONS.

CHIC TIP FIND CAVIAR AT SEAFOOD PURVEYORS, THROUGH MAIL-ORDER CATALOGS AND WEBSITES, OR AT FINE DEPARTMENT STORES INSTEAD OF THE GROCERY STORE. OUR FAVORITE IS PETROSSIAN.

CHIC TIP

Any time you're passing or placing a tray of items on skewers or toothpicks, make sure also to place a good-size lemon wedge on the tray so guests can plunge their discarded sticks into it.

CAVIAR TIP SHEET
HERE'S WHAT YOU SHOULD KNOW ABOUT THIS TREAT.

- BELUGA IS THE MOST DELICATE, EXPENSIVE, AND RARE OF ALL CAVIARS. IT'S OFTEN CALLED BLACK GOLD. BELUGA GRAINS ARE BEAUTIFUL: LARGE AND BUTTERY IN TASTE, RANGING IN COLOR FROM A LIGHT TO DARK GRAY. AT $1,600 PER POUND, BELUGA WILL SET YOU BACK.

- OSETRA IS HALF THE PRICE OF BELUGA. WITH A WARM GOLDEN HUE AND A SWEET, NUTTY FLAVOR, OSETRA IS TERRIFIC.

- SEVRUGA IS THE MOST COMMON TYPE OF CAVIAR. AT $550 PER POUND, IT'S LESS EXPENSIVE THAN OSETRA. DARK GRAY TO BLACK, SEVRUGA IS A BIT LESS SUBTLE IN FLAVOR AND A BIT MORE FISHY.

- NORTH AMERICAN CAVIAR IS MORE AFFORDABLE THAN IMPORTED CAVIARS. MOST OF YOUR GUESTS WILL NEVER TASTE THE DIFFERENCE.

- YOU CAN ALSO GET COLORFUL WITH RED SALMON CAVIAR, WHICH IS TASTY AND SALTY AND CHEAP, OR FLYING FISH ROE, WHICH IS GREEN AND SPICY, WASABI-FLAVORED.

SERVE CAVIAR WITH MELBA ROUNDS, TOAST POINTS, MINI PANCAKES, OR HOLLOWED-OUT BABY POTATOES. IF YOU'RE IN THE MOOD TO IMPRESS, ADD SIDE DISHES OF CRÈME FRAÎCHE, SOUR CREAM, MINCED ONIONS OR CHIVES, AND CHOPPED EGG.

For cocktail parties with a twist—or to add a twist to a classic affair—loosen up the menu and throw an unexpected edible in the mix. At a Kenneth Cole party we organized for the Reaction store opening on Fifty-seventh Street in Manhattan, the theme was "I Love New York." So we brought in hot-dog vendors, retro theater-style popcorn carts, and hot-pretzel stands. Offer one of those at your party, along with a toppings buffet with hot salsa, melted Cheddar, marinara sauce, and sweet mustard.

Other unusual but fun options include sliced and toothpicked Big Macs, buffalo wings with homemade blue cheese, or soup served in shot glasses. At the premiere for the movie *Men of Honor* at the Hudson Hotel in New York, we served tiny portions of mac and cheese in beautiful little porcelain glasses or dishes.

HERE ARE SOME OTHER FUN FOODS THAT FUNK UP THE MENU. JUST PRESENT THEM BEAUTIFULLY.

- MINIS. PEOPLE LOVE LITTLE THINGS. GIVE THEM TINY GRILLED BRIE OR GOAT CHEESE SANDWICHES ON GOURMET OR BAGUETTE BREAD; MINI GRILLED HOT DOGS, BURGERS, AND VEGGIE BURGERS; LITTLE PIZZA ROUNDS; AND BITE-SIZE BLTS SERVED IN HOLLOWED-OUT CHERRY TOMATOES.

- P B & J. FRESH PEANUT BUTTER AND JELLY SAND-WICHES ON SCONES OR CUT-UP SLICES OF OLD-FASHIONED WONDER BREAD.

- THE ELVIS. OFFER FRIED SLICED BANANAS AND PEANUT BUTTER ON WHITE BREAD. ADD FLUFF TO TASTE.

- CEREAL SOUP. THIS IS A CEREAL COCKTAIL OF CHEX, FRUIT LOOPS, CORN FLAKES, AND SPECIAL K, DRESSED UP WITH LOTS OF SEASONINGS; IT COMES FROM A GROOVY RESTAURANT IN BROOKLYN CALLED THAT BAR (SEE PAGE 219 FOR THE RECIPE).

TO LAUNCH SIMS ONLINE IN DECEMBER 2002 AT THE ALTMAN BUILDING IN NEW YORK CITY, THE FOOD, PREPPED BY OLIVIER CHENG CATERING & EVENTS, WAS ALL ABOUT COMBINING FLAVOR AND FUN. THIS IS WHAT WE SERVED.

PASSED HORS D'OEUVRES
Bite-size Spinach Quiche
Smoked-Salmon-Mousse Lollipops
Pigs-in-a-Blanket
Cheez Wiz on Triscuits
Celery Spears Stuffed with Peanut Butter
Warm Baked Artichoke Dip with Crackers

PASSED SWEETS
Mini Twinkies with Jack Daniel's Cream
Bite-size Ring Dings
Root Beer Floats with Malted Milk Ball Ice Cream

PLACED ON BARS
Chex Mix and Cheese Doodles

SPECIALTY BEVERAGE
The Sims Cocktail: Sour Apple and Pomegranate
    Cosmo

WHAT YOU NEED TO START YOUR PARTY OFF RIGHT: GREAT APPE-TIZERS. THESE MINI BLTS WERE CREATED FOR US BY OLIVIER CHENG OF OLIVIER CHENG CATERING & EVENTS IN NEW YORK CITY. PHOTO COURTESY OF PAUL COSTELLO.

DINNER'S ON!

No matter how you do it, a dinner party is an activity. It's entertainment. It's a show. It brings people together over one of our favorite pasttimes: eating. So whether you do it casually or formally, whether it's for family or for business reasons, keep in mind that you are producing your own bit of theater.

As with any party, begin by determining the theme and time of the dinner, as well as the number of guests, the budget, and the length of the party. These factors will help you plan the menu. Expect some guests to show up late and some to bring an unexpected guest (or two), so make sure you have extra food.

For instance, do you want a classic, three- to five-course meal at a lovely dining table at 8:00 P.M., a low-key dinner from 7:00 P.M. to 9:00 P.M. with gourmet food and a mellow atmosphere, a last-minute party thrown together at a whim, or a wild night that begins with a meal at 10:00 P.M. and lasts until the wee hours?

Once you know the kind of dinner you're going to have, come up with a menu that fits and then think about how to add spice to your dinner party with something memorable. Pick dishes that you think your guests will like, not just items you appreciate. At seated dinners, try to have something (preferably something that is served cold, like a salad with the dressing on the side) placed at the table so the guests have something to nibble when they take their seats. If money is tight, make a vegetable risotto dish. By the time you're finished, it will probably amount to ten dollars per person for a main dish that serves ten. Think about how you'll plate the food, as well. Instead of dividing the plate with a fish fillet in one third, vegetables in another, and mashed potatoes in the last, try layering the elements. Place the potatoes over a bed of greens and the fish on top of that. It will look like you know exactly what you're doing.

If you're not having the dinner at your own home, the food, drinks, and décor will probably be handled by someone else. And the best part is that you don't have to clean a thing. If the dinner is at home, however, you have to go through your kitchen to see what you need in terms of equipment and ingredients. If you're thinking of trying a new recipe, do a trial run to see if it works. Stick to simple things (i.e., no complicated sauces) if you're a novice. And buy your groceries days ahead of time. Assemble all of the ingredients and equipment you need in advance to prevent last-minute scrambling around the kitchen. Wash all of the vegetables for all of the dishes at once to save time. And don't kill yourself over making every little thing perfect.

BONNIE FULLER'S DINNER PARTY TIPS

BONNIE FULLER IS THE FORMER EDITOR-IN-CHIEF OF *GLAMOUR* MAGAZINE, *COSMOPOLITAN, US WEEKLY,* AND *MARIE CLAIRE* AND IS THE CURRENT EDITOR OF *THE STAR.* HERE ARE HER "DO'S" AND "DON'TS" FOR DINNER PARTY ENTERTAINING.

- ONLY INVITE PEOPLE WHO WILL TALK AND WHO WILL EAT.
- ALWAYS HAVE TOO MUCH FOOD. THE WORST CRIME IS TO INVITE PEOPLE AND TO SKIMP ON PORTIONS, SECONDS, APPETIZERS.
- DON'T IMPOSE YOUR DIET ON YOUR GUESTS. DON'T SERVE DRY, FAT-FREE FOOD. TASTE IS EVERYTHING.
- DO HAVE SOME TABLE CONVERSATION STARTERS YOU CAN THROW OUT TO GET PEOPLE TALKING.
- DON'T SEPARATE COUPLES BECAUSE MOST COUPLES BARELY GET TO SEE EACH OTHER THESE DAYS.
- DO HAVE SOME BACKGROUND MUSIC—IT KEEPS THE MOOD MORE CASUAL SO PEOPLE RELAX.
- MIX AND MATCH YOUR CHINA AND TABLE CLOTHS, ETC.
- *ALWAYS* HAVE APPETIZERS—PEOPLE CAN ARRIVE STARVING—AND DON'T LET DRINKS GO OVER AN HOUR BEFORE MOVING TO DINNER.
- DO MOVE DESSERT BACK TO THE LIVING ROOM TO BE MORE RELAXING.

It's okay to use store-bought and restaurant-bought food. You don't have to make it all from scratch, just whatever is easiest for you. Buy a bottle of salad dressing from the market, add some chopped fresh herbs to it, and serve it in a glass carafe. Use gourmet sauces from famous chefs. Nobu, Jean-Georges Vongerichten, Peter Luger (a world-renowned steak house in Brooklyn, New York), Giorgio's, and Rao's Restaurant all manufacture and sell their specialty sauces.

Once upon a time, there were strict rules about what you had to serve at dinner, but nowadays, putting a personal spin on the meal is more important. But there is still one thing all guests want, even the ones who are watching their weight: bread.

Always offer some form of baked concoction to start the meal. Put thin slices of garlic bread, long breadsticks—maybe those individually wrapped Italian ones—or cheese sticks in vases or bowls on the tables. You can provide decadent baskets of hot baked focaccia, or have servers offer guests a selection of breads, including raisin-nut, olive, and seven-grain. Order the bread from the very best bakery around, or a place known for its bread, like Eli Zabar's, a retail store and distributor in New York City.

CHIC TIP POUR OLIVE OIL FLAVORED WITH A FEW DROPS OF BALSAMIC VINEGAR INTO SMALL, PRETTY BOWLS AND PLACE THEM ON THE TABLE FOR GUESTS TO DIP THEIR BREAD IN. OFFER GOURMET FLAVORED BUTTER, AS WELL.

The only other dinner rule we like to stick to is: Don't make your guests labor over a meal that's too long. While no one likes to be rushed, three hours at the table is no fun, either. People get antsy. If you want to throw a party that starts late, say, after 9:00 P.M., you can try a different, more light-hearted approach to the food you serve, as the next section of the book explains.

AFTER HOURS

Parties that begin long after dark are usually more laid back and loose. The menu should be, too. Late at night, people are generally not likely to want a full meal (it's much harder to digest), so you don't have to offer anything too substantial and certainly not three or more courses. Play with the menu and give your guests things they don't normally expect.

Late night is a good time to turn fast food into something chic. (Who doesn't love a little calorie fest at midnight?) The trick to fabulous fast food preparation is plating it well, garnishing the platter with colorful drizzles of sauce, or serving it in a creative fashion.

- Follow Drew Barrymore's example and serve burgers from a local joint. Drew called In-N-Out burger, L.A.'s most popular fast food chain since 1948, and had them send a truck, called the Mobile Unit, to the set of *Charlie's Angels* to feed everyone as a surprise after long hours of filming. If you're not in L.A., find a burger chain near you.

ABOVE AND OPPOSITE: FAST FOOD CAN BE SOPHISTICATED, EVEN WHEN IT'S SERVED IN THE ORIGINAL PACKAGING. PRESENT IT ON GREAT TRAYS AND IN WOODED BOWLS LIKE THESE. PHOTOS COURTESY OF PAUL COSTELLO, SHOT AT THE HUDSON HOTEL PENTHOUSE IN NEW YORK CITY. BOWLS AND TRAYS COURTESY OF CALVIN KLEIN HOME.

- Serve recognizable items from McDonald's, Burger King, or Johnny Rockets, cut into quarters, on sleek silver trays.

- Get chili cheese fries and nachos from a local dive—and put them in great martini glasses.

- Order tacos from a place like Taco Bell and offer freshly made salsa and guacamole, along with a buffet table of toppings like goat cheese crumbles, shredded lettuce, sour cream, chopped tomatoes, and bell peppers.

- Get sassy with foot-long burritos and subs, and set them up on a long buffet table.

- Have a server pass chicken wings and chicken fingers, which can be wrapped in cloth napkins.

CHIC TIP ADD ONE OR TWO OF THESE FAST FOODS TO ANY PARTY, EVEN A FORMAL DINNER, TO JAZZ THINGS UP. EVERYONE LOVES MCDONALD'S FRIES.

Late night is also a good time to satisfy your guests' sugar cravings. Mix sweet and savory foods or just offer loads of fresh fruit and dessert platters, which we'll cover in the following chapter. Next, however, we tackle lunch.

WHAT'S YOUR FAVORITE PARTY FOOD?

- DAVID COPPERFIELD: "CHICKEN SATAY, BEEF SATAY, OR ANYTHING SATAY. LOVE THAT PEANUT SAUCE."

- DUCHESS OF YORK: "TOTAL VARIETY OF DIFFERENT TYPES OF FOOD. CHINESE, ITALIAN, COLD BUFFET."

- MICHAEL KORS: "MINIATURE BURGERS, GRILLED CHEESE, AND LOADS OF CAVIAR."

- AERIN LAUDER: "FRIED ZUCCHINI— NO ONE EVER SAYS NO TO IT."

- BOBBI BROWN: "BRICK OVEN MINI SIZE PIZZAS."

- HUGH JACKMAN: "A MOROCCAN FEAST . . . SITTING ON CUSHIONS ON THE FLOOR SURROUNDED BY CANDLES."

CHIC TIP IF YOU'RE SERVING WRAP SANDWICHES, REWRAP THEM IN ATTRACTIVE PAPER TO ADD A DESIGN-SAVVY ELEMENT TO THE FOOD PRESENTATION.

LUNCHEONS

Lunch food can be anything—pasta, salads, sandwiches, fajitas, chicken skewers—as long as it's not fussy. Some options are guacamole and chips to start, burritos, and sides of corn; or shelled lobster over a bed of chopped mango and greens with gazpacho soup and grilled vegetables.

Unless the party is a men's-club power meeting—in which case, serve up hanger steak—keep the food light. Midday meals shouldn't be too heavy. Lunch should also be short, no more than two hours for the actual meal. Match the food selections to the type of party you're having. Is it salads for a ladies' lunch; paninis and cupcakes for an office meeting; omelets with Brie, crabmeat, turkey bacon, and exotic mushrooms before a jaunt to the museum; or a buffet and a raw bar for a fashion show for charity?

Whatever you do, don't stress. Lunch should not be a high-maintenance affair. It's the perfect time to take something out from your favorite local place. At Harrison & Shriftman, we often host lunches in our conference room. We order sandwiches, soup, and sides of sautéed vegetables from a gourmet sandwich shop. We make sure to get a variety. Then we cut the sandwiches into quarters and place them on large trays, so our guests get to pick and choose. We take the side dishes out of the containers and use our own chic dishes. And we serve the soup from a large bowl, surrounded by individual soup cups. We make the conference table festive, change the lightbulbs, and bring out flavored iced tea and lemonade in beautiful pitchers to make an afternoon of it. There's nothing like conducting business in a lighthearted, fun setting.

CHIC TIP

Re-plate whatever food you order in and garnish the dish with fresh herbs, truffle or olive oil drizzle, orange slices, a few berries, or whatever works with what you're serving.

LETTUCE ENTERTAIN YOU!

The easiest lunch menus to pull off are salads, since they can be hearty, light, fancy, or as simple as chopped iceberg lettuce with blue cheese dressing, served in a bread or lettuce bowl. Here are some more healthy ideas.

- Purchase a selection of grilled vegetables from a good deli, then chop them fine and serve warm.

- Mix watermelon and goat cheese, a staple from the Ocean Club in the Bahamas, for a refreshing, summery salad (see page 224 for the recipe).

- Combine sliced hard-boiled eggs, Roquefort cheese, avocado, crumbled bacon, a few kinds of lettuce, and vinaigrette. Top with warm poached chicken or grilled shrimp and serve the salad in a large bowl.

- Chop iceberg lettuce, mozzarella cheese, salami, and marinated garbanzo beans fine enough to eat with a spoon. Add vinaigrette and you have the most-ordered dish from La Scala, a Los Angeles restaurant to the stars. Substitute tuna, turkey, chicken, or ham for salami if desired.

- Go Greek with crisp lettuce, chopped tomatoes, cucumbers, onion, bell pepper, feta cheese, and olives. Keep the dressing light: just balsamic vinegar, olive oil, and oregano.

- Arrange fresh or Italian canned tuna, French green beans, sliced Bermuda onions, boiled potatoes, Roma tomatoes, sliced hard-boiled eggs, and Niçoise olives to a bed of greens for a tuna Niçoise salad.

- Add pears, walnuts, raisins, and Gorgonzola cheese to a bed of spinach for a flavorful spinach salad. Add a sherry vinaigrette and you're set.

- Create a chopped salad bar: Set out bowls of varied chopped vegetables, garnishes, and dressings, and have a server toss up a selection for each guest. One of our favorite versions is the ultimate chopped salad from The Forge Restaurant, a classic restaurant in Miami Beach. It includes red peppers, red cabbage, iceberg lettuce, frisée lettuce, and butter lettuce all chopped into ¼-inch pieces, and Gorgonzola cheese to taste.

- Make a festive Caesar salad by adding marinated peppers, olives, and feta cheese for a Greek Caesar; baked tortilla chips, toasted pepitas, red chile croutons, and poblano pep-

BASIC FOOD IS ANYTHING BUT BASIC WHEN YOU PLATE IT WELL. NO NEED TO ASK SOMEONE FOR EXTRA GRATED PARMESAN CHEESE WHEN YOU ADD A HUNK OF CHEESE AND A MINI GRATER TO A BOWL OF CAESAR SALAD. PHOTO BY CARY SONGY/BARTON G. THE RESTAURANT.

pers for a Mexican Caesar; or jerk chicken and black beans for a Caribbean Caesar.

- Turn any salad into a sandwich by inserting it between two slices of bread.

- Marinate last night's vegetables in a great vinaigrette dressing all day for today's lunch.

- A quick and easy way to make any bed of greens more gourmet is to add walnuts, pine nuts, sliced avocado, and sun-dried tomatoes.

CHIC TIP

Order different types of food from different places to create a cross-country (or cross-city) meal. Just make sure you have the space to store everything properly. And remember that you don't have to think big and expensive for the food to be good. The little Chinese, Japanese, or Italian place in your town will do.

BARTON G.'S FOOD TIPS

BARTON G., WHO IS KNOWN AS AN ENTERTAINING VISIONARY, CATERS THE HOTTEST PARTIES FROM MIAMI TO LOS ANGELES, AND HIS MIAMI RESTAURANT, CALLED BARTON G. THE RESTAURANT, IS ONE OF OUR FAVORITES. NOT ONLY IS THE FOOD GREAT, BUT THE PRESENTATION IS UNIQUE: KITSCHY AND CHIC AT ONCE. HERE IS HIS ADVICE.

- SERVING FOOD IS NOT ABOUT HAVING THE MOST FABULOUS PLATTER. VENTURE OUT OF THE BOX AND MAKE USE OF FUN AND PLAYFUL THINGS, LIKE MINI OLD-FASHIONED MASON JARS FOR SHRIMP COCKTAIL, OLD MILK BOT-TLES, CRACKER JACK BOXES, CARDBOARD BOXES, AND BROWN PAPER BAGS CLOSED WITH CLOTHESPINS.

- PUT A MODERN TWIST ON BASIC COMFORT FOOD. FOR INSTANCE, ADD WHITE AND GREEN ASPARAGUS, EXOTIC MUSHROOMS, AND A POACHED EGG TO MACARONI AND CHEESE.

MAKE A CALL, AND THE MEAL IS READY

Ordering in food makes party production run more smoothly and takes a lot of pressure off you. Find a place that has a stand-out reputation and get something that blends with your party's concept. It will make the meal more memorable and will stimulate conversation: "Oh, where did you get this?" "From a little spot in Miami that Madonna loves." In fact, Joe's Stone Crab, the first restaurant in Miami Beach, established in 1913, will send their stone crabs, coleslaw, mustard sauce, Key lime pie, and bibs (!) anywhere. Embellish the menu at home by adding shrimp cocktail, coleslaw, and potatoes. For steaks, dial Omaha Steak, a hearty Nebraska mainstay famous for their juicy slabs of grade-A meat. See "Our Yellow Pages" or research online to find your own favorites. Read restaurant reviews in major papers and call the restaurants to see if they will ship.

ESSENTIAL TIPS OF THE TRADE

- CREATE A BALANCE OF HOT AND COLD DISHES.

- WRITE A COOKING AND SERVING TIMETABLE.

- ADD KOSHER SALT TO SEASON ANYTHING THAT'S BLAND.

- DRIZZLE TRUFFLE OIL OVER ANYTHING TO ADD SOME SOPHISTICATED FLAVOR.

- PLAN FOR THE AFTER-PARTY WITH AN ABUNDANCE OF CLEANING PRODUCTS AND SUPPLIES.

BECOME A CHEF, AT LEAST IN SPIRIT

ROCCO DISPIRITO IS THE CHEF AT NEW YORK CITY'S UNION PACIFIC AND ROCCO'S 22ND STREET. HE IS KNOWN FOR HIS UNIQUE FLAVOR COMBINATIONS.

WHAT IS YOUR IDEAL MENU FOR COCKTAILS?
"DRINKS AND SNACKS BY THE DOOR LIKE BOTTLES OF BEER OR A MAGNUM OF CHAMPAGNE ON ICE AND HUNKS OF PARMESAN CHEESE."

WHAT IS YOUR IDEAL MENU FOR LATE-NIGHT PARTIES?
"SELECT RECIPES YOU CAN PREPARE AHEAD. LIKE ONE HUNDRED SHRIMP ON THE LIP OF A BEAUTIFUL BOWL AND THE BEST COCKTAIL SAUCE YOU CAN FIND."

WHAT IS YOUR IDEAL MENU FOR LUNCH?
"GET YOUR FRIENDS TO HELP COOK. ESPECIALLY AT BARBECUES. THERE IS ALWAYS A GRILL MASTER, SO LET THAT PERSON DO THE WORK."

WHAT IS YOUR IDEAL MENU FOR BRUNCH?
"WHEN ALL ELSE FAILS, BREAK OUT THE CAVIAR."

FOOD FOR THOUGHT

Throughout the chapter, we list ideas for things to serve. We hope they will inspire your menu choices and parties, regardless of concept, time, and place. Feel free to incorporate any of our ideas into your own affair and tweak them to meet your needs.

CHAPTER SEVEN
SWEET TOOTH
DIET, SCHMIET!

SWEET TOOTH
DIET, SCHMIET!

Life is hard enough, so we think everyone should have dessert! Dessert is comforting, filling, rewarding: sugar, chocolate, vanilla extract, butter . . . what's not to love? And dessert is probably the easiest course to plan because it's the one course for which it's okay to break all the rules. Be childish: At a formal dinner party, bring in a cotton candy machine. For a proper work lunch, offer a S'mores fondue. Buy old-fashioned ice-cream cakes. Get creative with cupcakes. Dessert is fun!

At a late-night Malibu bash for *Harper's Bazaar,* we served Twinkies and other Hostess treats, cut into bite-size portions, to the likes of Rod Stewart, Matt Damon, Ben Affleck, and supermodel Gisele Bündchen. If you serve the simplest ingredients—store-bought Breyers mint ice cream, say—do it in an unexpected way: Layer it with whipped cream and chocolate sauce in a tall cocktail glass, complete with a tall chocolate cookie on the side. That's a trick we picked up from New York City's tony Gotham Bar & Grill. At a lavish dinner party at the restaurant Nick & Toni's in East Hampton to launch a new Mercedes-Benz, our dessert menu was simple: vanilla ice cream (from Häagen-Dazs) in a gorgeous silver bowl, along with fresh berries. Not a spoonful was left at the end of the night.

As with most elements of a party, dessert is all about presentation, whether the menu consists of nothing more than fresh fruit or offers classics like crème brûlée, chocolate raspberry soufflé, petits fours, or chocolate truffles. Do some research: Have dessert at a great bakery. Consult with the pastry chef at your favorite restaurant and try to make his or her creations at home. Buy a good cookbook (we list our favorites in "Our Yellow Pages") and make friends with your mixer. Or buy something premade from the bakery, the grocery store, or a restaurant you love or have heard about (remember many places will send food by FedEx to your doorstep; see "Our Yellow Pages" for names). There are lots of options to choose from. Your only goal: to give your guests—even the ones who think they simply can't swallow one more bite—a delicious reason to satisfy their sweet tooth.

In this chapter, you will find a list of what you need in your refrigerator, freezer, and pantry for dessert as well as the equipment you'll need when you're entertaining at home. Whether you're having a party at home, hiring a caterer, or entertaining at another venue, we provide serving options for desserts, including cakes, cookies, brownies, ice cream, pies, chocolates, and candy. We explain how to turn supermarket items into dessert delicacies, and we give sample dessert menus. In "Our Yellow Pages," we list our favorite bakeries around the country and give you the skinny on where to find the right tools, toppings, and accessories.

Our advice:

Indulge now, feel guilty later.

THE PERFECT END TO THE PERFECT PARTY IS ALWAYS THE PERFECT DESSERT, WHETHER IT'S COTTON CANDY AND COOKIES OR A PASTRY MASTERPIECE. PHOTO COURTESY OF DENISE TRUSCELLO/ WIREIMAGE.COM,

HOME SWEET HOME

There are a few ways to do dessert at home: Make it from scratch, whip up an easy concoction that requires no chef skills other than putting something in a dish, bring in something premade, or hire a caterer. If you plan to bake your heart out, you will need to make sure you're equipped with a mixer, a blender, proper trays and pans (i.e., cookie, brownie, Bundt cake, cupcake, and pie), cookie cutters, measuring cups and spoons, mixing bowls, and an apron (messes are to be expected). Consider asking a pastry chef—or someone in cooking school—to help you for a small fee (or in exchange for an invitation to your event). Make a day of baking with your friends (nothing like a flour fight to kick things off).

But entertaining at home does not mean you have to be Betty Crocker in the kitchen. If you don't feel like making a commitment to a preheated oven and hours of egg-yolk separating, keep it simple. Fresh fruit layered with crème fraîche will do the job, as will store-bought mini graham cracker pie crusts, filled with peanut butter and topped with warm chocolate sauce and Heath Bar crumbs (a concoction we picked up from a pastry-chef friend).

Mix and match different flavors of ice cream to create your own special sundaes. Layer crushed Oreos with whipped cream in a large glass bowl. Offer a pudding bar, with a selection of flavors. Or bring in dessert from a store or restaurant you adore and add your own touch with mounds of whipped cream, sprinkles, and sparklers. The key is making it look good. Make use of glass cylinders, silver bowls, martini glasses for ice cream, scooped-out melons and pineapples, and special plates.

HERE ARE SOME INGREDIENTS TO CONSIDER WHEN YOU'RE THINKING ABOUT DESSERT.

- Premade pie crusts—big or small—available at any grocery store
- Cookie and/or brownie mix
- Cake mix and icing
- Ice cream and/or sorbet
- Sprinkles
- Whipped cream
- Chocolate sauce
- Pudding and pudding mix
- Fresh seasonal fruit

If you plan to hire a caterer, he or she will bring all of the necessary dessert plates and serving ware, even napkins and silverware if you request it. But if you're doing it yourself, make sure you have the equipment and accessories. Whatever you don't have, you can most definitely rent, borrow from a friend, or find on the cheap at a discount store or flea market.

HERE ARE SOME OF THE PIECES YOU MIGHT NEED.

- A cake stand or a covered plate that can double as a cheese platter if need be
- Cake knives
- Gel cake-decorating pens to decorate the tops of cakes, cupcakes, brownies, cookies, and such
- Nonstick cookie sheets and liners. We recommend heavy-duty, double-insulated sheets because they distribute the heat evenly on the tray (you can also use them to cook chicken and roast vegetables)
- Cookie cutters in cute shapes
- An ice-cream scoop (let it sit in warm water before using it in order to soften ice cream while scooping)
- Ice-cream bowls (soup bowls will do the trick)
- An ice-cream machine for special occasions
- A blender for shakes (you can use the same one you used for drinks)

- Pie plates
- Cupcake liners/wrappers
- Great dessert plates, whether vintage china or classic white
- An hors d'oeuvre tray that holds bowls. These are great for samplers with, say, candy in one bowl, strawberries in another
- Serving bowls and platters
- Tiered plates for cookies, brownies, tartlets, chocolates, candy, or whatever you fancy
- A lazy Susan
- Spatulas
- A fondue set
- A culinary torch for crème brûlées and caramelization, if you want to go that extra mile
- Cocktail napkins
- Birthday candles and sparklers
- Doilies
- Straws

See "Our Yellow Pages" for details on where to buy these items.

For more unconventional presentation, place desserts on top of doilies and offer them buffet-style. Stack a couple of cookies in glass tumblers and tie a ribbon around each. Recycle small take-out soup containers (or buy them from a soup stand or restaurant) and fill them with individual servings of ice cream, pudding, whipped cream, chocolates, or candy and stick attractive labels on the containers. Serve chocolate mousse in a big glass bowl or a punch bowl with a ladle; surround it with Hershey's Kisses and a stack of small bowls for your guests to use. Popcorn boxes, flowerpots, and glass jars can hold cookies. Give each guest a cone-shaped party hat filled with treats. Use aluminum foil to create platters and bowls. Shop at a party store for fun props. Look around your home and see what else you can use. Then figure out how you want to dole out your treats, which leads us to our next point: Service.

AT YOUR SERVICE

As with drinks and food, there are three basic ways to serve desserts: passing them, placing them on tables, or a combination of both. There are, however, some fun options that can turn dessert into the memorable element of any party.

HIRE AWAY

We always love using servers, even if we're only serving dessert, so we have less to stress ourselves about. Servers also add a touch of chic to the simplest offerings: They make Hershey's Kisses or flavored marshmallows look lavish.

On the more formal end of entertaining, you can have servers pass trays of dessert at a cocktail party; at a formal dinner they can offer guests a choice of three desserts, taking orders and then serving them; or they can offer each guest a plated dessert at the end of the meal. You can also set up a buffet table with servers. Or you can try something fun. Servers can walk around with cookie jars and, using tongs, serve cookies to each person. Or they can hand out ice-cream cones. The legendary Beverly Hills Hotel does this and it's a perfect offering for a summer party. Here are more of our favorites.

IDEAS FOR SERVING DESSERT

- At a seated meal, give guests different desserts and extra forks and spoons—say, alternating flavors of soufflés, pear and apple tarts, or chocolate and vanilla cakes. That encourages people to interact as they share bites of dessert.

- Have a server place four types of dessert in front of every two to three people and tell them to share.

- Have one server offer ice cream or cake to each guest, while another server follows with toppings like hot fudge, whipped cream, and sprinkles.

- At Barry Diller's casual Oscar lunch, where guests hang out on his lawn, waiters passed huge trays, each holding a choice of five lavish desserts, so everyone could pick whatever they craved.

- Set up dessert stations with servers. One table could offer pies, another chocolate fondue, and yet another cupcakes.

- Get a trolley and have a server roll it around, offering dessert to guests. Very Harry Cipriani.

CHIC TIP

However you choose to serve desserts, offer little plates of chocolates, small cookies, or even candied ginger pieces at the dinner table, by the bar, or at coffee tables. It's nice to give everyone a sweet little nibble to pick at.

PLACE IT

If servers are not in your plan, you can still find decidedly elegant ways to offer dessert. Again, it's all in the presentation. Work with stylish platters. If you're having a sit-down dinner, think about setting up a separate area for your desserts. This way people can get up from the table, move around a bit, then help themselves to dessert. Or consider stationing large trays on the table, each tray holding several kinds of desserts. (Always try to offer people at least three types of dessert, with one being a light, somewhat healthy option like fruit.)

You can also leave the dining area after the main course. While guests relax and digest, you can clear the table, reset it with dessert, and then call everyone back when you're ready.

Variations on dessert buffets are plentiful and they are great for formal sit-down dinners, since they force people to mingle. You can place plated desserts throughout the party space—on the bar, counter, windowsill, and cocktail table. Or you can stack plates, forks, spoons, and napkins at one end of a table with an array of desserts to tempt your guests. Tiered platters always make superb buffet presentations. Each tier should be covered with a different dessert—for example, one with cake slices, one with cookies, and one with fruit—with whipped cream, plates, and other necessities on the side. A restaurant called the Lemon Tree in Capri, Italy, does this with a three-tiered table (that's right, a table) and it is just breathtaking.

WHAT'S FOR DESSERT?

Because the choices in desserts are endless, it's important to keep the menu focused on your affair's theme. Stick with holiday-appropriate desserts if you're having a holiday party. Gingerbread houses, cakes with green and red icing, or cookies cut in the shape of Santa and reindeer are great for Christmas. Get macaroons for Passover; red-hots, red velvet cake, and chocolate hearts for Valentine's Day; watermelon wedges and Key lime pie for Memorial Day; red, white, and blue Italian ices for the Fourth of July. If you're having an Italian dinner, offer cannolis, cream puffs, biscotti, or profiteroles, tiramisù, or gelato. (Consider getting these sweets from Ferrara's in New York City's Little Italy. Open since 1892, they are the oldest bakery in America and they ship anywhere. They also sell their cannoli shells frozen, so you can make them at home any time.) Or serve desserts from, say, Mexico, China, France, and Austria and call your party "around the world in a million calories." Host a spa party and offer nutritious, natural sweets, like fresh fruit, sugar-free and wheat-free pastries from a health-food store, and sorbet. For a summer barbecue, whip up apple pie à la mode.

At a cocktail party we organized to open a new Cartier store in downtown Manhattan, the theme of the jewelry collection was candy-colored baubles. So we placed masses of spring-colored hard candy in the store windows and served a rainbow of treats: pink and blue cotton candy in paper cones, mini ice-cream cones with different flavors of sorbet, and bins of candy.

Although we always like to provide our guests with two or three dessert choices, and we offer more than that if it's an all-dessert party, one dessert can still be fabulous. Ice cream or sorbet with fruit is simple and classic.

SIMPLE SWEETS YOU CAN MAKE AT HOME

- Crushed chocolate cookies layered with homemade whipped cream, served in a glass bowl with a ladle.

- Vanilla ice cream with berries and a drizzle of high-quality balsamic vinegar, a staple at New York's posh Le Cirque 2000.

- Fruit salad.

- Tollhouse cookies: Heat the cookies before serving by placing them in the toaster oven at 350 degrees for three to five minutes.

- Rice Krispie treats with add-ins, such as peanut butter, another kind of sugar cereal, and tiny colored marshmallows.

- Grilled sugar-coated fruit skewers.

- Many bakeries can now digitally scan a photo onto the top of a cake (see "Our Yellow Pages").

- Perfect slices of a store-bought pound cake on beautiful china with a dollop of whipped cream and a chocolate-covered strawberry.

- Fruit, caramel, or chocolate drizzle added to any kind of cake to make it look more sophisticated.

- Dessert ordered from a special bakery or restaurant.

- Polly's Cakes in Oregon will send by FedEx their ornately designed cakes in pieces in a cooler along with detailed sketches for correct assembly. Mrs. Beasley's in Los Angeles is famous for their lemon

cakes and Joe's Stone Crab in Miami is best known for its Key lime pie (see "Our Yellow Pages").

- Individual mini cakes with icing, sprinkles, M&Ms, crushed candy bars, and spatulas on the side. This is a great way to encourage people to get friendly.

 CHIC TIP IF YOU HIRE A CATERER AND ORDER A SPECIAL CAKE, THE CATERER WILL USUALLY PROVIDE TWO CAKES: A SHOW CAKE AND A RESERVE CAKE. ASK THE CATERER TO PRECUT THE RESERVE CAKE, SO DESSERT SERVICE IS SPEEDY AND SMOOTH AFTER THE SHOW CAKE IS SLICED.

COOKIES AND BROWNIES AND CHOCOLATES, OH MY!

What was your favorite dessert as a kid? If you were anything like us, it was cookies and brownies and chocolates. All at once! And there are so many great, easy ways to offer each one of them for dessert that your guests will feel like kids again.

You can pour the batter for chocolate-chip cookies or brownies into one large pan and make a big cake, or create a multilayer cake with icing. You can make fresh ice-cream sandwiches with cookies. Broken cookies, brownie bits, and bits of chocolate also make amazing ice-cream toppers. You can serve them gooey and warm with whipped cream in oversize or little bite-size portions. Buy or make cookie and brownie bars in a variety of flavors: marble, chocolate-chip truffle, peanut butter, caramel, coconut blondies. On a more playful note, find a bakery where you can custom order cookies or chocolates in the shape of shoes, playing cards, motorcycles, or anything that reflects your concept.

The creativity doesn't have to stop there. Serve fortune cookies dipped in chocolate or white chocolate. You can order them with fortunes that match the concept of your party (see "Our Yellow Pages"). Give each guest a chocolate rose, wrapped in red

MILK AND COOKIES ARE NOT JUST FOR KIDS. HERE'S A CLASSIC DESSERT THAT NO ONE CAN SAY NO TO. PHOTO COURTESY OF DENISE TRUSCELLO/WIREIMAGE.COM,

CHIC TIP TO TEST THE QUALITY OF CHOCOLATE, PRESS IT TO THE ROOF OF YOUR MOUTH. GRADE-A STUFF WILL MELT INSTANTLY.

CUPCAKE CULTURE

Serving cupcakes is a fun alternative to cake. Some of the most glamorous parties we've been to have featured tiers of cupcakes. Cupcakes are easy to eat and you can offer lots of variety. Our all-time favorite is a vanilla cupcake with sweet buttercream icing from Magnolia Bakery, a tiny sugar joint with a cult-like following in the West Village of Manhattan (see page 239 for the recipe).

or pink foil. Add a stylish box of chocolates to the dessert mix. Or put a couple of chocolates in a small Lucite box at each place setting. You can also personalize chocolate and find shapes that relate to your party's concept, such as champagne bottles, dollar signs, or tennis rackets. If you're doing a Las Vegas–themed party, give everyone chocolate poker chips. If the theme is Cuban, offer chocolate cigars. Get molds in different shapes like shoes, cars, or body parts, and make desserts that match the concept of your party.

You can even set up an entire "chocolate bar" with a menu, listing the different types of chocolate you're serving, like toasted almond clusters dipped in chocolate, chocolates with a butterscotch center, and layers of white and milk chocolate.

See "Our Yellow Pages" for our favorite chocolate stores and brands. If you don't have a fabulous chocolate shop near you, you can always order them online or possibly find them in an upscale department store like Neiman Marcus or Bloomingdale's.

TO MAKE YOUR DESSERT PRESENTATION SWEETER, ADD FLOWERS. HERE, A THREE-TIERED PLATTER WITH THREE FLAVORS OF MINI CUPCAKES. PHOTO BY JEFF VESPA/WIREIMAGE.COM.

TASTE BUDS WILL POP WITH CANDY-FLAVORED POPCORN. THIS IS PETERBROOKE'S CHOCOLATE RENDITION. YUM. PHOTO BY PAUL COSTELLO.

MIX HIGH AND LOW BY PLACING STORE-BOUGHT SYRUPS ON FAB-ULOUS CAKE STANDS SO YOUR GUESTS CAN DRESS UP THEIR DESSERTS IN STYLE. PHOTO BY PAUL COSTELLO.

GET SAUCY

TEN THINGS THAT DIP WELL IN CHOCOLATE (WHITE, MILK, DARK, AND ASSORTED)

- POPCORN
- PRETZELS (RODS, SUPERSIZE SOUR-DOUGH, AND MINIS)
- OREO COOKIES
- POTATO CHIPS
- RAISINS, NUTS, AND DRIED FRUIT
- ESPRESSO BEANS
- CARAMEL
- BERRIES AND CHERRIES
- GRAHAM CRACKERS
- MARSHMALLOWS
- CORNFLAKES CEREAL

I SCREAM, YOU SCREAM . . .

Ice cream is always a big hit at any party, whether it's ice-cream sandwiches (make your own wicked con-coction, like peppermint ice cream layered between chocolate cookies, rolled in crushed peppermint candy) or bars served on old-fashioned trays, an old-school theme ice-cream cake or a few scoops in a bowl, served with peppermint sticks.

CHIC TIP

Offer bowls of ice cream. On the table, place a few types of store-bought sauces (such as Reese's, Hershey's Magic Shell, and Hershey's chocolate syrup and strawberry syrup) on a beautiful cake stand.

ICE CREAM CONES ON TRAYS DESIGNED WITH HOLES ARE A REFRESHING WAY TO QUENCH SOMEONE'S SWEET TOOTH. PHOTO BY PAUL COSTELLO.

RACHEL HUNTER MAKES A WISH ON A DECADENT CHOCOLATE CAKE AT THE MORGAN BAR IN NEW YORK CITY. PHOTO COURTESY OF JEFF VESPA/WIREIMAGE.COM.

While the basic flavors of ice cream are fine, we like to liven things up with peanut butter, coconut, pistachio, or coffee and with more unusual tastes like green tea and cinnamon-raisin. Our own wild concoctions include potato chip and chocolate crunch and vanilla with apple pie filling. Go with whatever your mad-scientist sensibilities conjure.

 CHIC TIP POUR CONDENSED MILK OVER ICE CREAM, A CUBAN TRICK THAT SWEETENS THE DISH.

Offering a selection of mix-ins, either on the table or passed by a server, is also a sweet way to top things off. Think crushed candy bars galore, banana slices, rice pudding, coconut flakes, mint chips, macadamia nuts, peanut brittle, chocolate-covered pretzel bits, Rice Krispies, and more. Add Reese's and crushed pretzels to vanilla ice cream;

blend pecan pie filling and caramelized bananas with maple-flavored ice cream; mix coconut flakes and Nutella into coffee ice cream. Our favorite ice-cream chain, Cold Stone Creamery, adds mix-ins to any flavor of ice cream by mushing the ice cream and the mix-in together with aluminum uten-

FANCY FLAVORS THAT ROCK

- WHITE CHOCOLATE TREAT: A MIX OF WHITE CHOCOLATE ICE CREAM OR YOGURT WITH BROWNIE CHUNKS, CARAMEL DRIZZLE, COCONUT FLAKES, AND CHOPPED PECANS.
- MUDPIE: A CHOCOLATY BLEND OF COFFEE ICE CREAM, PEANUT BUTTER, BROKEN OREO COOKIES, ALMONDS, AND FUDGE SAUCE, TOPPED WITH WHIPPED CREAM.
- APPLE PIE À LA MODE: A COMFORTING CON-COCTION OF SWEET-CREAM ICE CREAM WITH APPLE PIE FILLING, CINNAMON, PIE-CRUST CHUNKS, AND CARAMEL DRIZZLE.
- SUGAR CEREAL: VANILLA ICE CREAM WITH COCOA PUFFS, GOLDEN GRAHAMS, AND COOKIE CRISP CEREAL.

TAKE TWO POP-TARTS, ADD ICE CREAM BETWEEN THEM, AND VOILÀ! THE BEST ICE-CREAM SANDWICH YOU'LL EVER HAVE. TOAST THE POP-TART BEFORE PREPARING AND SERVE INSTANTLY, AS THEY DO NOT FREEZE WELL. PHOTO BY PAUL COSTELLO.

cream and served with a bunch of spoons. Kids—and adults—love it. So go crazy and serve it before the meal. And while you're at it, why not serve it in a fishbowl? (See page 241 for the recipe.)

(See page 241 for the recipe.)

CHIC TIP SET UP MARTINI GLASSES FILLED WITH SOMETHING THAT REFLECTS THE FLAVOR OF ICE CREAM (I.E., MINTS, OR STRAWBERRIES AND WHITE CHOCOLATE) IN FRONT OF EACH FLAVOR YOU DESIGN.

LARA FLYNN BOYLE AND LARA SHRIFTMAN'S COLD STONE CREAMERY BIRTHDAY CAKES. SPONSORED BY CIROC VODKA. PHOTO COURTESY OF JEFF VESPA/WIREIMAGE.COM.

sils on a cold stone countertop. There's no reason you can't do something like that at your party, wherever it may be—in the living room, at a bar or club, or by the pool.

We've hired ice-cream trucks, rented soft-serve ice-cream machines from Mister Softee (Puff Daddy has been known to do this at his annual "white party" in the Hamptons), indulged our guests with fresh chocolate-covered waffle cones, and whipped up malteds and shakes, blended with Reese's Peanut Butter Cups. At any kind of party, it's fun to serve shakes in large vases or bowls with a multitude of spoons and straws. At Serendipity 3, a sweet shop on the Upper East Side of Manhattan that's been around since 1954, they're known for their frozen hot chocolate, a divine concoction topped with a mountain of whipped

I WANT CANDY!

We have a habit of serving candy at parties of all sorts. Candy is a great addition to traditional desserts because it's small, mess-free, and easy to eat. Another reason for its appeal: People love to have little nibbles. Every year, Scoop, one of our favorite stores in New York and Miami, has an all-night shopping party at which servers pass bowls of candy until dawn. Candy is also a great way of doing dessert if you don't have a budget for anything more. And, like everything else about entertaining, if you showcase it well, it will look just as chic as a trio of crème brûlées in white porcelain cappuccino cups.

THESE ARE OUR COLORFUL CANDY SCHEMES

- Fill glass bowls and vases with candy and place them on cocktail tables for cocktail, dessert, or late-night parties.

- Go old-school with Smarties, Wonka straws, Atomic FireBalls, mini hamburger gum, hot-chocolate lollis, and Ring Pops, placed in Lucite bins, giant bags, tins, serving (or cake) platters, or three-tiered plates.

- Place or pass little bags of candy, packaged in cellophane and tied with a ribbon. At a movie premiere for Joel Silver's *Ghost Ship,* we gave everyone in the audience mini boxes of truffles from Ethel M.

- Purchase See's lollipops in chocolate raspberry, vanilla, cinnamon, and sassafras and place them in bowls in the bathroom and on the tables. They're the most satisfying suckers on earth! They also make great host gifts.

- Place tall sticks of red licorice and/or Pixie Stix in glasses or jars at the bar.

- Color your life with custom-made candy. Did you know you could special order any color of M&Ms you can imagine? Just call M&M/Mars at 800-627-7852 for aqua, black, white, forest, hot pink, silver, teal, lime green. Using jars, vases, bottles, or martini glasses, layer M&Ms in colors that match your event: black and white, say, for a black-and-white ball. You can also order colored chocolate-covered Jordan almonds from Richart to match your party's color scheme. (See "Our Yellow Pages" for more information.)

- Pass bite-size chunks of toffee or frozen mini chocolate bars on a chic tray, as if they were delicacies.

- Order a heap of rocky-road fudge from a fudge store in lieu of a cake.

- Pass trays of caramel apples on sticks, rolled in nuts with dark and white chocolate drizzle. (See "Our Yellow Pages.")

- Offer candy-flavored popcorn. For the *Charlie's Angels* premiere at Henri Bendel in Manhattan, we set out bags of flavored popcorn and labeled them CHOCOLATE, CARAMEL, CINNAMON SUGAR, and POPCORN WITH M&MS.

- Scatter packaged candy—individually wrapped Swedish Fish, Gobstoppers, Pixie Stix, Sprees, Tootsie Rolls, and lollipops—on tables.

- Place "karma caramels" on the table or at each guest's plate. They are rich pieces of caramel, wrapped in velum and printed with karmically correct sayings. Consider it the new fortune cookie. (See "Our Yellow Pages.")

- Offer candy in a gift bag at the end of the night. Parting should always be such sweet sorrow.

One more reason to love candy: the sugar-based types (gummies, Chuckles, licorice) are fat-free, which leads us to our next point: desserts everyone can enjoy without feeling like it will go straight to their thighs.

LOOK, MA! NO GUILT!

It's always smart to offer your guests a dessert that won't leave a bad taste in their mouths, so to speak. There are always health- and food-conscious guests who are watching their waistlines. For them or for anyone who doesn't like chocolate (do they exist?) offer a guilt-free array of sorbet, frozen yogurt, dried fruit, power bars cut into bite-size pieces and arranged on trays with toothpicks, or sugarless candies in sweet little bags. The point is to serve something that's good for you without sacrificing flavor. Here are some other options.

- Baked apples

- Grilled pineapple chunks on skewers

- Sorbet and sorbet pops, served with champagne grapes

- Meringue cookies (they're fat-free and only 100 calories for four)

- Homemade fruit-flavored Popsicles (Just pour fruit juice into plastic popsicle molds and freeze.)

- Desserts from Weight Watchers, The Zone, or similar weight programs (Sunfare Zone Diet will customize and deliver these desserts to your door.)

- Store-bought fat-free cakes such as angel food cake

- Pie crusts filled with warm chunky applesauce, cinnamon, and a drop of whipped cream

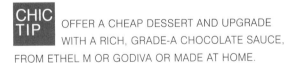

CHIC TIP OFFER A CHEAP DESSERT AND UPGRADE WITH A RICH, GRADE-A CHOCOLATE SAUCE, FROM ETHEL M OR GODIVA OR MADE AT HOME.

SUPER FINDS FROM THE SUPERMARKET

- Ice-cream bars, Moon Pies, and frozen Reese's Peanut Butter Cups, served on platters. At the Sony PlayStation2 party for Samantha and Charlotte Ronson's birthday, we served Ben & Jerry's bars—in the wrappers—on chic silver trays.

- Pints of ice cream for everyone. Just cover the labels with ribbons or color copies of photos of your guests.

- Hot pretzels and sweet dipping sauces

- Mini butter and sugar sandwiches on white bread, without the crusts

- Pressed peanut butter and jelly sandwiches. They'll melt in your hands—and in your mouth.

- Marshmallow Fluff, peanut butter, and fudge pies or sandwiches. Add sliced bananas to taste.

- Nutella and coconut flakes inside a warm soft tortilla (served hot) or baked Pillsbury dough

- A soft tortilla stuffed with white chocolate chips, macadamia nuts, and bananas

- Doughnuts on multitiered platters, enhanced with candy embellishment (see page 171 for a photo).

- McDonald's apple pie, heated and served with a scoop of vanilla ice cream, crushed nuts, and caramel drizzle

- Bread pudding with butterscotch, chocolate, and strawberry sauces on the side

- Pound cake from the supermarket. Cut it into diamond shapes and top it off with whipped cream and a berry to give it a sneaky haute-cuisine makeover.

THE MENU

Dessert should be as carefully plotted as everything else about your party. Below, we offer a list of parties and sample menus you could use. Of course you can serve any of the desserts any which way you want: with servers, by placing them on platters on tables, or via buffet. Eat up. And make sure you offer things for those who are dieting and those who are not.

A CLASSIC COCKTAIL PARTY

Most hosts don't serve dessert at cocktail parties, especially if it's between 6:00 and 8:00 P.M. But we think that's a mistake. People always crave something sweet. So give them two or three of the following.

- Chocolates or chocolate-covered strawberries

- Bite-size cookies and brownies

- Bite-size tarts filled with pecans, apple, caramel, or banana

- A milk shake bar

- Candy—gummies, truffles, mini chocolate bars—in bowls on all of the tables

SERVING FINGER FOOD AT COCKTAIL PARTIES MEANS NO MESS, NO STRESS.

DESSERT PLATTERS

Nobu makes the best ones: a round tray with green-tea ice cream, ice cream wrapped in rice paper, and other delicacies for all to share. At the New York City premiere of *Windtalkers,* starring Nicolas Cage, we did a seated dinner, offering a dessert platter of berries with crème fraîche, layered with whipped cream and served in a martini glass. On the table, there were also plates of rich lavish truffles.

TAKE IT ALL IN ONE BITE. SERVING SMALL PORTIONS OF DESSERTS (INCLUDING A MILK SHAKE) ON AN ELEGANT WHITE PLATTER IS DELICIOUSLY CHIC. PHOTO COURTESY OF DENISE TRUSCELLO/WIREIMAGE.COM.

LUNCHEON DESSERT OPTIONS

- A plate of mini cookies on the table

- A fruit plate in the middle of the table

- A salad of frozen grapes and a plate of biscotti

- Scoops of sorbet with fresh berries

- Mini portions of a light dessert, such as Key lime pie

DESSERT AND DANCING PARTY

Abundance is key, so go crazy with a buffet and servers, who pass treats such as individual portions of flavored crème brûlée served in espresso cups. For Jimmy Choo, we organized a buffet dinner party in the Hamptons and after dinner, servers passed trays with individual, bite-size desserts. There were two types of truffles, a brownie, an apple tart, and mini cookies on each tray. Try doing that yourself. Offer tarts and other sweet nibbles, brownie cakes, and platters holding one portion of five to ten types of desserts, so groups of people can share. Throw in dessert drinks, too, such as fruit-infused sake or liquor-infused gelato or sorbet.

Dessert is vital to any party that involves a full meal and it's always a nice addition to mid-afternoon teas, cocktail affairs, and late-night wildness. Think about it: Everyone loves to indulge,

MAKE YOUR OWN ICE-CREAM SANDWICHES AND THEN SPRINKLE WITH PEPPERMINT CANDY TO GIVE THEM A FRESH NEW FLAVOR. PHOTO COURTESY OF PAUL COSTELLO.

> **MAKE DESSERT MORE POTENT: ADD ALCOHOL**
>
> HERE ARE FOUR WAYS TO SPICE UP TRADITIONAL DESSERTS.
>
> - **MOJITO SORBET:** Pale green sorbet with fresh mint, lime, and rum. It tastes just like the Cuban drink of the same name. Make it at home with a blender or ice-cream maker. Or try to order it from a local sorbet maker. They will often allow you to create your own flavor if you order it in bulk.
>
> - **THE JACK DANIEL'S ICE-CREAM SODA:** A classic ice-cream soda with a splash of Jack.
>
> - **DRUNKEN FUDGE SAUCE:** Mix fudge sauce with Grand Marnier. Or try Mount Gay rum with caramel sauce. Just blend the sauce with the alcohol to taste, depending on how strong or weak you want it to be.
>
> - **YUMMY RUM:** Pour rum over pound cake to add the flavor of Barbados. Eyeball it to figure out how much to pour. Note: Too much alcohol will make the cake soggy.

even a little, even the pickiest of Atkins-only eaters. So make it amazing. Whether you have something shipped from an iconic restaurant or bakery from across the country, run out to the corner deli and cut up an Entenmann's cake and plate it in a sophisticated way with a scoop of ice cream and chocolate drizzle, or make an elaborate spread in your own kitchen, make dessert special. It doesn't have to be a large production, involve a great expense, or require you to spend hours mixing and separating egg yolks and whites. But it does have to leave an impression on your guests. Why? Well, it's the last thing you serve people at the end of the meal. So it's the perfect way to give your crowd something to remember before they go home.

Jody Buffalo

OH, BEHAVE!
MIND YOUR MANNERS

If you're talking with your mouth full, spilling wine all over the table, and making a general mess, people will talk. Trust us. Three years later, everyone will remember that you clearly skipped finishing school. As our mothers always said, "Act like a lady (or gentleman)." That requires a wee bit more poise and grace than simply flashing a perpetual smile, saying your "pleases" and "thank-yous" and not brushing your hair at the dinner table. Proper party protocol is a skill. Although there are generally two types of etiquette patterns in the world of entertaining—one for hosts and one for guests—some behavior tips, such as polishing your conversation repertoire, showing suitable table manners, learning how to make a toast, and knowing how to pose for a picture, are applicable to both. It's the host's job to know how to make seating assignments, set the table, introduce guests to one another, handle all misbehavers with grace, and handle any hired help and waitstaff. For guests, however, there is another code of conduct, which includes responding to the invitations, knowing what the appropriate attire is, understanding the difference between being fashionably late and way too late, taking a gift or some token of appreciation for the host, and polite mingling expertise. Thus, this chapter is broken up into proper host behavior, guest behavior,

and the kind of general behavior that's important for both.

Don't just skim; it's very poor manners.

THE HOST

Being a host carries a lot of responsibility. You have to be the producer, concierge, maître d', and chief social doyenne. So be prepared for mishaps, mayhem, and madness. Extra people pop in. There are always no-shows (count on five for every twenty-five to thirty positive responses). Something in the kitchen is bound to go awry. And you have to handle it all. Like a secret agent, you need to slickly deal with serving, food, drinks, seating, music (make sure it's not too loud or guests will not hear one another), chatting, and cleaning—without going gray, let alone breaking a sweat. There are three basic stages of party etiquette: before, during, and after the event.

Before you welcome your guests, you must know how to dress the table, arrange seating assignments and calm your nerves before the carousing begins. Let's start with setting the table. How many times have you wondered what fork to use for the cockles and what those little mother-of-pearl spoons are for? Your table, like your body, must be dressed to the nines, well kempt, and stylish, which won't be a problem if you follow the guidelines in this chapter.

SETTING THE TABLE IS AS MUCH A PART OF ETIQUETTE AS SENDING THANK-YOUS AND MINDING YOUR MANNERS. HERE IS A GORGEOUS TABLE SETTING. PHOTO BY SARA JAYE.

CHIC TABLE TIPS

- Have five extra place settings—and a lot of extra glasses—on hand, just in case.

- Don't jam the table with food and dishes you don't need.

- In advance, set up the tablecloth, napkins, candles, cutlery, wine and water glasses, salt, pepper, and flowers—make sure they aren't so tall that they'll obstruct views across the table.

- People use silverware from the outside in: appetizer fork leads to salad fork leads to entrée fork. So set the silverware appropriately. And know that it's okay to serve a salad before or after an entrée.

- Forks always reside on the left.

- Spoon, fish knives, and dinner knives should be placed on the right.

- Dessert spoon and fork rest above the place setting at the twelve-o'clock position.

- The bread and butter plate, which should be substantially smaller than the dinner plate, rests on the left of the dinner plate (with its own butter knife).

- Clear all unneeded plates between courses.

- Glasses progress by size from left to right: water, red wine, white wine, dessert wine.

- For informal settings, the napkin is placed to the left of the forks.

SET UP YOUR PLACE SETTINGS PROPERLY. SALAD FORK, THEN DINNER FORK ON THE LEFT. ENTRÉE DISH UNDER SALAD PLATE, WITH NAPKIN ON TOP. KNIFE TO THE RIGHT, FOLLOWED BY A SPOON. DESSERT FORK AND SPOON REST HORIZONTALLY, AT 12:00. AND THE GLASSES, RED WINE, WHITE WINE, AND WATER, STAND AT THE RIGHT CORNER. PHOTO BY PAUL COSTELLO.

TAKE A SEAT

There are three ways to deal with seating: Let your guests sit wherever and with whomever they choose, assign tables, or designate seats at the assigned tables. For parties that are smaller than ten, we usually don't bother with seating assignments, but you can. Sometimes people want to know where to sit and they'll look to the host to find out, so if you're not assigning seats, have a clear idea of where you want your guests to sit, because they will ask.

The second our guest lists creep up to two-digit numbers, we begin to get authoritative and instruct our guests where they should be seated, even at the most casual dinners (it's a perfect opportunity to set your friend up with someone new, enable two people to make a business connection, or put random people together in the hope of budding new friendships). The process of seat assignments, however, is a painstakingly delicate science, a daunting task that takes most professional party planners weeks—no, months!—to organize.

As the host, it's important to know some details about each guest: who doesn't care for whom, who's having troubled business relations with whom, who has a crush on whom. Think about it. How many parties have you been to where you couldn't stand the person to your left? And how many times have you slyly switched your name card with someone else's?

The tricks that work for us include putting people together who will have something to discuss, sitting people boy-girl-boy-girl, and making sure there is one funny person at each table (a laughing crowd is a happy one). We also like to make sure we have one social chameleon, someone who can talk to anyone about anything, at each table. It will ensure for lively conversation. In addition, think about each person's interests when you're seating them. If Bob is studying Indian culture, put him next to your friend who's really into yoga. If Brett's a personal trainer, seat him near someone sporty who may be in the market for some new gym moves. Sit an eligible guy next to the heartbroken girl who just broke up with her boyfriend.

As the person in charge of seating, you have to get into the minds of your guests to determine who would connect with whom. Charting out the seating plan has caused many a disaster. We've had friends who haven't slept for weeks just trying to make their seating assignments work. Over the years, we've developed a foolproof plan that makes this process a lot easier to control.

Here is our SEATING FORMULA, which works whether you're assigning seats by just table number or by table number and specific seats.

1. Get a FLOOR PLAN of the venue or make your own.
2. Find out HOW MANY TABLES there are, as well as the number of people each table can accommodate. If you're organizing a dinner for fifty, try to get five tables of ten (if the venue is not equipped with tables of that size, put together two tables of eight and say hello to intimacy).
3. ENLARGE THE DIAGRAM, number the tables, and laminate it (we'll explain why later).
4. Get small ROUND AVERY LABELS in two colors (one for boys, one for girls).
5. USING YOUR MASTER GUEST LIST AS A GUIDE, write each person's name on a label and place them in groups of six, eight, or ten, depending on the table situation. Be careful. Forgetting someone would be a major faux pas!
6. STICK LABELS ON THE CHART. Because you laminated it, it's easy to pull stickers off if you're not happy with the results.
7. MOVE THE LABELS around until you have something that works.
8. Then decide which tables you want near each other and NUMBER THEM. Table coordinates, which is where the tables are located within a space, are just as important as who's sitting at the seats around them. You never want to stick an A-list table in the back corner.
9. CHECK THE MASTER LIST again to ensure you seated everyone who has RSVP'd.
10. PHOTOCOPY THE CHART and check it all again.
11. Make sure you HAVE EXTRA CHAIRS nearby so you can seat extra guests who show up.

You can also seat people at specific tables without instructing them to take a particular seat. This is a slightly less formal way of seating assignments that we like to use for more casual affairs.

CHIC TIPS

- Cram if you have to. It keeps things COZY. You can always seat eight—or even ten—at a "six-top" (restaurant-speak for a "table for six").

- If the venue has EXTRA TABLES, dress them up with centerpieces, just in case you add people at the last minute.

- Place smokers near other smokers. The nicotine-addicted population is getting smaller and smokers like to know other smokers; it makes them feel less guilty about slipping out for a cigarette. If you can't stand those cancer sticks, CREATE A CIGARETTE LOUNGE, a place (near a window) where smokers can pollute their lungs in peace.

- ARRANGE PLACE CARDS IN ALPHA-BETICAL ORDER on a small table near the entrance. Each card must be labeled with the name of the guest on the outside and the table number on the inside.

- If you can arrange it, have someone HAND THE PLACE CARDS OUT TO EACH GUEST AS THEY ENTER. This way, a seating change can be handled discreetly.

- If you have less than beautiful penmanship, don't write the place cards yourself. Type them and print them from your computer or hire someone to write them. And make sure you have someone on site who can alter place cards and make them match with what you already have. George Christy, who has written about Hollywood parties for twenty-five years, has thrown an annual luncheon at the Toronto Film Festival every year for the past twenty years. He HAND-WRITES EACH PERSON'S NAME on place cards at each table setting. These cards have become an iconic symbol of his parties, something people always talk about.

- Bring extra pens, envelopes, and place cards. CRASHERS AND DROPOUTS will necessitate minor adjustments in the place cards.

- SORT SEATING CARDS by first names instead of last (it's easier to recall the spelling of "Karen" than "Robinovitz" when you're stressed and thinking of sixty-plus guests). If two people have the same first name, use their last initial.

- If you're SEATING COUPLES at the same table, let them share one place card. Speaking of couples, unless the pair is newly in love, it's okay to split them. It will enable them to mingle with new people. But if it's a large affair, create tables of couples to relieve your guests of the pressure of having to network.

- Don't know the name of a friend's date? Label that person's card like this: "Stephen Dorff and guest," or "GUEST OF MADONNA."

- Make sure someone is near the table card station to ANSWER QUESTIONS. Guests always have questions when it comes to their seats.

- Have a friend on hand to help. She may need to add a chair here or delete one there. (Give her the typed GUEST LIST, SEATING CHART, AND A CLIPBOARD so she looks professional.) This way, she's the one chasing waiters, not you, the host, who's very busy making sure everything else is perfect.

RELAX

Parties tend to work people into a tizzy. When there's so much to think about, it's easy to become anxious. We know. We've spent many evenings in severe states of anxiety. But after being behind the scenes of thousands of parties, we have come up with relaxing techniques that are soothing to the nerves—and to the party. As soon as you know you're having a party, we suggest enlisting a friend to be the undercover "subhost," the person who happily plays musical chairs when seating gets out of control, helps get the shy out of their shells, and copes with any faux pas when you're otherwise occupied. Then, if something small goes wrong, you don't have to drop everything and run to the rescue. We also recommend that every host be completely ready (hair, makeup, nails, outfit) at least fifteen to thirty minutes before people are expected to trickle in. Unfortunately, standing in the closet half-naked, picking through racks while sighing, will do you no good when your doorbell is ringing and your veal shank is burning to a crisp. If you're the type who always thinks, "I have nothing to wear," even though your closet would wholeheartedly disagree, pick out an outfit you feel good in long before the party begins. The last thing you need is to put on that one top that always makes you feel self-conscious about your belly. It's your party. You need to be at your best. And if you can't come up with anything new and saucy to wear (even at the Gucci boutique), stick to tried-and-true duds that you feel confident in, even if a few of your friends have already seen them ten times. (They'll forgive you. We promise.)

DURING THE PARTY

You've spent so much time and energy on making the party complete that you don't want to spoil it with some socially incorrect mannerisms. During the party, you need to be at full attention, ready to roll with the punches, and aware of a few simple rules, such as how to introduce people properly, manage an unwanted guest, take care of anyone who's had too much to drink, and handle any curve ball that comes your way. The first thing you need to realize is that not everyone in your crowd will be outgoing enough to strike up conversations with new people. It will be your job to make that kind of magic happen.

WHAT'S YOUR BIGGEST PARTY COMPLAINT?

- DAVID COPPERFIELD: "SMOKERS. AT A PARTY IT'S HARD TO GET AWAY FROM SMOKE. I HATE THE SMELL OF IT AND I HATE LEAVING A PARTY AND HAVING MY CLOTHES SMELL LIKE THEY WERE USED TO MOP DOWN THE BAR AT LOTUS."

- DUCHESS OF YORK: "WAITING IN LINE FOR COATS, FOOD, LAVATORIES, . . . WAITING IN LINE FOR ANYTHING."

- LARA FLYNN BOYLE: "GROUND THAT IS UNKIND TO STILETTOS."

- MICHAEL KORS: "V.I.P. ROOMS THAT ARE FILLED WITH NON-V.I.P.S."

- DONALD TRUMP: "BORING PEOPLE WHO DON'T KNOW WHEN IT'S TIME TO GO HOME."

- AERIN LAUDER: "TOO MANY PEOPLE."

FIVE COOL QUESTIONS THAT MAKE PEOPLE THINK—AND TALK.

- WHAT ARE YOUR FIVE FAVORITE MOVIES AND WHY?

- IF YOU COULD SEE ANY FIVE BANDS, DEAD OR ALIVE, WHAT WOULD THEY BE AND WHERE?

- WHAT WAS THE LAST GREAT BOOK YOU READ?

- WHAT ARE THE FIVE ITEMS YOU CANNOT LIVE WITHOUT?

- WHAT IS YOUR DREAM OCCUPATION?

BECOME THE MASTER INTRODUCER

When guests arrive, start by making them comfortable. Relieve them of their coats. Hand them a drink. And let the mingling begin. When you present one person to another, accentuate each guest's best attributes, i.e., "Stephen, this is Karen. She's the best writer in the world. And Stephen is a designer. You'd die over his clothes." Think of this part of the game as theater. You want to give your audience something to talk about, so highlight things that people have in common, whether it's politics, impulse shopping, or an ex. For example: "Elisa, let me introduce you to Joseph. Joseph, Elisa. You know, you're both major antique collectors. Elisa, tell Joseph about that piece you just picked up at the flea market." If your affair is ultra-formal, it's proper to say, "Allow me to introduce to you [someone's name]," rather than "allow me to introduce you to." Don't ask why. It just is. And when you're introducing a senior person to a junior person, always say the senior person's name first. For example: "Ralph Lauren, allow me to introduce to you Gisele Bündchen. She is a major supermodel. Gisele, this is Ralph Lauren, as in the lifestyle and clothing company." After you say your piece, it's okay to slink away and let your guests take over.

CHIC TIP TRY TO INTRODUCE EACH GUEST TO THREE NEW PEOPLE.

A GOOD HOST IS ALWAYS ALL SMILES. JUST ASK ELIZABETH HARRISON, SHOWN HERE WITH HEIDI KLUM AT THE *GLAMOUR* MAGAZINE MUSEUM OF NATURAL HISTORY EVENT. PHOTO COURTESY OF PATRICK McMULLAN/PMc.

WHO'S THAT GIRL . . . AND WHY IS SHE AT MY PARTY?

While you're scanning the scene, it's not uncommon to spot an uninvited guest. If you want to expel the unwanted one, you need to handle the situation like a pro (read: without an attitude). If you have servers on hand, you can always instruct one to pull the old "we don't have enough prepared food or drinks to serve you, I'm so sorry" routine. Otherwise, it's time—yet again—for your subhost to step in and do your dirty work. If the unwanted one is the guest of an invited friend, you have two choices: let it slide (and politely ignore the unwarranted invader for the rest of the evening) or ask your guest to make that person disappear (in kinder terms, of course) because it's technically his or her responsibility.

You may want to watch out for guests who may have had too much to drink. There's always one at every party. This person tends to hand out business cards while repeatedly announcing, "I love you. Do you know how much I love you?" This person can also be recognized by an untucked shirt, wobbly high heels, a sweaty brow, smeared lipstick, or an excessively loud voice. First of all, do not let this person drive home. If the party is at your house, make sure you have extra bedding and a place for this person to sleep, even if it's a sleeping bag on the floor of your bedroom. It's your party. You have to act responsibly! If your party is not at home, rely on your subhost. The two of you should always have a plan for those who've had too much to drink, be it a car or taxi service or a friend who's agreed to remain sober and ferry people home. If you have friends who are known for being badly behaved with alcohol, talk to them in advance. Let them know that they shouldn't drink at your party because you don't want to deal with the "kissing incident" again (they will have no clue what you're talking about, but they'll be way too ashamed to ask). It might get them to drink less, but still keep the number of a taxi service on hand.

PARTING IS SUCH SWEET SORROW

Your party is coming to an end, which means that it's time to pay the fiddler. Whether you're having a party at home or at another venue, there will almost always be people to pay: the caterer, the staff, the bar. Know how you're paying for everything in advance and be prepared with a fistful of cash, checks, or credit cards, whatever method of payment was agreed upon. When the bill comes, if you're at a place where you'd get a bill—wait! The bill shouldn't come. Hand someone your credit card well before the end of the party or give your credit card number on the phone in advance. You never want your guests to see you paying a bill or leaving a tip. Now, let's talk tipping.

Being gracious is key for any self-respecting host. So don't stiff a waiter, even if he technically deserves it. You should always leave between 15 and 20 percent (25 percent if the service is amazing) for waiters and bartenders. An easy way to figure out how much that is: Move the decimal point one number to the left. So for $145.20, that would be $14.52, which is 10 percent of the total. Then take half of that amount, which would be $7.26, and add it to the 10 percent amount ($14.52). In this case, that's $21.78. Round it up to $22 and you'll be set to jet. For 20 percent, just double the 10 percent amount ($14.52). And voilà! At a restaurant, the tip is typically included for parties of eight or larger (ask first to make sure that it is, so you don't double tip or skip out on tipping altogether). If tip is included and the waitstaff is extraordinary, throw in an extra twenty-dollar bill or two. Leave the coat checker one dollar for each coat. Give the valet two to five dollars per car (unless you've hired a valet service to man your entire party, in which case, the head valet should get the requisite 15 to 20 percent, which he or she will divvy up for the staff).

And it's always wise to give an extra bit of a tip to those who have made your party easy along the way: the barback you hired, the wine sommelier (15 percent of the wine bill), the furniture delivery men who brought the rentals, the super who allowed you to party on the roof of your building even though it's against the rules of the lease. It's nice to slip fifty dollars to the maître d' who helped you out; but you can also just send a thank-you note or a little gift. We like to put our tips in tiny

---

MORE MANNERS TO MIND

- IF YOU CATCH A COUPLE PUTTING YOUR BEDROOM (OR BATHROOM) TO USE, JUST CLOSE THE DOOR AND PRETEND IT NEVER HAPPENED. MAKE A MENTAL NOTE OF THE INCIDENT SO YOU CAN DECIDE IF THE GUESTS ARE WORTHY OF A FUTURE INVITATION.
- FEED THE PEOPLE WHO WORK FOR YOU. YOU CAN'T EXPECT WAITSTAFF OF ANY KIND TO DO A GOOD JOB WITHOUT SOME PROTEIN. GIVE THEM SANDWICHES, CHIPS, DIP, CRUDITÉ, SODA, AND WATER.
- EAT PROTEIN—TURKEY, CHICKEN, FISH, OR TOFU—BEFORE THE PARTY BEGINS. A HOST NEVER HAS TIME TO EAT AT HER OWN BASH, AND THAT MEANS IT WILL TAKE LESS ALCOHOL TO GET YOU DRUNK. YOU CAN'T DO YOUR JOB IF YOU'RE TIPSY, SO BE SURE TO NOURISH YOURSELF IN ADVANCE.
- IF YOU YAWN IN MID-CONVERSATION, BLAME IT ON LACK OF SLEEP, EVEN IF THE REAL REASON IS BOREDOM.
- MAKE SURE DINNER IS SERVED AT A REASONABLE TIME. IN OTHER WORDS, DON'T INVITE GUESTS TO ARRIVE AT 8:00 AND WAIT TWO HOURS TO SERVE FOOD.
- EMPTY GARBAGE BAGS AS THE NIGHT PROGRESSES. AND ALWAYS HAVE A HUGE STASH OF EXTRA BAGS AT YOUR DISPOSAL.
- IF YOU'RE USING SOMEONE ELSE'S SPACE OR HOME, MAKE SURE YOU RETURN IT TO ITS ORIGINAL, CLEAN SPLENDOR. WHEN YOU'RE USING SOMEONE'S HOME, YOU DON'T WANT TO LEAVE ANY SIGNS THAT THERE WAS A PARTY; OTHERWISE, YOU'LL LOSE YOUR PRIVILEGES FOREVER.
- RETURN ALL BORROWED GOODS THE NEXT DAY, AND ENCLOSE A THANK-YOU NOTE.

envelopes, along with a note, like the ones provided at a hair salon or spa. It's a tactful way to hand someone money. While you're thanking everyone, it's important to acknowledge your sub-host. Give her or him a thoughtful gift: flowers, lingerie, a gift certificate for a pedicure, a book about her favorite artist, gift certificates to the movies, homemade cupcakes and a stack of her favorite magazines so she can hibernate for a day.

 CHIC TIP IF YOU ARE TERRIBLE AT MATH, JUST WRITE "20%" ON THE GRATUITY SECTION OF THE BILL; THE RESTAURANT WILL ADD IT UP FOR YOU.

As the host, you never stop working, even the day after your party. Send a thank-you to every person who gave you a gift. (In fact, you should send a thank-you for all gifts, period. Even if the gift you get is a thank-you gift!) Also send one to the bartender, photographer, florist, assistant, and your friend's younger brother who carried the drunkard to the taxi at the end of the night. The only rule to sending a thank-you is that you must send one, and within two to three days of your event. (Weddings are not included in this rule. A bride has up to three months for such endeavors.)

HERE'S THE NO-BRAINER FORMULA BEHIND ALL SUCCESSFUL THANK-YOU NOTES.

- Hand-write it, even if you don't have the best penmanship (on stationery is best).

- Don't worry about length. Brevity is the soul of a note! But no one-liners.

- Identify the reason you're thanking someone. Write "The fruitcake was delish!" even if the only thing that ate it was the garbage disposal.

WHAT TO SAY IN A THANK-YOU NOTE? ASK CRANE'S. THIS IS THEIR GUIDE. CRANE'S BLUE BOOK OF STATIONARY, EDITED BY STEVEN L. FEINBERG.

- Say something about how the gift makes you feel or what you'll do with it (i.e., "That Warhol catalog looks fabulous on my coffee table. Now, where are my fifteen minutes?").

- Make a reference to seeing that person soon (i.e., "Looking forward to seeing you soon!")

- Be aware of how to sign off at the end of the note. If you're friends but not close enough to use the word "love," just draw a happy face or write "xoxo" to stand for hugs and kisses. The phrase "best," "all my best," or "cheers" is a casually cool ending for friendly acquaintances, work "friends," and people you don't know well but would like to. "Respectfully," "yours," "yours truly," "sincerely," and "regards" work for anyone you have a formal relationship with.

- Include your full return address, especially if you don't know the recipient well.

THANK-YOU BASICS

There are no hard-and-fast rules when it comes to writing thank-you notes. We prefer to follow this rough guideline.
1. Write the thank-you note. 2. Affix stamp. 3. Mail it.
Of course, we'd prefer if you wrote it on Crane's stationery.

If you'd like a few more useful tips on the actual writing of the thank-you, we've been using this formula for years and have yet to have one note returned. If you are the succinct type, a correspondence card works perfectly, as does a small foldover note. Punctuality counts – and it certainly appears more sincere. Generally speaking, the message is brief and usually consists of four parts.

1. The greeting.
   Dear Barbara,
2. An appreciation of the item or favor.
   Thank you for the wonderful Italian phrase book.
3. Mention how useful it will be.
   It should come in handy when I'm looking for a man in Rome.
4. Sign off with a suggestion of a future meeting.
   I look forward to seeing you when I return from the trip, happily engaged. Ciao.

That's it. Save the mention of your puppy's amazing new trick for another letter. Unless, of course, your puppy was the gift you're thanking them for.

SOME OF OUR FAVORITE THANK-YOU NOTES

Dear Elizabeth,

Thank you for your help this weekend. It was a beautiful event.

Warm regards,

John & Fisher

[anne bruno] FLORAL & EVENT DESIGN, NEW YORK, T. 212 766 5660

ROBERT WOOD JOHNSON IV

Dear Lara —

Thanks for your help.
Hope to see you Sunday.

Best
Woody

A BUSINESS THANK-YOU NOTE ON OFFICIAL STATIONERY IS
INFORMAL WHEN IT'S HAND-WRITTEN.

BLAINE TRUMP

Dear Lara and Elizabeth,   September 30, 1998

Thank you very much for the wonderful job your team did for The Race to Deliver. It was a pleasure working with you both. We are so thankful for all the support, it makes our mission at God's Love We Deliver a bit easier. Please come down and see us soon. Thank you again for making the race such a success. Best Wishes. ——Blaine

---

nov. 1999

dear lara,

Thank you so much for having me be a part of such a lovely evening.
It was truely an exquisite party that exuded such class, elegance and "good energy." ☺ i had a great time!
... and what can i say, i LOVE my watch!! it is so beautiful !!!

Thank you Lara ... for everything !!

hope to see you soon,
all my love, paula.

PAULA USED CUTE STATIONERY—AND FABULOUS
PENMANSHIP—TO THANK US.

KELLY KILLOREN BENSIMON
240 CENTRE STREET NEW YORK, N.Y. 10013

22 November 2003

Tinsley—

Thank you so much for sending the beautiful Delman shoes. What a special treat!
Many thanks. Kelly

Dear Elizabeth,
It was such a pleasure working with you this season! Thank you for all your support.

Peter Som

ABOVE, CENTER: BLAINE TRUMP'S NOTES ARE BEAUTIFUL
BECAUSE THEY ARE SO DETAILED AND PERSONAL. ABOVE,
BOTTOM: AS WITH KELLY BENSIMON'S NOTE, LEAVE YOUR PER-
SONAL MARK WITH BEAUTIFUL HANDWRITING AND A LINE
THROUGH YOUR NAME. COURTESY OF KELLY KILLOREN BENSIMON.

ABOVE AND TOP LEFT: THESE THANK-YOU NOTES CAME WITH
MASSIVE FLOWER ARRANGEMENTS. THE FLORIST MAY HAVE
WRITTEN THEM, BUT YOU CAN WRITE YOUR OWN AND DELIVER IT
TO THE FLOWER SHOP.

Details

Daniel Peres
Editor-in-Chief

February 2004

Lara,

There aren't enough words in all of the world's languages for me to express my gratitude for your boundless generosity and hospitality.

You will forever remain unrivaled in terms of being the ultimate hostess. As soon as I open an envelope with your return address, I know I'm destined for one of the more memorable evenings of my life. Unfortunately, a simple thank you will have to suffice for all of the kindness you've shown me.

With all the love in my heart,

Dan

TO PERSONALIZE A GRACIOUS THANK-YOU LETTER, TYPED ON YOUR COMPANY'S LETTERHEAD, SIGN IT BY HAND, LIKE DAN PERES, EDITOR-IN-CHIEF OF *DETAILS* MAGAZINE. COURTESY OF DAN PERES, EDITOR-IN-CHIEF, *DETAILS* MAGAZINE.

WRITE A THANK-YOU NOTE WITH STYLE

- IN YOUR POCKET, PURSE, OR BEDROOM, DURING THE PARTY KEEP AN ONGOING LIST OF THOSE YOU WANT TO THANK SO YOU DON'T FORGET.
- IF YOU DON'T HAVE MONOGRAMMED STATIONERY, GET CREATIVE AND MAKE YOUR OWN CARD. USE THE BACK OF A PHOTO FROM THE PARTY OR A PIECE OF COLORFUL PAPER WITH YOUR LIPSTICK PRINT.
- INVEST IN *WRITING THANK-YOU NOTES: FINDING THE PERFECT WORDS* BY GABRIELLE GOODWIN AND DAVID MACFARLANE. IT'S AN EXCELLENT RESOURCE (SEE PAGE 260 OF "OUR YELLOW PAGES" FOR A SELECTION OF HELPFUL BOOKS).

GUEST BEHAVIOR

Rules and protocols for guests differ from those of the host. All guests should remember that being invited to a party is an honor and it should be respected, especially if you want to remain on guest lists of all kinds in the future. If you're a badly behaved guest, you can kiss future invitations good-bye. Your host will probably not want your presence at the next party, and other guests will remember your poor manners when they're having parties of their own. Minding your manners is mandatory. Similar to host manners, guest manners can be broken down to three phases: before, during, and after the party.

For a guest, good manners begin the second you get an invitation. As a rule, a guest should always respond to a party within one to five days of receiving the invitation. For one, it's important to let the host know that his or her invitation arrived in your mailbox safe and sound. And, all hosts put substantial time and energy into producing parties, so it is considerate to inform them if you will or will not be attending. This way, the host can prepare and provide food, drinks, and seats for the right number of people. Otherwise, someone will be stuck nibbling on whatever got burned in the kitchen because you forgot to make one measly phone call.

 CHIC TIP SAVE THE INVITATION AND BEFORE YOU LEAVE, DOUBLE-CHECK THE TIME, DATE, PLACE, AND DRESS SO YOU KNOW WHERE TO GO, WHEN TO GET THERE, AND HOW TO LOOK.

Before leaving your home, make sure you have a little token of appreciation for the host, especially if the party is at her or his home. One should never show up at a party at someone's home empty-handed (unless a gift was sent before the party). That doesn't mean you need to kill yourself finding the perfect gift. Candles, a bottle of wine, or champagne will do. But—yawn! That's so cliché. And flowers? While we all love to get flowers, it's one of the worst gifts to take to a party. Your host will have to drop everything, find a vase, and arrange them to fit the décor. We also like to avoid giving food that the host will feel obligated to serve at the party. So when it comes to gifts, try to be original.

If you're not sure if you can attend a party, notify your host of your tentative status as soon as possible and try to solidify your plans immediately. And if you have an out-of-town visitor, don't just assume he or she can go with you to the party. It's polite to ask the party-thrower if having a "plus one" is acceptable. Your host will probably say, "the more, the merrier," unless, of course, you want to take an entourage of three or more people. (If the people are famous, however, by all means, ask to take them; they'll be an excellent addition to the social circle.)

SIDE NOTE: Guests of guests should never bring guests!

In addition to responding in a timely manner, guests shouldn't call the host the day of the party. Hosts are very busy before the party begins; the pressure is on. Calling them to ask about where the party is, what you should wear, or anything that's not an emergency will only exasperate them. So be prepared. And be sure to show up at the party in proper attire. When you're a guest, you're not the star of the party, so there's no need to outshine everyone. Just wear something appropriate and flattering. If you're not sure what kind of dress certain parties call for, we have created a guide that will allow you to match up the kind of party with the kind of outfit it would call for.

HERE ARE SOME OF OUR FAVORITE GIFTS FOR HOSTS.

- A tin of caviar, with a mother-of-pearl spoon. Or chip in with a bunch of friends for "Six Months of Caviar," which is a salty package of caviar-to-taste each month (see page 259).

- A certificate for a manicure and pedicure or massage treatment at a local day spa.

- Present a basket filled with everything your friend will need to treat herself to a sinful breakfast in bed in the A.M.

- Bath products galore: Kiehls, Lady Primrose, Fresh, H2O+, Bath & Body Works, Frederick Fekkai.

- The host's favorite movie on DVD and microwave popcorn.

- A chic journal with profound inspirational quotes on the cover.

- A crystal vodka ice cooler with matching vodka flutes.

- Out-of-print or first-edition vintage books of art, photography, fashion, or design.

- Silver picture frames.

- A pair of boxing gloves and a private boxing lesson.

- A yoga instructor for an at-home lesson or a gift certificate to a class, along with a yoga mat.

- A beach towel in a basket with flip-flops, SPF, and the new Jackie Collins novel (good for beach or outdoor parties).

- Anything monogrammed: pajamas, vases, picture frames, napkins, stationery, dictionaries, photo albums, leather-bound books of quotable sayings.

- A set of vintage coasters, glass ashtrays, or a swanky lighter.

- Customized stationery. You can ever have enough.

- A gift certificate for the gumball-of-the-month or chocolate-of-the-month club. Give toothpaste with the card.

IT'S NOT WHO YOU ARE, IT'S WHAT YOU WEAR THAT COUNTS!

- **A POOL, BEACH, OR BACKYARD PARTY** Wear a bathing suit under a graphic sarong, nice shorts, or a little skirt and a tank top. Bring a fitted sweatshirt for later, when it could get chilly.

- **A LOW-KEY BRUNCH OR AFTERNOON TEA** Wear a fabulous T-shirt and jeans or flat-front, straight-leg black pants. Think about wearing perfectly pressed, untattered denim with a cashmere top and high heels. The vibe you're going for is "studied casual." Sundresses and sandals work for seventy-five-degree weather and wool skirts and high boots do the trick in the cold.

- **A FORMAL LUNCHEON** Wear a chic suit (all white for summer), a pencil skirt and polished blouse, or the kind of thing you'd envision wearing to meet your new boyfriend's parents at the country club. The point is to be polished.

- **A COCKTAIL PARTY OR GROOVY DINNER** Wear something fun yet stylish. A one-shouldered top with elegant slacks, sky-high heels, and chunky earrings. Your image should be good-time-girl with sophistication.

- **A PROPER DINNER PARTY** Keep the jeans in the closet! It's time to wear the posh designer dress you splurged on, a cashmere sweater and silk chiffon skirt, or the kind of tasteful ensemble you'd spot in the society pages of *Vogue*.

- **A WILD BASH** Wear whatever! Leather pants, a lace dress, that micro-miniskirt you've been afraid of. Get out the so-high-you-can-hardly-walk-in-them heels. Play. Show some skin. Express yourself. This is the time to experiment with a crazy something you love and never had an occasion to pull off.

JOAN AND MELISSA RIVERS ON WHAT TO WEAR

WHAT IS YOUR FAVORITE THING YOU HAVE EVER SEEN SOMEONE WEAR TO A PARTY?
JOAN: "A FRIEND ONCE ARRIVED TOTALLY IN RED."
MELISSA: "THE PERFECT BLACK SUIT WITH INCREDIBLE JEWELRY."

WHAT'S THE BEST ADVICE YOU COULD GIVE SOMEONE WHO DOESN'T KNOW WHAT TO WEAR TO A PARTY?
JOAN: "PUT ON SOMETHING THAT CAN START A CONVERSATION—AN ETHNIC BROACH, AN UNUSUAL NECKLACE—SOMETHING YOU CAN TALK ABOUT OR BE ASKED ABOUT."
MELISSA: "KEEP IT SIMPLE AND CHIC. STICK TO ONE COLOR OR TONE ON TONE. YOU CAN'T GO WRONG."

WHAT'S THE BEST THING A HOST CAN SAY TO SOMEONE WHO COMES TO A PARTY WEARING THE WRONG ATTIRE?
JOAN: "RELAX, I JUST DID THE SAME THING LAST WEEK AT ____'S HOUSE."
MELISSA: "TELL THEM NOT TO WORRY ABOUT IT. LAUGH WITH THEM. IT'S THE HOST'S JOB TO PUT THAT PERSON AT EASE."

WHAT IS AN INEXPENSIVE WAY TO MAKE YOUR OUTFIT STAND OUT AT A PARTY?
JOAN: "A SIMPLE DRESS AND A FABULOUS SHOW-STOPPING PIN OR NECKLACE. IT DOESN'T HAVE TO BE EXPENSIVE OR REAL!"
MELISSA: "A GREAT ACCESSORY."

WHAT IS THE BEST COCKTAIL PARTY OUTFIT?
JOAN: "A WELL-FITTING BLACK DRESS AND SEXY, SEXY, SEXY SHOES."
MELISSA: "YOUR FAVORITE LITTLE BLACK DRESS."

WHAT IS YOUR FAVORITE DINNER PARTY OUTFIT?
JOAN: "A LOW-CUT DRESS. THEY'LL ONLY BE SEEING YOUR TOP HALF FOR MOST OF THE EVENING."
MELISSA: "CHIC YET COMFORTABLE PANTS WITH A FABULOUS TOP AND GREAT SHOES."

Once you know what to wear, it's time to know when you should make your entrance. For life's important appointments—job interviews, business meetings, blind dates—it's good to be early, but when it comes to parties, showing up early is uncool (unless, of course, the host asks you to). All hosts could use an extra fifteen minutes to prepare. If you're the neurotic type who likes to arrive everywhere twenty minutes before call time, ignore your compulsion, because walking into a party early puts an undue amount of pressure on a host to be all smiles when there are still last-minute chores to deal with. It's best to arrive fifteen minutes late, especially if the party is taking place over a short period of time, like two to four o'clock, or six to eight o'clock, and so on. If you're going to be more than thirty minutes late, call the host to give your estimated time of arrival. On the other end of the party, you may have to check out on the early side. If you're at a large gathering, don't run up to the host to say, "I'm leaving now." Just slip away quietly, or at most, tell the host when you arrive that you may leave early. That way, you won't feel guilty leaving without saying good-bye and the host won't feel pressured to entertain you as you walk out the door.

CHIC TIP IF YOU JUST PLAIN FORGOT TO TAKE A GIFT, SEND FLOWERS OR SOMETHING THOUGHTFUL AFTER THE FACT.

DURING THE PARTY . . .

You've responded. You've dressed. You've shown up, gift in hand. And now you're in the thick of the party. It's time to relax and enjoy. We'll begin with introductions. Parties are the best places to meet new people. So after a proper introduction to someone new, the best gesture you can make is to reach out for a handshake. Don't give one of those fishy, wimpy shakes where you barely hold on to someone's appendage. Shake with strength. It's a sign of self-assuredness and it's a surefire way to make a strong first impression. The art of a firm handshake lies in the bit of skin that extends between your thumb and pointer finger. That part of the hand should connect with the same part of someone else's hand. Once contact is made, slightly jerk your hand up and down, while making eye contact and saying hello. Then add, "So nice to meet you," or something similarly cordial.

Kissing on the cheek isn't a bad move either, especially if you've been dying to meet someone and your friend has been trying to introduce you for years. But don't do the double-cheek kiss unless you're European or the person you're meeting is European. Otherwise, you'll seem affected. (If you just returned from a trip to Europe, you're excused out of what we call "the habit rule," which means that you probably got into the habit of double-cheek kissing while you were away and you have at least fourteen days to return to normal American procedures.)

As the party goes on, you will probably forget a name—or ten! If you're passing by someone you just met, smile and say "Hi," and you'll be fine. Ask the host later who the person is, just so you know for future reference. And if you just met someone and already forgot his or her name, it's okay to admit it and ask. You're human. Chances are, he or she may have forgotten your name, too. Now, if you're the introducer and you can't remember someone's name, that's another story. You have to play it off in a subtle, laid-back sort of way. Give friends a signal—an ear tug, a slight rub of the chin with your thumb and forefinger, a hair-twirl—which means, "Have no clue who this person is. Introduce yourself!" Or say, "Oh, have you two met?" The second you say that, the two parties will probably introduce themselves and you'll be off the hook and fine for the rest of the night.

AFTER THE PARTY

Whether you make a habit out of sending people thoughtful cards for no reason at all or not, thank-you notes are an important part of any well-mannered personality. Thank the person who threw the party. Your host worked hard to pull something together and a little written appreciation is always nice. Mail it within a week of the party. While it's acceptable to send an e-mail or make a phone call to say thank you, taking the time to hand-write a message, even if it's no longer than three lines, will mean a lot to your host.

And while you're being well-mannered, send an e-mail to anyone who gave you his or her card at the party. It's a savvy way to build your network, make a new friend, and be remembered as someone who's polite and poised.

AND NOW, GOOD BEHAVIOR FOR ALL

There are some rules of etiquette that apply to both hosts and guests and if you aren't aware of them, you may find yourself struggling to get through conversations, offending someone at the dinner table, suffering from stage fright while making a toast, or ruining your favorite blouse while trying to remove an ugly Merlot stain. These are useful tips not just for parties, but for any social situation. Consider this the practical guide to the good life.

TÊTE-À–TÊTE

Brush up on your conversation skills, because just looking good is not enough to keep a party going. Talking about the weather is a bit cliché, we think, as it's the topic everyone turns to during drab dialog moments. How often have you been in a painfully dry conversation, in which you've felt like a dentist pulling teeth, and suddenly asked, "So, how about that heat?" To avoid such awkwardness, read (or skim) *Time, Newsweek,* even the *National Enquirer* and your newspapers' gossip columns. Then try starting a conversation on the latest economic crisis in corporate America or the alien baby born to Oprah. Surprise people by talking wisely about current events one minute and celebrity gossip the next. If gossip isn't your thing, consider catching up on CNN or rent an old Fellini movie before the big day. That way, you'll be able to intelligently bring up some topic beyond the local weather. During conversation lulls (statistically, there's one every eleven minutes), ask people thought-provoking questions or talk about plans for the holidays or the summer, or ask guests how they met the host. Also, compliment people. If you love someone's dress, tell her and find out where she got it (there's always a story behind chic clothes). Furthermore, don't fear debates; they make for fiery cocktail fodder. And never, ever ignore anyone.

TABLE MANNERS, DEAR

Some table-manner rules are obvious, like don't floss at the table or clean out your nails with a fork prong, but others are more esoteric and subtle. And it is those manners, the ones that go by unnoticed, that make the best impressions.

- Whenever serving people, plates should be served from the left and removed from the right.

- At a restaurant, close your menu when you're ready to order.

- Never slouch or slump (consult your chiropractor if you don't believe us).

- Put your napkin in your lap as soon as the host(ess) does. At a restaurant, open it as soon as you sit down. That will signify the beginning of the meal. If you have to get up in midmeal, place your napkin on your chair, not the table, so you don't get in your neighbor's way.

- Don't eat until each person has food on their plates. Premature eating is not something Mother would approve of.

- Chew your food (don't just swallow it whole) and put down your fork between bites.

- Avoid slurping at all costs.

- Use silverware from the outside in if you're not sure what fork goes with what dish.

- If you drop silverware, leave it and just ask the nearest waiter for a replacement. If you're at an informal party at someone's home, pick up the piece, wipe it with a napkin, put it on the table, and ask for a new one.

- Keep elbows off the table while you—and everyone else—eat.

- Unless there's a fire, talking with your mouth full is prohibited.

- Playing with your food is a no-no. So is pushing that last bit of rice on your fork with your finger. (That's what knives are for!)

- Be polite to waiters and servers. They have feelings, too.

- Don't pour water onto your napkin, even if you splattered olive oil on your favorite top. Use the restroom to tend to your spill.

- When you're finished, neatly place your fork and knife at the four-o'clock position on your plate.

- Any time you're at someone's private home (and they don't have hired help), offer to take dirty dishes into the kitchen. The host will probably say "No thanks," but the offer is what counts; and it will ensure you a place in the good-guest Rolodex forever.

TOAST OF THE TOWN

Toast time is usually reserved for transition periods between courses of a meal or rounds of cocktails. If you're making a speech, keep it short and snappy. Prepare what you want to say in advance. You don't need to read word-for-word off of a piece of paper (if you do, however, make sure you pause to make eye contact with your audience). Nor do you have to sound flawlessly fluid. Act natural. Make a joke about being nervous, as it is something everyone can relate to. For more help, consult page 260 and find a list of books with toast tips.

A GOOD TOAST ALWAYS CALLS FOR ONE THING: GOOD FRIENDS! HERE ARE FRIENDS MARIA MENOUNOS, JARON LOWENSTEIN, RACHEL ZALIS, AND ANDREA ORBECK. PHOTO BY JEFF VESPA/WIREIMAGE.COM.

HERE ARE A HANDFUL OF OUR FAVORITE TOASTS. RAISE YOUR GLASS AND HAVE A GO!

HERE'S TO LYING, CHEATING AND STEALING
LIE TO LIE TO SAVE A FRIEND
CHEAT TO CHEAT TO CHEAT DEATH
STEAL TO STEAL THE HEART OF SOMEONE YOU LOVE
—UNKNOWN

FOR BETTER OR FOR WORSE, BUT NEVER FOR GRANTED.
—UNKNOWN

THREE BE THE THINGS I SHALL NEVER ATTAIN: ENVY, CONTENT, AND SUFFICIENT CHAMPAGNE.
—DOROTHY PARKER

MAY YOU LIVE AS LONG AS YOU WANT
AND MAY YOU NEVER WANT AS LONG AS YOU LIVE.
—UNKNOWN

MAY ALL YOUR JOYS BE PURE JOYS,
AND ALL YOUR PAIN CHAMPAGNE.
—UNKNOWN

I THINK THAT GOD IN CREATING MAN SOMEWHAT OVERESTIMATED HIS ABILITY.
—OSCAR WILDE

HERE'S TO STEAK WHEN YOU'RE HUNGRY,
WHISKEY WHEN YOU'RE DRY,
ALL THE GIRLS (BOYS) YOU EVER WANT,
AND HEAVEN WHEN YOU DIE.
HERE'S TO THOSE THAT LOVE US,
AND HERE'S TO THOSE THAT DON'T,
A SMILE FOR THOSE WHO ARE WILLING TO,
AND A TEAR FOR THOSE WHO WON'T.
—UNKNOWN

AMOR VINCENT OMNIA. (LOVE CONQUERS ALL.).
—UNKNOWN

"LOVE DOESN'T MAKE THE WORLD GO 'ROUND, BUT IT SURE MAKES THE RIDE WORTHWHILE."
—MAE WEST

PICTURE PERFECT

If you ever wondered why models, socialites, and celebrities always look so good in magazines, it's not because they have perfect genes, but rather, because they know how to pose for a picture. You don't have to look like Grace Kelly to be photogenic. You just need to know a few little tricks. That way, when the camera flash goes off, you'll be prepared—and glamorized forever.

- Wearing glasses? Slightly tip your head down to avoid the glare.

- Stand with one foot in front of the other to make your hips appear smaller. Crossing one leg in front of the other will give you a narrow appearance, as well.

- Turn forty-five degrees to the left or right and face your shoulders to the camera. This gives the illusion of a little waist.

- Suck in your stomach by using your core ab strength and pulling your belly button inward, as if you're trying to make it reach your spine.

- Hold your chin slightly downward while looking up. It was Princess Di's standard photo-op move. It also helps hide double chins.

- Look directly into or slightly above the camera for piercing eye contact.

- Keep your shoulders down by using your scapula muscles (where your wings would be if you had them) to elongate your neck, camouflage that double chin, and convey confidence.

- Put your arm around your friend's waist instead of shoulders. It will make your arms appear thinner.

- Got a drink in your hand? Hide it behind the person next to you.

A MANNEQUIN AT A LACOSTE EVENT AT BARNEYS, NYC, POSING PROPERLY. PHOTO COURTESY OF PATRICK McMULLAN/PMc.

- Don't stand next to someone who puts her arm around your shoulders—with a drink in hand. It will look very bad if you wind up running for office one day.

- Whatever you do, do not say "cheese." It's cheesy.

CHIC TIP SALT SOMETHING AS SOON AS YOU STAIN IT. LET THE SALT SIT, AS IT IS SAID TO ABSORB THE STAINS. TAKE THE GARMENT TO THE DRY CLEANER AS SOON AS POSSIBLE.

FOR HOW TO SMILE FOR THE CAMERA

- FOR SOMEONE WHO DOESN'T FREQUENT THE RED CARPET, STOP AND STRIKE A POSE AND HOLD IT.

- THE MOST FLATTERING ANGLE FOR A POSE VARIES, BUT USUALLY STRAIGHT ON WITH HIPS TO THE SIDE A BIT WORKS.

- THE BEST THING TO WEAR FOR A PICTURE IS COLOR.

- MATTE MAKEUP TENDS TO LOOK BETTER IN PHOTOS.

- TO LOOK THINNER IN A PICTURE, BE IN THE MIDDLE AND PUT OTHERS SLIGHTLY IN FRONT, WEAR DARKER COLORS, AND DEFINITELY WEAR SLEEVES OR A BOA, OR A STOLE.

- AS A RULE, YOU SHOULD ALWAYS SMILE, BUT NOT TOO MUCH.

OUT! OUT! DAMN SPOT!

There's wine on your felt carpet and salad dressing on your best white top. It's called party aftermath, sweetheart, and there's no getting around it. There are three kinds of stains: earth (fruit juices, wine, and cola—yes, cola!), protein (blood, sweat, milk), and oil (greasy stains left by any oil, mascara, lipstick). While most people believe that club soda is the cureall to stains, it actually isn't. There is a specific remedy for each kind of stain, respectively: soap, distilled or bottled water, and clear vinegar (the acidity of vinegar helps remove stains); soap, distilled or bottled water, and a bit of ammonia; and any citrus-based stain remover. When you're trying to remove the stain, do not rub the fabric or you will set the stain instead of remove it. Instead, dab lightly with a towel and let it dry. If the stain is not 100 percent removed, repeat the process again.

Practice your skills while you're at dinner with friends. Consider videotaping yourself while you eat so that you can see, first-hand, what you need to improve (this is for obsessive-compulsive types only). And brush up on your general social manners, whether you're a host or a guest. Thank everyone who has helped you make the night memorable. And remember this: There is no such thing as being too polite, only not polite enough. We recommend many etiquette books, which are listed in "Our Yellow Pages."

CLOCKWISE FROM ABOVE LEFT: STANDING WITH ONE LEG IN FRONT OF THE OTHER OFFERS A SLIM SILHOUETTE, AS EVIDENCED BY THE EVER-SO-SLIM JULIE BOWEN, IMAN, AND RENE RUSSO AT THE CELINE ABT GALA DINNER AT SOTHEBY'S; SHOW OFF YOUR BEST SIDE (AND DAINTILY HOLD YOUR HANDBAG), JUST LIKE LUCY SYKES DID AT THE CARTIER DELICES LAUNCH AT THE SOHO CARTIER STORE; MICHAEL MICHELLE'S PERFECT POSE: STRAIGHT ON, WITH THE HIPS FORWARD, ONE LEG IN FRONT OF THE OTHER; LOOK ANGELIC BY GAZING—NOT STARING—AT THE CAMERA, JUST LIKE CHARLIE'S ANGELS, SHOWN HERE PERFECTING THE LOOK AT THEIR PREMIER AT HENRI BENDEL; FLASH A HUGE SMILE AND STAND WITH YOUR LEGS SLIGHTLY APART IN A CASUAL WAY AS ANGIE HARMON DOES AT THE HUDSON HOTEL IN NEW YORK; SOMETIMES A LITTLE SLOUCH GOES A LONG WAY, BUT ONLY FOR TALL PEOPLE SUCH AS DONOVAN LEITCH AND MAGGIE RIZER, SHOWN HERE AT THE CELINE ABT GALA DINNER AT SOTHEBY'S. PHOTOS COURTESY OF PATRICK McMULLAN/PMc.

CHAPTER NINE
ANALYZE THIS!
CASE STUDIES TO STUDY

ANALYZE THIS!
CASE STUDIES TO STUDY

People always ask us how to throw a party from beginning to end. So we broke down some of our favorite parties to let you behind the velvet ropes of our thinking, planning, plotting, and producing processes. Each party will cover concept, location, invitations, décor, drinks, food, dessert, music, and cheap tricks. You may want to replicate a party from beginning to end or use it as a template and add your own twist. You can adapt our basic party principles from these case studies, which include a classic Hamptons-style clambake, a Barbie-and-Ken-themed birthday bash, a big-budget roller-skating party, an afternoon tea at a friend's house for the launch of her jewelry line, a manicure-pedicure party, an owner's-box sports party designed for guys to enjoy, an Indian dinner for ten, and a hangover brunch. Just remember: Even though we used the beach as a location for one of our parties doesn't mean you have to. Our concepts will work anywhere—a backyard, a park, a nightclub, a roof deck, a restaurant, wherever you can imagine—and for any number of people. Just because we put together an event for fifty doesn't mean you can't do it for ten—or for a hundred. So feel free to switch locations, take décor ideas from one party and use them for another, tweak the menu, and mix and match to your heart's content. There is only one rule: Your party should represent you and a concept you love. If you're looking for resources that we mention, they will be listed in "Our Yellow Pages." And in the meantime, take what you like from each of these cases, leave what you don't, and party on.

THE GANGS ALL HERE—REAPING ALL THE REWARDS OF SERIOUS PLANNING! JERRY O'CONNELL, ESTELLA WARREN, LARA SHRIFTMAN, AND DAVID SPADE AT THE GQ LOUNGE. PHOTO COURTESY OF JEFF VESPA/WIREIMAGE.COM.

CLAMBAKE
TRADITIONAL HAMPTONS-STYLE

A TRADITIONAL HAMPTONS-STYLE CLAMBAKE
FOR FIFTY AT SUNSET

THE CONCEPT
WE PLANNED A CHIC, SOPHISTICATED ALL-WHITE AFFAIR. WE WANTED TO KEEP EVERYTHING SIMPLE SO THE BEACH WOULD STAND OUT AS THE MAIN ATTRACTION.

THE LOCATION
A PLOT OF SAND ON THE BEACH

THE INVITATION
WE HAND-DELIVERED TO EACH GUEST A LARGE SHELL WITH THE INVITATION WRITTEN ON IT IN BLUE CALLIGRAPHY. EACH SHELL WAS PACKAGED IN A GLOSSY WHITE, SAND-FILLED BOX TIED WITH A BEAUTIFUL BLUE RIBBON.

SOME OTHER IDEAS
- Printing an invitation on velum paper and attaching a small shell with a white ribbon to the top of the page
- Mailing everyone a deflated beach ball, which they have to blow up to read and bring to the party for playtime
- Buying a beach-themed invitation from a stationery store. If you have extra funds, package the invites with a pair of flip-flops, a towel, or suntan lotion.
- A classic white card with ocean-blue script for the party specifics

DÉCOR
THE OUTDOOR LOUNGE
The only downside to a beach is that there's no furniture already in place. So we started from scratch and created a sleek, all-white beach lounge. We used the following:

OUR INSPIRATION BOARD. WE SIFT THROUGH HUNDREDS OF MAGAZINES AND CATALOGS TO COME UP WITH IDEAS FOR OUR PARTIES AND HOW WE VISUALIZE THEM. PHOTO BY PAUL COSTELLO.

- White picnic tables and patio-type furniture, which we rented along with large umbrellas
- White beanbag chairs that we bought at Ikea
- Plush wicker lounge chairs, which we rented
- A bevy of cozy seating areas (consisting of bought, rented, or borrowed futons and mattresses encased in white terry-cloth and denim slip covers)
- Large hammocks (rented or bought)
- White blankets and lots of oversize floor pillows on the sand
- One long rented buffet table under a rented canopy to serve food and one table for the bar

---

FURNITURE FIXES FOR THE STYLISH—BUT BROKE—BEACH HOST
- INNER TUBES, STREWN ABOUT. THEY WON'T POP.
- COVER WOODEN CRATES (ASK THE MANAGER OF A GROCERY STORE IF YOU CAN HAVE THE EMPTY FRUIT CRATES) AND CARDBOARD BOXES WITH TOWELS AND FABRICS AND—PRESTO!—COCKTAIL TABLES.
- GET TREE TRUNKS FROM A LOCAL LUMBERYARD AND USE THEM AS COCKTAIL TABLES AND SMALL STOOLS. SOME LUMBERYARDS HAVE THEM IN STOCK.
- LAY OUT A PATCHWORK DESIGN OF BRIGHTLY COLORED INDIAN-INSPIRED WOVEN BEACH MATS.
- BORROW FOLDABLE CHAIRS FROM YOUR FRIENDS, NEIGHBORS, MAYBE YOUR GRANDMA (YOU KNOW SHE HAS THEM FOR PLAYING BRIDGE).
- BUILD YOUR OWN CANOPY (SEE PAGE 27 FOR INSTRUCTIONS).

TABLETOP

A party, like a Chanel suit, isn't complete without the right accessories. So we dressed up our tables, sticking to our all-white color scheme, with:

- Scattered white starfish.
- Large, clean seashells for salt and pepper.
- Floating gardenias and candles in glass bowls.
- White cloth napkins (hell hath no fury like wind against a paper napkin) and linens.
- Heavy-duty, transparent polycarbonate tumblers and punch bowls. They have the weight of crystal and are good for the beach: more durable than plastic, not as fragile as glass.
- A list of "today's specials" on a blackboard near the buffet table.
- Wet wipes and lemon wedges in fishbowls.
- One large white flower on each person's plate. By the end of the party, all of the girls were wearing the flowers behind their ears.

LIGHT ON!

The moonlight goes only so far, so we added artificial lighting to our décor.

- We lined the path to our party with tiki torches.
- The driveway to the beachfront house was lined with lumis, which are sand-filled, white paper bags—decorated with cut-out shapes of stars and moons—that hold votive candles. (They're easy to make if you want to do it yourself. Just cut up white paper bags, fill them with sand, dirt, or rocks so they won't tip over, and place candles inside.)
- We built a bonfire and wrapped white lights around legs of the buffet table and the poles of the canopy. (The party was close enough to the house to run extension cords.)
- Paper lanterns, hanging from trees, strung between umbrellas, and scattered on tabletops, made the mood resort-like and sexy.

THE SOUND OF MUSIC

For the first part of the party, we hired a saucy samba band. And after dinner, a deejay played everything from reggae to eighties pop classics. If you are using high-tech sound equipment, rent a generator so you can plug in outside.

DRINK UP!

On the beach, the less fuss the drinks are, the better. We served:

- Red and white wine
- Bottles of beer and wine coolers, placed in four galvanized tubs of ice, so guests could help themselves. (This also works with traditional coolers.)
- Bottled water, served out of the bottle, with crazy straws
- Mojitos
- Fruit ceviche (a refreshing snack with a buzz)

FRUIT CEVICHE
RECIPE COURTESY OF ERIKA KOOPMAN
SERVES 12 TO 16

INGREDIENTS
2 BANANAS, PEELED AND SLICED
2 CUPS CUBED AND SEEDED WATERMELON
2 ORANGES, PEELED AND SECTIONED
1 GRAPEFUIT, PEELED AND SECTIONED
4 STRAWBERRIES, HULLED AND THINLY SLICED
1/3 CUP SHREDDED COCONUT
1/3 CUP SLIVERED ALMONDS
2 TABLESPOONS SUGAR
1/4 CUP DARK RUM
1/4 CUP BRANDY

INSTRUCTIONS
- COMBINE THE FRUIT, COCONUT, AND ALMONDS IN A LARGE BOWL.
- IN A SMALL BOWL, MIX THE SUGAR INTO THE RUM AND BRANDY UNTIL IT DISSOLVES.
- POUR THE RUM MIXTURE OVER THE FRUIT MIXTURE. CHILL FOR 2 HOURS, STIRRING OCCASIONALLY.

FOOD, GLORIOUS FOOD!

In the Hamptons, the stylish set swears by The Clam Man, a catering company. Naturally, they catered our party. The menu was:

- Clams and mussels steamed in herbs and white wine, served with toasted French bread
- Seared marinated tuna served with a soy dipping sauce, wasabi, and pickled ginger
- 1¼-pound steamed lobsters with melted butter
- Grilled free-range chicken with a citrus barbecue glaze
- Rosemary herbed red potatoes or fries
- Corn on the cob

 CHIC TIP WE ADDED TO THE MENU BY FIRING UP THE GRILL AND ALSO OFFERING HOT DOGS, BURGERS (HAMBURGERS, TURKEY, AND VEGETABLE), AND GRILLED PORTOBELLO MUSHROOMS.

SWEET TOOTH

We eschewed finicky desserts that required the use of—gasp—silverware. Servers passed plates of mini desserts that guests could eat in just one bite. This is what we offered:

- Cut-up watermelon, with a little cup for seed-spitting.
- Fudge brownies
- Key lime tartlets
- Gooey, warm chocolate chip cookies
- Marshmallows, graham crackers, and chocolate bars so people could make their own s'mores by the bonfire.

CHIC TIP

Have skewers of marshmallows ready for the fire. This is a great addition for any cocktail party where there's a fireplace, as it forces people to interact and get playful.

GOOD SERVICE

- We placed platters of shrimp cocktail and oysters on cocktail tables before the party started.
- We set up mojito bottle service at the tables, while a server passed other drinks.
- Waitresses, dressed in long, white beach coverups, served food at the buffet table.
- Servers passed plates of cookies and the s'more fixins.

CHIC TIP WE PROVIDED RED-AND-WHITE-CHECKED BIBS FOR EATING THE SEAFOOD.

THE LOO

We rented a port-o-potty trailer with four stalls. We enhanced the bathrooms with scented candles galore and hung photos of seashells. We even hired an attendant and provided beauty products for guests to freshen up.

OVER-THE-TOP ADDITIONS

- Remember the "wet banana," the long yellow plastic sheath that, when wet, was the best homemade water slide? Get one!
- People get dirty after a few hours of beach action. Rent or buy a portable outdoor shower.
- Provide individual insect-repelling misting fans for each guest.
- Keep outdoor heaters on hand, as it gets cold by the ocean after dark.
- Build a dance floor.
- At Aerin Lauder's beach party, guests parked their cars at a valet lot and four Suburban trucks chauffeured people to and from the beach. It was an extravagant touch.

BARBIE AND KEN
THEME PARTY

BARBIE AND KEN THEME PARTY
YOU CAN USE THIS TEMPLATE FOR ANY THEME YOU COME UP WITH.

A WILD PARTY FOR LARA AND HER FRIEND TAMARA BECKWITH'S JOINT BIRTHDAYS, WITH A SEATED DINNER FOR SIXTY AND AN AFTER-DINNER PARTY OF DESSERT, DRINKS, AND DANCING FOR THREE HUNDRED MORE FRIENDS.

THE CONCEPT BARBIE AND KEN. USE THIS TEMPLATE FOR ANY PARTY YOU LIKE. JUST APPLY THE BASIC CONCEPTS TO THE THEME

THE LOCATION A HOT NEW RESTAURANT-LOUNGE. BECAUSE THE CLUB WAS NEW, THE HOSTS WERE ABLE TO NEGOTIATE A GOOD DEAL WITH THE OWNERS.

THE INVITATION MAKE SURE THE INVITATION TELLS PEOPLE HOW TO DRESS. AT LARA AND TAMARA'S PARTY, PEOPLE DRESSED AS GLITTER BARBIE, VINTAGE CHANEL BARBIE, TENNIS BARBIE, CONCERT DATE KEN, GI JOE KEN, AND THEN SOME. EVEN THE STAFF WAS RELEGATED TO WEARING BARBIE MALIBU T-SHIRTS—AND WIGS!

OTHER INVITATION OPTIONS
- A store-bought invitation with the right theme.
- Design the card on your computer. Print it from home. And seal the envelope with an appropriate sticker.
- A white card with pink handwriting.
- If you want to be extreme, you could send a Barbie doll.

HOW TO DO IT
- SCAN AN IMAGE INTO YOUR COMPUTER OR SEARCH FOR IMAGES ONLINE. CONVERT IT FROM FOUR-COLOR TO ONE-COLOR. WE CHOSE SHADES OF PINK À LA BARBIE. (FOUR-COLOR IMAGES COST AN ARM AND A LEG TO PRINT.)
- TWEAK THE IMAGE SIZE SO THAT IT WORKS AS A FIVE-BY-SEVEN-INCH HORIZONTAL INSTEAD OF A FOUR-BY-SIX-INCH VERTICAL.
- FIND A BARBIE-ESQUE FONT ON THE COMPUTER ("PARTY LET" ON A MAC).
- TYPE IN THE COPY FOR THE INVITE (FONT SIZE 12) AND CENTER IT. MAKE UP SOMETHING SASSY, LIKE: "COME PLAY IN THE DOLLHOUSE. DRESS AS YOUR FAVORITE BARBIE OR KEN."
- WHEN YOU'RE DOING A DINNER AND AN AFTER-PARTY, MAKE SURE THE CARD SAYS 9 P.M. SHARP FOR DINNER. OTHERWISE, YOU'LL HAVE DINNER GUESTS COMING IN AFTER TEN O'CLOCK AND THERE WON'T BE MUCH TIME FOR THEM TO SIT DOWN AND EAT.
- PRINT THE INVITATIONS AT AN AFFORDABLE COPY SHOP. IT COST ABOUT $150 FOR 300 CARDS ON WHITE GLOSSY STOCK.
- BUY MATCHING PINK ENVELOPES.
- USE LABELS (OURS WERE PRINTED WITH THE SAME BARBIE-STYLE FONT) ON THE BACK FLAP OF THE ENVELOPE FOR RETURN ADDRESSES.
- TYPE EACH GUEST'S ADDRESS ON WHITE OVERSIZE LABELS; WE INCLUDED A SCANNED IMAGE OF BARBIE IN THE CORNER. MAKE THE FONT SIZE OF THE TOP LINE (THE GUEST'S NAME) 14 POINTS AND THE FOLLOWING LINES 12 POINTS IN ALL CAPITAL LETTERS.
- PRINT LABELS FROM THE COMPUTER, USING THE SAME STYLE FONT AS THE INVITE.
- FIND CAMPY "HAPPY BIRTHDAY" STAMPS AT THE POST OFFICE.
- SEAL THE ENVELOPES WITH A STICKER.

BARBIE'S PINK PARADISE. MATTEL WOULD BE PROUD. PINK M&MS, FLASHING BARBIE BRACELETS AS NAPKIN RINGS, PINK MENUS (MADE ON THE COMPUTER), PINK VOTIVE CANDLES, PINK TABLECLOTHS, AND MARILYN BARBIE AS A CAMPY CENTERPIECE ADD TO THE FUN TABLE DÉCOR. © CESARE BONAZZA.

Dress as your favorite Barbie or Ken
for
Lara Shriftman & Tamara Beckwith's
Birthday Bash

Saturday, April 20, 2002
Dinner, Cocktails & Dancing
8 o'clock in the evening

Tangier
2138 Hillhurst Avenue

DJ San Ranson

RSVP Harrison & Shriftman 917-351-8686

Special thanks to Barbie, Krispy Creme, Coffee Bean & Tea Leaf, Perrier, Alpine Creative

DÉCOR

WELCOME TO THE DOLLHOUSE!

The décor for this kind of party can be simple or elaborate, as long as it's "Barbie." Think of it as a bubblegum-pink fantasyland. Get kitschy with retro Barbie dolls, accessories, cars, and toys. And keep everything as girlie as possible.

NAME CARDS

We assigned tables (but not specific seats) to prevent mayhem. And we dolled up the name-card table and made it an integral part of the décor by covering it with a shiny pink cloth and placing it near the entrance. This is how to do it:

- On the tabletop, place three-by-five white envelopes, with guests' names written with a pink calligraphy pen.
- Seal the envelope with Barbie stickers.
- Lara and Tamara named each table after a different doll: Western Barbie, Marilyn Barbie, and so on.
- Inside, on pink paper that matches the envelopes of the invitations, a note, with the same Barbie font used throughout, should read: "You're seated at Diva Barbie," or whatever table the guest is assigned to. Use the specific dolls as the centerpiece of each table so guests can find their seats.

CHIC TIP

To save money, print four cards on each page, then cut them to size after.

TABLETOP

- Pink tablecloths and napkins will keep things flirty.
- Make your life easier and ask the venue's manager to order pink cloths from the distributor, where you're likely to get them at a discount or at no charge.
- Valley of the Dolls! Use Barbies preserved in their boxes to create fabulous centerpieces for tables.
- Sprinkle some joy on the tables with pink rose petals and glittery heart-and-star metallic pink confetti.
- Traditional napkin rings? No thanks. Tie each napkin with a flashing Barbie bracelet or a pink ribbon, to add some flavor to the room.
- Drape pink fabric over the chairs and tie the back with a large pink ribbon.
- Type menus at home on bright pink paper. Use them as table décor, placing one at each setting. In big letters, write: "Barbie and Ken Bash" and the date in the same font used on the invitation. Print four menus on each page and cut them to size (four by six inches).

LEFT: CHINA CHOW AS CHANEL BARBIE. RIGHT: ZOE CASSAVETES AND TRACEY ROSS AS CHANEL BARBIES.
© CESARE BONAZZA.

Princess of the Nile Barbie

Concert Date Ken

Western Ken

Malibu Barbie

BARBIE'S BIG BOUQUET, DESIGNED BY ERIC BUTERBAUGH FLOWER DESIGNS. © CESARE BONAZZA.

FLOWERS

Eric Buterbaugh, L.A.'s florist to stars such as Paul McCartney, Arnold Schwarzenegger, and Will Smith, created a psychedelic floral pastel paradise for Lara and Tamara's party. Barbie and Ken dolls hung off flower pots, vases, and containers, which were embellished with grosgrain ribbon. You can do the same trick at home with ribbon, a glue gun, and one trip to a toy store.

BECOME A FABULOUS FLORIST!

Choose pink roses in different sizes, shapes, colors, and stages of development. Arrange them like a puffy cloud of mismatched sizes, imperfectly perfect. Use floral foam to make some roses extra tall. Wrap pink fabric around a container or vase and use a glue gun to make it stick.

With the glue, attach Barbie dolls and Barbie accessories to the same container. Spray the whole arrangement with Aerosol Diamond Dust to give it that luscious Barbie glow.

THE REST OF THE ROOM

- Eye candy! Fill glass bowls of specially ordered pink M&Ms (see "Our Yellow Pages").
- On tables around the perimeter of the restaurant, place pink cans of Chupa Chup lollipops, our favorite candy (see "Our Yellow Pages").
- Blow up pink helium balloons with curled ribbons, cut at all different lengths, to transform the ceiling into a sky of pink clouds.
- Tack lengths of pink chiffon to the ceiling, draping them to fall in front of all doorways.
- Buy or rent pink shag rugs to give the room a shagadelic retro aura.

THE LOO

- Keep the bathroom as sweet and sassy as the rest of the décor.
- Place a photo of Barbie on the girls' room door and a photo of Ken on the boys' room door.
- Fill cylinders with Barbie pink lipsticks.
- Place bowls of pink sucking candies.
- In the stalls, hang sexy fifties-style bordello images of Barbie, photocopied from art books and vintage posters.
- Use pink toilet paper.

CHIC TIP

- Always use carpet runners when you're putting down rugs. Otherwise, someone is bound to slip and break a leg. And guess who's getting sued.

- Make the space glow by surrounding the area with pink votive candles.

- To give the whole room a rosy hue, provide pink lightbulbs and ask the restaurant manager to use them instead of regular bulbs.

THE SOUND OF MUSIC

Get a deejay to whip up a crazy cocktail of seventies, eighties, hip-hop, and techno-pop music. Or find out what kind of sound system the restaurant has. They're probably equipped with the type of stereo that mixes dozens of CDs. If they're not, bring or rent one. Cue up girl-rockers and fierce soundtracks like:

- the Go-Go's
- the Bangles
- Joan Jett
- Pat Benatar
- ABBA
- Donna Summer
- *Saturday Night Fever*
- *Carlito's Way*
- *Boogie Nights.*

DRINK UP!

We wanted the bar to be fun and mostly self-service in order to cut down on staffing costs. You can do the same by:

- Passing pretty pink Bellinis (made with rosé champagne) before dinner. Fruity, fizzy things get people giggly.
- Serving champagne, white wine, and water at dinner.
- Making Barbie's dream drink: a whimsical yet functional ice sculpture, lit by fluorescent pink lights, through which flowed Ketel One vodka. The sculpture chills alcohol as it flows along an ice path to fill cocktail glasses, rimmed with pink sugar. Check on the Internet to see where you can order ice sculptures.
- Offering Smirnoff Ice, the citrus-flavored malt beverge. It's easy to serve, straight from the bottle. Hire a server to hand them out with pink straws.
- Having mini bottles of flat and sparkling water and champagne.

SARAH WYNTER AS WORKOUT BARBIE AND JENINE LEIGH AS HAWAIIAN BARBIE. © CESARE BONAZZA.

BARBIE'S DREAM DRINK, A KETEL ONE ICE SCULPTURE. © CESARE BONAZZA.

THE BARB-A-LICIOUS COCKTAIL WITH PINK COCKTAIL CANDY. YUM. © CESARE BONAZZA.

FOOD, GLORIOUS FOOD

When you're serving dinner for sixty, it's important to keep the menu basic, so there's something for everyone. This is how we satiated our crowd.

- Fifteen minutes before it was time for guests to be seated, a server placed a mixed green salad at each setting so it was ready the second everyone sat.
- At dinnertime, we ushered guests through the pink chiffon curtains to the dining room by doing the old theater "lights-on-and-off" trick.
- We had platters of hummus and herbed goat cheese with garlic bread and breaded cala- mari with spicy rémoulade sauce on the table for premeal nibbling.
- We preselected three entrées to keep the price down and the chef sane: chicken curry, salmon steak, and New York strip steak. A waiter offered each person the choice of one or a taste of each.
- A selection of side dishes (garlic spinach, fries, haricots vert) was placed family-style on the tables, for everyone to indulge. Sharing forces people—even timid types—to interact.

SWEET TOOTH

We gave everyone a sugar high with the sweetest treats on earth.

- Cake for sixty? Oh, the pressure. Instead, we served pink cupcakes with buttercream frost- ing in a Barbie cupcake wrapper.
- In addition, we placed heart-shaped choco- lates, wrapped in pink foil, and edible silver and pink lip gloss on all of the tables.
- Barbie's a bit too skinny, don't you think? So we ordered a sinful glazed doughnut cake, made of layers of doughnuts arranged on a huge tiered platter. To keep the cake kitschy, we added colorful Barbie accessories to the tiers.
- We also had servers pass individual pink glazed doughnuts.
- Our servers were dolls. Literally. They were dressed as Barbie and they passed pink Jell-O shots, in pink cups, all night long.

BARBIE'S PINK-GLAZED, ACCESSORY-EMBELLISHED KRISPY KREME CAKE—AND TAMARA AND LARA, THE DOLLS OF THE NIGHT. © CESARE BONAZZA.

ROLLER-SKATING
MOROCCAN THEME PARTY

MOROCCAN ROLLER-SKATING PARTY
THIS CASE STUDY ACTUALLY WILL GIVE YOU IDEAS FOR TWO PARTIES: A ROLLER-SKATING BASH AND A PARTY WITH A MIDDLE EASTERN THEME.

THE CONCEPT
A GROOVY ROLLER-SKATING PARTY WITH DANCING ON WHEELS, ALONG WITH SNACKS AND COCKTAILS. FOR A LAVISH PRODUCT LAUNCH, WE CREATED A MOROCCAN LAIR WITH MIDDLE EASTERN FOOD AND DÉCOR. YOU CAN USE THIS TEMPLATE FOR ANY THEME YOU COME UP WITH. JUST APPLY THE BASIC CONCEPTS WE USED AND MAKE SURE THEY CORRESPOND TO YOUR THEME.

THE LOCATION
A ROLLER RINK. CHOOSE A ROLLER RINK THAT IS EQUIPPED WITH SAFETY BARS ALONG THE PERIMETER OF THE RINK AND LOCKER ROOMS FOR THE SHOES. NO RINK NEAR YOU? NO PROBLEM. FIND A NIGHT CLUB OR ANY VENUE THAT HAS A BIG, BARREN, OPEN FLOOR AND SET UP A "SHOE CHECK" RATHER THAN A COAT CHECK.

CHIC TIP
If there's a locker room, get someone to be in charge of a master key.

SAVE THE DATE
- A month before the party, we sent a save-the-date notice on a piping-hot-pink roller-skate wheel.
- We wrote the details of the party's date, time, and place in black lettering on the wheel. We mailed it in a white cardboard box and marked the date on the label that sealed it closed.

THE INVITATION
- The invitation was printed on a scroll of antique-looking paper (knock it off by soaking the paper in tea) and complete with stylized lettering that said, "Boogie down at a Moroccan-style disco." To match the concept, we included two sticks of sweet incense and a disco-ball keychain.

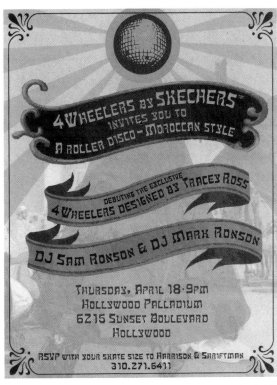

LEFT: THE SAVE-THE-DATE WAS PRINTED ON A WHEEL. YOU CAN DO THAT OR PRINT A LABEL ON THE COMPUTER AND STICK IT ON. THEN PACKAGE IT WELL—WITH A DETAILED LABEL AND YOUR PARTY 411 RUNNING ACROSS THE BOX. STILL LIFE: DEVON JARVIS OPPOSITE: KEEP ON ROCKIN' IN A FREE WORLD, THANKS TO ELIANE HENRI OF HARRISON & SHRIFTMAN, WHO PUT THIS SHINDIG TOGETHER. PHOTO BY DONATO SARDELLA/WIREIMAGE.COM.

DÉCOR
MARRAKECH EXPRESS

We shopped flea markets, fabric stores, and out-of-the-way ethnic boutiques to scrounge up the goods, which included:

- A floor collage of mismatched Moroccan area rugs and oversize pillows
- Seats and sofas covered with exotic fabrics
- Copper flowerpots, ceramic art, mosaic tables, glowing lanterns, and squishy leather ottomans lending a North African look
- Oversize hookah pipes as decorative sculptures
- Woven baskets and bowls scattered throughout
- Rich reddish orange fabric, draped from the ceiling, for a sultry tent effect
- Palm trees and lush plants
- Moroccan silks draped to camouflage a hideous deejay booth
- Black velum around the walls of the room
- Sarongs for the entire staff, even the men
- We transformed the center of the rink into a plush den by hiring a carpenter to build wooden platforms on different levels and throwing futon mattresses, covered with rugs, fabrics, and pillows, on top of them. Knock

this concept off by bringing in cushions, sofas, and mattresses and even getting slabs of wood from a lumberyard to make your own inexpensive platform levels.

LIGHT ON!

- Moroccan-style lanterns radiated serenity.
- We changed the lightbulbs to amber, gold, pink, and yellow to give the space an exotic glow. Warning: Avoid candles! People are clumsy on skates!

DRINK UP!

Skates may put your guests' limbs at risk. To avoid drunk skating accidents, we kept the alcohol quotient low and offered

- A soda bar with a variety of flavors
- Milkshakes and malteds, served with two straws for couples
- Cosmopolitans and vodka cocktails at the bar (we instructed the bartender to serve tipsy skaters Cosmos that were heavy on the cranberry juice).

STEP INTO OUR LAIR. INSTEAD OF SOFAS, WE MADE A HODGE-PODGE PATCHWORK OF EXOTIC RUGS, SCATTERED OTTOMANS, POOFS AND CUSHIONS, AND LOW COCKTAIL TABLES. PHOTO COURTESY OF DONATO SARDELLA/WIREIMAGE.COM.

HIRE WAITRESSES ON WHEELS À LA *HAPPY DAYS*.

FOOD, GLORIOUS FOOD!
It's all about finger food at a party like this, where the energy is high and no one wants to sit down to eat a multicourse meal. So we served
- Pigs-in-a-blanket
- Chicken fingers with an assortment of dips (blue cheese, mustard, ketchup)
- Pita points with hummus and tabbouleh

CHIC TIP
Splurge for a stylist to Moroccanize the buffet area to make it look like something from the grand bazaar. Can't afford this? Get an assistant chef from a local restaurant to do it for you, or ask your artiest friend.

SWEET TOOTH
After working off hundreds of calories around the rink, everyone was starving for dessert, so we went all out with
- Homemade ice-cream sandwiches, which were passed. (A cheaper alternative: supermarket-bought Good Humor sandwiches, cut up and served with toothpicks.)
- A make-your-own-sundae bar. We placed vats of ice cream next to bowls of M&Ms, Reese's Peanut Butter Cups, Kit Kat bars, Captain Crunch, peanut-butter brittle, Oreos, crushed graham crackers, hot fudge, caramel sauce, whipped cream, and fresh fruit . . . just for starters.
- We served warm homemade Toll House cookies and brownies. (No time to bake? Just use the microwave to heat a store-bought variety.)

THE SOUND OF MUSIC
NEW YORK CELEBRITY SIBLING DEEJAYS MARK AND SAMANTHA RONSON AMPED UP THE HOUSE AT OUR PARTY. THIS WAS PART OF THEIR SOULFUL, ECLECTIC PLAYLIST:
STEVIE WONDER: "ALL I DO"
MARVIN GAYE: "GOT TO GIVE IT UP"
MICHAEL JACKSON: "PYT"
NO DOUBT: "HELLA GOOD"
MADONNA: "INTO THE GROOVE"
SOFT CELL: "TAINTED LOVE"
N'SYNC (FEATURING NELLY): "GIRLFRIEND" REMIX
NIKKA COSTA: "EVERYBODY GOT THEIR SOMETHING"

OVER THE TOP "NOT SO CHEAP" TRICKS
Because we had a big budget to play with, we were able to kick things up a notch with extravagant additions. So we
- Gave Skechers Four Wheeler skates to every guest as a gift.
- Supplied colorful socks in case people forgot to bring their own.
- Screened the movie *Xanadu*.
- Hired congo drummers to groove to the music.
- Found a professional troupe of skaters, who showed up wearing leg warmers, head bands, and *Flashdance*-style cut sweatshirts, to get the party rolling.

ANALYZE THIS!

175

CHILLING OUT IN THE MIDDLE OF THE RINK WAS EASY—WITH MATTRESSES, COVERED WITH RUGS AND THROWS, AND GROOVY PALM TREES. A TENTED CEILING AND SULTRY LANTERNS ADDED TO THE SEXY, WARM VIBE. PHOTO COURTESY OF DONATO SARDELLA/WIREIMAGE.COM.

AFTERNOON TEA
AN A-LIST EVENT ON A Z-LIST BUDGET

AN OUTDOOR AFTERNOON TEA

THE TEA WAS PLANNED TO LAUNCH SAMANTHA KLUGE'S JEW-ELRY LINE TO FRIENDS, CELEBRITIES, AND THE PRESS. WORKING WITH HER, WE CAME UP WITH AN A-LIST PARTY ON A Z-LIST BUDGET, WITH A *MOD SQUAD* SEVENTIES FLAIR.

THE LOCATION
SAMANTHA KLUGE'S BACKYARD, POOLSIDE.

THE INVITATION
FORGET FANCY PAPER, EXPENSIVE ENGRAVINGS, AND THE EXPENSE OF GOING POSTAL. WE SENT A FAX SCRAWLED WITH FANCIFUL CALLIGRAPHY. WE PURPOSELY DIDN'T INCLUDE THE ADDRESS ON THE INVITATION, AS IT FORCED PEOPLE TO CALL FOR DIRECTIONS . . . AND RSVP.

Siblings Samantha Kluge
and
John W. Kluge, Jr.
cordially invite you to the unveiling of

213505 love

Family Jewels

One of a kind pieces

Thursday, February 28th, 2002
11:30 AM brunch

RSVP/address/directions:
Harrison & Shriftman
(310) 271-6411

A FAXED INVITATION IS CHEAP BUT CHIC WHEN YOU USE DECO-RATIVE CALLIGRAPHY. THIS WAS DESIGNED BY CALLIGRAPHER STEPHANNIE BARBA, WHO CALLS THE FONT "TONI SWEET AND SASSY." COURTESY OF STEPHANNIE BARBA, WWW.STEPHANNIEBARBA.COM. OPPOSITE: USE INDOOR FURNITURE OUTSIDE TO MAKE THINGS COMFORTABLE AND COZY. RIGHT: LOW, COLORFUL, BUG-REPELLANT CANDLES, LINING THE PERIMETER OF THE POOL, ARE A GROOVY TOUCH. PHOTOS BY JEFF VESPA/WIREIMAGE.COM.

DÉCOR
A GROOVY MODERN LOUNGE
ON THE PATIO

Sam has a groovy backyard filled with lime-green, white, and powder-blue furniture from the seventies. She just enhanced it with a few decorative elements.

- An artful sign-in book Sam decorated herself. This is a good way to make guests feel welcome and to help the host remember the day forever.
- Blue and green citronella candles lined the perimeter of the pool.
- Gardenias floated in water-lily bowls of different sizes.
- Watercolor portraits hung on the walls and leaned against the house in the backyard.
- Why spend a fortune custom-ordering matchbooks? We cut costs by getting Fire Chief matchbooks and decorating them with labels, using the same font that appeared on the invitation.

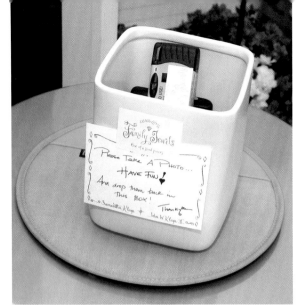

PHOTO BY JEFF VESPA/WIREIMAGE.COM.

SPRUCE UP THAT CERAMIC VASE.

1. PLACE IT ON A PRETTY TRAY.

2. FILL IT WITH DISPOSABLE KODAK CAMERAS.

3. PUT A HANDWRITTEN NOTE ON THE CONTAINER, INSTRUCTING PEOPLE TO CAPTURE THEIR KODAK MOMENTS AND THEN RETURN ALL CAMERAS BACK TO THE VASE.

4. SEND PICTURES TO YOUR FRIENDS WITH A THANK-YOU NOTE AFTER THE PARTY.

HERE'S HOW TO KNOCK OFF THE LOOK.

- RENT A COUPLE OF PIECES OF CHIC MID-CENTURY MODERN FURNITURE FROM A LOCAL FURNITURE DEALER.
- BUY BEANBAG CHAIRS COVERED IN COLORFUL VINYL, OR GO WITH BLOW-UP FURNITURE.
- SCORE VINTAGE COASTERS FROM GARAGE SALES, TAG SALES, AND ANTIQUE STORES.
- GET BRIDGE-STYLE FOLDING TABLES AND CHAIRS, AND USE VINYL TABLECLOTHS.
- INSTEAD OF WATERCOLOR PAINTINGS OF YOUR FRIENDS, COLOR COPY PHOTOGRAPHS, ENLARGE THEM, AND HANG THEM ON WALLS.

DRINK UP!

Who says you need alcohol to have fun? Afternoon teas should be healthy and well-mannered. So we offered

- Coffee Bean & Tea Leaf's Ice Blendeds, which are the drink of choice in L.A. See page 247 for the recipe.

- Every kind of hot tea imaginable: English Breakfast, Earl Grey, Chai, Japanese Cherry, Blood Red Orange, Indian Assam, Tropical Passion, and Moroccan Mint.

- Tea-licious iced teas infused with fresh fruit.

- Refreshing water mixed with cucumber and mint.

A SELF-SERVICE BAR WITH A MULTITUDE OF PITCHERS OF FLAVORED WATER AND ICED TEA. PHOTO BY JEFF VESPA/WIREIMAGE.COM.

GOOD SERVICE

Although a drink buffet isn't typically first on the sophisticate's list, this is how we added chic to it.

- We served iced tea and "agua frescas" (water mixed with cucumber and mint) in three or four clear glass pitchers, placed at the center of two buffet tables.

- We surrounded the pitchers with a hodge-podge of vintage glasses from the fifties.

- We lined up bottles of water, flat and fizzy, in a semicircle.

- Glass cylinders of fresh fruit—green apples, strawberries, lemons, limes—added a shot of decorative color.

FOR TEA AND SYMPATHY, OFFER TEAS WITH MEDICINAL PROPER-TIES, SUCH AS

- CHAMOMILE MADE FROM AN EGYPTIAN HERB. FOR CENTURIES, IT HAS BEEN USED AS A CURE-ALL FOR DIGESTIVE PROBLEMS, FEVERS, FLU SYMPTOMS, AND ANXIETY.
- MOROCCAN MINT, WHICH IS SAID TO STIMULATE THE MIND.
- PEPPERMINT, A COOL FLAVOR THAT ALLEVIATES PMS, HEADACHES, AND DIGESTIVE PROBLEMS.
- LEMON VERBENA, A SOOTHING, CALM-ING, AND MEDITATIVE FLAVOR THAT IS GOOD FOR BATTLING STRESS.
- ROOIBOS OR "RED BUSH," A SOUTH AFRICAN TEA THAT IS RICH IN VITAMIN C. IT HELPS EASE INSOMNIA, HEADACHES, AND MORNING SICKNESS FOR PREGNANT WOMEN.
- GREEN TEA, A FAVORITE IN JAPAN. A DOCTOR WE KNOW SWEARS IT HELPS GET YOUR METABOLISM GOING IN HIGH GEAR. HE SAYS THAT IF YOU REPLACE COFFEE WITH GREEN TEA, YOU'LL LOSE WEIGHT.

TO SET UP A SIGN-IN TABLE, MAKE SURE YOU HAVE PENS AND DECORATE THE TABLE WITH FLOWERS OR WHATEVER WORKS FOR YOUR PARTY. PHOTO BY JEFF VESPA/WIREIMAGE.COM.

TABLE DÉCOR DOESN'T HAVE TO BE POSH. CANDLES, FLOATING GARDENIAS IN SMALL GLASS BOWLS, AND POTTED GRASS HAVE A FRESH, SUMMERY APPEAL. PHOTO BY JEFF VESPA/WIREIMAGE.COM.

FOOD, GLORIOUS FOOD

Tea time means civilized eating. So we kept the menu light by offering

- TEA SANDWICHES: spinach and olive sandwiches as well as smoked chicken sandwiches. We had ours catered, but you can forgo a caterer and make them at home.

- SLICED BRIE and Roma tomatoes on melba-toast rounds.

A TRADITIONAL MENU FOR AN AFTERNOON TEA

FROM CLARIDGE'S LONDON, THE LUXURY BRITISH HOTEL THAT EPITOMIZES GRAND ENGLISH STYLE, THE CLASSICS ARE:
SANDWICHES, SANS CRUST, SLICED IN QUARTERS AND FILLED WITH
EGG SALAD AND WATERCRESS
SWEET CHICKEN SALAD ON
    MARBLE RYE
EUROPEAN CUCUMBER AND
    DILL CREAM
FRESH ASPARAGUS AND BOURSIN
SCOTTISH SMOKED SALMON ON
    PUMPERNICKEL
BLACK CURRANT AND CINNAMON-
    ALMOND SCONES, SERVED WITH
    DEVONSHIRE CREAM AND JAMS
LEMON CAKE
DRIED FRUIT CAKE
PISTACHIO SHORTBREAD COOKIES
COCONUT MACAROONS
FLORENTINE COOKIES
A HUGE SELECTION OF HOT TEAS

- THIS MENU IS SERVED IN COURSES, ALONG WITH INDIVIDUAL STEEPING POTS OF TEA. THE FIRST COURSE IS THE SANDWICHES; THE SECOND COURSE IS THE SCONES AND PASTRIES. THIS KIND OF MENU WORKS FOR LUNCH OR BETWEEN 4:00 AND 6:00 P.M.

LEFT: THE KEY INGREDIENTS OF A GREAT TEA? MIX COFFEE BEAN & TEA LEAF ICE BLENDEDS AND A VERY STELLAR CROWD. HERE, GWYNETH PALTROW & SAM KLUGE AT KLUGE'S AFTERNOON JEWELRY LAUNCH EVENT. RIGHT: ELIZABETH BERKLEY AND REBECCA ROMIJN-STAMOS. PHOTOS BY JEFF VESPA/WIREIMAGE.COM.

MEDITERRANEO ICED TEA

SPICE UP REGULAR ICED TEA BY ADDING THESE INGREDIENTS. IT HAS SUCH A LUXE APPEAL, YOUR GUESTS WILL WONDER HOW YOU DID IT. RECIPE COURTESY OF MEDITERRANEO.

MAKES 1 DRINK

INGREDIENTS
1 REGULAR TEA BAG
1 CURRANT TEA BAG
½ AN ORANGE
2 STRAWBERRIES
1 TEASPOON SUGAR

INSTRUCTIONS
BOIL ALL INGREDIENTS TOGETHER THEN STRAIN, CHILL, AND SERVE.

SWEET TOOTH

We bought mini Bundt cakes from the grocery store, sliced them, and served them on elegant Lucite, silver, and glass trays. Everyone wanted the recipe!

THE SOUND OF MUSIC

This party isn't about the music, it's about the people. So we kept the sounds down-tempo with a jazzy compilation CD from Pottery Barn that was chock-full of classic songs by Ella Fitzgerald, Chet Baker, Nat "King" Cole, Nina Simone, and Peggy Lee.

MUSICIAN **MOBY** AND KELLY TISDALE, HIS PARTNER IN **TEANY**, THEIR SWANKY TEA SALON IN MANHATTAN, GAVE US THIS PLAYLIST FOR A HIPPER TEA PARTY.

THE SIXTHS: "AS YOU TURN TO GO"
BRIAN ENO: "ON SOME FARAWAY BEACH"
SUPER FURRY ANIMALS: "IT'S NOT THE END OF THE WORLD"
ROXY MUSIC: "OH YEAH"
THE WALKMEN: "THEY'RE WINNING"
LADYTRON: "DISCOTRAXX"
THE FLAMING LIPS: "WHAT IS THE LIGHT?"
BLUR: "BLUE JEANS"
MAGNETIC FIELDS: "LONG-FORGOTTEN FAIRYTALE"
TELEPOPMUSIK: "BREATHE"
CLINIC: "THE SECOND LINE"
SIOUXSIE AND THE BANSHEES: "DEAR PRUDENCE"
THE JAM: "THE BITTEREST PILL"
THE SHINS: "NEW SLANG"
BOARDS OF CANADA: "JULIE AND CANDY"

CHIC TIP HIRE A PIANIST AND VIOLINIST TO PERFORM, LIVE.

THE FAMILY JEWELS DISPLAY. PHOTO BY JEFF VESPA/WIREIMAGE.COM.

CHEAP TRICKS

- Turn your guest book into a raffle. We put the names of our seventy-five guests in a jar and picked out a name. The prize at Samantha Kluge's party: a monogrammed jewelry box.

- No Parking Zone. No parking was available at this house, and the road was too long and windy to create a parking zone. So a friend stood at the top of the street and instructed guests to park in a nearby lot. There, rented golf carts shuttled everyone to and from.

OVER-THE-TOP ADDITIONS

Hire a bathroom attendant. When guests emerge from bathroom stalls, the attendant informs them that their sink is ready. This means the sink is three-quarters full of lukewarm water. The attendant should offer to pump liquid soap on the guests' hands and then offer linen napkins.

BEAUTY PARTY
MANI-PEDIS, HAIR, AND MAKEUP

A MANI-PEDI BEAUTY PARTY
FOR TWENTY OF OUR FRIENDS

THE CONCEPT
MANIS AND PEDIS FOR EVERYONE! YOU CAN KNOCK THIS PARTY OFF AT ANY NAIL SALON. OR YOU CAN DO IT AT HOME.

THE LOCATION
BUFFSPA, A POSH, UPSCALE NAIL SPA IN BERDGORF GOODMAN.

THE INVITATION
WE CREATED A CLASSIC, TIFFANY-STYLE GLOSSY WHITE INVITATION PACKAGED WITH A BOTTLE OF NAIL POLISH AND A NAIL FILE.

OTHER INVITATION OPTIONS
- An invitation printed on the back of a nail polish color chart
- Printing the party details on a label, which you stick to an actual bottle of nail polish
- A plain card, with a nail accessory of any sort tucked in the envelope

OPPOSITE: BEAUTY BEGINS AT YOUR FEET! HERE, ANGELA BASSETT GETS A PEDICURE FROM CLIVE (FROM THE BUFFSPA) AT THE JUICY DAY OF INDULGENCE IN LOS ANGELES. PHOTO COURTESY OF LESTER COHEN/WIREIMAGE.COM.

ESTEE LAUDER'S ALL-ACCESS PASS CARD/INVITATION WAS ALL ABOUT THE CUTE COPY, WHICH OUTLINED A SCHEDULE OF EVENTS FOR INVITED REVELERS DURING THE SUNDANCE FILM FESTIVAL: 12:00, MEET WITH YOUR AGENT. 1:00, GET YOUR NAILS DONE AT THE ESTEE LAUDER HOUSE. STILL LIFE: DEVON JARVIS. INVITATION COURTESY OF ESTEE LAUDER.

DÉCOR
A DELUXE ESCAPE
Our favorite nail suite is BuffSpa, an all-white manicure mecca with a private pedicure room. The staff uniform includes Jimmy Choo sandals, which are for sale. You can also get a pedicure with polish that matches the lining of the shoe of your choice. Their foot treatments involve an intense salt scrub exfoliation, a foot mask, and an extended massage. It's bliss. We like to have business meetings and parties at BuffSpa, where we order light bites from Bergdorf's café, sip Champagne, drink iced coffee out of wineglasses, and pamper ourselves— and our friends—to perfection. The only décor element we add is scented votive candles.

DRINK UP!
Our drinks menu was the most ladylike:

- Champagne
- Iced coffee and tea
- Mini bottles of Fiji water

CHIC TIP SERVE GUESTS DRINKS AS THEY ARRIVE AT THE PARTY. USE WINEGLASSES INSTEAD OF TUMBLERS. AND HAVE PITCHERS ON HAND FOR REFILLS.

FOOD, GLORIOUS FOOD!
To go with our beauty theme, the menu was healthy and spa-like.
- Crudités
- Hors d'oeuvre plates with small portions of poached salmon with watercress; cucumber salad; celeryroot rémoulade; cold shrimp with brandy sauce and caramelized pearl onions; asparagus vinaigrette

CHIC TIP

We placed plates on tabletops so people could nibble between appointments or while their feet were soaking. We also hired servers and typed a menu on the back of a nail-polish color chart.

Entrées were served on trays so that we could eat while we had our pedicures.

- Trio of poached salmon with watercress sauce, gravlax served with Scandinavian dill sauce, and salmon tartare and cucumber salad.
- Gotham salad, the Bergdorf Goodman special everyone loves. It is made of diced chicken breast, ham, Gruyère cheese, tomatoes, beets, bacon, hard-boiled egg, and iceberg lettuce tossed with their signature Thousand Island dressing.

OVER-THE-TOP EXTRAS!

- Hire reflexologists or masseurs to pamper guests during and between treatments.
- Offer friends a neck and shoulder massager that fits around the neck. A hand control operates the heat, sound, and vibration functions.
- Because nothing's worse than smudging a perfect pedicure, give your guests flip-flops.
- Put out bowls of Altoids mints and lollipops.
- Give everyone a gift bag of nail supplies.

SWEET TOOTH!

After all of that healthy food, it was time to splurge.

- Vanilla-bean poached pear with almond biscuit and chocolate sauce
- Crème brûlée
- Assorted cookies placed on the table for guests to choose

FEET GOOD ENOUGH TO EAT! COOKIES BY DESIGN MADE US THE BEST COOKIES, SHAPED LIKE HANDS, FEET, AND NAIL POLISH. PHOTO BY PAUL COSTELLO.

 CHIC TIP OFFER ONE LARGE PLATTER FOR ALL TO SHARE OR HAVE A WAITER TAKE INDIVIDUAL ORDERS.

THE SOUND OF MUSIC

We went with the classics that made everyone sing along: Lionel Ritchie's love songs, Madonna from her *Like a Virgin* years, and soundtracks from *Pretty in Pink, Valley Girl,* and *The Breakfast Club.* But you can play anything—classical music, jazz, reggae—that makes you happy.

MIXING MUSIC AND FRIENDS: KIDADA JONES AND NAOMI CAMPBELL PLAY DEEJAYS AT THE GET LUCKY WITH LOLA EVENT AT THE LOLA BOUTIQUE IN LOS ANGELES. COURTESY OF DONATO SARDELLA/WIREIMAGE.COM.

TURN YOUR NEIGHBORHOOD SALON INTO THE BUFF EXPERIENCE!

- HAVE THE PARTY AFTER HOURS AND POST A SIGN ON THE FRONT DOOR THAT SAYS "PRIVATE PARTY."

- CREATE A RECEPTION AREA IN WHICH GUESTS CAN MINGLE AS THEY ARRIVE. REMOVE OLD RATTY MAGAZINES AND REPLACE THEM WITH GLOSSY NEW EDITIONS AND RESTORATIVE BOOKS LIKE THE "IF" BOOK SERIES AND GUIDES TO FENG SHUI AND THE ZEN LIFE.

- BRING CANDLES, FLOOR PILLOWS, EVEN COMFY CHAIRS TO MAKE IT COZY.

- HANG CHIFFON FROM THE CEILING TO CREATE A PRIVATE PEDICURE AREA IN THE BACK OF THE ROOM.

- REARRANGE THE MANICURE STATIONS SO THAT THERE'S ONE LONG TABLE FOR NAILS. THIS IS WHAT BUFFSPA DOES, AND IT'S CONDUCIVE TO CONVERSING.

- TRY TO ARRANGE THE PEDICURE AREA SO THAT CHAIRS FACE ONE ANOTHER.

- SERVE DRINKS AND PASSED HORS D'OEUVRES SIMILAR TO THOSE FOUND AT BERGDORF'S OR CREATE YOUR OWN MENU. ORDER IN CHINESE, SUSHI, EVEN CUT-UP SUBWAY SANDWICHES.

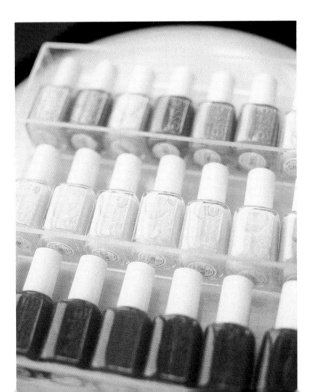

TAKE BUFFSPA TO YOUR HOUSE!

- HIRE TECHNICIANS FROM YOUR FAVORITE NAIL SALON OR LOCAL COSMETOLOGY SCHOOL. ASK THEM TO WEAR MATCHING OUTFITS (BLACK PANTS, WHITE T-SHIRTS) AND BRING THEIR OWN TOOLS.

- ARRANGE NAIL TOOLS IN WHITE PLASTIC BASKETS.

- IF YOUR BUDGET IS LOFTY, RENT A LONG NARROW TABLE AND ERGONOMICALLY CORRECT CHAIRS FOR THE MANICURE STATION. OTHERWISE, MAKE DO WITH YOUR KITCHEN TABLE, DESK, OR WHATEVER YOU HAVE.

- GET CUTICLE WAX, TOP-NOTCH NAIL FILES, VITAMIN E FOR MOISTURIZING THE SKIN, AND NAILTIQUE, THE TOP-SHELF BRAND OF TOP COAT.

- RENT QUICK-DRY NAIL DRIERS, JUST LIKE THE ONES FROM SALONS.

- BUY WHITE BASINS TO USE AS FOOT SOAKS AND FILL THEM WITH ROUND ZEN-INSPIRED ROCKS AND A CUTE SPONGE.

HERE'S HOW TO MAKE BUFFSPA'S SALT SCRUB.

INGREDIENTS
1 CUP KOSHER SALT
1/4 CUP SUGAR
1/4 CUP OLIVE, PEANUT, OR SIMILAR OIL
FRESH HERBS, CHOPPED, OR A FEW DROPS OF YOUR FAVORITE ESSENTIAL OIL

INSTRUCTIONS
MIX TOGETHER. IN A BATH OR SHOWER, APPLY WITH HAND TO FEET, ELBOWS, AND KNEES IN A CIRCULAR MOTION TO SOFTEN AND EXFOLIATE SKIN.

POLISHED! ESSIE'S FANTASTIC COLLECTION OF COLORS.
PHOTO BY PAUL COSTELLO.

SHOPPING AND PAMPERING: EVERY GIRL'S DREAM! JENNIFER LOVE HEWITT, BRITTANY MURPHY, AND MENA SUVARI AT THE JUICY DAY OF INDULGENCE, WHERE GUESTS GOT BUFFED, MANICURED, AND DRESSED IN EVERYTHING JUICY AT THE CHATEAU MARMONT IN LOS ANGELES. PHOTOS BY LESTER COHEN/WIREIMAGE.COM.

MANI-PEDI PARTY TIP

INSTEAD OF DOING THE USUAL FOR A BRIDAL SHOWER OR BACHELORETTE PARTY, PAMPER YOUR GIRLFRIENDS WITH A SPA-INSPIRED PARTY. START WITH A MINI YOGA CLASS OR INDIVIDUAL TEN-MINUTE MASSAGE SESSIONS, THEN GIVE EVERYONE THE OPTION OF GETTING THEIR MAKEUP, NAILS, OR HAIR DONE. AT THE END OF THE DAY, SEND EACH GUEST HOME WITH HER OWN TERRY CLOTH ROBE AND SLIPPERS.

OVER-THE-TOP ADDITIONS

Get lavish by adding extra spa-like treatments to the mix.

- Get paraffin kits, which condition the skin like nothing else, for hands and feet.

- Offer nail art. Don't make a face! Nail art doesn't have to mean mall-chick. Chichi spas like BuffSpa and Rock Spa at the Hard Rock Hotel in Las Vegas offer fashion-forward nail art—say, the signature Burberry check plaid, lace-like overlays, and Swarovski crystals.

- Hire an eyebrow expert to sculpt everyone's eyebrows. Or get a do-it-yourself eyebrow-shaping kit.

- Fill gift bags with nail treats.

- Hire an astologer or a tarot card reader.

ONLY REVLON MAKES IT, BUT YOU MAKE THE PARTY UNFORGETTABLE! HERE, A BASKET OF NAIL MUST-HAVES BY REVLON. PHOTO BY PAUL COSTELLO.

LUCKY MAGAZINE AND LOLA COSMETICS CELEBRATE A DAY OF BEAUTY AND SHOPPING AT THE GET LUCKY WITH LOLA EVENT IN LOS ANGELES. CLOCKWISE FROM UPPER LEFT: HERE, CHRIS MCMILLAN STRAIGHTENS AMY SMART'S TRESSES. MONET MAZUR GETS COIFFED. BIJOU PHILLIPS GETS MADE UP. RACHEL HUNTER PICKS OUT SOME THREADS. PHOTOS BY DONATO SARDELLA/WIREIMAGE.COM.

AN INDIAN FEAST
FOR TEN, FOR UNDER $200

AN INDIAN FEAST
FOR TEN, FOR UNDER $200

THE LOCATION

A FRIEND'S CHIC LOFT APARTMENT. THIS WORKS JUST AS WELL AT AN INDIAN RESTAURANT. SOMETIMES THEY'RE SO OVER-THE-TOP—IN THE BEST POSSIBLE WAY—THAT YOU WON'T NEED TO BRING IN ANY DÉCOR OF YOUR OWN.

THE INVITATION

A CARD WITH GOOD KARMA. HERE'S HOW:

- We found inexpensive cards emblazoned with the image of an Indian god at Godvina's in L.A. (see "Our Yellow Pages"), but you can get them at any Indian store.
- We printed the invitation copy, using a computer, on velum paper, which was about seventy-five cents per page. We used a Mac's "cut-out" font.
- Then we glued old-fashioned photo corners on the inside of each card and inserted the printed velum, cut to size, within.
- We found groovy envelopes at a paperie and hand-wrote the addresses with a shimmery gold paint pen.

LEFT: LARA DRINKS TO THE FÊTE ACCOMPLI. IT LOOKS LAVISH, BUT EVERYTHING WAS BOUGHT ON THE CHEAP. WE BEGGED A FRIEND TO LET US USE HIS APARTMENT FOR THE PARTY, BORROWED SARIS FOR THE DÉCOR, AND TURNED DECORATIVE WRAPPING PAPER INTO PLACE MATS. LOFT COURTESY OF ARI HOROWITZ. PHOTO BY PAUL COSTELLO.

OTHER INVITATION OPTIONS

- PRINT YOUR INVITATION ON EXOTIC, INDIAN-LOOKING FABRIC.
- PRINT THE INVITATION ON VELUM PAPER AND ATTACH IT, BY PUNCHING A HOLE AND USING STRING, TO A TAROT CARD.
- ANY KIND OF INVITATION THAT SAYS "GET SPICY AT AN INDIAN DINNER"—ALONG WITH A SMALL BOTTLE OF CURRY SEASONING. WE FOUND IT AT A SMALL INDIAN SHOP IN L.A., BUT YOU CAN EASILY DOWNLOAD IMAGES OFF THE INTERNET.

DÉCOR
THIS WAY TO BOMBAY

Our loft space ended up resembling a small Indian restaurant in Manhattan's East Village. This is how we did it:

- We cut graphic wrapping paper into large rectangles and used them as place mats.
- We used the Indian-inspired font from the invite and printed name cards and menus on gold paper. We saved trees by printing two to four menus per page and cutting them to size. If you have a color printer, make all the names purple; purple and gold make a fabulous combination.
- We used children's gold bangle bracelets as napkin rings.
- We found goldenrod paper plates and matching goldenrod paper napkins.
- We wrapped forks and knives in the napkins and placed them, upright, in glass vases on the table.
- We used big gold plastic serving trays, found at a cheap décor store in Los Angeles.
- We spread gold doilies and golden confetti on the table for a splashy Bollywood vibe.
- We placed a gold foil–wrapped chocolate rose on each plate.

YOU ARE INVITED TO AN INTIMATE INDIAN FEAST

THURSDAY, JUNE 13TH, 2002 8 O'CLOCK SHARP

FOR GOOD KARMA R.S.V.P. HARRISON & SHRIFTMAN 917-351-8687

ROLLING SILVERWARE IN PAPER NAPKINS AND STUFFING THEM IN A GLASS VASE LOOKS ELEGANT ON THE BUFFET TABLE.

BLACK-AND-GOLD BUD VASES FILLED WITH WHITE ROSES, CUT DOWN, LOOK SOPHISTICATED AND SWANKY. THIS VASE WAS FROM AN INEXPENSIVE INDIAN STORE AND THE FLOWERS WERE $1 EACH.
PHOTOS BY PAUL COSTELLO.

CHIC TIP MIX AND MATCH OLD SERVING TRAYS FROM PAST EVENTS. AN ECLECTIC HODGEPODGE GIVES A SOULFUL APPEARANCE.

TO GIVE THE ROOM AN AUTHENTIC ETHNIC SPIN, WE

- Lit heavenly woodsy scented incense, which we placed in gold incense holders.
- Played with Indian-ish hues: purple, gold, rich reddish brown.
- Borrowed fabrics from our bohemian friends to Indianize the ambiance, including saris, scarves, and sheets. We draped fabric on sofas, tables, and chairs and used scarves to cover glass vases.
- Turned Indian-looking tapestries and bedspreads into wall and table embellishments.
- Leaned pictures of Indian gods against the wall.
- Filled simple vases with single white or pink roses.

FLOWER CHILD

ERIC BUTERBAUGH SHOWED US A WONDERFUL INDIAN FLOWER TRICK. CREATE MOUNDS OF ORANGES, COMPLETE WITH THEIR LEAVES IF POSSIBLE. PLACE STICKS OF INCENSE THROUGHOUT (JUST POKE THEM RIGHT IN THE ORANGES). THEN SPRINKLE A FEW BRIGHT FLOWERS LIKE ANEMONES THROUGHOUT THE ARRANGEMENT. NO NEED FOR WATER; IT'S AN ARRANGEMENT FOR THE NIGHT, FOR LOOKS ONLY! IT MAKES A CHEAP AND CHIC CENTERPIECE.

LIGHT ON!

- We changed the lightbulbs to sixty-watt amber bulbs, which made the ambiance sultry.
- We placed white, red, and orange votive candles on every surface.
- Flower-shaped candles floating in glass bowls added a feminine flair to tabletops.

DRINK UP!

We set up the bar on a table in the center of the room, giving our guests easy access to the drink selection, which included:

- Wa-taj, our own version of Indian agua fresca. It's water mixed with cinnamon and Indian spices such as curry powder.
- Kingfisher beer
- Spicy Indian pineapple punch (see page 193 for the recipe)
- Smirnoff Vanilla Twist vodka, mixed with tonic, ginger ale, or Red Bull. We named the drink "The Indiantini."
- Herbal and Indian Assam teas
- Kombucha cold tea, a digestive Indian beverage

THE MENU WAS PRINTED ON GOLD-LEAF PAPER AND ENHANCED WITH A GOLD-FOIL WRAPPED ROSE. PHOTOS BY PAUL COSTELLO.

FOOD, GLORIOUS FOOD!

We had food delivered from an inexpensive Indian restaurant and served the following to start:

- Sumptuous Indian breads, like naan, cheese puri, and paratha, which we placed on the table before the guests arrived
- Vegetable pakora, also known as vegetable fritters
- Samosas, which are fried dough, stuffed with potatoes, peppers, and other savories
- Onion Bhajia, deep-fried sliced onions

ENTREES INCLUDED

- Chicken Curry
- Beef Curry
- Vegetable Tikka
- White rice with an assortment of Indian dipping sauces. General rule: There should be at least three different colors of sauces to choose from: something refreshing, cool, and green; something hot, spicy, and red; and something brown with vinegar and onions.
- Green salad (for non-Indian-food lovers)

INDIAN FOOD FROM A DIVE IN NEW YORK CITY'S EAST VILLAGE, SERVED ON GREAT SILVER TRAYS.

SERVERS

We paid our interns overtime and asked them to wear saris and serve drinks and food. They passed appetizers on small trays in the beginning and then worked the buffet table serving food to our guests. Before the meal, we educated our servers, so they were able to explain the ingredients and preparation of each dish.

SWEET TOOTH

Our dessert gave our guests a taste of American classics, just to mix things up. We offered

- Carvel Flying Saucers in assorted flavors, passed on fabulous trays

- Gourmet truffles and chocolates in a box topped with an arrangement of roses

- White Rabbit cream candies and ginger candies in little bowls

- Bowls of seedless grapes and grilled pine-apple chunks on skewers

GROOVY ETHNIC BEATS ADDED TO THE SULTRY VIBE.
PHOTO BY PAUL COSTELLO.

THE SOUND OF MUSIC

We kept the music light, airy, and oh-so-Asian with random Indian CDs.

CHIC TIP

You can find Asian-inspired music at a yoga studio or online.

CHEAP TRICKS

- We offered gift bags with jasmine- and amber-scented incense, cinnamon mints, and ginger candies.

OVER-THE-TOP ADDITIONS

We didn't blow our budget, but if you want to go above and beyond yours, here are some things to add to the party.

- Hire someone to offer henna tattoos; they're very Madonna-in-her-spiritual-phase and they're temporary.

- Bring in a psychic with a crystal ball.

- Give each female guest a sarong and have someone on hand to teach people the art of wrapping.

PHOTO BY PAUL COSTELLO.

THE PINEAPPLE DRINK PACKS A BIG PUNCH. ADD A FLOATING GARDENIA TO GIVE IT A BOOST. PHOTO BY PAUL COSTELLO.

LOT 61 SPICY PINEAPPLE PUNCH
RECIPE COURTESY OF LOT 61

SERVES 2

INGREDIENTS
2 CUPS PINEAPPLE JUICE
¼ TEASPOON CINNAMON
6 WHOLE CLOVES
6 CARDAMOM PODS
1½ TEASPOONS CHOPPED FRESH MINT LEAVES
½ CUP BRANDY

INSTRUCTIONS
- PUT 1 CUP OF WATER, 1 CUP OF THE PINEAPPLE JUICE, THE CINNAMON, CLOVES, CARDAMOM PODS, AND MINT INTO A SAUCEPAN. BRING THE MIXTURE TO A BOIL, COVER THE PAN, AND SIMMER GENTLY FOR 20 MINUTES.
- REMOVE FROM THE HEAT AND ALLOW IT TO COOL. KEEP THE PAN COVERED. STRAIN THE DRINK AND ADD THE REMAINING CUP OF PINEAPPLE JUICE AND THE BRANDY. SERVE HOT OR COLD.

THE $200 INDIAN DINNER PARTY FOR 10

BUDGET:

INVITES	$ 11.50
MENUS	$ 6.00
FOOD	$ 70.00
SERVICE	$ 20.00
RED BULL	$ 12.00
PUNCH	$ 14.00
GINGER CANDIES	$ 3.00
NAPKINS, PLATES	$ 5.00
NAPKIN RINGS	$ 7.50
PLACEMATS	$ 5.00
DOILIES	$ 2.00
CENTERPIECE	$ 2.50
POSTERS	$ 15.00
VASE	$ 6.00
INCENSE	$ 3.00
STATUE	$ 2.50
INDIAN CD	$ 14.99

RING IT
LITTLE GIRLS' BRACELETS BECAME NAPKIN RINGS (75 CENTS EACH AT GOVINDA'S).

HANG IT
KITSCHY, CARTOONY POSTERS ($5 TO $10 AT GOVINDA'S) OF INDIAN GODS HELPED MORPH THE LOFT INTO SOMETHING MORE MYSTICAL.

SERVE IT
INDIAN BREADS (LIKE *NAAN*) COCONUT *POORI, SAMOSAS* (FRIED DOUGH STUFFED WITH POTATOES AND PEPPERS), CHICKEN AND BEEF CURRY, VEGETABLE *PAKORA* (INDIAN FRITTERS), AND RICE FOR 10 COST $70 FROM NEW YORK CITY'S ROSE OF BOMBAY.

EAT IT
LARA SPREAD OUT SNACKS LIKE GINGER CANDIES ($3 A BAG AT A LOCAL HEALTH FOOD STORE).

READ IT
LARA TYPED UP A MENU USING A QUIRKY COMPUTER FONT ON GOLD LEAFED PAPER ($6 AT PARTY ON LA CIENAGA). THE FOIL-WRAPPED FLOWERS ADDED ROSE OF INDIA CHARM—AND WERE FREE SINCE THEY WERE A GIFT.

A HANGOVER BRUNCH
AT HOME OR IN A GREAT RESTAURANT

A HANGOVER BRUNCH
KEEP THE PARTY GOING

THE CONCEPT
A HANGOVER BRUNCH FOR FIFTEEN FRIENDS. WE FIRST DID THIS PARTY AT 4 A.M. AT THE MOTOROLA C.A.A. PARTY AT THE SUNDANCE FILM FESTIVAL IN 1999, AND WE REPEATED IT IN 2001 ON A PRIVATE YACHT IN ST. BARTH'S THE MORNING AFTER LARA'S BIRTHDAY.

THE LOCATION
HOME SWEET HOME. YOU CAN DO THIS ANY-WHERE.

THE INVITATION
A MESSAGE IN A BOTTLE. A BEER BOTTLE, THAT IS. BUT WITH A PARTY LIKE THIS, ANYTHING GOES. HERE ARE SOME OTHER OPTIONS.

- A prescription bottle, filled with candy and covered with a label detailing your party's information. Or you can use a candle that looks like a real prescription bottle.
- A packet of Advil enclosed with any type of invitation—boxed, homemade, classic.
- A simple white notecard with a Band-Aid at the top and a note that says something funny, like "We always overdo it on Saturday night. Come nurse your hangover at . . ."

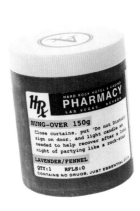

OPPOSITE: THE BEST WAY TO CURE A HANGOVER? A PARTY WITH FIRST-AID KITS AS CENTERPIECES, ASPIRIN FOR ALL, HANGOVER PILLS, AND H2O+ EYE GEL MASKS. PHOTO BY PAUL COSTELLO. LEFT: GET AN AROMATHER-APY CANDLE WITH A RELAX-ING SCENT AND WRAP IT WITH A LABEL, EQUIPPED WITH THE DETAILS OF YOUR PARTY. HARD ROCK HOTEL & CASINO'S HANGOVER CANDLE. STILL LIFE: DEVON JARVIS.

DÉCOR
HOSPITAL CHIC
We got inventive with bandages, gauze, and all sorts of doctor supplies. First-aid kits have never looked so good.

- As a reminder of the night before, we hung a disco ball above the table.

- We used "towers" of stacked Aspirin bottles as centerpieces, along with Glaceau vitamin water, and Ouch bubblegum that comes in a pseudo Band-Aid box, which we found at a drug store.

- We stuck Band-Aids on each drinking glass in the shape of an X.

- We served bagels, breads, and muffins in empty plastic emergency kit cases.

- Wrapping Ace bandages around chair backs and writing menus (with red ink) on gauze enhanced the pharmaceutical effect.

- Empty vodka bottles became water pitchers (this frightened everyone at first).

- Wooden tongue depressors were used instead of butter knives for spreading cream cheese ("Open your mouth and say 'ah'").

- Beer bottles held single sunflowers, which brightened the table.

- Hangover Ender pills were placed on each plate.

- We infused the room with the scent of lavender, which promotes relaxation, something everyone needed that Sunday morning.

BAND-AIDS ON CHAMPAGNE GLASSES, FILLED WITH OJ.
PHOTO BY PAUL COSTELLO.

DRINK UP!

There are two ways to nurse a hangover: Drink more or get healthy. We opted to give our friends a choice from two drink menus.

THE ALCOHOLIC MENU

- Mimosas
- Bloody Marys
- A potent mixture of your own. Call it something humorous, like "Corpse Reviver."

THE NONALCOHOLIC ROAD TO RECOVERY

- Whole, fat-free, soy, and chocolate milk, arranged in clear glass jars and labeled with Band-Aids
- Freshly squeezed orange, grapefruit, watermelon, or carrot juice. (We like to mix OJ and grapefruit juice for a vitamin-packed concoction of our own.)

- Water made with packets of Emergen-C in tropical, strawberry, and orange flavors
- Coffee (decaf, regular, flavored, and iced)
- Coke, Diet Coke, Ginger Ale
- V-8 juice with stalks of celery

OPTIONS FOR THE HEALTH CONSCIOUS

- WHEAT-GRASS SHOTS OR MIXED DRINKS OF WHEAT GRASS AND GINGER OR WHEAT GRASS AND MINT, SERVED IN TEST TUBES
- CARROT, APPLE, AND GINGER JUICE FOR ENERGY
- GINGER TEA, A NATURAL STOMACH SOOTHER
- FRESHLY MADE JUICES MIXED WITH ENERGIZERS, LIKE SPIRULINA, BEE POLLEN, AND PROTEIN POWDER

THE SECRET OF HEALING? H_2O+ EYE GEL MASKS MAKE GREAT PARTING GIFTS. PHOTO BY PAUL COSTELLO.

ABOVE: SUGAR CEREAL, CANDY CIGARETTES, AND BAND-AIDS MAKE FOR A HEALTHY BUFFET. BELOW: H$_2$O+ EYE GEL MASKS WILL RELIEVE YOUR GUESTS AFTER A NIGHT OF PARTYING.

ABOVE: SET THE TABLE WITH HANGOVER HELPER TABLETS AND CLEVER COASTERS. BELOW: ASPIRIN, BEROCCA, HANGOVER HELPER, EMERGEN-C, AND DETOX TEA FROM TRADITIONAL MEDICINALS ARE JUST WHAT THE DOCTOR ORDERED. PHOTOS COURTESY OF PAUL COSTELLO, SHOT AT THE HUDSON HOTEL PENTHOUSE IN NEW YORK CITY.

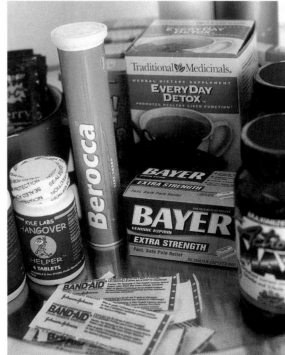

COOKIES BY DESIGN MADE US SPECIAL COOKIES, SHAPED AS ALCOHOL BOTTLES AND OVER-THE-COUNTER DRUGS. PHOTO BY PAUL COSTELLO.

FOOD, GLORIOUS FOOD!

Brunch options are endless. You can set up omelet bars with a huge selection of ingredients, such as cheeses, vegetables, potatoes, shrimp, chicken, sausage, bacon, caviar, smoked salmon, which is what the Four Seasons Hotel brunch is famous for. You can go crazy with every brand of cereal in the supermarket, homemade oatmeal with fresh fruit, and French-toast sandwiches— peanut butter and jelly, goat cheese and apple slivers, cream cheese and jam, barbecued chicken, even macaroni and cheese. For our hangover brunch, we offered two mini menus, one for those who craved carbs and fats and the other for those who were nutritiously correct.

FOR CARB-O-PHILES

- Deluxe bread baskets with cinnamon buns, heated muffins, flavorful croissants, bagels, Hostess apple pies, mini brioche rolls, and Krispy Kreme doughnuts

- A selection of cream cheese flavors, home-made jams, and butter

- Pop Tarts, placed beautifully on a platter

- Baked apples, stuffed with walnuts and dried cranberries

- Cereal, from granola to Trix, placed in glass cylinders, along with milk served in glass carafes

- A pancake bar, at which a server whipped up a fresh batch of hotcakes with a variety of fixins, such as cheese and scrambled eggs; cinnamon and raisins, cream cheese and banana; coconut flakes and vanilla frosting (straight from the can), and Nutella and Rice Krispies.

 CHIC TIP NAME YOUR PANCAKES AFTER FRIENDS OR QUIRKY THINGS, SUCH AS THE SOUTHERN BELLE (FOR ANYTHING WITH CORNMEAL), THE HAWAIIAN PUNCH, AND THE FAT BOY.

FOR A BIT OF PROTEIN, WE ADDED

- Omelets with fillings galore
- Breakfast burritos: scrambled eggs tossed with black beans, guacamole, pistachio nuts, spinach, and goat cheese, all wrapped in a soft tortilla
- Bacon and sausage
- Turkey sausage, chicken sausage, and tofu sausage

FOR OUR HEALTH-MINDED FRIENDS

- Organic eggs
- Light egg steamers and fresh herbs, scrambled without butter or oil and with a choice of steamed broccoli, onions, shiitake mushrooms, tomatoes, or spinach
- Scrambled tofu with salsa, served in whole wheat pita
- Pickled veggies like cucumbers, tomatoes, and peppers
- Seven-grain and spelt bread
- Baked potatoes with fixins like cottage cheese, goat cheese, and grilled eggplant
- Wheat-free and sugar-free pastries
- Frozen grape salad (just freeze seedless white and green grapes and serve them after thawing them out for five minutes)

JEWISH SOUL FOOD

OFFER A TRADITIONAL BRUNCH ANY NICE JEWISH MOTHER WOULD APPROVE OF BY SERVING FRESH BAGELS, SENT TO YOUR HOME FROM NEW YORK'S RENOWNED H&H BAGELS OR ZABAR'S FOOD EMPORIUM; A SPREAD OF LOX, WHITEFISH, SABLE, AND HERRING; POTATO KNISHES AND APPLESAUCE; SIX FLAVORS OF CREAM CHEESE (WALNUT RAISIN, CHIVE, NOVA SPREAD, TOFU, AND SO FORTH); SIDE DISHES OF CAPERS AND SLICED TOMATOES AND ONIONS; AND "MOMMER'S FRIED MATZOH," LARA'S GRANDMOTHER'S SECRET.

MOMMER'S FRIED MATZOH

THIS IS LARA'S GRANDMA'S "SECRET" RECIPE AND IT'S GREAT FOR A BREAKFAST OR BRUNCH PARTY. SWEETEN IT UP WITH A SIDE OF APPLESAUCE.

SERVES 2

INGREDIENTS

CANOLA OIL
MATZOH (USE THIN MATZOH; 2 PIECES PER PERSON)
1 EGG FOR EACH PIECE OF MATZOH
KOSHER SALT

INSTRUCTIONS

- BREAK THE MATZOH INTO LARGE PIECES. AND PLACE IN A BOWL. ADD COLD WATER TO COVER AND SOAK FOR 2 TO 3 MINUTES. DRAIN THE WATER COMPLETELY.
- BREAK THE EGGS INTO A SEPARATE BOWL AND MIX WELL. ADD KOSHER SALT TO TASTE.
- ADD THE EGGS TO THE MATZOH PIECES.
- TO A LARGE FRYING PAN OVER MEDIUM HEAT, ADD THE OIL. WHEN THE OIL IS HOT, ADD THE MATZOH MIX. FRY THOROUGHLY ON ONE SIDE. THEN TURN THE MATZOH OVER AND FRY THE OTHER SIDE UNTIL BROWN.

THE SOUND OF MUSIC

Whatever it is, the music at a hangover brunch must be soft and mellow. We went with an eclectic mix of Billie Holiday, Enya, Johnny Cash, and soothing white noise like rain and ocean waves.

CHEAP TRICKS

We made gift bags by using old-fashioned brown paper lunch bags, filled with Emergen-C, mini bottles of vodka and aspirin, and bagels.

 CHIC TIP THIS ENTIRE PARTY WORKS JUST AS WELL LATE AT NIGHT OR AT 4 A.M. AS IT DOES FOR BRUNCH.

A GUYS' NIGHT OUT
CREATE YOUR OWN OWNER'S BOX

A GUYS' NIGHT OUT
GUYS JUST WANT TO HAVE FUN, TOO

THE CONCEPT
CREATE YOUR OWN "OWNER'S BOX" FOR THE SUPER BOWL (OR ANY OTHER SPORTING EVENT).

THE LOCATION
A LIVING ROOM, A SPORTS BAR WITH A KILLER TELEVISION SETUP, OR OUTSIDE BY THE POOL (BRING IN BIG-SCREEN TVS FOR THE NIGHT).

THE INVITATION
SOMETHING HASSLE-FREE, OUT OF THE BOX, THAT BLENDS WITH THE SPORTS THEME

ALSO TRY
- An invitation printed with your team's colors
- An invitation designed to resemble a scoreboard
- The old-fashioned phone line. Call everyone two weeks before so they can save the date. Follow up with reminder calls, first a week before and then the day before the party.
- An e-vite online

DÉCOR
SOMETHING TED TURNER WOULD BE PROUD OF
To keep the party as high-spirited as the teams, you can follow our game plan.

- Use a color scheme that matches your team.

- Get silly with metallic football balloons and latex balloons that say FIRST DOWN! We attached metallic curling ribbon to the balloons and weighted them with barbells. It gave the boys something to grip when someone charged down the whatever yard line. We also scribbled messages—and players' names—on the balloons with markers.

- Go with plastic and paper goods that match the team's colors. Or get kitschy with paper plates adorned with footballs and team-related themes.

- Accessorize the buffet with kitschy toothpicks topped with footballs.

- Hang a FIRST DOWN sign on the bathroom door.

- Buy Silly String in the team's color. Supply one bottle per guest, to use at will.

- Use confetti as part of the décor. Although confetti can be messy, it's also a blast. Spread sparkles in your team's color on a table.

- Top off cakes with football-shaped candles and sparklers.

- Fill glass bowls with whistles (one for everyone) and football bottle openers.

OPPOSITE: POPCORN SHRIMP POPS IN AN OLD-FASHIONED POPCORN BOX, TURNED ON ITS SIDE, OVERFLOWING WITH CRISPY SHRIMP AND MOVIE THEATER POPCORN. PHOTO BY CARY SONGY/BARTON G. THE RESTAURANT.
LEFT: CUTE ROBIN MAGUIRE INVITATIONS WILL HELP YOU GATHER UP THE GUYS. ROBIN MAGUIRE IS A DIVISION OF THE CHATSWORTH COLLECTION.

DRINK UP!

We kept the bar simple with

- Beer, beer, and more beer, please.
- Margaritas. Tint the salt with the team's colors. Green for the Jets, blue for the Cowboys, et cetera.
- A potent Screwdriver, served in giant fishbowls with multiple straws for sharing.
- Snow cones spiked with liquor. We used food coloring to turn the ice into our team's colors.
- Shots, passed when your team scores.
- Soda and water.

FOOD, GLORIOUS FOOD!

There are two types of guys: the ones who crave old-fashioned junk food and the ones who appreciate gourmet goods. We created menus for both. You can mix and match.

GREASY GOOD-TIME FOOD THAT GUYS WANT

- Popcorn, pretzels, and chips for nibbling
- Subway sandwiches, cut to mini hand-held portions
- Buffalo wings or chicken fingers. Kentucky Fried Chicken served on a sophisticated platter, along with dipping bowls of ketchup, mustard, blue cheese, and honey mustard.
- Hot dogs with a spread of toppings: sauerkraut, onions, peppers, grated cheese
- French fries, served in either cone-shaped party hats or newspaper cones

CHIC TIP ALWAYS HAVE A HEALTHY OPTION FOR THE LADIES, IF THEY ARE PRESENT.

TOP: TEA SANDWICHES ARE TEA-LICIOUS. LINE THEM UP ON A TRAY AND SERVE. ABOVE: CUT CELERY ON THE BIAS AND PUT PEANUT BUTTER IN A PASTRY BAG TO SQUEEZE IT ON FANCIFULLY. PHOTOS BY PAUL COSTELLO.

IT'S ALL IN THE CARDS. DEBRA MESSING AND BROOKE SHIELDS GETTING THEIR DIRTY TAROT CARDS READ. PHOTOS COURTESY OF DONATO SARDELLA/WIREIMAGE.COM.

FOR GLAM BOYS WHO LIKE TO GO GOURMET

- A Brie and goat cheese platter with fruit and Carr's crackers
- Cut-up sandwiches filled with smoked chicken and apple bacon, smoked salmon and dill, and seared tuna with miso-ginger dressing, served on hot focaccia
- Chicken, beef, and vegetable satay on skewers
- Homemade waffle fries, served in waffle cones, along with sauces (mayo, French dressing, blue cheese, ketchup, honey mustard) to dip
- Homemade brownie–ice-cream sandwiches, mini crème brûlée, or individual-size cheesecakes
- Mrs. Field's cookies (heated, please)
- Strawberries and crème fraîche served in a martini glass
- Richard chocolates, topped with scanned-in photos of the team players

SWEET TOOTH

Greasy good-time guys get Ben & Jerry's ice-cream bars and a big ice-cream cake, decorated to honor your team. How about a Jets football, a Knicks basketball, a Rangers crest, a picture of the boxer or wrestler of the night. You could serve cupcakes (even if they're from Hostess) decorated with the name of your team. And don't forget bowls and bowls of candy as far as the eye can see (eye candy!).

CHIC TIP OFFER SHARON'S SORBET POPS FOR THE GIRLS.

CHEAP TRICKS

- We provided gift bags chock-full of treats, including a pad to be used for keeping score or for writing down bets (we slipped in a list of each player's stats); a hat; and team memorabilia.

OVER-THE-TOP ADDITIONS

We kicked the party up a notch by
- Bringing in a manicurist to keep the women occupied.
- Hiring a masseuse for half-time R&R.
- Handing out cigars, along with shiny silver Zippo lighters engraved with the date of the bash.
- Buying team jerseys for the women. We supplied scissors, sequins, and laces, so the girls could cut their jersey into sexy halters or muscle tees with lacing up the side.

CHAPTER TEN
EAT, DRINK & BE MERRY
RECIPES GALORE

EAT, DRINK & BE MERRY
RECIPES GALORE

DURING THE COURSE OF OUR PARTY-PLANNING (AND ATTENDING) LIVES, WE HAVE BEEN TO THOUSANDS OF RESTAURANTS, TRIED COUNTLESS DISHES AND DELICACIES, AND GATHERED MORE RECIPES THAN THERE ARE VOLUMES IN YOUR LOCAL LIBRARY. SOME OF THE RECIPES ARE EASY TO FOLLOW, WHILE OTHERS ARE MORE CHALLENGING. MANY WERE GIFTS WE RECEIVED FROM FRIENDS, FAMILY MEMBERS, AND THE COUNTRY'S MOST NOTEWORTHY CULINARY GURUS. THIS CHAPTER INCLUDES RECIPES FOR DRINKS, FOOD, AND DESSERTS THAT YOUR GUESTS WILL DEVOUR. MAKE THEM ALL WITH LOVE. IT'S THE BEST INGREDIENT FOR ANY EVENT.

DRINKS

HARRY'S BAR CIPRIANI'S BELLINI 207
CHATEAU MARMONT KIR ROYALE 207
MYNT MYNTINI 208
NOBU FRENCH MARTINI 208
BOND STREET SAKETINI 209
THOM'S BAR AT 60 THOMPSON THOM MARTINI 209
METRO APPLE MARGARITA 209
ISLE DE FRANCE JERRY'S PLANTER'S PUNCH 210
BEVERLY HILLS SCORPION BOWL 210
ASIA DE CUBA TIKI PUKA PUKA & MAMBO KING 211
BUNGALOW 8 STRAWBERRY MOJITO 212
MATUSALEM ULTIMATE MOJITO 212
SUITE 16 PARTY MONSTER 213
ELIZABETH'S JELL-O SHOTS 213
CAPRI LIMONCELLO 214
VILLA DOLCE CARAMELLA 214
DA SILVANO SGROPPINO 215
TANQUERAY NO. TEN SMOOTHIE 215
STEIN ERIKSEN LODGE KEOKI COFFEE 216
LAS VENTANAS ICED TEA 216

READY (PLAN, SHOP), SET (THE TABLE, THE DÉCOR), COOK (AH, THE RECIPES)! PHOTO COURTESY OF PAUL COSTELLO, SHOT AT THE PENTHOUSE OF THE HUDSON HOTEL IN NEW YORK CITY.

FOOD

ROSA MEXICANO GUACAMOLE 217
CALIFORNIA PIZZA KITCHEN SPINACH ARTICHOKE DIP 218
THAT BAR SAM AND STEVEN'S CEREAL SOUP 219
STEIN ERIKSEN LODGE CHEESE FONDUE 220
THE CLIFF TUNA TARTARE 221
BARTON G. TOMATO SOUP 222
PINK TACO MEXICAN GRILLED-TURKEY CHOPPED SALAD 223
DUNE AT THE OCEAN CLUB WATERMELON–GOAT CHEESE SALAD 224
WHOLE FOODS EGGLESS TOFU SALAD 225
TUSCAN STEAK HOUSE SALAD 226
ASIA DE CUBA CALAMARI SALAD 227
SOUTHAMPTON PRINCESS DINER GREEK SALAD DRESSING 228
BERGDORF GOODMAN THOUSAND ISLAND DRESSING 229
SILVER PALATE COOKBOOK APRICOT AND CURRANT CHICKEN 230
TUSCAN STEAK CHICKEN PICATTA AND ANGEL HAIR PASTA 231
RAOUL'S STEAK AU POIVRE 232
AGO WHITEFISH 232
NOBU BLACK COD WITH MISO 233
THE CLIFF THAI CURRY SHRIMP WITH CORIANDER RICE AND FRIED BASIL 234
DA SILVANO RISOTTO AL CARCIOFI (ARTICHOKE RISOTTO) 235
JOE'S STONE CRAB CREAMED SPINACH 236
THE FORGE HARICOTS VERTS 236
JOE'S STONE CRAB HASH BROWNS 237

DESSERTS

LE CIRQUE 2000 PETIT FOURS 238
MAGNOLIA BAKERY VANILLA CUPCAKES 239
MAGNOLIA BAKERY BUTTERCREAM VANILLA ICING 240
DELANO HOTEL BAKED APPLE 240
SERENDIPITY 3 FROZEN HOT CHOCOLATE 241
MOMMY'S RUGALACH 242
INDOCHINE ROASTED BANANA WITH COCONUT SAUCE 243
BEVERLY HILTON GRIFF'S BAKED ALASKA 244
DELANO HOTEL WHITE CHOCOLATE YOGURT 244
BUBBIE'S ICE CREAM MICROWAVE MOCHI 245
THE IVY STICKY TOFFEE PUDDING 246
KATHLEEN'S BAKESHOP CHOCOLATE CHIP COOKIES 247
THE COFFEE BEAN & TEA LEAF® VANILLA ICE BLENDED® 247

DRINK RECIPES

CHAMPAGNE DRINKS
HARRY'S BAR

CIPRIANI'S BELLINI

CIPRIANI'S IS KNOWN TO ATTRACT THE BIGGEST MOGULS AND PLAYERS IN THE WORLD, FROM DONALD TRUMP TO RONALD PERELMAN AND RALPH LAUREN. IT'S GREAT FOR BRUNCH, TOO. IF YOU CAN'T FIND WHITE PEACH PURÉE, MAKE IT THE OLD-FASHIONED WAY BY PURÉEING PEACHES WITH A FOOD MILL OR A FOOD PROCESSOR. RECIPE COURTESY OF *THE HARRY'S BAR COOKBOOK* BY ARRIGO CIPRIANI.

SERVES 5

INGREDIENTS
⅔ CUP WHITE PEACH PURÉE
1 BOTTLE CHILLED PROSECCO (ITALIAN VERSION OF CHAMPAGNE)

MIXING INSTRUCTIONS
IN THE BOTTOM OF EACH CHAMPAGNE FLUTE, POUR 4 TEASPOONS OF THE PEACH PURÉE. JUST BEFORE SERVING, POUR THE PROSECCO UNTIL THE GLASS IS FULL AND STIR.

CHATEAU MARMONT

KIR ROYALE

YOUR GUESTS WILL FEEL LIKE ROYALTY SIPPING THIS SWEET LIBATION FROM THE CHATEAU MARMONT, AN UBER-HIP CELEBRITY MAGNET BOUTIQUE HOTEL IN LA-LA LAND. RECIPE COURTESY OF CHATAEU MARMONT.

SERVES 1

INGREDIENTS
5 OUNCES PREMIUM CHILLED ROSE CHAMPAGNE
½ OUNCE CASSIS
FRESH LEMON TWIST, FOR GARNISH

MIXING INSTRUCTIONS
FILL FLUTE WITH CHAMPAGNE. ADD CASSIS. GARNISH WITH FRESH LEMON TWIST.

MARTINIS

MYNT
MYNTINI

MYNT IS THE HOTTEST CLUB IN MIAMI, WITH LINES AROUND THE BLOCK TO HEAR LARA'S BROTHER DEEJAY AND CATCH PUFF DADDY ON THE DANCE FLOOR. THE MINT FLAVOR GIVES A ZESTY KICK TO THIS COCKTAIL. WE CALL IT A CLASSIC WITH A TWIST. RECIPE COURTESY OF NICOLA SIERVO OF MYNT MIAMI/MYNT LOUNGE MIAMI.

SERVES 1

INGREDIENTS
2 LIME WEDGES
2 TABLESPOONS SUGAR
6 LEAVES OR 2 SPRIGS OF FRESH MINT, PLUS LEAVES
  FOR GARNISH
4 OUNCES VODKA

MIXING INSTRUCTIONS
MUDDLE THE LIME, SUGAR, AND MINT IN A GLASS. TOP IT OFF WITH ICE AND ADD THE VODKA. SHAKE IT UP AND STRAIN INTO A CHILLED MARTINI GLASS. GARNISH WITH A FEW LEAVES OF MINT.

NOBU
FRENCH MARTINI

MIX UP MARTINIS IN A WHOLE NEW WAY. ADDING AN EXTRA INGREDIENT HERE AND THERE IS A SUREFIRE WAY TO TAKE THE BAR FROM DRAB TO FAB. THIS IS A FAVORITE AMONG THE CELEBRITY-FILLED MALIBU SET WHO SWEAR BY NOBU. PINEAPPLE COCKTAIL CANDY AROUND THE RIM MAKES A SPECTACULAR FINISHING TOUCH. RECIPE COURTESY OF NOBU MALIBU.

SERVES 1

INGREDIENTS
2 OUNCES RAZBERI
2 OUNCES STOLI VODKA
1 OUNCE PINEAPPLE JUICE
1 OUNCE CHAMBORD

MIXING INSTRUCTIONS
SHAKE WELL WITH ICE AND STRAIN INTO A MARTINI GLASS.

SAKETINI

THIS SUPER-SULTRY SUSHI RESTAURANT IN MIAMI AND NEW YORK HAS A CROWD AS BEAUTIFUL AS ITS SUSHI. THE SAKE LIST HERE IS KNOWN AS ONE OF THE BEST, AND THIS DRINK IS THEIR MOST FAMOUS. RECIPE COURTESY OF INDOCHINE.

SERVES 1

INGREDIENTS
1¼ OUNCES VODKA
1¼ OUNCES SAKE

MIXING INSTRUCTIONS
SHAKE WITH ICE, STRAIN, AND SERVE UP IN A CHILLED COCKTAIL GLASS OR ON THE ROCKS.

THOM'S BAR AT 60 THOMPSON

THOM MARTINI

NEW YORKERS FLOCK TO THOM'S BAR AT THE BOUTIQUE, CHIC 60 THOMPSON HOTEL IN GREENWICH VILLAGE FOR ITS PLUSH VIBE, GROOVY ENERGY, AND THE SWEET, CITRUS-INFUSED MARTINIS. SO WHIP THESE UP, CUE UP THE LOUNGE TUNES, AND LINGER INTO THE NIGHT. COURTESY OF JASON POMERANC OF 60 THOMPSON.

SERVES 1

INGREDIENTS
4 OUNCES SKYY CITRUS VODKA
2 OUNCES FRESH LIME JUICE
SPLASH OF SIMPLE SYRUP
FRESH MINT

MIXING INSTRUCTIONS
SHAKE ALL INGREDIENTS IN A SHAKER. POUR INTO A CHILLED MARTINI GLASS AND SERVE.

METRO

APPLE MARGARITA

FOR A SEXY COCKTAIL THAT'S SWEET AND TART AND PERFECTLY TASTY, WE HAVE THREE WORDS: METRO APPLE MARGARITA. IT'S MADE WITH ROSE'S COCKTAIL INFUSIONS SOUR APPLE TO GIVE IT THAT EXTRA ZING. THIS APPLE MARGARITA RECIPE IS FROM METRO RESTAURANT. RECIPE COURTESY OF METRO KITCHEN, ONE OF THE FIRST BOUTIQUE HOTELS IN SOUTH BEACH.

SERVES 1

INGREDIENTS
4 OUNCES MR & MRS T MARGARITA MIX
2 OUNCES TEQUILA
2 OUNCES ROSE'S COCKTAIL INFUSIONS SOUR
    APPLE MIX

MIXING INSTRUCTIONS
IN A BLENDER, COMBINE INGREDIENTS AND BLEND WITH 2 CUPS OF CRUSHED ICE FOR AT LEAST 15 SECONDS UNTIL SLUSHY. POUR INTO SALT-RIMMED MARGARITA GLASS AND GARNISH WITH A LIME SLICE, IF DESIRED.

ISLE DE FRANCE

JERRY'S PLANTER'S PUNCH

THE GRENADINE AND THE MYERS'S RUM GIVE A RAINBOW EFFECT TO THE PLANTER'S PUNCH. JERRY PREPARES HIS PUNCH AHEAD OF TIME TO GIVE THE VANILLA AND CINNAMON TIME TO INFUSE THE DRINK, MINGLING WITH THE FRUIT AND RUM. THIS IS THE MOST REFRESHING SUMMER DRINK FOR BEACH PARTIES. RECIPE COURTESY OF CASE DE L'ISLE RESTAURANT AT THE LUXURY ISLE DE FRANCE HOTEL IN ST. BARTH'S.

SERVES 2

INGREDIENTS
1⅓ OUNCES ORANGE JUICE
1⅓ OUNCES GUAVA JUICE
1⅔ OUNCES PINEAPPLE JUICE
1 VANILLA POD
SPRINKLING OF GROUND CINNAMON
1 OUNCE PAILLE ST. JAMES RUM
1 OUNCE MOUNT GAY RUM

FOR DECORATION
GRENADINE
MYERS'S RUM
¼ PINEAPPLE RING
1 CHERRY

MIXING INSTRUCTIONS
MIX ORANGE, GUAVA, AND PINEAPPLE JUICE IN A GLASS. SPLIT THE VANILLA POD AND SCRAPE THE SEEDS INTO THE JUICES. STIR IN THE CINNAMON, AND ADD THE PAILLE ST. JAMES AND MOUNT GAY RUMS. DIVIDE THE PUNCH BETWEEN TWO GLASSES. TOP WITH A SPASH OF GRENADINE, THEN FLOAT A DROP OF MEYERS'S RUM ON TOP. GARNISH WITH THE PINEAPPLE AND CHERRY.

BEVERLY HILLS

SCORPION BOWL

TRADER VIC'S IS A FESTIVE POLYNESIAN RESTAURANT. IT'S KNOWN FOR ITS DRINKS, WHICH ARE SERVED IN GIANT GLASSES OR HUGE BOWLS, ALONG WITH A FLEET OF STRAWS. THIS IS A FAMILY-STYLE DRINK. MEANING: IT'S MEANT TO BE SHARED. SO SPICE UP ANY DINNER PARTY, EVEN THE MOST CONSERVATIVE KIND, AND GIVE YOUR GUESTS A FUN WAY TO INTERACT. RECIPE COURTESY OF TRADER VIC'S, MERV GRIFFIN'S BEVERLY HILTON HOTEL, BEVERLY HILLS, CALIFORNIA.

SERVES 4

INGREDIENTS
3 OUNCES ALMOND SYRUP
6 OUNCES LEMON JUICE
8 OUNCES ORANGE JUICE
8 OUNCES LIGHT RUM
4 OUNCES BRANDY

MIXING INSTRUCTIONS
POUR ALL OF THE INGREDIENTS INTO A BLENDER WITH ICE AND BLEND UNTIL COMBINED. POUR INTO A LARGE BOWL. PLACE AN EDIBLE FLOWER IN THE MIDDLE FOR DECORATION.

ASIA DE CUBA

ASIA DE CUBA, THE HIGH-ENERGY ASIAN-CUBAN FUSION RESTAURANT IN NEW YORK, LOS ANGELES, AND LONDON, MAKES POTENT COCKTAILS. THESE ARE TWO OF OUR FAVORITES. IF YOU DON'T SERVE THEM FOR THE TASTE (SWEET, ALMOST CANDY-LIKE; THE KIND OF DRINKS THAT ARE SO GOOD, SOME PEOPLE COMPLETELY OVERLOOK THE FACT THAT THEY'RE GETTING DRUNK), SERVE THEM FOR THE AMAZING NAMES. RECIPES COURTESY OF ASIA DE CUBA.

TIKI PUKA PUKA

SERVES 2 OR 3

INGREDIENTS
2 OUNCES BACARDI LIMÓN
2 OUNCES BACARDI LIGHT
2 OUNCES TRIPLE SEC
2 OUNCES GOSLING'S BLACK RUM
2⅓ OUNCES CRANBERRY JUICE
2⅓ OUNCES ORANGE JUICE
2⅓ OUNCES PINEAPPLE JUICE
SPLASH OF LIME JUICE

MIXING INSTRUCTIONS
MIX TOGETHER AND SHAKE, SHAKE, SHAKE!

MAMBO KING

SERVES 1

INGREDIENTS
GRENADINE
SUGAR
1½ OUNCES RASPBERRY VODKA
SPLASH OF CHAMPAGNE

MIXING INSTRUCTIONS
DIP THE RIM OF A CHAMPAGNE FLUTE IN GRENADINE TO MAKE IT MOIST AND THEN PRESS IT INTO SUGAR TO LINE THE GLASS WITH SOMETHING SWEET. POUR THE RASPBERRY VODKA INTO THE GLASS AND THEN ADD THE CHAMPAGNE TO TOP IT OFF.

STRAWBERRY MOJITO

WELCOME TO THE SUPER–HIGH BROW LOUNGE, WHERE THE FILM PREMIERE AFTER-PARTIES LINGER LATE INTO MOST NIGHTS AND THE VELVET ROPE CLIPBOARD GATE-KEEPERS ARE SO STRICT, YOU NEED A KEY CARD (OR GEORGE CLOONEY BY YOUR SIDE) TO GET IN. RECIPE COURTESY OF BUNGALOW 8.

SERVES 1

INGREDIENTS

2 OR 3 FRESH STRAWBERRIES, PLUS 1 FOR GARNISH
3 SPRIGS FRESH MINT
1½ TO 2 TABLESPOONS BROWN SUGAR
3 LIME WEDGES
4 OUNCES CAPTAIN MORGAN'S SPICED RUM

MIXING INSTRUCTIONS

MASH THE STRAWBERRIES, MINT, BROWN SUGAR, AND LIME WEDGES WITH THE RUM. ADD ICE AND SHAKE. STRAIN INTO A COCKTAIL GLASS AND GARNISH WITH A JUICY STRAWBERRY.

ULTIMATE MOJITO

THIS CLASSIC CUBAN COCKTAIL WAS A HIT AT HIGH-PROFILE EVENTS LIKE SUPER SATURDAY IN THE HAMPTONS, THE *GLAMOUR* MAGAZINE EQUALITY NOW BENEFIT, THE *LEGALLY BLONDE 2* PREMIERE AFTER-PARTY IN THE HAMPTONS, AND THE 4TH ANNUAL LOVE HEALS BENEFIT. IT'S A GREAT SIGNATURE DRINK. RECIPE COURTESY OF MATUSALEM RUM.

SERVES 1

INGREDIENTS

4 TABLESPOONS SUGAR
4 FRESH LIMES, JUICED
2 OUNCES MATUSALEM PLATINO RUM
A SPLASH OF SODA WATER
A SPLASH OF MATUSALEM GRAN RESERVA 15 YEAR
2 SPRIGS FRESH MINT

MIXING INSTRUCTIONS

POUR SUGAR, LIME JUICE, AND THE MATUSALEM PLATINO RUM IN A COCKTAIL GLASS. STIR UNTIL THE SUGAR DISSOLVES. FILL THE GLASS WITH ICE AND TOP WITH SODA WATER. STIR AGAIN AND ADD A FLOATER OF MATUSALEM GRAN RESERVA 15 YEAR. GARNISH WITH THE FRESH MINT.

PARTY MONSTER

A FAVORITE OF BRITNEY SPEARS, IT'S THE PERFECT WAY TO WELCOME GUESTS, OR IT CAN BE PASSED AROUND BY A SHOT GIRL. RECIPE COURTESY OF SUITE 16.

SERVES 2

INGREDIENTS
1½ OUNCES PATRON SILVER TEQUILA
SPLASH OF LIME JUICE

MIXING INSTRUCTIONS
MIX INGREDIENTS AND SHAKE.
SERVE VERY COLD.

ELIZABETH'S
JELL-O SHOTS

YOU MAY THINK THAT THIS IS "JUNIOR" OR EVEN TOO FRATERNITY. BUT AT A PERSONAL DINNER ELIZABETH THREW FOR HER CLOSE FRIENDS, WHERE THE MOST ELEGANT OF MEALS WAS SERVED, IT WAS THE JELL-O SHOTS PASSED ON FORMAL SLEEK TRAYS THAT WERE THE TALK OF THE NIGHT—AND FOR WEEKS TO COME. THE PLASTIC SOUFFLÉ CUPS ARE AVAILABLE AT PARTY STORES.

SERVES 16

INGREDIENTS
3 PACKAGES JELL-O WITH SUGAR
3 CUPS BOILING WATER
2 CUPS VODKA OR EVERCLEAR GRAIN ALCOHOL,
    CHILLED IN THE FREEZER SO IT'S NICE AND COLD

MIXING INSTRUCTIONS
POUR THE BOILING WATER OVER THE JELL-O IN A LARGE BOWL AND STIR UNTIL DISSOLVED. ADD THE VODKA AND MIX. POUR INTO SHOT GLASSES OR 2-OUNCE PLASTIC SOUFFLÉ CUPS. PLACE THE GLASSES ON A TRAY OR IN AN EMPTY PIZZA BOX (SO THEY DON'T SPILL) AND CHILL IN THE FREEZER UNTIL FIRM.

CAPRI

LIMONCELLO

ONE TRIP TO THE EXQUISITE ISLE OF CAPRI AND YOU'LL GET HOOKED ON LIMONCELLO, A TRADITIONAL DRINK ON THE ITALIAN RIVIERA. IT IS SOMETHING THE NATIVES INDULGE IN AT PARTIES. AND IT'S SURE TO BRING THAT JET SET EURO-VIBE TO ANY SOIREE.

SERVES 10

INGREDIENTS
8 LEMONS
1 LITER VODKA
1 LITER LUKEWARM WATER
1 KILO SUGAR

MIXING INSTRUCTIONS
ZEST THE LEMONS WITH A FINE ZESTER AND COMBINE THE ZEST AND THE VODKA IN A JAR. WAIT 4 DAYS. PREPARE A SYRUP BY BLENDING THE LUKEWARM WATER AND THE SUGAR. ADD THE VODKA INFUSION AND MIX. WAIT 10 MINUTES. FILTER THE MIXTURE AND SERVE THE LIMONCELLO OVER ICE.

VILLA DOLCE

CARAMELLA

A SINFUL TREAT, MADE WITH THE SAME RICH GELATO THAT CELEBRITY CHEF WOLFGANG PUCK USES AT HIS CLASSIC AND FAMOUS BOÎTE, SPAGO. RECIPE COURTESY OF MONTE MARCACCINNI.

SERVES 1

INGREDIENTS
2 SCOOPS VILLA DOLCE CARAMEL GELATO
2 OUNCES MYERS'S DARK RUM
1 OUNCE KAHLÚA
CRUSHED ICE
CHOCOLATE SYRUP, FOR GARNISH

MIXING INSTRUCTIONS
MIX ALL INGREDIENTS EXCEPT THE CHOCOLATE SYRUP IN A BLENDER. GARNISH A LARGE WINEGLASS BY POURING FOUR STRIPS OF CHOCOLATE SYRUP INSIDE THE GLASS. POUR IN THE DRINK MIXTURE AND SERVE.

SGROPPINO

LEMON SORBET BLENDED WITH PROSECCO IS A TRADITIONAL VENETIAN DRINK. AT DA SILVANO—AN ITALIAN RESTAURANT IN NEW YORK CITY KNOWN AS A MEDIA POWER CENTER, FREQUENTED BY ARTISTS, CELEBRITIES, AND FASHION MOGULS SUCH AS ANNA WINTOUR, CALVIN KLEIN, AND CAROLINA HERRERA—THEY SERVE A VERSION MADE WITH VODKA. IT'S EASY TO MAKE AND SUPER POTENT. RECIPE COURTESY OF *DA SILVANO COOKBOOK: SIMPLE SECRETS FROM NEW YORK'S FAVORITE ITALIAN RESTAURANT* (BLOOMSBURY) BY SILVANO MARCHETTO.

SERVES 4

INGREDIENTS
1⅓ CUPS LEMON SORBET
1 CUP PREMIUM VODKA

MIXING INSTRUCTIONS
PLACE 4 CHAMPAGNE FLUTES IN THE REFRIGERATOR TO CHILL. PUT THE SORBET AND VODKA IN A BLENDER. BLEND ON HIGH SPEED UNTIL SMOOTH. POUR INTO THE CHILLED FLUTES AND SERVE IMMEDIATELY.

NO. TEN SMOOTHIE

A LITTLE TANQUERAY GIVES THE WORD "SMOOTHIE" A WHOLE NEW MEANING. WE SERVED IT AT THE OPENING OF THE SWANKY EQUINOX GYM IN LOS ANGELES. IT'S NOT THE HEALTHIEST OF DRINKS, BUT WE HEARD NO COMPLAINTS! RECIPE COURTESY OF TANQUERAY.

SERVES 4

INGREDIENTS
2 OUNCES TANQUERAY NO. TEN
6 OUNCES PINEAPPLE JUICE
6 OUNCES FRESHLY SQUEEZED ORANGE JUICE
3 OUNCES ORANGE SHERBET
3 OUNCES FROZEN STRAWBERRIES
3 OUNCES FROZEN BANANAS

MIXING INSTRUCTIONS
MIX ALL OF THE INGREDIENTS TOGETHER IN A BLENDER WITH ICE AND BLEND UNTIL SMOOTH.

KEOKI COFFEE

IN UTAH, STEIN ERIKSEN IS CONSIDERED ONE OF THE MOST ELEGANT AND POSH OF ALL SKI RESORTS. POURING ONE OF THEIR FAMOUS AFTER-DINNER DRINKS IS THE BEST WAY TO WARM UP YOUR CROWD FOR AN AFTERNOON SOIREE. HOT TUBS AND SNOW NOT INCLUDED. RECIPE COURTESY OF STEIN ERIKSEN LODGE.

SERVES 2

INGREDIENTS
1 OUNCE BRANDY
¾ OUNCE KAHLÚA
5 OUNCES HOT, FRESH COFFEE
FRESH WHIPPED CREAM

MIXING INSTRUCTIONS
COMBINE THE BRANDY, KAHLÚA, AND COFFEE IN A MUG. TOP WITH WHIPPED CREAM AND SERVE.

LAS VENTANAS

ICED TEA

THIS IS A NON-TRADITIONAL WAY TO OFFER CLASSIC ICED TEA. AT LAS VENTANAS, A LUXURIOUS RESORT IN LOS CABO, MEXICO, IT'S THE MOST REVITALIZING DRINK BECAUSE THE WEATHER IS SO HOT. GIVE YOUR GUESTS A TASTE OF MEXICO—AND BUY ICE CUBE TRAYS FOR THE RINGS. ADD AN EXOTIC TWIST BY BLENDING DIFFERENT FLAVORS OF TEA TO CREATE SOMETHING REFRESHING. AND SERVE IT UP WITH PETIT FOURS. RECIPE COURTESY OF LAS VENTANAS AL PARAISO, LOS CABOS, MEXICO.

SERVES 8

ORANGE ICE CUBES

INGREDIENTS
3 CUPS OF ORANGE JUICE
1 CUP OF WATER
¾ CUP OF SUGAR

INSTRUCTIONS
BOIL THE WATER. ADD SUGAR TO SWEETEN. ADD ORANGE JUICE. STIR UNTIL DISSOLVED. LEAVE IT UNTIL IT BECOMES COLD. PLACE IN AN ICE TRAY TO FREEZE. WHEN THE ICE CUBES HAVE FORMED, SERVE IN GREEN TEA WITH A SAGE BRANCH.

PINEAPPLE ICE CUBES

INGREDIENTS
3 CUPS OF PINEAPPLE JUICE
1 CUP OF WATER
¾ CUP OF SUGAR

INSTRUCTIONS
BOIL THE WATER. ADD SUGAR TO SWEETEN. ADD PINE-APPLE JUICE. STIR UNTIL DISSOLVED. LEAVE IT UNTIL IT BECOMES COLD. PLACE IN AN ICE TRAY TO FREEZE. WHEN THE ICE CUBES HAVE FORMED, SERVE IN GREEN TEA WITH A SAGE BRANCH.

PARTY FOOD

APPETIZERS

ROSA MEXICANO

GUACAMOLE

THIS RENOWNED MANHATTAN RESTAURANT SERVES MARGARITAS THAT ARE AS BEAUTIFUL AS THE PATRONS. THE RESTAURANT IS ALSO KNOWN FOR ITS GUACAMOLE, WHICH IS PREPARED TABLESIDE WITH A *MOLCAJETE Y TEJOLETE* (A MORTAR AND PESTLE MADE OF VOLCANIC ROCK). RECIPE COURTESY OF *ROSA MEXICANO*.

SERVES 2

INGREDIENTS

3 TABLESPOONS CHOPPED WHITE ONION
½ TEASPOON CHOPPED SERRANO CHILES
1½ TEASPOONS FINELY CHOPPED FRESH CILANTRO
½ TEASPOON SALT
1 RIPE HASS AVOCADO
1 SMALL CHOPPED RIPE TOMATO (DISCARD JUICE AND SEEDS)

INSTRUCTIONS

- IN A SMALL BOWL, THOROUGHLY MASH 1 TABLESPOON OF THE CHOPPED ONION, THE SERRANO CHILES, ½ TEASPOON OF THE CILANTRO, AND THE SALT UNTIL IT IS A JUICY PASTE. AND NOTE THAT YOU CAN ADJUST THE AMOUNT OF SERRANO CHILES IN THE RECIPE FOR MILD, MEDIUM, OR HOT GUACAMOLE.

- SPLIT THE AVOCADO IN HALF AND REMOVE THE PIT. SLICE THE AVOCADO LENGTHWISE IN ⅛- TO ¼-INCH STRIPS. THEN CUT IT ACROSS TO FORM CUBES. SCOOP THE AVOCADO OUT OF ITS SKIN WITH A SPOON (DON'T MASH OR SCRAPE IT). ADD THE AVOCADO TO THE PASTE AND FOLD TO COMBINE.

- SLOWLY ADD THE TOMATOES AND THE REMAINING ONION AND CILANTRO, FOLDING GENTLY. BY NOT MASHING, YOU'LL KEEP THE GUACAMOLE NICE AND CHUNKY.

- ADD EXTRA SALT TO TASTE.

SPINACH ARTICHOKE DIP

THIS IS THE BEST DIP EVER—ALL OF YOUR GUESTS WILL GO CRAZY FOR IT. RECIPE FROM *CALIFORNIA PIZZA KITCHEN COOKBOOK,* BY LARRY FLAX AND RICK ROSENFIELD, HUNGRY MINDS INC.

SERVES 8 TO 10

INGREDIENTS

¼ CUP OLIVE OIL

2 TABLESPOONS UNSALTED BUTTER

¾ CUP DICED WHITE OR YELLOW ONION

1½ TABLESPOONS MINCED GARLIC

½ CUP ALL-PURPOSE FLOUR

1½ CUPS CHICKEN STOCK (PREFERABLY HOMEMADE)

1½ CUPS HEAVY CREAM

¾ CUP FRESHLY GRATED PARMESAN CHEESE

2 TABLESPOONS DEHYDRATED CHICKEN STOCK BASE
   OR CRUMBLED BOUILLON CUBES

1½ TABLESPOONS FRESHLY SQUEEZED LEMON JUICE

1 TEASPOON SUGAR

¾ CUP SOUR CREAM

12 OUNCES FROZEN SPINACH, DEFROSTED, DRAINED,
   WRUNG OUT BY HAND, AND COARSELY CHOPPED

6 OUNCES CANNED ARTICHOKE BOTTOMS, DRAINED
   AND CUT INTO ⅛-INCH SLICES

1 CUP FINELY SHREDDED MONTEREY JACK CHEESE

¾ TEASPOON TABASCO SAUCE

BLUE AND WHITE CORN TORTILLA CHIPS

INSTRUCTIONS

■ IN A LARGE SAUCEPAN, WARM OLIVE OIL AND BUTTER TOGETHER OVER MEDIUM HEAT. WHEN THE BUTTER HAS MELTED, ADD THE ONION AND COOK, STIRRING OCCASIONALLY, UNTIL SOFT, 3 TO 4 MINUTES. STIR IN THE GARLIC AND COOK 2 TO 3 MINUTES LONGER, STIRRING FREQUENTLY AND STOPPING BEFORE THE ONION AND GARLIC BROWN.

■ SPRINKLE IN THE FLOUR AND CONTINUE COOKING, STIRRING CONTINUOUSLY, UNTIL THE MIXTURE TURNS A GOLDEN BLOND COLOR, 10 TO 15 MINUTES. THEN, WHISKING CONTINUOUSLY, SLOWLY POUR IN THE STOCK UNTIL IT IS SMOOTHLY INCORPORATED. WHEN THE MIXTURE BEGINS TO SIMMER, STIR IN THE CREAM. LET IT RETURN TO A SIMMER.

■ REMOVE FROM THE HEAT, ADD THE PARMESAN, CHICKEN BASE OR BOUILLON CUBES, LEMON JUICE, AND SUGAR, AND STIR UNTIL THOROUGHLY BLENDED.

■ ADD THE SOUR CREAM, SPINACH, ARTICHOKE BOTTOMS, CHEESE, AND TABASCO SAUCE, AND STIR UNTIL THE INGREDIENTS ARE THOROUGHLY COMBINED AND THE CHEESE HAS MELTED.

■ TRANSFER TO A WARMED SERVING BOWL AND SERVE IMMEDIATELY, ACCOMPANIED BY BLUE AND WHITE CORN TORTILLA CHIPS.

SAM AND STEVEN'S CEREAL SOUP

THIS RECIPE WORKS AT ANY PARTY—AS AN APPETIZER OR SOMETHING FOR YOUR GUESTS TO NIBBLE THROUGHOUT. NOT ONLY IS IT SO QUIRKY THAT IT'S A GREAT CONVERSATION PIECE, BUT YOU CAN WHIP IT UP IN A JIFFY WITHOUT SPENDING A LOT OF MONEY. WARNING: HIGHLY ADDICTIVE. RECIPE COURTESY OF SAM FIRER AND STEVEN HALL OF THAT BAR.

SERVES 6 TO 8 PEOPLE

INGREDIENTS

2 18-OUNCE BOXES OF YOUR FAVORITE CEREAL (CHEX, FROOT LOOPS, CORN FLAKES, SPECIAL K, ETC.)
3 CUPS DRIED CRANBERRIES
½ POUND (2 STICKS) BUTTER
¼ CUP GARLIC POWDER
1 TABLESPOON CAYENNE PEPPER
3 TABLESPOONS DARK CHILI POWDER
SALT AND PEPPER TO TASTE

INSTRUCTIONS

■ MIX THE CEREAL WITH THE DRIED CRANBERRIES.

■ IN A SKILLET, MELT THE BUTTER. ADD THE GARLIC POWDER, CAYENNE PEPPER, CHILI POWDER, AND SALT AND PEPPER TO TASTE.

■ POUR THE SPICED BUTTER OVER THE CEREAL AND TOSS WELL. EAT UP!

CHEESE FONDUE

MID-WINTER, FONDUE IS THE ULTIMATE INDULGENCE. WARM, HEARTY, SATISFYING, IT'S NO WONDER IT'S THE RITZY STEIN ERIKSEN LODGE'S APRÈS-SKI SPECIALTY. BRINGING THIS TO THE TABLE AT ONE OF YOUR PARTIES IS A GREAT WAY TO GET YOUR GUESTS TO MINGLE—AND FEEL A BIT DECADENT AS THEY DIP FRUIT AND BREAD INTO THE CROCK OF MELTED CHEESE. GET A SECOND POT—AND GO FOR CHOCOLATE FONDUE AFTER DINNER. RECIPE COURTESY OF EXECUTIVE CHEF ZANE HOLMQUIST, STEIN ERIKSEN LODGE.

SERVES 6 TO 8

INGREDIENTS

1 GARLIC CLOVE, CHOPPED IN HALF
1 CUP CREAM
1½ CUPS DRY WHITE WINE
1 TO 1½ TABLESPOONS CORNSTARCH MIXED WITH
    1 TO 1½ TABLESPOONS COLD WATER TO MAKE A
    SLURRY
5 OUNCES EMMENTALER CHEESE, GRATED
4 OUNCES GRUYÈRE CHEESE, GRATED
½ TEASPOON NUTMEG
SALT TO TASTE
FRESHLY GROUND WHITE PEPPER TO TASTE
2 OUNCES KIRSCHWASSER
CUBED COUNTRY BREAD, FOR SERVING
DICED APPLES, FOR SERVING
DICED PEARS, FOR SERVING

INSTRUCTIONS

- RUB A HEAVY-BOTTOMED PAN WITH THE GARLIC HALVES. ADD THE CREAM AND WHITE WINE AND BRING TO A BOIL.

- THICKEN THE MIXTURE WITH 1½ TABLESPOONS OF THE CORNSTACH SLURRY AND THEN SLOWLY ADD THE CHEESES; KEEP STIRRING UNTIL ALL THE CHEESE IS MELTED. ADJUST THE CONSISTENCY WITH MORE OF THE SLURRY OR MORE WINE.

- ADD THE NUTMEG, SALT, AND PEPPER. FINISH WITH THE KIRSCHWASSER.

- DIP THE BREAD AND FRUIT INTO THE FONDUE AND SERVE.

TUNA TARTARE

THE CLIFF IS CONSIDERED THE PREEMINENT RESTAURANT IN BARBADOS. THIS ELEGANT DISH IS SURPRISINGLY SIMPLE TO MAKE AT HOME—AND A GREAT THING TO SERVE DURING THE SUMMER, WHILE PICNICKING IN THE PARK OR EATING POOLSIDE AT SUNSET. SERVE IT AS A PASSED APPETIZER OR PLATED FOR SEATED DINNERS. FOR ADDITIONAL DECORATION, ADD FRIED WONTON SKINS AND FRIED NORI SEAWEED. RECIPE COURTESY OF *THE CLIFF RECIPES* (MILLER) BY PAUL OWENS, THE CLIFF, BARBADOS.

SERVES 1

INGREDIENTS

12 OUNCES FINELY DICED SUSHI-GRADE TUNA

2 TABLESPOONS LEMON JUICE

PINCH OF CHILI POWDER

SALT AND FRESHLY GROUND BLACK PEPPER TO TASTE

1 TEASPOON TOASTED BLACK SESAME SEEDS

1 TEASPOON CHOPPED FRESH CILANTRO, PLUS A FEW LEAVES FOR GARNISH

OLIVE OIL TO TASTE

ASIAN VINAIGRETTE, FOR DRIZZLING

CHILI OIL, FOR DRIZZLING

SESAME–SOY EMULSION, FOR DRIZZLING

FRESH CHIVES, CHOPPED

TOMATO, SEEDS REMOVED, DICED

INSTRUCTIONS

■ GENTLY TOSS THE TUNA WITH THE LEMON JUICE, CHILI POWDER, SALT AND PEPPER, SESAME SEEDS, CHOPPED CILANTRO, AND OLIVE OIL. TASTE FOR SEASONING AND SPICINESS AND REFRIGERATE.

■ TO ASSEMBLE THE DISH, PLACE A 2- X 1-INCH PASTRY CUTTER IN THE CENTER OF THE PLATE AND FILL WITH THE TUNA TARTARE MIXTURE. REMOVE THE PASTRY CUTTER AND DRIZZLE THE TUNA AROUND THE ASIAN VINAIGRETTE, A LITTLE CHILI OIL, AND THE SESAME-SOY EMULSION.

■ SPRINKLE CHOPPED CHIVES, TOMATO, AND CILANTRO LEAVES AROUND THE PLATE AND SERVE.

ASIAN VINAIGRETTE

INGREDIENTS

1 CUP LIME JUICE

1 CUP CHOPPED SHALLOTS

¼ CUP SOY SAUCE

3 TABLESPOONS GRATED GINGER

¼ CUP CHOPPED FRESH JALAPEÑO

1 TABLESPOON CHOPPED GARLIC

¼ CUP HONEY

3 TABLESPOONS RED CURRY PASTE

2½ CUPS SESAME OIL

2½ CUPS OLIVE OIL

INSTRUCTIONS

THREE DAYS IN ADVANCE OF WHEN THE VINAIGRETTE IS NEEDED, COMBINE ALL INGREDIENTS. STORE IN THE REFRIGERATOR UNTIL NEEDED.

SESAME-SOY EMULSION

INGREDIENTS

¾ CUP SOY SAUCE

¼ CUP HONEY

¼ CUP SESAME OIL

½ RED ONION, DICED

1 TABLESPOON MINCED GARLIC

1 CUP OLIVE OIL

SALT AND PEPPER TO TASTE

INSTRUCTIONS

COMBINE ALL INGREDIENTS, EXCEPT THE OLIVE OIL, SALT, AND PEPPER, IN A BLENDER. BLEND FOR 1 MINUTE. DRIZZLE IN THE OLIVE OIL, CONTINUING TO BLEND UNTIL EMULSIFIED. ADD SALT AND PEPPER TO TASTE. STORE IN A SQUEEZE BOTTLE AND KEEP REFRIGERATED.

TOMATO SOUP

IN MIAMI, RESTAURANT OWNER BARTON G. IS THE MOST WELL-KNOWN, SOUGHT-AFTER (AND EXPENSIVE!) CATERER. HE'S BEEN KNOWN TO GO SO FAR AS TO BRING IN GIRAFFES FOR AN EVENT! THE BEST WAY TO SERVE THIS SOUP—THE BEST TOMATO SOUP ON EARTH—IS IN MINI CUPS AS AN APPETIZER OR FROM A HUGE POT ON A BUFFET TABLE. RECIPE COURTESY OF BARTON G., THE RESTAURANT

SERVES 15

SEASONING MIX
2 TABLESPOONS CHOPPED FRESH ROSEMARY
½ TEASPOON GROUND NUTMEG
1 TABLESPOON SUGAR
2 CUPS ROASTED AND CHOPPED GARLIC

FOR THE SOUP
1 CUP HEAVY CREAM
2½ TABLESPOONS UNSALTED BUTTER
1½ CUPS CHOPPED ONIONS
½ CUP CHOPPED CELERY
11 CUPS PEELED AND CHOPPED VERY RIPE TOMATOES
   (ABOUT 16)
1½ CUPS CHICKEN STOCK
½ CUP CHOPPED FRESH BASIL

INSTRUCTIONS

- COMBINE THE INGREDIENTS FOR THE SEASONING MIX IN A SMALL BOWL AND SET ASIDE.

- BRING THE CREAM JUST TO THE BOILING POINT IN A SMALL SAUCEPAN. REMOVE FROM THE HEAT AND SET ASIDE.

- MELT THE BUTTER IN A HEAVY THREE-QUART NON-REACTIVE POT (DON'T USE CAST IRON) OVER HIGH HEAT AND ADD THE ONIONS AND CELERY. COOK, STIRRING OCCASIONALLY, FOR 12 MINUTES OR UNTIL SOFT. STIR IN THE TOMATOES AND SEASONING MIX, COVER, AND BRING TO A ROLLING BOIL. WHEN THE MIXTURE BOILS, UNCOVER THE POT, STIR WELL, AND COOK FOR APPROXIMATELY 3 MORE MINUTES. STIR IN THE CHICKEN STOCK, COVER, REDUCE THE HEAT TO LOW, AND SIMMER FOR 10 MINUTES.

- RAISE THE HEAT TO HIGH AND COOK, UNCOVERED, FOR 10 MORE MINUTES. STIR IN THE BASIL, THEN REMOVE FROM THE HEAT.

- PUT THE SOUP INTO A FOOD PROCESSOR (IN TWO BATCHES) AND PROCESS UNTIL COARSELY PURÉED, BUT NOT QUITE SMOOTH.

- POUR THE SOUP INTO A LARGE BOWL AND STIR IN THE CREAM. SERVE WARM.

PINK TACO

MEXICAN GRILLED-TURKEY CHOPPED SALAD

THIS IS OUR FAVORITE THING TO EAT WHILE LOUNGING AT THE ELABORATE POOL OF THE HARD ROCK HOTEL & CASINO IN LAS VEGAS. IT'S THE PERFECT LUNCH AND A BUFFET MUST-HAVE, ESPECIALLY FOR MEXICAN-THEMED PARTIES. RECIPE COURTESY OF THE PINK TACO AT THE HARD ROCK HOTEL & CASINO.

SERVES 1

INGREDIENTS

4 OUNCES CHOPPED HEARTS OF ROMAINE LETTUCE
4 OUNCES ACHIOTE-MARINATED GRILLED TURKEY BREAST
2 OUNCES DICED ROMA TOMATO
2 OUNCES DICED RED ONION
2 OUNCES DICED PEELED GRANNY SMITH APPLES
2 OUNCES YELLOW HOMINY
2 OUNCES FRESH POBLANO PEPPER, ROASTED, PEELED, AND CHOPPED
1 OUNCE BROKEN TORTILLA CHIPS
1 OUNCE TOASTED PEPITAS
2 OUNCES CUMIN VINAIGRETTE
SALT AND BLACK PEPPER TO TASTE
SLICED HASS AVOCADO

INSTRUCTIONS

- COMBINE LETTUCE, TURKEY, TOMATO, ONION, APPLES, HOMINY, POBLANO PEPPER, TORTILLA CHIPS, AND PEPITAS IN A LARGE BOWL. MIX WELL.

- ADD VINAIGRETTE AND TOSS AGAIN. SEASON TO TASTE WITH SALT AND PEPPER.

- PLACE SALAD IN A LARGE SERVING BOWL AND GARNISH WITH AVOCADO SLICES.

THE ACHIOTE MARINADE

INGREDIENTS

1 POUND ACHIOTE PASTE
1/2 CUP RED WINE VINEGAR
1/2 CUP GARLIC PURÉE
2 CUPS OLIVE OIL
KOSHER SALT TO TASTE
BLACK PEPPER TO TASTE

INSTRUCTIONS

CRUMBLE THE ACHIOTE PASTE WITH YOUR HANDS UNTIL NO LUMPS REMAIN. WHISK IN VINEGAR AND GARLIC PURÉE AND MIX WELL. WHISK IN THE OLIVE OIL SLOWLY UNTIL ALL IS INCORPORATED. SEASON TO TASTE. MARINATE CHICKEN, TURKEY, BEEF, OR FISH FOR AT LEAST 2 HOURS.

THE CUMIN VINAIGRETTE

INGREDIENTS

1 OUNCE WHITE WINE VINEGAR
3 TABLESPOONS GROUND CUMIN
1 TABLESPOON KOSHER SALT
1/2 TABLESPOON FRESHLY GROUND BLACK PEPPER
3 OUNCES OLIVE OIL

INSTRUCTIONS

IN A LARGE BOWL, MIX THE VINEGAR, CUMIN, SALT, AND PEPPER. SLOWLY WHISK IN THE OLIVE OIL UNTIL THE INGREDIENTS ARE EMULSIFIED.

WATERMELON–GOAT CHEESE SALAD

IT MAY BE A CINCH TO PULL OFF THIS RECIPE, BUT IT IS SUCH A GOURMET COMBINATION OF FLAVOR AND TEXTURE THAT IT'S SURE TO IMPRESS EVERYONE, EVEN YOUR MOST FINICKY FRIENDS. THEY'LL THINK YOU'RE A MAD GENIUS IN THE KITCHEN. RECIPE COURTESY OF JEAN-GEORGES, DUNE.

SERVES 2

INGREDIENTS

1 RED WATERMELON
1 YELLOW WATERMELON
1 LOG OF FRESH COACH FARM GOAT CHEESE
PINCH OF FLEUR DE SEL
CRACKED WHITE PEPPERCORNS TO TASTE
EXTRA-VIRGIN OLIVE OIL TO TASTE

INSTRUCTIONS

- CUT THE WATERMELONS INTO PIECES ½ X ½ X 3½ INCHES. STACK ON A PLATTER.

- CRUMBLE LARGE PIECES OF THE GOAT CHEESE OVER THE WATERMELON.

- SPRINKLE THE WATERMELON AND CHEESE WITH THE FLEUR DE SEL AND CRACKED WHITE PEPPER. DRIZZLE WITH OLIVE OIL AND SERVE.

EGGLESS TOFU SALAD

HERE IS A VEGETARIAN FAVORITE FROM WHOLE FOODS, THE ULTIMATE HEALTH-FOOD EMPORIUM. IT'S FABULOUS FOR THE CARNIVOROUSLY CHALLENGED. RECIPE © WHOLE FOODS MARKET, INC., 2003.

MAKES 1 POUND

INGREDIENTS

TWO BLOCKS OF FIRM TOFU
2 TO 3 TEASPOONS GROUND TURMERIC
VEGETABLE OIL
½ WHITE ONION, MINCED
SALT AND FRESHLY GROUND BLACK PEPPER
¼ BUNCH OF SCALLIONS, SLICED
2 CELERY STALKS, MINCED
¼ BUNCH OF FLAT-LEAF PARSLEY, MINCED
1 TO 2 CUPS MAYONNAISE, TO TASTE

INSTRUCTIONS

- PLACE TOFU IN A COLANDER IN THE SINK, COVER WITH PLASTIC WRAP, AND PLACE A CAN ON TOP. LEAVE FOR ABOUT AN HOUR; THIS WILL HELP DRAIN OUT ANY WATER. THEN CRUMBLE THE TOFU INTO FINE CHUNKS.

- STIR THE TURMERIC IN ¼ CUP WATER TO MAKE A SLURRY.

- PLACE A LITTLE OIL INTO A SAUTÉ PAN OVER A MEDIUM-LOW FLAME. ADD THE ONION ALONG WITH SALT AND PEPPER FOR FLAVOR. SAUTÉ THE ONION UNTIL TRANSLUCENT, 3 TO 4 MINUTES. THEN ADD IN THE TOFU, CONSTANTLY STIRRING TO PREVENT STICKING. ONCE THE TOFU IS NICE AND HOT, POUR THE SLURRY INTO THE PAN.

- STIR FOR 2 TO 3 MINUTES. AT THIS POINT, IT SHOULD RESEMBLE SCRAMBLED EGGS.

- REMOVE THE TOFU MIXTURE FROM THE PAN AND SPREAD IT ON A COOKIE SHEET. REFRIGERATE FOR A FEW HOURS AND THEN STIR IN THE SCALLIONS, CELERY, PARSLEY, AND MAYO. SERVE CHILLED.

TUSCAN STEAK
HOUSE SALAD

SERVE IT FAMILY-STYLE IN A BIG BOWL WITH SALAD TONGS. THE RECIPE FOR THIS MOUTHWATERING ITALIAN FAVORITE IS COURTESY OF TUSCAN RESTAURANT IN MIAMI.

SERVES 3

INGREDIENTS

8 OUNCES MIXED BABY GREENS
4 OUNCES CHOPPED ROMAINE LETTUCE
¼ CUP GREEN BEANS, BLANCHED AND CUT INTO
    1-INCH PIECES
1 OUNCE PEPPERONI, JULIENNED
1 OUNCE SALAMI, JULIENNED
½ CUP MEDIUM-DICE PLUM TOMATO
¼ CUP MEDIUM-DICE CUCUMBER
2 TABLESPOONS BLACK OLIVES, ROUGHLY CHOPPED
2 TABLESPOONS GREEN OLIVES, ROUGHLY CHOPPED
⅓ CUP CHICKPEAS, WASHED AND KEPT WHOLE
2 PEPPERONCINI
⅓ CUP MEDIUM-DICED MOZZARELLA CHEESE
SALT AND FRESHLY GROUND BLACK PEPPER TO TASTE
FLORENTINE VINAIGRETTE

INSTRUCTIONS

TOSS ALL INGREDIENTS IN A LARGE BOWL AND SERVE.

FLORENTINE VINAIGRETTE

INGREDIENTS

2 TABLESPOONS DRIED OREGANO
2 TABLESPOONS CHOPPED GARLIC
1¼ CUPS RED WINE VINEGAR
¼ CUP WATER
¼ POUND PARMIGIANO-REGGIANO, GRATED
SALT AND FRESHLY GROUND BLACK PEPPER TO TASTE
2 CUPS OLIVE OIL

INSTRUCTIONS

IN A LARGE BOWL, COMBINE ALL OF THE INGREDIENTS EXCEPT THE OLIVE OIL. WHEN THE INGREDIENTS ARE WELL INCORPORATED, SLOWLY WHISK IN THE OLIVE OIL. ADJUST THE SEASONING WITH SALT AND PEPPER.

CALAMARI SALAD

THIS IS THE KIND OF THING THAT YOU SHOULD PUT IN A GIANT BOWL WITH A LADLE AND SERVE FAMILY-STYLE. A GREAT STARTER FOR ANY MEAL ANY TIME OF YEAR. RECIPE COURTESY OF ASIA DE CUBA.

SERVES 6 TO 8

INGREDIENTS

18 OUNCES CALAMARI CUT INTO ⅝-INCH RINGS AND TENTACLES, WASHED AND DRAINED WELL

9 TABLESPOONS FLOUR MIX

OIL, FOR DEEP-FRYING

3 HEADS OF CHICORY, CUT INTO 1-INCH PIECES

2 HEADS OF RADICCHIO, CUT INTO A CHIFFONADE

2 BUNCHES OF FRISÉE, CUT INTO 1-INCH PIECES

1½ CUPS HEARTS OF PALM, CUT INTO ½-INCH DICE

1½ CUPS CHAYOTE, CUT INTO ½-INCH DICE, BLANCHED

1¼ CUPS CASHEWS, ROASTED AND CHOPPED

1½ CUPS RIPE BANANAS, CUT INTO ½-INCH DICE

9 OUNCES ORANGE–SESAME DRESSING

INSTRUCTIONS

■ DREDGE THE CALAMARI IN THE FLOUR MIX. SHAKE OFF THE EXCESS FLOUR AND DEEP-FRY THE CALA-MARI AT 350°F.

■ ONCE THE CALAMARI IS GOLDEN BROWN, REMOVE IT FROM THE FRYER AND DRAIN ON PAPER TOWELS. SEASON WITH SALT AND PEPPER. SET ASIDE.

■ IN A LARGE MIXING BOWL, MIX THE CHICORY, RADICCHIO, FRISÉE, HEARTS OF PALM, CHAYOTE, CASHEWS, BANANAS, AND THE DRESSING. ADD THE CALAMARI AND TOSS IT ALL TO MIX IT UP EVENLY. CHECK FOR SEASONING.

FLOUR MIX

THIS COATING IS ALSO DELICIOUS ON CHICKEN OR FISH FILLETS. TOGARASHI, A HOT RED JAPANESE CHILE, IS AVAILABLE AT ASIAN MARKETS

INGREDIENTS

1 CUP ALL-PURPOSE FLOUR

2 OUNCES CORNSTARCH

1 TEASPOON KOSHER SALT

1 TEASPOON TOGARASHI

SALT AND FRESHLY GROUND BLACK PEPPER TO TASTE

INSTRUCTIONS

COMBINE THE INGREDIENTS IN A MEDIUM BOWL AND SET ASIDE.

ORANGE–SESAME DRESSING

INGREDIENTS

1 QUART ORANGE JUICE CONCENTRATE, THAWED

1½ OUNCES YELLOW MISO PASTE

3 OUNCES HONEY

1 TEASPOON GINGER

1 TEASPOON CHOPPED GARLIC

SALT AND FRESHLY GROUND BLACK PEPPER TO TASTE

2 TABLESPOONS SESAME OIL

3 CUPS CANOLA OIL

3 OUNCES CHILE OIL

INSTRUCTIONS

WITH A MIXER, COMBINE THE ORANGE JUICE CONCEN-TRATE, MISO PASTE, HONEY, GINGER, GARLIC, SALT, AND PEPPER. SLOWLY BLEND IN THE OILS TO EMULSIFY.

GREEK SALAD DRESSING

OUR FAVORITE SALAD DRESSING COMES FROM THE SOUTHAMPTON PRINCESS DINER IN SOUTHAMPTON, WHERE THEY MAKE THE BEST GREEK SALAD. SERVE THIS OVER CHOPPED ROMAINE, TOMATO CHUNKS, CUBES OF FETA CHEESE, AND GREEK OLIVES. RECIPE COURTESY OF THE SOUTHAMPTON PRINCESS DINER.

MAKES 3 CUPS

INGREDIENTS

4 CUPS OLIVE OIL

2 CUPS RED WINE VINEGAR

2 GARLIC CLOVES, MINCED

2 TEASPOONS DRIED OREGANO

JUICE OF 1 LEMON

SALT AND FRESHLY GROUND BLACK PEPPER TO TASTE

PINCH OF SUGAR

INSTRUCTIONS

BLEND ALL OF THE INGREDIENTS. ADD A PINCH OF SUGAR, IF NEEDED, AND SEASON WITH SALT AND FRESHLY GROUND PEPPER.

THOUSAND ISLAND DRESSING

BERGDORF GOODMAN'S RUSSIAN DRESSING IS THE TOPPER OF THE FAMOUS GOTHAM SALAD, A CHOPPED SALAD WHICH INCLUDES ICEBERG LETTUCE, HAM, TOMATOES, CHICKEN, GRUYERE CHEESE, AND BEETS. RECIPE COURTESY OF HENRY LAMBERT AND MICHAEL FOX, OPERATORS OF BERGDORF GOODMAN CAFES.

MAKES 1¾ CUPS

INGREDIENTS

1 TABLESPOON FINELY CHOPPED ONION
2 TABLESPOONS SWEET RELISH
½ CUP CHILI SAUCE
1½ TABLESPOONS TARRAGON VINEGAR
¼ TEASPOON CHOPPED FRESH TARRAGON OR
    PARSLEY (OR ⅛ TEASPOON DRIED)
1 CUP MAYONNAISE (RECIPE FOLLOWS)
SALT AND PEPPER TO TASTE

INSTRUCTIONS

COMBINE THE ONION, RELISH, CHILI SAUCE, VINEGAR, TARRAGON (OR PARSLEY), MAYONNAISE, SALT, AND PEPPER IN A BOWL AND MIX WELL.

MAYONNAISE

INGREDIENTS

1 EGG YOLK
2 TEASPOONS TARRAGON VINEGAR
¼ TEASPOON LEMON JUICE
½ TEASPOON DIJON MUSTARD
½ TEASPOON SALT
⅛ TEASPOON WHITE PEPPER TO TASTE
¾ CUP SAFFLOWER OIL
¼ CUP OLIVE OIL
2 TABLESPOONS FINELY CHOPPED ONION (OPTIONAL)

INSTRUCTIONS

IN A LARGE BOWL, WHISK THE EGG YOLK. THEN ADD THE VINEGAR, LEMON JUICE, DIJON MUSTARD, SALT, AND PEPPER. COMBINE THE OILS, THEN WHISK A FEW DROPS OF THEM INTO THE EGG YOLK MIXTURE. BLEND WELL. ADD A FEW MORE DROPS, WHISKING CONTINUOUSLY, UNTIL THE DRESSING BEGINS TO THICKEN. THEN POUR IN THE REMAINING OIL IN A SLOW, STEADY STREAM, WHISKING CONSTANTLY. STIR IN THE ONIONS. (IF THIS BECOMES TOO THICK, ADD A FEW DROPS OF WATER AND WHISK TO THIN IT OUT. IF IT SEPARATES AS YOU ADD OIL, HEAT A TABLESPOON OF WATER TO A BOIL AND PUT IT IN A SEPARATE BOWL. SLOWLY WHISK IN THE SEPARATED MIXTURE, THEN WHISK IN THE REMAINING OIL IN A SLOW, STEADY STREAM.)

SILVER PALATE COOKBOOK

APRICOT AND CURRANT CHICKEN

A REALLY QUICK AND EASY GOURMET DISH. IT'S ALWAYS A HIT AND LOOKS GORGEOUS ON THE PLATE. RECIPE FROM *THE SILVER PALATE COOKBOOK* BY SHEILA LUKINS AND JULIE ROSSO.

SERVES 6 TO 8

INGREDIENTS

2 CHICKENS (2½ TO 3 POUNDS EACH), QUARTERED
SALT AND FRESHLY GROUND BLACK PEPPER TO TASTE
1 TEASPOON GROUND GINGER
1½ CUPS BITTER ORANGE MARMALADE
⅓ CUP APPLE JUICE
⅓ CUP FRESH ORANGE JUICE
8 OUNCES DRIED APRICOTS
8 OUNCES DRIED CURRANTS
¼ CUP BROWN SUGAR

INSTRUCTIONS

- PREHEAT THE OVEN TO 375°F.

- PLACE THE CHICKEN PIECES, SKIN SIDE UP, IN A SHALLOW ROASTING PAN AND SPRINKLE GENEROUSLY WITH SALT AND PEPPER AND THEN GINGER. SPREAD THE MARMALADE OVER THE CHICKEN AND POUR THE APPLE AND ORANGE JUICES INTO THE PAN.

- BAKE UNCOVERED FOR 20 MINUTES. REMOVE FROM THE OVEN AND ADD THE APRICOTS AND CURRANTS TO THE PAN, MIXING THE FRUIT EVENLY. SPRINKLE THE FRUIT WITH THE BROWN SUGAR AND RETURN TO THE OVEN.

- BAKE, BASTING THE CHICKEN FREQUENTLY, UNTIL THE CHICKEN IS GOLDEN BROWN AND SHINY ON TOP, 40 TO 45 MINUTES. REMOVE THE CHICKEN, APRICOTS, AND CURRANTS TO A WARMED SERVING PLATTER. POUR SOME OF THE PAN JUICES OVER THE TOP AND POUR THE REMAINING JUICES INTO A SAUCEBOAT. SERVE IMMEDIATELY.

CHICKEN PICATTA AND ANGEL HAIR PASTA

WE ORDER THIS WHENEVER WE GO TO TUSCAN STEAK BECAUSE IT'S THE EPITOME OF AN ITALIAN CLASSIC MEAL THAT WORKS WELL FAMILY-STYLE. A CROWD-PLEASING FAVORITE. GARLIC BREAD IS A MUST! RECIPE COURTESY OF TUSCAN STEAK IN MIAMI.

SERVES 10

INGREDIENTS

14 EGGS
¼ CUP MINCED GARLIC
½ CUP LEMON JUICE
1 POUND PARMIGIANO-REGGIANO CHEESE, GRATED
1 BUNCH OF BASIL, ROUGHLY CHOPPED
SALT AND FRESHLY GROUND BLACK PEPPER TO TASTE
10 SKINLESS, BONELESS CHICKEN BREASTS
FLOUR, FOR DREDGING
¾ CUP OLIVE OIL
4 POUNDS ANGEL HAIR PASTA (DRY)
5 OUNCES CAPERS
¾ CUP FRESH LEMON JUICE
3¼ CUPS CHICKEN STOCK
3 CUPS CHOPPED GARLIC
SALT AND FRESHLY GROUND BLACK PEPPER TO TASTE
¾ STICK BUTTER
1 BUNCH OF BASIL CUT INTO A CHIFFONADE

INSTRUCTIONS

- IN A BOWL, MIX THE EGGS, GARLIC, LEMON JUICE, PARMIGIANO-REGGIANO, BASIL, SALT, AND PEPPER. MIX UNTIL WELL INCORPORATED.

- DREDGE EACH CHICKEN BREAST IN FLOUR, SHAKE OFF THE EXCESS, AND DIP INTO THE SEASONED EGG MIXTURE.

- HEAT THE OLIVE OIL IN A SAUTÉ PAN. THEN PLACE THE CHICKEN GENTLY IN THE PAN. COOK THE CHICKEN UNTIL IT'S GOLDEN BROWN, THEN TURN UNTIL BROWNED ON THE OTHER SIDE AND COOKED THROUGH, ABOUT 10 MINUTES TOTAL.

- MEANWHILE, COOK THE PASTA IN SALTED BOILING WATER UNTIL AL DENTE. DRAIN AND SET ASIDE.

- IN A HOT SAUTÉ PAN, COMBINE THE CAPERS, LEMON JUICE, CHICKEN STOCK, GARLIC, SALT, AND PEPPER. COOK FOR 2 MINUTES, OR UNTIL THE INGREDIENTS HOMOGENIZE. ADD THE PASTA TO THE PAN AND FINISH BY ADDING THE BUTTER.

- PLATE THE PASTA ON A LARGE PLATTER AND TOP IT OFF WITH THE COOKED CHICKEN. GARNISH WITH FRESH BASIL ON TOP.

RAOUL'S

STEAK AU POIVRE

THERE'S NOTHING LIKE A GOOD STEAK, ESPECIALLY WHEN YOU SERVE IT WITH FRENCH FRIES—THE PERFECT BLEND OF CHIC SOPHISTICATION AND GUILTY PLEASURE. RECIPE COURTESY OF RAOUL'S.

SERVES 10

INGREDIENTS

8 POUNDS SHELL STEAK (OR TUNA STEAK)
2 CUPS CRUSHED BLACK PEPPERCORNS
½ CUP (2 STICKS) PLUS 1 TEASPOON BUTTER
½ CUP OIL
KOSHER SALT
¼ CUP BRANDY
½ CUP DEMI-GLACE (AVAILABLE AT ANY GOURMET
   FOOD STORE)

INSTRUCTIONS

- PAT THE UNCOOKED STEAK IN THE CRUSHED PEPPERCORNS.

- PLACE ½ CUP OF THE BUTTER AND ALL OF THE OIL IN A LARGE SAUTÉ PAN. HEAT THE PAN OVER MEDIUM-HIGH HEAT AND ADD THE STEAK. SALT TO TASTE. SEAR THE STEAK ON BOTH SIDES.

- SCRAPE THE FAT OFF OF THE STEAK AND THEN FLAMBÉ IT WITH BRANDY UNTIL THE FIRE BURNS OUT.

- ADD THE DEMI-GLACE. WHEN IT STARTS TO THICKEN, SWIRL IN THE REMAINING TEASPOON OF BUTTER. SERVE THE STEAK HOT AND PASS THE SAUCE.

AGO

WHITEFISH

AGO RESTAURANT, A CLASSIC IN LOS ANGELES AND MIAMI, IS FREQUENTED BY ROBERT DE NIRO, GEORGE CLOONEY, HUGH GRANT, KATE HUDSON, AND ALMOST EVERY MAJOR STUDIO HEAD. RECIPE COURTESY OF AGO.

SERVES 1

INGREDIENTS

8 OUNCES WHITEFISH FILLET
4 TEASPOONS EXTRA-VIRGIN OLIVE OIL
4 TO 6 BABY ARTICHOKES, SLICED
2 GARLIC CLOVES
JUICE OF ½ LEMON
1 POUND SPINACH LEAVES, WASHED, DRIED,
   AND STEMMED
1 TEASPOON CHOPPED FLAT-LEAF PARSLEY

INSTRUCTIONS

- SAUTÉ THE WHITEFISH FILLET IN 2 TEASPOONS OF THE EXTRA-VIRGIN OLIVE OIL UNTIL GOLDEN.

- IN A SEPARATE PAN, SAUTÉ THE ARTICHOKES WITH 1 TEASPOON OF THE OLIVE OIL AND 1 CLOVE OF GARLIC. WHEN THE ARTICHOKES ARE TENDER, ADD THEM TO THE WHITEFISH AND SIMMER TOGETHER FOR 3 TO 5 MINUTES WITH THE LEMON JUICE.

- IN A CLEAN PAN, SAUTÉ THE SPINACH WITH THE OTHER CLOVE OF GARLIC AND THE REMAINING TEASPOON OF OLIVE OIL JUST UNTIL WILTED AND PLACE IT ON A SERVING DISH. TOP IT OFF WITH THE WHITEFISH AND THEN THE ARTICHOKES. GARNISH WITH A SPRINKLE OF FRESH PARSLEY.

BLACK COD WITH MISO

THIS DISH IS OUR OBSESSION—AND ROBERT DE NIRO'S. THE FISH MUST MARINATE FOR 2 TO 3 DAYS, SO PREPARE IT WELL IN ADVANCE. ONE OF ITS KEY FLAVORS IS THE HAJIKAMI GINGER ROOT, WHICH IS AVAILABLE IN ASIAN MARKETS. THIS RECIPE WORKS WELL WITH BEEF AND SALMON, TOO. NOTE: ONE OF OUR FAVORITE WAYS TO EAT THIS BLACK COD IS IN SMALL PORTIONS, WRAPPED IN BUTTER LETTUCE. RECIPE COURTESY OF NOBU.

SERVES 4

INGREDIENTS

4 BLACK COD FILLETS, ABOUT ½ POUND EACH
3 CUPS NOBU-STYLE SAIKYO MISO
1 STALK OF HAJIKAMI PER SERVING

NOBU-STYLE SAIKYO MISO

INGREDIENTS

¾ CUP SAKE
¾ CUP MIRIN
2 CUPS WHITE MISO PASTE
1¼ CUPS SUGAR

INSTRUCTIONS

- IN A MEDIUM SAUCEPAN OVER HIGH HEAT, BRING THE SAKE AND MIRIN TO A BOIL.

- BOIL FOR ABOUT 20 SECONDS TO EVAPORATE THE ALCOHOL.

- REDUCE THE HEAT TO LOW AND ADD THE MISO PASTE, MIXING WITH A WOODEN SPOON.

- WHEN THE MISO HAS DISSOLVED COMPLETELY, RAISE THE HEAT TO HIGH AGAIN AND ADD THE SUGAR, STIRRING CONSTANTLY WITH THE WOODEN SPOON TO THE BOTTOM OF THE PAN SO THE SAUCE DOES NOT BURN.

- REMOVE THE SAUCE FROM THE HEAT ONCE THE SUGAR IS COMPLETELY DISSOLVED AND COOL TO ROOM TEMPERATURE.

PREPARING THE FISH

- PAT THE FILLETS THOROUGHLY DRY WITH A PAPER TOWEL.

- SLATHER THE FISH WITH THE NOBU-STYLE SAIKYO MISO AND PLACE IN A NONREACTIVE DISH OR BOWL. COVER TIGHTLY WITH PLASTIC WRAP. LEAVE TO STEEP IN THE REFRIGERATOR FOR 2 TO 3 DAYS.

COOKING INSTRUCTIONS

- PREHEAT THE OVEN TO 400°F. PREHEAT THE GRILL OR BROILER.

- LIGHTLY WIPE OFF ANY EXCESS MISO CLINGING TO THE FILLETS, BUT DO NOT RINSE IT OFF.

- PLACE THE FISH ON THE GRILL, OR IN A BROILER PAN, AND GRILL OR BROIL UNTIL THE SURFACE OF THE FISH TURNS BROWN.

- TRANSFER FILLETS TO AN OVENPROOF PAN OR BAKING DISH AND BAKE FOR 10 TO 15 MINUTES, UNTIL OPAQUE.

- AFTER THE FISH IS COOKED, ARRANGE THE BLACK COD FILLETS ON INDIVIDUAL PLATES AND GARNISH THEM WITH HAJIKAMI.

- ADD A FEW EXTRA DROPS OF NOBU-STYLE SAIKYO MISO TO EACH PLATE.

EAT, DRINK & BE MERRY

THAI CURRY SHRIMP WITH CORIANDER RICE AND FRIED BASIL

FROM THE CLIFF RESTAURANT IN BARBADOS COMES THIS SUMPTUOUS CURRY. RECIPE COURTESY OF *THE CLIFF RECIPES* (MILLER) BY PAUL OWENS, THE CLIFF, BARBADOS.

SERVES 1

SHRIMP
¼ CUP VEGETABLE OIL
2 13½-OUNCE TINS OF UNSWEETENED COCONUT MILK
2 TO 3 TABLESPOONS THAI GREEN CURRY PASTE
2 TABLESPOONS SUGAR
4 TABLESPOONS THAI FISH SAUCE
24 LARGE SHRIMP
KOSHER OR SEA SALT
1 CUP FRESH BASIL LEAVES, SHREDDED

GARNISH
4 PORTIONS OF CORIANDER RICE
1 RED BELL PEPPER, CORED, SEEDED, AND CUT INTO STRIPS
1 YELLOW BELL PEPPER, CORED, SEEDED, AND CUT INTO STRIPS
1 GREEN BELL PEPPER, CORED, SEEDED, AND CUT INTO STRIPS
1 CUP WHOLE BASIL LEAVES
VEGETABLE OIL, FOR FRYING
1 EGGPLANT, SLICED CROSSWISE AND GRILLED

INSTRUCTIONS
- HEAT THE OIL IN A SAUCEPAN AND ADD A LITTLE OF THE COCONUT MILK AND ALL OF THE CURRY PASTE. COOK OVER HIGH HEAT UNTIL IT SEPARATES.

- ADD THE SUGAR, FISH SAUCE, AND THE REST OF THE COCONUT MILK AND BRING TO A BOIL. ALLOW TO SIMMER FOR 15 TO 20 MINUTES.

- POACH THE SHRIMP IN SALTED WATER UNTIL JUST COOKED, ABOUT 3 MINUTES. DRAIN AND ADD IT TO THE SAUCE.

- ADD THE BASIL. SERVE WITH RICE AND TOP WITH THE FRESH PEPPERS.

- TO FURTHER GARNISH, FRY THE WHOLE BASIL LEAVES IN HOT OIL UNTIL CRISP, ABOUT 40 SECONDS. DRAIN ON PAPER TOWELS. SPRINKLE ON THE TOP OF THE CURRY AND SERVE WITH GRILLED EGGPLANT.

CORIANDER RICE

INGREDIENTS
1 CUP WHITE RICE
2 CUPS WATER
1 CUP CHOPPED FRESH CORIANDER (CILANTRO)

INSTRUCTIONS
- COMBINE THE RICE WITH THE WATER IN A POT. COOK OVER HIGH HEAT UNTIL WATER COMES TO A BOIL AND THEN LOWER TO MEDIUM-LOW FLAME AND LET THE RICE SIMMER, COVERED, UNTIL THE WATER IS ABSORBED, ABOUT 20 MINUTES.

- REMOVE FROM THE HEAT AND ADD THE CHOPPED CORIANDER WHEN THE RICE IS COOL.

RISOTTO AL CARCIOFI
(ARTICHOKE RISOTTO)

YOU'LL TASTE ARTICHOKE IN EVERY BITE OF THIS RISOTTO BECAUSE, BY COOKING THE ARTICHOKES IN THE POT BEFORE ADDING THE RICE AND STOCK, THE ENTIRE DISH BECOMES INFUSED WITH THEIR FLAVOR. THIS WORKS WELL AS AN APPETIZER, TOO. RECIPE FROM *DA SILVANO COOKBOOK: SIMPLE SECRETS FROM NEW YORK'S FAVORITE ITALIAN RESTAURANT* (BLOOMSBURY) BY SILVANO MARCHETTO.

SERVES 4 TO 6

INGREDIENTS

1 LEMON, HALVED

8 BABY ARTICHOKES

2 QUARTS CANNED LOW-SODIUM BEEF BROTH OR CHICKEN OR VEGETABLE STOCK

5 TABLESPOONS OLIVE OIL

1 LEEK, WHITE PART ONLY, WASHED WELL AND MINCED

1 GARLIC CLOVE, MINCED

1 POUND (2 CUPS) CARNAROLI OR ARBORIO RICE

½ CUP DRY WHITE WINE

1 TABLESPOON UNSALTED BUTTER

1 CUP FRESHLY GRATED PARMIGIANO-REGGIANO

FINE SEA SALT

FRESHLY GROUND BLACK PEPPER

INSTRUCTIONS

- FILL A STAINLESS-STEEL OR CERAMIC BOWL LARGE ENOUGH TO HOLD THE ARTICHOKES WITH COLD WATER. SQUEEZE THE JUICE FROM THE LEMON HALVES INTO THE BOWL.

- CLEAN AND TRIM THE ARTICHOKES DOWN TO THE HEART BY CUTTING OFF THE STEMS AND SNAPPING BACK AND REMOVING ALL THE TOUGH OUTER LEAVES. QUARTER THE HEARTS AND PLACE THEM IN THE BOWL WITH THE LEMON WATER TO KEEP THEM FROM DISCOLORING.

- POUR THE BROTH INTO A POT AND BRING IT TO A BOIL OVER HIGH HEAT. LOWER THE HEAT AND ALLOW THE BROTH TO SIMMER.

- WARM THE OLIVE OIL OVER MEDIUM HEAT IN A HEAVY-BOTTOMED POT LARGE ENOUGH TO HOLD ALL THE INGREDIENTS. ADD THE LEEK AND GARLIC AND SAUTÉ FOR 3 MINUTES.

- WHILE THE LEEK AND GARLIC ARE COOKING, DRAIN THE ARTICHOKE HEARTS AND PAT THEM DRY WITH PAPER TOWELS. ADD THE ARTICHOKE HEARTS TO THE LEEK AND GARLIC AND COOK UNTIL THE ARTICHOKE HEARTS BEGIN TO COLOR, ABOUT 5 MINUTES. ADD THE RICE AND STIR TO COAT IT WITH OIL. FRY THE RICE, STIRRING CONSTANTLY, UNTIL IT TURNS OPAQUE IN THE CENTER, 3 TO 4 MINUTES. ADD THE WINE AND STIR UNTIL IT EVAPORATES, ABOUT 1 MINUTE.

- ADD ABOUT 1 CUP OF THE SIMMERING BROTH AND COOK, STIRRING CONSTANTLY, UNTIL THE RICE IS ALMOST DRY. CONTINUE TO ADD BROTH BY THE LADLEFUL, STIRRING AS YOU COOK AND ADDING MORE BROTH ONLY AS THE PREVIOUS ADDITION HAS BEEN ABSORBED. AFTER ABOUT 15 MINUTES, BEGIN ADDING THE BROTH IN SMALLER INCREMENTS UNTIL YOU REACH THE DESIRED CONSISTENCY, WITH THE RICE FULLY COOKED BUT STILL A BIT AL DENTE AND WITH A SLIGHTLY CREAMY CONSISTENCY.

- JUST BEFORE SERVING, ADD THE BUTTER AND PARMIGIANO-REGGIANO, SEASON WITH SALT AND PEPPER, AND STIR VIGOROUSLY UNTIL THE RISOTTO IS CREAMY. SERVE FAMILY-STYLE FROM A LARGE SERVING BOWL OR DIVIDE AMONG INDIVIDUAL BOWLS.

SIDES

JOE'S STONE CRAB
CREAMED SPINACH

A FAMOUS SIDE DISH FROM A FAMOUS RESTAURANT IN MIAMI. THIS RECIPE IS REPRINTED FROM *EAT AT JOE'S: THE JOE'S STONE CRAB RESTAURANT COOKBOOK* PUBLISHED BY BAY BOOKS (© 2000).

SERVES 4

INGREDIENTS

2 10-OUNCE BOXES OF FROZEN CHOPPED SPINACH, THAWED
1½ CUPS LIGHT CREAM (OR ¾ CUP EACH HEAVY CREAM AND MILK)
1 TEASPOON SALT
¼ TEASPOON NUTMEG, OR TO TASTE
2 TABLESPOONS UNSALTED BUTTER
2 TABLESPOONS ALL-PURPOSE FLOUR

INSTRUCTIONS

- GENTLY SQUEEZE THE SPINACH, DISCARDING EXCESS WATER. PLACE IT IN A NONALUMINUM SAUCEPAN AND COOK OVER LOW HEAT, STIRRING CONSTANTLY, FOR 5 MINUTES OR UNTIL IT BEGINS TO BECOME TENDER BUT IS STILL BRIGHT GREEN. ADD THE CREAM, SALT, AND NUTMEG AND SIMMER FOR 5 MINUTES OR UNTIL THE CREAM HAS BUB-BLED AND REDUCED SLIGHTLY.

- MEANWHILE, MELT THE BUTTER IN A SMALL SKIL-LET; ADD THE FLOUR AND COOK OVER LOW HEAT, STIRRING FOR 3 TO 4 MINUTES, UNTIL OPAQUE. STIR THIS ROUX INTO THE SPINACH MIXTURE. SIMMER FOR 4 OR 5 MINUTES, UNTIL CREAMY AND SMOOTH BUT STILL BRIGHT GREEN. CORRECT THE SEASONINGS AND SERVE HOT.

THE FORGE
HARICOTS VERTS

YES, THEY'RE JUST GREEN BEANS, BUT THEY SOMEHOW SOUND MUCH MORE INTERESTING WHEN YOU CALL THEM HARICOT VERTS, ESPECIALLY WITH THIS RECIPE FROM ONE OF MIAMI'S BEST RESTAURANTS. THEY MAKE GREAT PREMEAL "PICKING FOOD." RECIPE COURTESY OF THE FORGE RESTAURANT, OWNER SHAREEF MALNIK.

SERVES 2

INGREDIENTS

¼ CUP CANOLA OIL
1 CUP HARICOTS VERTS, RINSED AND STEMS REMOVED
1 TABLESPOON CHOPPED GARLIC
2 TABLESPOONS SOY SAUCE

INSTRUCTIONS

IN A SAUTÉ PAN, HEAT OIL OVER MEDIUM-HIGH HEAT UNTIL IT JUST BEGINS TO SMOKE. ADD THE BEANS (MAKE SURE THEY ARE DRY OR THE OIL MIGHT FLAME UP) AND GARLIC AND COOK UNTIL THE GARLIC IS GOLDEN BROWN, APPROXIMATELY 3 MINUTES. REMOVE FROM HEAT AND IMMEDIATELY ADD SOY SAUCE.

HASH BROWNS

YOU MAY THINK OF THESE HASH BROWNS AS SOMETHING THAT GOES ONLY WITH BRUNCH, BUT WE LOVE TO SERVE THEM WITH DINNER TO ADD AN ELEMENT OF SURPRISE, WHETHER WE'RE SERVING STEAK TARTARE OR BLACKENED CATFISH. YOUR GUESTS WILL GOBBLE THESE UP ANY TIME. RECIPE FROM *EAT AT JOE'S: THE JOE'S STONE CRAB RESTAURANT COOKBOOK* PUBLISHED BY BAY BOOKS (© 2000).

SERVES 4

INGREDIENTS

3 MEDIUM IDAHO POTATOES (ABOUT 1¼ POUNDS)

SALT

5 TABLESPOONS VEGETABLE OIL, OR MORE AS NEEDED

SALT AND FRESHLY GROUND BLACK PEPPER

INSTRUCTIONS

- PEEL THE POTATOES AND HALVE THEM LENGTH-WISE. COOK IN BOILING SALTED WATER UNTIL TENDER BUT NOT MUSHY, 25 TO 30 MINUTES. DRAIN AND COOL. CUT THE POTATOES UP ROUGHLY, SLICING THEM IN THIN, IRREGULAR PIECES. THE PIECES DON'T HAVE TO BE EVEN, BUT THEY SHOULDN'T BE ANY LARGER THAN A QUARTER.

- HEAT 2½ TABLESPOONS OF THE OIL IN A 7- OR 8-INCH NONSTICK SKILLET OVER MEDIUM HEAT. (IF YOU ARE USING A CAST-IRON OR OTHER HEAVY SKILLET, YOU MAY NEED A LITTLE MORE OIL.) WHEN THE OIL IS HOT BUT NOT SMOKING, ADD THE POTATOES; THEY SHOULD COVER THE BOTTOM EVENLY, AND THE PAN SHOULD BE ABOUT THREE-QUARTERS FULL. SEASON THE POTATOES WITH SALT AND PEPPER. WITH A WOODEN SPOON OR SPATULA, TURN THE POTATOES OVER TO IMPREGNATE WITH OIL. GENTLY SMOOTH OUT THE MIXTURE IN THE PAN, PRESSING IT AROUND THE EDGES TO FORM A NEAT ROUND EDGE. SPRINKLE WITH A LITTLE MORE SALT AND PEPPER, AND DRIZZLE WITH A LITTLE MORE OIL.

- LET THE POTATOES COOK, WITHOUT MOVING THEM, UNTIL YOU CAN SEE THAT THE EDGES ARE BROWN, 10 TO 12 MINUTES. ADJUST THE HEAT, IF NECESSARY, TO MAINTAIN A STEADY, GENTLE SIZZLE. GIVE THE PAN A LITTLE SHAKE NOW AND THEN TO PREVENT STICKING, WITHOUT DISTURBING THE POTATOES. AND IF NEEDED, ADD A LITTLE MORE OIL IN THE CENTER OF THE PAN.

- WHEN THE EDGES ARE BROWN, INVERT A FLAT DINNER PLATE OVER THE SKILLET. HOLDING THE SKILLET WITH A POT HOLDER OR KITCHEN TOWEL, INVERT THE POTATOES DECISIVELY OVER THE PLATE. PLACE THE SKILLET BACK ON THE BURNER, ADD 2 TABLESPOONS MORE OIL, AND CAREFULLY SLIDE THE POTATOES BACK INTO THE SKILLET WITH THE BROWNED SIDE UP. SPRINKLE WITH A LITTLE MORE SALT AND PEPPER.

- LET THE POTATOES SIZZLE FOR ABOUT 30 SECONDS. MAKE A FEW CUTS IN THE POTATOES WITH THE SIDE OF THE SPOON. COOK THE SECOND SIDE, ADJUSTING THE HEAT AS NECESSARY, UNTIL NICELY BROWNED, ABOUT 10 MINUTES LONGER.

- NOW HOLD A SERVING PLATE OVER THE SKILLET, AND INVERT THE HASH BROWNS ONTO THE PLATE SO THAT THE JUST-BROWNED SIDE IS UP. SERVE HOT.

DESERTS
LE CIRQUE 2000
PETIT FOURS

PERHAPS MANHATTAN'S MOST FAMOUS, CLASSIC WATERING HOLE, LE CIRQUE 2000 IS STEEPED IN TRADITION. PETIT FOURS ARE ALMOST ALWAYS SERVED AT FINE, FOUR-STAR RESTAURANTS, WHETHER YOU ORDER DESSERT OR NOT. SO SERVING A PLATE OF THESE CONFECTIONARY TREATS WITH MINI COOKIES AND CHOCOLATES IS A CHIC WAY TO ADD A TOUCH OF ELEGANCE TO ANY AFFAIR. RECIPE COURTESY OF LE CIRQUE 2000.

MAKES APPROXIMATELY 50 PETIT FOURS OR 12 TO 15 MUFFINS

INGREDIENTS

4½ CUPS SUGAR
1 CUP FLOUR
1 CUP ALMOND POWDER OR OTHER NUT POWDER
2¼ CUPS EGG WHITES
½ CUP HONEY
3½ TABLESPOONS KIRSCH
2 CUPS BROWNED BUTTER
POWDERED SUGAR, FOR DUSTING

NOTE: TO MAKE NUTTY-TASTING BROWN BUTTER, SIMPLY BRING THE BUTTER TO A BOIL IN A SAUCEPAN AND LET IT TURN A DEEP BROWN. WATCH IT CAREFULLY TO MAKE SURE IT DOESN'T BURN.

INSTRUCTIONS

- PREHEAT THE OVEN TO 350°F.

- IN A LARGE MIXING BOWL, MIX THE SUGAR, FLOUR, ALMOND POWDER, AND EGG WHITES UNTIL SMOOTH. ADD THE HONEY AND KIRSCH. STIR IN THE BROWN BUTTER AND POUR THE BATTER INTO 1 X 1½ X ¾-INCH MOLDS FOR PETIT FOURS OR MUFFIN TINS WITH A 2-INCH DIAMETER. SPRINKLE WITH POWDERED SUGAR. BAKE FOR 8 MINUTES, OR UNTIL THE CENTER SPRINGS BACK WHEN TOUCHED.

- ALLOW THE PETIT FOURS OR MUFFINS TO COOL ON A RACK, THEN TURN THEM OUT OF THEIR MOLDS. DUST WITH MORE POWDERED SUGAR BEFORE SERVING.

MAGNOLIA BAKERY
VANILLA CUPCAKES

THE LINES AROUND THE CORNER FOR MAGNOLIA, THE BAKERY WITH THE MOST FAMOUS CUPCAKES IN NEW YORK, ARE INSANE! WE LOVE CUPCAKES—THEY'RE ALMOST BETTER THAN CAKE—BECAUSE THEY'RE EASY TO SERVE (NO CUTTING FIASCOES TO STRESS OVER) AND NO ONE CAN HAVE JUST ONE. REPRINTED WITH PERMISSION OF SIMON & SCHUSTER FROM *THE MAGNOLIA BAKERY COOKBOOK* BY JENNIFER APPEL AND ALLYSA TOREY.

MAKES 24 CUPCAKES OR 1 THREE-LAYER 9-INCH CAKE

INGREDIENTS

1 CUP (2 STICKS) UNSALTED BUTTER, SOFTENED
2 CUPS SUGAR
4 LARGE EGGS, AT ROOM TEMPERATURE
1½ CUPS SELF-RISING FLOUR
1¼ CUPS ALL-PURPOSE FLOUR
1 CUP MILK
1 TEASPOON VANILLA EXTRACT

INSTRUCTIONS

■ PREHEAT THE OVEN TO 350°F. GREASE AND LIGHTLY FLOUR TWO 12-CUP MUFFIN TINS AND THEN LINE WITH CUPCAKE PAPERS.

■ IN A LARGE BOWL, USING AN ELECTRIC MIXER AT MEDIUM SPEED, CREAM THE BUTTER UNTIL SMOOTH. ADD THE SUGAR GRADUALLY AND BEAT UNTIL FLUFFY, ABOUT 3 MINUTES.

■ ADD THE EGGS ONE AT A TIME, BEATING WELL AFTER EACH ADDITION.

■ COMBINE THE FLOURS AND ADD IN 4 PARTS, ALTER-NATING WITH THE MILK AND THE VANILLA EXTRACT, BEATING WELL AFTER EACH ADDITION.

■ SPOON THE BATTER INTO THE PREPARED CUPS UNTIL ABOUT THREE-QUARTERS FULL. BAKE UNTIL THE TOPS SPRING BACK WHEN LIGHTLY TOUCHED, 20 TO 22 MINUTES. REMOVE THE CUPCAKES FROM THE PANS AND COOL COMPLETELY ON A RACK BEFORE ICING.

BUTTERCREAM VANILLA ICING

THE FLAVOR OF THIS ICING IS HEAVENLY! REPRINTED WITH PERMISSION OF SIMON & SCHUSTER FROM *THE MAGNOLIA BAKERY COOKBOOK* BY JENNIFER APPEL AND ALYSSA TOREY.

MAKES ENOUGH ICING FOR 1 THREE-LAYER 9-INCH CAKE OR 24 CUPCAKES

INGREDIENTS

1 CUP (2 STICKS) UNSALTED BUTTER, SOFTENED
8 CUPS CONFECTIONERS' SUGAR
½ CUP MILK
2 TEASPOONS VANILLA EXTRACT

INSTRUCTIONS

- PLACE THE BUTTER IN A LARGE MIXING BOWL. ADD 4 CUPS OF THE SUGAR AND THEN THE MILK AND VANILLA EXTRACT. BEAT UNTIL SMOOTH AND CREAMY.

- GRADUALLY ADD THE REMAINING SUGAR, 1 CUP AT A TIME, UNTIL THE ICING IS THICK ENOUGH TO BE OF GOOD SPREADING CONSISTENCY. ADD A FEW DROPS OF FOOD COLORING IF DESIRED. USE AND STORE ICING AT ROOM TEMPERATURE, AS ICING WILL SET IF CHILLED. NOTE: YOU CAN STORE THIS ICING IN AN AIRTIGHT CONTAINER FOR UP TO 3 DAYS.

BAKED APPLE

AT A BRUNCH, ON A DESSERT BUFFET TABLE, OR AS AN APPETIZER WITH A SALAD, BAKED APPLES HAVE A HEARTY, DOWN-HOME APPEAL. MAKE THEM EVEN SWEETER WITH HOMEMADE OR STORE-BOUGHT CARAMEL DIPPING SAUCE ON THE SIDE. RECIPE COURTESY OF BLUE DOOR AT THE DELANO HOTEL.

SERVES 12

INGREDIENTS

1/4 CUP ALMOND PASTE
1/2 CUP SOFT BUTTER
2 CUPS DRIED CRANBERRIES
3 TABLESPOONS HONEY
2 TABLESPOONS VANILLA
1/4 TEASPOON SALT
2 CUPS TOASTED WALNUTS
12 GRANNY SMITH APPLES, CORED

INSTRUCTIONS

- TO MAKE THE FILLING, MIX THE ALMOND PASTE, BUTTER, AND CRANBERRIES TOGETHER. ADD THE HONEY, VANILLA, AND SALT. COMBINE HALF OF THE BERRY MIXTURE AND HALF OF THE NUTS IN A FOOD PROCESSOR AND PURÉE. TOSS THE PURÉE WITH THE REMAINING BERRY MIXTURE AND NUTS.

- FILL EACH APPLE WITH 2 TABLESPOONS OF THE FILLING AND PLACE IN A BAKING DISH. COVER AND BAKE FOR 25 MINUTES AT 250°F.

FROZEN HOT CHOCOLATE

THIS IS ONE OF THE CLASSIC DESSERTS NEW YORK CITY IS KNOWN FOR. WE'VE GULPED THEM DOWN AND SERVED THEM UP AT MANY A PARTY—AFTER LUNCH, DINNER, OR IN THE MIDDLE OF THE NIGHT AFTER DANCING FOR HOURS. ONE OF THE REASONS IT WORKS SO WELL IS BECAUSE OF ITS SIZE: LARGE! IT'S A COMMUNAL DESSERT THAT'S MEANT TO BE SHARED. FREEZE THE OVERSIZED GLASS BEFORE SERVING AND GO HEAVY ON THE WHIPPED CREAM. RECIPE USED WITH PERMISSION FROM STEPHEN BRUCE, OWNER OF SERENDIPITY 3.

SERVES 2

INGREDIENTS

1 GENEROUS LADLEFUL OF SERENDIPITY'S SECRET
    FROZEN HOT CHOCOLATE BLEND (RECIPE
    FOLLOWS)
½ PINT MILK
½ QUART CRUSHED ICE
WHIPPED CREAM
GRATED CHOCOLATE

INSTRUCTIONS

PLACE ALL THE INGREDIENTS IN A QUART-SIZE BLENDER. BLEND UNTIL IT'S THICK AND CREAMY. THEN POUR IN A LARGE BOWL (A GRAPEFRUIT BOWL IF YOU HAVE ONE) AND TOP IT WITH A MOUND OF WHIPPED CREAM AND GRATED CHOCOLATE. INSERT STRAWS FOR SIPPING AND ICED-TEA SPOONS FOR DIPPING.

SERENDIPITY'S SECRET FROZEN HOT CHOCOLATE BLEND

INGREDIENTS

1½ LEVEL TEASPOONS EACH OF SWEETENED VAN
    HOUTON COCOA AND DROSTE COCOA
1½ TEASPOONS SUGAR
1 TABLESPOON UNSALTED BUTTER
½ OUNCE EACH OF THE FOLLOWING CHOCOLATES:
    CALLEBAURT, VALRHONA, LINDT, CADBURY, ANTON
    BERG, FREIA, MARABU, GHIRARDELLI, AND CACAO
    BARRY
½ CUP MILK

INSTRUCTIONS

IN THE TOP OF A DOUBLE BOILER OVER BOILING WATER, MELT THE FIRST TWO COCOAS WITH THE SUGAR AND BUTTER, CREAMING TO A SMOOTH PASTE. ADD THE REMAINING CHOCOLATES AND CONTINUE MELTING, SLOWLY DRIBBLING IN THE MILK WHILE STIRRING. COOL TO ROOM TEMPERATURE AND FOLLOW THE RECIPE FOR FROZEN HOT CHOCOLATE, SUBSTITUTING ½ CUP MILK FOR ½ PINT OF MILK.

NOTE: YOU CAN ALSO BUY THE BLEND RIGHT FROM SERENDIPITY 3 OR FROM WILLIAMS-SONOMA AND HAVE IT DELIVERED TO YOUR DOOR. SEE "OUR YELLOW PAGES" FOR ORDERING INFORMATION.

EAT, DRINK & BE MERRY

MOMMY'S
RUGALACH

THERE IS NOTHING LIKE HAVING YOUR MOTHER'S SECRET RECIPE TO MAKE A
DESSERT SPECIAL, AND THIS ONE HAS BEEN IN LARA'S FAMILY FOR GENERATIONS.
THEY'RE SO GOOD, THEY GIVE PASSOVER A WHOLE NEW RELIGIOUS MEANING. IF
THERE ARE ANY LEFTOVERS, YOU CAN FREEZE THEM.

MAKES 64 PIECES

INGREDIENTS

2 PACKAGES DRY YEAST
3 CUPS SIFTED FLOUR
1 CUP SWEET BUTTER, SOFTENED
3 EGG YOLKS
1 CUP SOUR CREAM
1 CUP SUGAR
1 CUP FINELY CHOPPED PECANS
3 TABLESPOONS CINNAMON
4 TABLESPOONS MELTED SWEET BUTTER
MINI–NESTLE CHOCOLATE CHIPS
NUTS
WHITE RAISINS
HONEY
APRICOT PRESERVES
RASPBERRY PRESERVES

INSTRUCTIONS

■ IN A LARGE BOWL, SPRINKLE THE YEAST ON THE
FLOUR. CUT IN THE SOFT BUTTER AND BLEND. STIR
IN THE EGG YOLKS AND SOUR CREAM, AND CON-
TINUE MIXING UNTIL THE DOUGH IS STIFF. ROLL
THE DOUGH INTO A BALL, WRAP IN WAX PAPER,
AND REFRIGERATE OVERNIGHT.

■ PREHEAT THE OVEN TO 325°F.

■ DIVIDE THE DOUGH INTO 4 PARTS. COMBINE THE
SUGAR, PECANS, AND CINNAMON AND SPRINKLE A
QUARTER OF THE MIXTURE ONTO A PASTRY TABLE.
ROLL ONE PART OF THE DOUGH ON TOP OF THE
MIXTURE INTO A 12-INCH CIRCLE. BRUSH WITH
MELTED BUTTER AND SPREAD ON YOUR CHOICE OF
THE CHOCOLATE CHIPS, NUTS, WHITE RAISINS,
HONEY, APRICOT PRESERVES, AND RASPBERRY
PRESERVES OR A COMBINATION.

■ CUT INTO 16 PIE-SHAPE WEDGES, STARTING AT THE
WIDER EDGE. ROLL UP AND GENTLY CURVE INTO
CRESCENTS.

■ REPEAT WITH THE REMAINING DOUGH AND
SUGAR/NUT MIXTURE, VARYING THE FILLING IF YOU
LIKE. BAKE ON A GREASED COOKIE SHEET FOR 25
TO 30 MINUTES. WHEN WARM, BRUSH TOPS WITH
HONEY.

ROASTED BANANA WITH COCONUT SAUCE

AT EVERY DINNER PARTY WE'VE EVER HOSTED AT INDOCHINE—A DIMLY LIT, EXTREMELY SULTRY DOWNTOWN INDONESIAN RESTAURANT IN NEW YORK CITY THAT ATTRACTS FASHION INDUSTRY INSIDERS AND CELEBRITIES—WE ALWAYS PURPOSELY OVER-ORDER THE ROASTED BANANA, A WARM MOUTHWATERING BURST OF CARAMEL AND BANANAS. MAKE IT AT HOME AND WE PROMISE YOUR GUESTS WILL CONSTANTLY ASK YOU WHAT IT WAS—AND WHERE YOU GOT IT. RECIPE COURTESY OF INDOCHINE, NEW YORK.

SERVES 6

INGREDIENTS

8 OUNCES JAPANESE SWEET STICKY RICE (PLUM
    BLOSSOM BRAND IS A GOOD ONE)
½ CAN (8 OUNCES) COCONUT MILK
4 TEASPOONS SUGAR
PINCH OF SALT
1 TABLESPOON HONEY
6 VERY RIPE BANANAS
12 BANANA LEAVES, ABOUT 8 INCHES SQUARE
COCONUT TAPIOCA SAUCE

COCONUT TAPIOCA SAUCE

INGREDIENTS

8.4 OUNCES TAPIOCA, SOAKED IN COLD WATER FOR
    ABOUT 10 MINUTES UNTIL SOFT
7 TEASPOONS SUGAR
2 CANS COCONUT MILK
1 PINCH OF SALT

INSTRUCTIONS

SIMMER ALL INGREDIENTS WITH TAPIOCA FOR ABOUT
20 MINUTES. LET COOL.

INSTRUCTIONS

- COOK THE RICE IN THE COCONUT MILK, SUGAR, SALT, AND HONEY OVER MEDIUM HEAT FOR 15 TO 20 MINUTES, UNTIL RICE IS SOFT AND TRANSPARENT, STIRRING OFTEN. TRANSFER RICE TO A STEAMER FOR 30 MINUTES. DIVIDE STEAMED RICE INTO SIX PORTIONS, SPREADING EACH PORTION ONTO A PIECE OF PLASTIC WRAP.

- PEEL AND CUT BANANAS INTO 5-INCH PIECES. PLACE ONE PIECE OF BANANA ON EACH PORTION OF RICE AND, USING THE PLASTIC WRAP AS A GUIDE, ROLL THE RICE AROUND THE BANANA. REMOVE THE PLASTIC WRAP. REPEAT WITH REMAINING BANANA AND RICE SQUARES.

- WRAP THE BANANA AND RICE ROLLS IN THE BANANA LEAVES, FOLDING THE ENDS LIKE GIFT WRAP TO SECURE, AND STEAM 5 TO 10 MINUTES (LONGER IF THE BANANAS ARE NOT TOO RIPE).

- TO SERVE, CUT OPEN THE TOP PART OF THE BANANA LEAF AND SERVE WITH COCONUT TAPIOCA SAUCE. OPTIONAL: SPRINKLE WITH CRUSHED PEANUTS AT SERVING TIME.

BEVERLY HILTON
GRIFF'S BAKED ALASKA

FLAKY, CRISP, MOIST, AND RICH, GRIFF'S BAKED ALASKA HAS ALWAYS BEEN A HOUSE FAVORITE AT THE BEVERLY HILTON, THE OLD-WORLD ESTABLISHMENT THAT EPITOMIZES HOLLYWOOD GLAMOUR. RECIPE COURTESY OF MERV GRIFFIN'S BEVERLY HILTON HOTEL, BEVERLY HILLS, CALIFORNIA.

SERVES 4

INGREDIENTS

SPONGE CAKE (HOMEMADE OR STOREBOUGHT)
1 PINT HÄAGEN-DAZS VANILLA ICE CREAM
MERINGUE (RECIPE FOLLOWS)
MARASCHINO CHERRIES

INSTRUCTIONS

- BAKE A SPONGE CAKE IN A SHEET PAN AND USE A 3-INCH ROUND BISCUIT CUTTER TO MAKE 4 INDIVIDUAL CAKES. (WANT TO SIMPLIFY YOUR LIFE? BUY A CAKE FROM THE SUPERMARKET AND CUT IT INTO THREE-INCH ROUNDS).
- PLACE ONE SCOOP OF HÄAGEN-DAZS VANILLA ICE CREAM ON TOP OF EACH CAKE ROUND AND FREEZE FOR A FEW HOURS, OR UNTIL HARD.
- BEFORE SERVING, USE A PASTRY BAG TO PIPE ON FRESH MERINGUE (RECIPE FOLLOWS). USE A HAND-HELD TORCH TO BROWN THE MERINGUE. GARNISH WITH A CHERRY.

MERINGUE

INGREDIENTS

1 PINT EGG WHITES
1 POUND SUGAR

INSTRUCTIONS

IN THE LARGE BOWL OF AN ELECTRIC MIXER, BEAT THE EGG WHITES ON MEDIUM SPEED UNTIL SOFT PEAKS FORM. CONTINUE TO BEAT AND GRADUALLY ADD THE SUGAR, BEATING UNTIL STIFF, GLOSSY PEAKS FORM.

DELANO HOTEL
WHITE CHOCOLATE YOGURT

A DECADENT BREAKFAST THAT'S SWEET ENOUGH FOR DESSERT. IT'S EASY—AND INEXPENSIVE—TO MAKE AND IT STORES WELL OVERNIGHT. RECIPE COURTESY OF THE DELANO IN MIAMI BEACH.

MAKES 2¼ CUPS

INGREDIENTS

8 OUNCES WHITE COUVETURE CHOCOLATE OR CALLEBAUT 60/40 WHITE-CHOCOLATE SHAVINGS
10 OUNCES PLAIN OR NONFAT YOGURT
1½ OUNCES VELDA FARMS HEAVY CREAM

INSTRUCTIONS

MELT THE WHITE CHOCOLATE IN A DOUBLE BOILER. ADD THE YOGURT AND CREAM. MIX WELL AND REMOVE FROM THE HEAT. POUR THE MIXTURE INTO A BOWL. COVER AND REFRIGERATE FOR 4 HOURS BEFORE USING.

MICROWAVE MOCHI

MOCHI IS A JAPANESE PASTRY, MADE FROM RICE THAT HAS BEEN POUNDED INTO A FLEXIBLE DOUGH. IT IS OFTEN FLAVORED WITH COCONUT OR FILLED WITH ICE CREAM OR RED-BEAN PASTE (OR RED-BEAN ICE CREAM, FOR THAT MATTER). THIS IS THE MOCHI RECIPE THE CHEF USES AT NOBU, COURTESY OF BUBBIES HOMEMADE ICE CREAM AND DESSERTS IN AIEA, HAWAII. THEY'RE ALWAYS A BIG HIT ON DESSERT PLATTERS AFTER SUSHI. SERVE WITH FRESH FRUIT AND CUT INTO QUARTERS RIGHT AS YOU'RE ABOUT TO SERVE. TWO CUPS OF JUICE (PASSION FRUIT, ORANGE, STRAWBERRY–GUAVA, OR GUAVA) CAN BE SUBSTITUTED FOR THE COCONUT MILK FOR A FRUITY FLAVOR. CORNSTARCH CAN BE SUBSTITUTED FOR THE MOCHIKO FLOUR. RECIPE COURTESY OF BUBBIES ICE CREAM.

MAKES 24 MOCHI BALLS

INGREDIENTS

2 CUPS MOCHIKO FLOUR
1½ CUPS SUGAR
1 16-OUNCE CAN OF COCONUT MILK AND WATER TO
    EQUAL 2¼ CUPS OF LIQUID
A FEW DROPS OF FOOD COLORING (OPTIONAL)
POTATO STARCH OR CORNSTARCH, FOR ROLLING

INSTRUCTIONS

- MIX THE MOCHIKO FLOUR, SUGAR, MILK, AND FOOD COLORING IN A BOWL USING A WHISK.

- BASTE THE CONE OF A 3-QUART MICROWAVE TUBE PAN WITH MARGARINE AND POUR IN THE BATTER.

- COVER WITH PLASTIC WRAP AND MICROWAVE ON HIGH FOR 12 MINUTES.

- LET IT SIT FOR A FEW MINUTES. THEN, PULL THE MOCHI FROM THE SIDES OF THE PAN AND INVERT IT ONTO A BOARD THAT HAS BEEN DUSTED WITH POTATO STARCH OR CORNSTARCH.

- LET IT COOL AND THEN SLICE IT INTO ¼-INCH PIECES. ROLL THE OUTSIDE IN THE STARCH.

THE IVY
STICKY TOFFEE PUDDING

THE IVY IS ONE OF LONDON'S BEST RESTAURANTS. TO MAKE THE STICKIEST, MOST GOOEY AND ADDICTIVE PUDDING, ADD PLENTY OF SAUCE BETWEEN THE LAYERS SO IT ALL SOAKS THROUGH. RECIPE COURTESY OF *THE IVY, THE RESTAURANT AND ITS RECIPES* (TRAFALGAR SQUARE) BY A. J. GILL.

SERVES 4 TO 6

INGREDIENTS

FOR THE SPONGE CAKE

¾ CUP PITTED DATES
3 CUPS UNSALTED BUTTER AT ROOM TEMPERATURE,
    PLUS MORE TO GREASE PAN
¾ CUP SOFT DARK BROWN SUGAR
2 LARGE EGGS, LIGHTLY BEATEN
1 CUP SELF-RISING FLOUR
ICE CREAM, SOUR CREAM, OR CRÉME FRAÎCHE TO
    SERVE

FOR THE TOFFEE SAUCE

2 CUPS HEAVY CREAM
1¾ CUPS SUPERFINE SUGAR
4¾ CUPS UNSALTED BUTTER

INSTRUCTIONS

- SIMMER THE DATES IN 1⅓ CUPS OF WATER OVER LOW HEAT FOR ABOUT 10 TO 15 MINUTES OR UNTIL THEY ARE SOFT AND THE WATER HAS ALMOST EVAPORATED. TRANSFER MIXTURE TO A BLENDER AND PURÉE UNTIL SMOOTH. IF THE PURÉE IS TOO THICK (IT SHOULD BE A GOOD SPOONABLE CONSISTENCY), ADD A LITTLE MORE WATER. SET ASIDE TO COOL.

- PREHEAT THE OVEN TO 325ºF.

- BUTTER A 6 X 5 X 2½ INCH RECTANGULAR CAKE PAN OR BAKING DISH, AND LINE WITH PARCHMENT PAPER. SET ASIDE.

- TO MAKE THE TOFFEE SAUCE: POUR 1 CUP OF THE CREAM, THE SUGAR, AND THE BUTTER INTO A HEAVY-BOTTOMED PAN AND MIX WELL. BRING TO A BOIL, STIRRING WITH A WOODEN SPOON, AND CONTINUE TO BOIL UNTIL THE MIXTURE IS GOLDEN

BROWN (ABOUT 8 TO 10 MINUTES). REMOVE THE SAUCE FROM THE HEAT, ALLOW IT TO COOL FOR ABOUT 10 MINUTES, THEN WHISK IN THE REMAINING CREAM.

- TO MAKE THE SPONGE CAKE: CREAM THE BUTTER AND SUGAR TOGETHER UNTIL LIGHT AND FLUFFY. ADD THE EGGS SLOWLY, TAKING CARE THAT THE MIXTURE DOES NOT SEPARATE. (IF THIS DOES HAPPEN, ADD A LITTLE OF THE FLOUR AND CONTINUE MIXING FOR A MINUTE OR SO.) FOLD IN THE FLOUR GENTLY WITH A LARGE METAL SPOON UNTIL THOROUGHLY MIXED. ADD THE DATE PURÉE AND MIX WELL.

- SPREAD THE CAKE MIXTURE IN THE BAKING PAN AND BAKE FOR 50 TO 60 MINUTES, OR UNTIL FIRM TO THE TOUCH. ALLOW IT TO COOL IN THE PAN. KEEP THE OVEN ON.

- REMOVE THE CAKE FROM THE PAN AND TRIM THE OUTSIDE EDGES AND THE TOP IF NECESSARY FOR A NEAT APPEARANCE. CUT THE CAKE HORIZONTALLY INTO 4 LAYERS, THEN REASSEMBLE IN THE BAKING PAN (LINED WITH FRESH PARCHMENT PAPER), SPREADING TWO-THIRDS OF THE WARM SAUCE BETWEEN THE SPONGE LAYERS. THE SAUCE MAY NEED TO BE WHISKED AGAIN UNTIL SMOOTH BEFORE USE.

- ONCE YOU HAVE ASSEMBLED THE PUDDING, REHEAT IT IN THE OVEN FOR 15 TO 20 MINUTES, THEN CUT IT INTO 4 TO 6 EQUAL SERVINGS AND TOP WITH THE REMAINING TOFFEE SAUCE. SERVE WITH ICE CREAM, SOUR CREAM, OR CRÈME FRAÎCHE.

CHOCOLATE CHIP COOKIES

THESE ARE REALLY EASY TO MAKE AT HOME. THEY'RE A KNOCKOUT DESSERT FOR ALMOST ANY PARTY. RECIPE COPYRIGHT © KATHLEEN KING, FROM *KATHLEEN'S BAKESHOP COOKBOOK*. REPRINTED BY PERMISSION OF ST. MARTINS GRIFFIN.

MAKES 4½ DOZEN 3-INCH COOKIES

INGREDIENTS

2 CUPS ALL-PURPOSE FLOUR

1 TEASPOON BAKING SODA

1 TEASPOON SALT

1 CUP BUTTER

¾ CUP GRANULATED SUGAR

¾ CUP FIRMLY PACKED DARK BROWN SUGAR

1 TEASPOON WATER

1 TEASPOON VANILLA EXTRACT

2 EGGS

2 CUPS SEMISWEET CHOCOLATE CHIPS

INSTRUCTIONS

- PREHEAT OVEN TO 350°F. PREPARE GREASED COOKIE SHEETS.

- IN A LARGE BOWL, STIR TOGETHER THE FLOUR, BAKING SODA, AND SALT.

- IN ANOTHER LARGE BOWL, CREAM THE BUTTER AND SUGARS. ADD THE WATER AND VANILLA AND MIX UNTIL COMBINED. ADD THE EGGS AND MIX LIGHTLY. STIR IN THE FLOUR MIXTURE. FOLD IN THE CHOCOLATE CHIPS. DON'T OVERMIX.

- DROP ONTO PREPARED COOKIE SHEETS USING TWO TABLESPOONS. COOKIES WILL SPREAD, SO SPACE THEM AT LEAST 2 INCHES APART.

- BAKE FOR 12 MINUTES, OR UNTIL EDGES AND CENTER ARE BROWN. REMOVE COOKIES TO A WIRE RACK TO COOL.

VANILLA ICE BLENDED®

EVERYONE IN L.A., FROM THE STUDIO HEADS TO THE STRUGGLING ACTORS, IS OBSESSED WITH THESE ICED BLENDEDS. YOU CAN GET THE MIX AND MAKE THEM ANYWHERE. SEE "OUR YELLOW PAGES" FOR ORDERING INFORMATION. RECIPE COURTESY OF COFFEE BEAN & TEA LEAF.

SERVES 1

INGREDIENTS

12 OUNCES ICE

3 OUNCES NONFAT MILK

3 OUNCES COFFEE BEAN & TEA LEAF PURE COFFEE EXTRACT, REGULAR OR DECAFFEINATED

⅓ CUP COFFEE BEAN & TEA LEAF FRENCH DELUXE VANILLA

WHIPPED CREAM, FOR SERVING

INSTRUCTIONS

- POUR THE ICE, MILK, COFFEE EXTRACT AND VANILLA INTO A BLENDER AND BLEND UNTIL SMOOTH.

- TOP WITH A DOLLOP OF WHIPPED CREAM AND ENJOY.

EVENT BUDGET TEMPLATE
CALCULATE THE COST OF YOUR ULTIMATE PARTY

EVENT BUDGET TEMPLATE

SUBJECT	ESTIMATE	ACTUAL	SUBJECT	ESTIMATE	ACTUAL
LOCATION			DRINKS		
Location / Venue Fee			Beer		
Room Rental Charge			Wine		
Plating Charge			Champagne		
INVITATIONS			Hard Alcohol		
Save-the-Date Cards			Mixers		
Design			Soda / Soft Drinks		
Printing or Calligraphy			Bottled Water		
Stationery / Boxed Invitations			Glasses (paper / plastic)		
Envelopes / Tube mailers			Condiments (olives, lemons, etc.)		
Caligraphy of Envelopes			Ice		
Mailing Labels			Bar Tools		
Stuffing / Sealing			Coffee & Tea		
Postage			Bartender(s)		
Messenger Services			Barback(s)		
Mail House Fee			Tipping for Servers		
FOOD			DÉCOR		
Placed Food			Indoor Lighting (candles / lightbulbs / spotlights / disco balls)		
Hors d'Oeuvres					
Main Course			Outdoor Lighting		
Plates and Bowls			Tent		
Utensils			Flowers		
Serving Dishes / Trays			Florist		
Caterer / Chef			Place cards / Name cards		
Chef's Assistant			Tablecloths		
Waitstaff			Napkins		
Busboys			Napkin holders		
Staff Uniforms			Table Décor		
Desserts			Furniture / Rentals		
Delivery / Pick-up			Fabric		
Staff			Pillows		
Food Servers			Balloons		
Tipping for Servers			Confetti		
			Printed Matchbooks		
			Banners, Posters, & Signs		

SUBJECT	ESTIMATE	ACTUAL
SOUND		
Deejay		
Band		
Entertainment		
Audio Equipment		
CDs		
Staging		
MISCELLANEOUS EXPENSES		
Event Planner		
Staff		
Check-in Staff		
Doorman		
Coat-Check Attendant(s)		
Valet		
Security		
Insurance		
Permits		
Space Heaters		
Fans		
Porta-Johns		
Toilet Paper / Bathroom Accessories		
Cleanup		
Garbage Pickup		
Photographer		
Film & Processing		
B-Roll Crew		
Video Crew		
Disposable Cameras		
Press Wall		
Ropes, Stations, etc.		
Tax		
Delivery		
Generator / Power		
Gift Bags		
Gift Item(s)		
Bag		
Tissue Paper		
Tipping for Staff		

SUBJECT	ESTIMATE	ACTUAL
PERSONAL EXPENSES		
Phone / Cell Phone		
Messenger		
Federal Express		
Account Supplies		
Transportation		
Thank-You Cards		
Thank-You Gift		
TOTAL		

USING THIS AS A TEMPLATE, YOU'LL BE ABLE TO CALCULATE YOUR BUDGET. But remember, not all of these elements apply to every party. If you're having an intimate gathering of eight for dinner, you probably won't need to hire a valet service, rent a coat rack, or buy extra glasses. But you should still factor in the cost of minor things, like nice pens (if you're hand-writing your invitations) and garbage bags. Photocopy this spread, or recreate it according to your own party needs.

CHIC TIP

Most people tend to go about 10 percent over their budget, so when you're figuring out how much you're spending for every aspect of the party, leave at least 10 percent of the total budget unallocated, so you have extra cash for whatever unexpected costs pop up.

CHAPTER ELEVEN
OUR YELLOW PAGES
ALL THE CONTACTS YOU EVER WANTED BUT WERE AFRAID TO ASK FOR

THIS RESOURCE GUIDE IS DIVIDED BY CHAPTERS, WHICH ARE THEN ORGANIZED BY SUBSECTION.

Bryan Lourd, Steve Martin,
Ron Meyer, Jim Wiatt and Rita Wilson

invite you to celebrate the release of

man eater

a novel by

gigi levangie grazer
Published by Simon & Schuster

Champagne & Hors d'oeuvres
Thursday, May 29th, 2003

7:00 - 9:00 p.m.

RSVP
Harrison & Shriftman
310 271 6411

■ **BOOKS WE RECOMMEND:**
Be My Guest: Theme Party Savoir-Faire, Rena Kirdar Sindi.

FOR LESS EXPENSIVE CLASSIC OPTIONS, TRY:
■ CRANE'S. They've been around for over two hundred years: www.crane.com or call 800-572-0024.
■ WILLIAM ARTHUR: www.thegoldenquill.invitations.com or 877-879-6776.

CHAPTER TWO: WHERE'S THE PARTY?
■ GIORGIO BALDI RISTORANTE, a famous Italian restaurant in Los Angeles. Great for dinner parties. 310-573-1660.
■ Charter a yacht through WWW.YACHTSTORE.COM.

CHAPTER THREE: YOU'RE INVITED!
CLASSIC CUSTOM-ORDER INVITATIONS
To splurge on the best custom-made and printed invitations on thick, water-marked paper that's decorative and hand-finished with borders, check out:
■ CARTIER at www.cartier.com or call 800-CARTIER.
■ TIFFANY & CO. at www.tiffany.com or 800-843-3269.
■ SMYTHSON OF BOND STREET, established in 1887, is the place where British style cognoscenti get "proper stationery": www.smythson.com or 877-769-8476.
■ MRS. JOHN L. STRONG makes beautiful stationery: 212-838-3775 or www.mrsstrong.com.

IN THE BOX: PRE-PACKAGED CLASSIC STATIONERY
Can't deal with all the hassle of picking out the paper and thinking about time-consuming things like cardstock and envelope lining?
■ ANNA GRIFFIN at www.annagriffin.com or call 404-817-8170 to find out about her invitations that slide into embossed sleeves and fit into a larger envelope. Ribbons are optional. Very Victorian and Southern Belle.

PRINTING
■ KINKO'S at 1-800-2KINKOS or www.kinkos.com.
■ ALPINE CREATIVE GROUP. Harrison & Shriftman swears by this printing company! 212-989-4198.

OUT OF THE BOX
■ CANDY CARDS makes great greeting cards with candy attached: www.candycardgreetings.com.
■ MERI MERI makes cute invitations that pull out of envelopes that resemble purses, shoes, champagne buckets, golf bags, and such. They're a bit pricey, but such a conversation piece: 650-525-9200.

CALLIGRAPHY
■ Take a calligraphy class at the LEARNING ANNEX in New York City: 212-371-0280 or www.learningannex.com.
■ Download Lucida, a classic calligraphy font, for $22 at WWW.FONTS.COM.
■ STEPHANIE BARBA, calligrapher extraordinaire, will make a calligraphy font for you or hand-write something classy, no matter where you're located: 212-327-0100 or 415-437-6001.
■ For special hand-made invitations and calligraphy, try ERICA MCPHEE, PAPERWHITE STUDIO: www.paperwhitestudio.com or 207-892-7815.
■ BERNARD MAISNER CALLIGRAPHY AND FINE STATIONERY does beautiful calligrapy: 212-477-6776.

Hugh M. Hefner
& Christie Hefner
invite you to celebrate
Playboy's 50th Anniversary

Thursday, December 4, 2003
9pm-1am / 11pm Tribute

The New York State Armory
Lexington Avenue at 26th Street

This invitation admits two
Non-transferable / Photo ID Required
Dress to Kill

RSVP to Harrison & Shriftman
917 351 8684
No cameras allowed

HANDS-ON

Get good paper.
- GEORGE STANLEY PAPER: 800-627-2648 or www.mara-mi.com.
- THE PAPER COMPANY: 800-525-3196.
- KATE'S PAPERIE: www.katespaperie.com or 888-941-9169.
- SOOLIP PAPERIE AND PRESS: 310-360-0545.
- AITOH for Japanese-inspired paper and origami: 650-866-3814 or www.aitoh.com.
- THE GOOD LIFE at PARTY ON LA CIENEGA IN L.A. for great stationery and party items in general: 310-659-8717.
- THE PAPER SOURCE is a great place to find do-it-yourself invitations, paper, and envelope liners, along with adhesives, glue sticks, and tools. They also offer workshops on printing, making cards, and gift wrapping. 773-525-7300 or www.papersource.com.

- QUOTABLE CARDS are cards with quotes from cultural icons. Contact www.quotablecards.com or 212-420-7552.
- ROBIN MAGUIRE has quirky, brightly colored, fun blank notes and invitations, save-the-date and response cards, as well as place cards: www.robin-maguire.com or 800-998-0323.
- STUDIO Z MENDOCINO sells cheeky black cards with gold-foiled motifs and cute letterpress phrases: www.studio-z.com or 707-964-9448.
- PREPPY CARDS makes adorable cards you can have customized. They're available at Pomegranate in New York City. 212-288-4409 or at www.preppycards.com.
- ITTY BITTY COMPANY has invitations for every occasion: 229-438-5555 or www.ittybittycompany.com.

GIMMICK-A-GO-GO

- PETERBROOKE to order invitations printed on chocolate: 904-398-2488 or www.peterbrooke.com.
- SOOLIP for chocolate-covered cookies with custom fortunes: 310-360-0545.
- DYLAN'S CANDY BAR for edibles: www.dylanscandybar.com or 646-735-0078.
- FRIDGE FUN offers puzzles and other kitschy items: www.fridgefun.com or 800-845-8320 (Crane's has them, too).
- POP SHOTS STUDIOS has pop-up cards: info@popshotsstudios.com or 800-852-7677.

PENS WE SWEAR BY

- The PENTEL fountain or sign pen, in an array of colors: www.pentel.com or 800-231-7856.
- SHARPIE calligraphy pens: 800-323-0749 or www.sharpie.com.

INVITATION ACCESSORIES

- AVERY labels, available at Staples: www.staples.com or 800-3-STAPLE.
- EMBOSSER, available through Martha by Mail: www.marthabymail.com or 800-950-7130.
- To avoid paper cuts on the tongue, get the PENTEL ROLL 'N GLUE through www.pentel.com or 800-231-7856 or visit www.officeworld.com. Martha by Mail also makes a good item called Lick & Stick.
- INSCRIBE, the first personalization system, a computerized calligraphy machine that features a real chisel-tip calligraphy pen, hand-mixed ink, and letterforms designed by masterful calligraphers. Use for printing envelopes, invitations, place cards, menus, anything. You can also use it to create camera-ready art for offset printing. Forty styles of printing and sixty-nine colors are available. At about $8,000, it's expensive, but it's perfect for those who entertain all the time. To find out more, visit www.inscribe.com or call 781-933-3331.

BOOKS WE RECOMMEND

- *Invitations*, by Marc Friedland and Betty Goodwin.

FÊTE ACCOMPLI!

CHAPTER FOUR: **PARTY PRODUCTION**

PLANNING
■ Visit WWW.THEPLUNGE.COM for help with your party. This site walks you through all the aspects of a party and gives great reasons to have a party.

FURNITURE
■ Ikea has it all: seating, tables, ottomans, pillows, rugs, bath mats (for outdoor parties), even lights, candles, and other such accessories—at smart prices. Available at www.ikea.com or by calling 800-434-IKEA.
■ Everything you need to furnish your house, you'll find at FOREMOST FURNI-TURE. www.foremostfurniture.com or 866-694-6678.

DÉCOR ITEMS
■ Find Astroturf (fake grass) at C.I.T.E DESIGN in New York City: www.cite-design.com or 212-431-7272.
■ Funky wallpaper or wrapping paper for place mats, from HOME DEPOT at 800-430-3376.
■ AMSCAN for everything—decorative bags, confetti, candles, favors, gimmicks, and more: www.amscan.com or 800-284-4333.

LET THERE BE LIGHT
■ CALVIN KLEIN HOME has chic white candles in glass hurricanes on a fabulous silver plate: 800-294-7978.
■ KARMA candles to boost your mood at www.supplycurve.com.
■ MARC JACOBS gardenia-scented candles, sold at SAKS FIFTH AVENUE: www.saksfifthavenue.com or

877-551-SAKS.
■ LAVA has great country orchid floating candles, scented gel candles, and pillar candles: 858-451-7030
■ RESTORATION HARDWARE makes flicker flame lights: www.restoration hardware.com or 800-816-0901.
■ VOTIVO'S aromatherapy glass candles are our favorite. Get Red Currant! www.morningfarm.com or www.thelittlecandleshop.com.
■ URBAN OUTFITTERS sells disco balls: www.urbanoutfitters.com or 800-282-2200.
■ Try BATH & BODY WORKS' Cucumber Melon plug-ins to make your party smell good: www.bathandbody works.com.
■ BED BATH & BEYOND provides all the essentials for your bathroom, bedroom, kitchen, and dining room: 1-800-GO-BEYOND or www.bedbathand beyond.com.
■ LUMI BAGS are bags you put sand and candles in. They are great for outdoor lighting. Subtle, chic, and inexpensive: www.luminarias.com.
■ PHILIPS makes great lightbulbs for entertaining. They come in an assortment of colors and you can find them anywhere. Go to www.philips.com for more information.
■ Set the mood with votive candles in glass holders. INDIANA GLASS COMPANY has traditional white votives and holders. Available at www.lancaster colony.com

FLOWER POWER

■ 1-800-FLOWERS.COM: where a dozen roses can be found for under $10.

■ ERIC BUTER-BAUGH, a Los Angeles florist: 310-247-7120.

■ We've found orchids at TARGET for around $5, available at www.target.com or by calling 800-440-0680.

SOUND FACTORY: COOL COMPILATIONS
■ CAFÉ DEL MAR: www.cafedelmar music.com.
■ HOTEL COSTES: www.plaza101.com, www.saksfifth avenue.com, and www.smokecds. com.
■ FUTURE LOUNGE 03: www.kelkoo.com (UK option).
■ LA MUSIQUE DE PARIS DERNIÈRE: www.kelkoo.com (UK option).
■ MAXIM'S DE PARIS: www.kelkoo. com (UK option).
■ THE STANDARD HOTEL COMPILA-TION: 323-650-9090.
■ Paris's world-renowned BUDDHA BAR is a club with an excellent reputation and its range of CDs is held in similarly high regard. Available from amazon.com or contact 011-33-1-53-05-90-00 or www.buddha bar.com.
■ VH1 sells great compilation '80s CDs. You can find them at most music stores or online at www.vh1.com.
■ Drew's Famous Hula Party: www.drews famous.com (Note: DREW'S FAMOUS makes tons of compilations for any occasion.)

■ WWW.KAZAA.
COM
■ WWW.MP3.COM
■ WWW.LIVEWIRE.
COM

SOUND
FACTORY:
GOING LIVE
■ JUILLIARD
SCHOOL OF
MUSIC:
www.juilliard.edu or
212-799-5000, ext.
313. Ask them for a
referral near you.

SOUND FACTORY: OTHER PLACES TO SHOP FOR MUSIC

■ WWW.AMAZON.COM
■ WWW.BORDERS.COM
■ WWW.BILLBOARD.COM
■ COLETTE, the most famous fashion boutique in Paris, has the coolest CDs: www.colette.tm.fr.
■ JEFFREY NEW YORK, a high-fashion department store where they stock Gucci and groovy music. Call 212-206-1272.
■ POTTERY BARN: www.pottery barn.com or 888-779-5176.
■ WWW.UNIVERSALCLASSICS.COM.
■ WWW.VH1DIVAS.COM.
■ VOYAGE, a chic clothing store in London, makes a great CD. Call the store at 011-44-20-7823-9581 for info.
■ BASE in Miami has a great selection of music for anyone. Go to www.base world.com or go to the store at 939 Lincoln Road, Miami Beach, FL, 305-531-4982.

CHEAP TRICKS

■ Get MOTOROLA hand-held "Talka-bout" walkie-talkies to communicate with your staff during the party. Available at www.motorola.com or by calling 866-289-6686.
■ CLICK CLACK MINTS has tins you can customize: www.clickclack.com or 312-951-1222.
■ SMART ALEX for cheeky party tags, horoscope coasters, and more: www.smartalexinc.com or 773-244-9275.

CHEAP TRICKS: GAMING

■ WWW.BOARDGAMES.COM has old-school games, such as Twister and Connect Four.
■ CRATE & BARREL'S six-in-one game box includes a felt-lined wooden box with metal knobs, chess, checkers, crib-bage, dominoes, backgammon, and cards; the box reverses and doubles as a game board from backgammon to chess/checkers. Contact www.crateandbarrel.com or 800-967-6696.
■ POTTERY BARN also has good game boxes with chess, checkers, dominoes, tic-tac-toe, dice, cards, and more, available at www.potterybarn.com or by calling 888-779-5176.
■ RESTORATION HARDWARE has magnetic darts, game boxes, poker-chip sets, craps, and more at www.restorationhardware.com or 800-816-0901.
■ LAGOON GAMES has everything from mind games to drinking games: www.thelagoongroup.com or 617-437-7285.

OVER-THE-TOP ADDITIONS

■ THE CONTAINER STORE, leading retailer of storage and organization products. For a store near you, please visit www.containerstore.com or call 800-786-7315.

CHAPTER FIVE: WE'LL DRINK TO THAT

GLASSWARE

- IKEA: www.ikea.com or 800-434-IKEA.
- POTTERY BARN: www.pottery barn.com or 888-779-5176.
- PIER 1 has great coasters, wine charms, and bar tools: 800-245-4595 or www.pier1.com.

BAR ACCOUTREMENTS

- Try IKEA, CRATE & BARREL, POTTERY BARN, and TARGET for can and bottle openers, corkscrews, spoons, knives, pitchers, and more: www.ikea.com or 800-434-IKEA; www.crateandbarrel.com or 800-323-6499; www.potterybarn.com or 888-779-5176; www.target.com or 800-440-0680.
- BLENDERS: The WARING PROFESSIONAL and the HAMILTON BEACH PROFESSIONAL are the best. Contact www.waringproducts.com or 800-4-WARING; www.hambeach.com or 800-851-8900. Cuisinart's version is also good: www.cuisinart.com or 800-726-0190.
- BLACK AND DECKER has great tools for the kitchen from blenders to food processors: www.blackanddecker.com.
- Margarita salts and mixes: WWW.SPECTRUMGOURMET.COM.
- CALIENTE MARGARITA SALTER from CRATE & BARREL: www.crateand barrel.com or 800-323-6499.
- FROZEN DRINK MACHINE. Available at WWW.FRONTGATE.COM or 800-626-6488.
- ICE SHAVER: HAWAII ICE is a retro-looking number that turns blocks of ice into fluff. Available at Back to Basics: 800-688-1989 or www.backtobasics products.com.
- SNO-MOTION SNOW CONE KIT from BACK TO BASICS comes with an ice shaver and all the things you need for snow cones, including a recipe book: www.backtobasicsproducts.com or 800-688-1989.
- ORIGINAL SMOOTHIE MAKER is available at BACK TO BASICS: www.backtobasicsproducts.com or 800-688-1989; or TARGET, www.target.com or 800-440-0680.
- LICKITY SIP ICE-POP MAKERS, complete with a built-in spout that churns out four drinks per package. See TARGET at www.target.com or 800-440-0680.
- The SHOT STEWARD, a revolving shot-pouring contraption that holds four or six bottles at once, from www.front gate.com or 800-626-6488.
- PROGRESSIVE INTERNATIONAL is a leading designer of a diversified kitchen ware and entertaining tool: 800-426-7101 or www.progressiveintl.com.

SERVERS

- ABC BARTENDING SCHOOLS, since 1977. There are locations across the country: www.abcbartending.com or 888-COCKTAIL.

MIXERS/TONICS

- MR & MRS T's makes great mixers. From Daiquiris to Bloody Marys, you can't go wrong: www.motts.com.
- Try HOLLAND HOUSE mixers: www.hollandhouse.com.
- Escape to paradise with MARGARITA-VILLE MARGARITA MIX: www.motts.com.

WACKY WAYS TO GO BOTTOMS-UP

- 7-Eleven Slurpees at 7-ELEVEN: www.711.com.
- Litecubes, light-up cubes to illuminate drinks: WWW.LITE CUBE.COM.
- To serve drinks with a professional finish, rim the glasses with COCKTAIL CANDY from Planet Sugar. It is available in the following flavors: Apple, Banana, Blueberry, Cherry, Chocolate, Coffee, Cranberry, Grape, Lemon, Lime, Mango, Peach, Pineapple, Raspberry, Strawberry, Tangerine, Vanilla, and Watermelon: www.cocktail candy.com or 323-276-3905.
- Personalize your margaritas with CHAMBORD: 800-523-3811 or www.chambord online.com.

■ EL PASO CHILE COMPANY makes Martini 101 Kits and Freezaritas, where you just add the alcohol and freeze, and a BBQ 101 Kit with all the BBQ essentials: 888-4-SALSAS or www.elpasochile.com.

■ ROSE'S COCKTAIL INFUSIONS are a great addition to any cocktail menu. They come in Cranberry Twist, Blue Raspberry, and Sour Apple. Mix one part infusions with one part vodka or the spirit of your choice. Available at www.rosesinfusions.com.

BEER

■ SAMUEL ADAMS CHOCOLATE BOCK will be the talk of your party. It includes an exclusive blend of Scharffen Berger chocolate made solely for this beer. Consumers can most likely find it at grocery stores, supermarkets, liquor stores, and beer distributors.

WINE

■ Go to WWW.WINE.COM to buy wine. You can also go to the party planner and it will figure out how much wine you will need and what kind of wine to serve with the food you are serving.

■ MIO VINO makes wine charms, bracelets that tie around the bottom of the neck of the glass and act as markers so your guests can keep track of their drinks: www.mywinejewels.com or 425-210-4043.

COCKTAILS AND CANDY

■ CADBURY ADAMS makes Swedish Fish and Sour Patch Kids. They are great additions to spice up cocktails.

You can find them at any candy store. They are also perfect for placing in glass bowls at any party. For more information, call 877-492-3267.

BOOKS WE RECOMMEND

■ *The Complete Idiot's Guide to Mixing Drinks,* by Alan Axelrod and The Players.

■ *The Pocket Idiot's Guide to Bartending,* by Alan Axelrod.

■ *The New York Bartender's Guide,* by Sally Ann Berk.

■ *Shaken Not Stirred: A Celebration of the Martini,* by Jared M. Brown and Anastatia R. Miller.

■ *Mr. Boston Official Bartender's and Party Guide,* by Renee Cooper and Chris Morris.

■ *The Bartender's Bible: 1001 Mixed Drinks and Everything You Need to Know to Set Up Your Bar,* by Gary Regan.

■ *Savoy Cocktail Book* by Henry Craddock. A classic book of cocktails that dates back to 1930. You will find it at Bergdorf Goodman: 800-558-1855 or www.bergdorfgoodman.com.

COFFEE, TEA, OR ME?

■ ELIXIR TONICS AND TEAS, 8612 Melrose Avenue, West Hollywood, California 90049, 310-657-9300.

■ Contact COFFEE BEAN & TEA LEAF to order Ice Blended Kits: 800-TEA-LEAF or www.coffeebean.com.

CHAPTER SIX: FOOD, GLORIOUS FOOD

ALL KINDS OF FOOD
■ Bread and cheese sticks: WWW.CHEESESTICKS.COM or 800-643-0573.
■ HADLEY'S DRIED FRUIT: www.hadley fruitorchard.com or 800-854-5655.
■ E.A.T., a division of Eli Zabar's, has the best appetizers and breads: www.elizabar.com
■ TERRA CHIPS are the perfect snacks for parties. They have a huge assortment of chips: www.terrachips.com.
■ CARRS crackers: 269-961-2000 or www.carrs-online.com.
■ For amazing gourmet food from France, try WWW.FAUCHON.COM.
■ ACAPULCO TO-GO: www.acapulco restaurants.com or 800-735-3501.
■ BAJA FRESH: www.bajafresh.com.
■ DOMINOS: www.dominos.com or 888-DOMINOS.
■ H&H BAGELS: www.handhbagel.com or 800-49-BAGEL.
■ IN-N-OUT BURGER: www.innout burger.com or 800-786-1000.
■ JOE'S STONE CRAB: www.joesstonecrab.com.
■ JOHNNY ROCKETS: www.johnny rockets.com.
■ MCDONALD'S: www.mcdonalds.com or 800-244-6227.

■ BURGER KING: www.burgerking.com.
■ KENTUCKY FRIED CHICKEN: www.kfc.com or 800-225-5532.
■ TACO BELL: www.tacobell.com.
■ NOBU in New York: 212-941-1976. (Note: There are also locations in Las Vegas, London, Malibu, and Miami.)
■ OMAHA STEAKS: www.omaha steaks.com or 800-960-8400.
■ ZABAR'S: www.zabars.com or 212-787-2000.

WELL EQUIPPPED
■ CALVIN KLEIN HOME has great dishes, serving trays, and glassware: 877-256-7373.
■ Caviar spoons, toast point trays, and accompaniments: WWW.PET ROSSIAN.COM or 800-828-9241.
■ The Pop-Up Hotdog Cooker for gimmicky food: At HAMMACHER SCHLEMMER: www.hammacher. com or 800-543-3366
■ CRATE & BARREL for plates, bowls, serving trays, etc.: www.crateand barrel.com or 800-967-6696.
■ TARGET for everything you'd need in a kitchen . . . and then some: www.target.com or 800-862-1973.
■ REAL LIFE BASIC in Miami Beach, Florida, is a store that carries great serving dishes for appetizers and dinners: 305-604-1984 or www.reallife basic.com.

COOKBOOKS WE RECOMMEND
■ *Chef Daniel Boulud: Cooking in New York City,* by Daniel Boulud and Peter Kaminsky.
■ *The Barefoot Contessa Cookbook: Secrets from the East Hampton Specialty Food Store for Simple Food and Party Platters You Can Make at Home,* by Ina Garten.
■ *Top Secret Restaurant Recipes: Creating Kitchen Clones from America's Favorite Restaurant Chains,* by Todd Wilbur.
■ *The Balthazar Cookbook,* by Keith McNally, Riad Nasr, and Lee Nanson.

SAUCES
■ JEAN-GEORGES VONGERICHTEN: www.starchefs.com.
■ NOBU: 212-941-1976.
■ PETER LUGER (steak sauce): www.peterluger. com or 718-387-7400.
■ RAO'S Italian sauces: www.raos.com.
■ GIORGIO BALDI sauces include White Truffle Oil, Tomato Basil, and Arrabbiata. Available at 310-573-1660 or www.gior giobaldi.com.

CHAPTER SEVEN: SWEET TOOTH

HAVE YOUR CAKE AND EAT IT, TOO

■ BASKIN-ROBBINS for picture cakes: www.baskinrobbins.com or 800-859-5339.

■ FERRARA BAKERY in Little Italy, New York City, where you can get Italian pastries and ice cream: www.ferrara cafe.com or 212-226-6150.

■ HANSEN'S CAKES in Los Angeles, where all celebs get their cakes: 323-936-4332.

■ JOE'S STONE CRAB for the best Key lime pie: www.joesstonecrab.com or 800-260-CRAB.

■ LITTLE PIE COMPANY, a New York City staple that's known for their sour cream apple walnut pie and pumpkin cheesecake: www.littlepiecompany.com or 877-872-PIES.

■ MAGNOLIA BAKERY in New York City makes the best cupcakes: 212-462-2572.

■ MASTURBAKERS in New York City sells custom-order cakes shaped like body parts: www.masturbakers.com or 212-475-0476.

■ MRS. BEASLEY'S in Los Angeles has gift baskets, cookies, and cakes for every holiday and occasion: www.mrs beasleys.com or 800-710-7742.

■ POLLY'S CAKES in Ohio designs cakes however you want them. Some of their cakes have won awards! www.pollyscakes.com or 503-230-1986.

■ BOULEY BAKERY in New York City: 212-964-2525.

■ PUBLIX has amazing cakes at great prices. Go to www.publix.com to find the Publix closest to you.

COOKIES AND BROWNIES AND CHOCOLATES, OH MY!

■ COOKIES BY DESIGN for bouquets of theme-shaped cookies with great saying, which make great desserts as well as gifts: www.cookiesbydesign.com or 800-945-2665.

■ MADELAINE has good cheap chocolate in fun shapes—dollars, gaming chips, etc.—for theme parties: www.madelainechocolate.com or 800-322-1505.

■ MARTINE'S CHOCOLATE, in BLOOMINGDALE'S. They make high-end, seasonally themed chocolate: www.martineschocolate.com or 212-705-2347.

■ MRS. FIELD'S, a classic cookie place that sells decorative cookie cakes, which is a good substitution for a birthday cake: www.mrsfields.com or 800-COOKIES.

■ PETERBROOKE CHOCOLATE for chocolate-covered popcorn, among other chocolate-covered treats: www.peterbrooke.com or 904-398-2488.

■ RICHART chocolates is a high-end, decorative chocolatier. You can have photos and words scanned on your chocolate: www.richart.com or 888-RICHART.

■ SCHARFFEN BERGER baking chocolate from Williams-Sonoma and many grocery stores: www.williams sonoma.com or 877-812-6235.

■ TATE'S BAKE SHOP for the best chocolate chip cookies and muffins. It is in the Hamptons: 631-283-9830.

A COOKBOOK WE RECOMMEND

■ *The Buttercup Bake Shop Cookbook: More Than 80 Recipes for Irresistible, Old-Fashioned Treats*, by Jennifer Appel.

HOME, SWEET HOME

■ Alphabet letter molds: WWW.SUG ARCRAFT.COM.

■ WILLIAMS-SONOMA for animal cookie cutters, cookie presses, cookie sheets, bowls, cake pans and stands, cream whippers, fondue kits, measuring cups and spoons, mixers, ice-cream makers, spatulas, knives, and more: www.williams sonoma.com or 877-812-6235.

■ CRATE & BARREL stocks all sorts of dessert and kitchen supplies, fondue sets, birthday kits, platters, utensils, a tasting set, and more: www.crate andbarrel.com or 800-323-6499.

■ KRUPS for mixers: www.krups. com or 800-526-5377.

■ Pretzel Fun Kit from AUNTIE ANNE'S: www. auntieannes.com or 717-442-4766.

■ TEUSCHER chocolates. They are known for their champagne truffles: www.teuscher.com or 800-554-0924 or 212-246-4416.

■ POPCORN FACTORY has a wide assortment of popcorn available in many colors and flavors, such as Kettle Corn, Caramel, and White Cheddar: www.popcornfactory.com, 800-541-2676.

■ BINDI DESSERTS can be found at www.bindidessert.com and are also available at www.neimanmarcus.com.

■ Macadamia Hearts from LA CONVER-SATION in Los Angeles: 310-858-0950.

■ FAIRY TALE BROWNIES have brownies that come in 12 Fairy Tale flavors. They taste great, you can freeze them and they make great gifts: www.brownies.com, 1-800-FAIRYTALE

I SCREAM, YOU SCREAM . . .

■ COLD STONE CREAMERY: www.cold stonecreamery.com or 480-348-1704.

■ CIAO BELLA'S GELATO: www.ciaobellagelato.com or 800-GELATO-3.

■ MISTER SOFTEE: 856-939-4103.

■ SERENDIPITY 3's Frozen Hot Chocolate: 800-672-9466 or 212-838-3531 or purchase from Williams-Sonoma at www.williams sonoma.com or 877-812-6235.

■ GOOD HUMOR ICE CREAM HELPER: www.goodhumor.com.

■ Ice cream with berries or aged vinegar from LE CIRQUE 2000 in New York City: 212-303-7788. But you can make it at home!

■ CARVEL ice cream for their famous Flying Saucers: www.carvel.com.

I WANT CANDY!

■ AMSCAN. Call 914-345-2020 or go to www.amscan.com for cute bags to put the candy in for your guests.

■ DYLAN'S CANDY BAR, a chic candy shop in New York City where you can find rare candy concoctions as well as bulk everything, amazing prepackaged baskets, and a party room for rent: www.dylanscandybar.com or 646-735-0078.

■ M&M'S COLOR WORKS to order M&Ms in custom colors: www.mmmars.com or 800-627-7852.

■ MICHAEL RECCHIUTI marshmallows at WILLIAMS-SONOMA: www.williams sonoma.com or 877-812-6235.

■ Paper candy cups and peppermint snaps from WILLIAMS-SONOMA.

■ CITY BAKERY in Manhattan for marshmallow treats: 212-366-1414.

■ ROCKY MOUNTAIN FUDGE COM-PANY: www.rockychoc.com or 604-298-2462.

■ Impress your guests with FAUCHON'S fancy French candy: www.fauchon.com.

■ GOOD KARMAL sells sweet caramels wrapped in fortunes at www.good karmal.com

■ NEIMAN MARCUS has amazing candy apples by Mrs. Prindables. They are available covered in chocolate and caramel, and make great gifts. www.mrsprindables.com.

LOOK, MA! NO GUILT!

■ Froze Fruit: 888-700-4700.

■ Fruit from Whole Foods: www.whole-food.com (also makes a great gift!).

■ Sharon's Sorbet: www.sharons-sorbet.com, or contact your local supermarket to see if they sell this tasty treat.

■ Tasti D-Light: www.tastidlite.com or 212-685-0210.

■ The Zone bars: 888-343-8661 or www.zone perfect.com.

■ World of Nuts for sugar-free chewies: 212-724-5319.

■ Weight Watchers for healthy snack options: www.weight watchers.com.

Dear Elisabeth,

Thank you for your weekend. It was a bea[...]

warm regards,

John & Fisher

[anne bruno] FLORAL & EVENT DESIGN, NEW YORK, T. 212 766 5[...]

CHAPTER EIGHT: OH, BEHAVE!

GUEST BEHAVIOR: HOUSEWARMING AND THANK-YOU GIFTS

- CRYSTAL VODKA ice cooler with matching vodka flutes at a home supply store or www.petrossian.com or 800-828-9241.
- HADLEY'S dried fruit and nuts: www.hadleyfruitorchard.com or 800-854-5655.
- Money cards from ROBIN MAGUIRE that say "Just a little $omething," and "A Gift for You" in groovy fonts: www.robin-maguire.com or 800-922-2259.
- MONOGRAMMED ANYTHING: pajamas, vases, picture frames, cocktail napkins, stationery, dictionaries, leatherbound books of quotable sayings. Log on to WWW.TRACEYROSS.COM or see the Monogram Shop in East Hampton (631-329-3379) for details. Also POMEGRANATE: 212-288-4409 Note: Lara's favorite gift is MEYER'S LUGGAGE'S leather-bound black, brown, or green photo album, monogrammed with something personal. Call 561-655-5644 in Palm Beach to order.
- MRS. BEASLEY'S THANK-YOU GIFT BASKETS contain everything from yummy combinations of muffins and cookies to wine for $24.95 to $89.95. Available at www.mrsbeasleys.com or by calling 800-710-7742.
- MRS. FIELD'S cookies-of-the-month, a new cookie each month: www.mrs fields.com or 800-COOKIES.
- Pottery from THE IVY AT THE SHORE in L.A. for $16 to $100: 310-393-3113.
- KITSON in Los Angeles has the perfect gift for any hostess: 310-859-2652.
- FRED SEGAL in L.A. has great gift options from a great apothecary, from infant gifts to housewares: 323-651-4129.
- RON HERMAN, with a location in Fred Segal, also has great gifts, including Jet T-shirts: 323-651-4129.
- FREDERIC FEKKAI products: www.fekkai.com.
- RALPH LAUREN chrome picture frames at Ralph Lauren at BLOOMINGDALE'S and any Ralph Lauren boutique.
- Silk-screened gift cards and retro notebooks from KATE'S PAPERIE: www.katespaperie.com or 888-941-9169.
- "Six Months of Caviar," a salty package of caviar-to-taste each month, $650 at WWW.PETROSSIAN.COM or by calling 800-828-9241. Chic tip: Petrossian's caviar solitaire, a 50-gram serving of caviar with a mother-of-pearl spoon, is also a great gift.
- SMYTHSON'S BESPOKE STATIONERY GIFT SET includes 100 engraved cards and printed envelopes for $456: www.smythson.com or 877-769-8476.
- SEE'S boxed lollipops: www.sees.com or 800-347-7337.
- Sweets! ETHEL M.'S gift plan: January is dreamy whites, February is truffle hearts, March is fruit chews and jelly beans, April is satin cremes, May is pecan and caramel, June is almond butter crisps, July is chocolate sauce, August is peanut brittle, September is nuts and caramel, October calls for caramel apples, November is about silk truffles, and December is a deluxe assortment. Twelve, six, or three months of chocolate treats from $50 to $300: www.ethelm.com or 800-438-4356.

BOOKS WE
RECOMMEND
■ *A Gentleman
Entertains: A
Guide to Making
Memorable
Occasions
Happen,* by John
Bridges and
Bryan Curtis.
■ *Esquire's
Handbook for
Hosts.*
■ *Gentleman's
Guide to Life:
What Every Guy
Should Know
About Living
Large, Loving
Well, Feeling
Strong, and
Looking Good,*
by Steve
Friedman.
■ *Things You
Need to Be Told*
by the Etiquette
Girls.
■ *Emily Post's
Etiquette,* by
Peggy Post.
■ *Emily Post's
Entertaining: A
Classic Guide to
Adding Elegance
and Ease to Any
Festive
Occasion,* by
Peggy Post.
■ *Toasts,* by Paul
Dickson.
■ *Town & Country
Social Graces:
Words of Wisdom
on Civility in a
Changing
Society,* edited
by Jim Brosseau.

■ The New York breakfast basket from ZABAR'S comes with fresh bagels, nova lox, cream cheese, chocolate babka, cinnamon rugalach, raisin and health breads, preserves, Irish oatmeal, cinnamon granola, yogurt, coffee, and a coffee mug, packaged in a wooden crate with Hebrew National mustard. Available at www.zabars.com.
■ Yummy facial, beauty, nail, goddess, or bathtub kits for $30 to $40 each at WWW.JAQUAGIRLS.COM.
■ Try a basket filled with gourmet organic food, elegant coffee, or wine and cheese from WHOLE FOODS: www.wholefoods.com.
■ SCOOP is a chic clothing store famous for its assortment of designers and Juicy Couture, as well as gift certificates and cute accessories from other chic designers: www.scoopnyc.com.
■ LINKS OF LONDON, a store in New York City, frames for glasses: 212-867-0258.
■ THE GOLD KIOSK is a great place to find interesting gifts. Gold Kiosk stores can be found in Ian Schrager's hotels, including the Mondrian in Los Angeles and the Delano in Miami Beach: 305-673-2535.
■ AQUA SPA, the rooftop spa at the Delano in Miami Beach, has amazing products that are perfect gifts: www.ianschragerhotels.com or 305-672-2000.
■ MALIBU COLONY COMPANY is the cutest gift shop in Malibu and has amazing gifts: 310-317-0177 or 23410 Civic Center Way, Malibu, CA 90265.
■ LADY PRIMROSE has perfect gifts, including lotions, bath salts, and perfumes: www.ladyprimrose.com.

■ Go above and beyond as a guest. Show your hostess that you really appreciate her hospitality. Go to WWW.MAC.COM and you can personalize an iPod as a gift.
■ TASCHEN has amazing coffee table books that we like to give as hostess gifts. You can find a book to fit any hostess at www.taschen.com.
■ Having HEWLETT PACKARD digital cameras and printers at your party is like having a photographer on hand. They are easy to use and guests will love playing with them. Take pictures and print them out to send home with guests: www.hp.com.
■ C.Z. Guest candles by SLATKIN & CO. come in assorted scents, such as Jardin de Fleurs (green, $28.00), Jardin de Roses (pink, $28.00), and Templeton (small, $34.00; large, $65.00). Available at Neiman Marcus: 800-937-9146.

TÊTE-À-TÊTE
BRUSH UP ON YOUR CONVERSATION SKILLS
■ WWW.NYTIMES.COM for current events.
■ THE NEW YORK *POST'S* "Page Six" for celebrity dirt, www.pagesix.com.
■ *US WEEKLY* for pages and pages of celebrity dirt; visit www.usmagazine.com for subscription info.
■ *L. A. CONFIDENTIAL* magazine, *HAMPTONS* magazine, and *GOTHAM* magazine: 800-566-3622.

OUT! OUT! DAMN SPOT!
■ MADAME PAULETTE DRY CLEANERS in Manhattan sells the best stain removal kit, 212-838-6827.

BOOKS WE
RECOMMEND
FOR THANK
YOU NOTES
■ *Crane's Blue
Book of
Stationery: The
Styles and
Etiquette of
Letters, Notes,
and Invitations*,
by Steven L.
Feinberg.
■ *Writing Thank
You Notes:
Finding the
Perfect Words,*
by Gabrielle
Goodwin and
David
MacFarlane.
■ *The Art of the
Handwritten
Note,* by
Margaret
Shepard.

CHAPTER NINE: ANALYZE THIS!

CLAMBAKE

DÉCOR: THE OUTDOOR LOUNGE

■ Eleven-foot-tall outdoor canopy from HAMMACHER SCHLEMMER: www.hammacher.com or 800-321-1484.

■ Cube structured beanbags from POTTERY BARN: www.potterybarn.com or 888-779-5176.

■ Nantucket table and chairs, Carmel table and chairs, fiesta striped umbrella, all from CRATE & BARREL: www.crate andbarrel.com or 1-800-323-6499.

DÉCOR: TABLETOP AND SUCH

■ Boston Warehouse Skewers in stainless steel from ZABAR'S: www.zabars.com or 800-697-6301.

■ CRATE & BARREL'S lobster napkins, galvanized tubs, and Oceanique dishtowels: www.crateandbarrel.com or 800-323-6499.

■ SEA SHELL WORLD, shells from $7.99 to $9.99: www.seashellworld.com or 888-9-SHELLS.

■ Table linens from WHOLESALE TABLE LINENS at www.wholesale-table-linens.com or 866-827-4177.

■ Transparent polycarbonate tumblers, pitchers, and punch bowls from FRONTGATE: www.frontgate.com or 800-626-6488.

■ SOLO PLASTIC CUPS: www.solo cup.com.

FOOD, GLORIOUS FOOD!

■ HAMPTON CLAMBAKE AND CATERING COMPANY: www.hampton clambake.com or 631-324-8620.

■ THE CLAM MAN: www.theclam man.com or 610-874-5694.

■ TATE'S BAKE SHOP, Southampton: 631-283-9830.

THE SOUND OF MUSIC

■ YAMAHA GENERATOR for outdoor equipment: www.yamaha.com or 800-88-YAMAHA.

OVER-THE-TOP ADDITIONS

■ French Resort Solar Shower, an outdoor shower, a personalized water playground, and an outdoor heater, all from HAMMACHER SCHLEMMER: www.hammacher.com or 1-800-321-1484.

■ Hammocks from CRATE & BARREL: www.crateandbarrel.com or 800-323-6499.

■ Residential misting fan from FRONTGATE: www.frontgate.com or 800-626-6488.

■ ORIENTAL TRADING COMPANY has tons of party favors and a great selection of products for your clambake: 800-875-8480 or www.oriental trading.com.

BARBIE AND KEN THEME PARTY

PRINTING AND INVITATIONS

■ ALPINE PRINTING, New York City: 212-989-4198.

■ HALLMARK store, $4.99 for a card with Barbie's face, Barbie stickers at www.hallmark.com.

■ JAM PAPER AND ENVELOPES in New York City; a pack of envelopes is just $25: 212-255-4593.

■ KINKO'S: 1-800-2KINKOS, www.kinkos.com.

LIGHT ON!

■ Candle torches, galvanized star lights, tapered fiber outdoor lights, and paper lanterns, all from CRATE & BARREL: www.crateand barrel.com or 800-323-6499.

■ Christmas lights from CHRISTMAS LIGHTS ETC. at www.christmas lightsetc.com or 1-866-XMAS-ETC.

■ LAVA CANDLES: www.lavacandle. com or 1-800-6-CANDLE.

■ Multi-fuel brass lanterns, HAMMACHER SCHLEMMER: www.hammacher. com or 800-321-1484.

■ Stainless steel and copper garden torches from FRONTGATE: www.frontgate.com or 800-626-6488.

DÉCOR: WELCOME TO THE DOLLHOUSE
- Barbie dolls: WWW.TOYSRUS.COM.
- Confetti, pink votive candles, and pink helium balloons from AMSCAN: www.amscan.com or 800-284-4333.
- KETEL ONE ice sculpture: www.ketelone.com.

SWEET TOOTH
- ETHEL M. pink chocolates, edible silver, and pink lip gloss: 800-438-4356 or www.ethelm.com.
- KRISPY KREME doughnuts or stacked cake (cake starts at $250): www.krispykreme.com.
- M&Ms in pink: 800-627-7852 or www.mmmars.com.

AN AFTERNOON TEA
TABLEWARE AND FAVORS
- Clear glass pitchers, citronella candles, and glass bowls for water lilies and floating flowers, all from CRATE & BARREL: 800-323-6499 or www.crate andbarrel.com.
- Disposable KODAK cameras at RITE AID or TARGET: www.riteaid.com or 800-RITE-AID; www.target.com or 800-440-0680.
- To make the ice cubes like they do at Las Ventanas, buy ice trays that make ice cubes shaped as rings and sticks at WWW.PROGRESSIVEINTL.COM. They also have cool products like ice-cream sandwich makers, ice shavers, and just about anything you can think of to use in the kitchen.

DRINKS
- Make your own COFFEE BEAN & TEA LEAF ICE BLENDEDS (makes eight 16-ounce drinks): 32 ounces coffee extract ($11.95), 20 ounces powder ($7.50); order HBH coffee extract at 800-TEA-LEAF or www.coffeebean.com.

FURNITURE
- Buy from DESIGN WITHIN REACH (Jasper Morrison's Air Chair, $75) or the Eros chair by Philippe Starck for Kartel, $370): 800-944-2233 or www.dwr.com.
- Rent famous pieces like the lip sofa and the bubble chair at WWW.AID20C.COM.

LIGHTING
- Citronella candles: square stoneware cachepots and candles in aqua and blue, $15.95 at CRATE & BARREL: 800-323-6499 or www.crateandbarrel.com.

FLOWERS
- Water-lily bowls in different sizes (12.5 x 4.5 inches is $21.95) at CRATE & BARREL: 800-323-6499 or www.crate andbarrel.com.

MUSIC
- POTTERY BARN *Dinner at 8* jazz compilation CD ($28) includes twenty-four songs by jazz greats Ella Fitzgerald, Chet Baker, Nat "King" Cole, Nina Simone, and Peggy Lee: 888-779-5176 or www.potterybarn.com.

FLOWERS
- Eric Buterbaugh, L.A. florist: 310-247-7120.

LIGHTING
- Pink votive candles at Amscan: www.amscan.com or 800-284-4333.

A BEAUTY PARTY
INVITATIONS
- ROBIN MAGUIRE (www.robin-maguire.com or 800-998-0323) and Studio Z Mendocino (www.studio-z.com or 707-964-9448).

PRODUCTS AND SUCH FOR HANDS AND FEET
- ALMAY'S 5 Days to Grow Nail Conditioning Solution ($6.99), Well-Conditioned Cuticle Oil ($6.99), Massage & Grow Nail and Cuticle Wax ($6.99), or Fluoride Plus Shatter Proof Top-Coat: www.almay.com or 800-992-5629.
- Base-coat polish by NAILTIQUE: www.cvs.com or your local drugstore.
- BLISSLAB'S FrigiFeet Foot Mask, $22 and Hot Salt Scrub, $38: www.bliss world.com or 888-243-8825.
- BUFFSPA for manicure or pedicure: Bergdorf Goodman, 212-872-8624 (phone) or 212-872-2797 (fax).
- Colored polish from ESSIE: www.essie.com or 718-726-5000; SALLY HANSEN: www.sallyhansen.com or 800-953-5080; or REVLON: www.revlon.com or 800-473-8566. $3.49 to $7.50.
- CONAIR'S Remote Control foot spa, $69.99 at Target: www.target.com or 800-440-0680.
- DESIGN-A-NAIL kit for $29.99 at Target: www.target com or 800-440-0680.
- DESIGN-A-NAIL BY DEE for creating nail art at home: www.as-seen-on-tv-discounts.com.
- JOHNSON & JOHNSON Q-tips and cotton balls, $1.69: www.jnj.com.
- LA CROSS cuticle trimmers and pushers and Smooth-It Foot Wand: www.cvs.com.
- NAIL ART at New York spas like Buff, Rescue Aromatherapy: 212-431-3805.
- Nail drier by HAMMACHER SCHLEMMER and paraffin kit for hands and feet for $179.95: 800-543-3366 or www.hammacher.com.
- Peppermint Foot Lotion for $14 at BODY SHOP: www.thebodyshop.com.
- REVLON nail clippers ($2.39) and REVITASPA footbath ($49.99): www.revlon.com or www.target.com.
- SALLY HANSEN Acetone Free Nail Polish Remover pads. Nails and Cuticles Crème, $5.95, and Mega Shine Extended Wear Top Coat ($5.95): www.sallyhansen.com.
- Toesie Brush and Pumice by LA CROSS: www.cvs.com.
- H_2O+ makes fab water-based skin-care products: www.h2oplus.com or 800-242-2284.
- AQUA SPA is a great spa with amazing products for mani-pedi parties at the Delano Hotel in Miami Beach: 305-672-2000.
- REVLON has all the tools necessary for your own mani-pedi party: www.revlon.com.
- ORLY not only has great polish for your mani-pedis, they also have great mani-pedi kits: www.orlyproducts.com.

BEAUTY KITS
■ ESSIE SPA PEDICURE MINI KIT with marine sea salts, an exfoliating foot scrub, a hydro-masque, and a ylang ylang foot and massage oil for $35: www.essie.com or 718-726-5000.
■ JAQUAGIRLS prepacked paint cans are filled with products like aro-matherapy soaks, scrubs, toe sepa-rators, nail files, and a pumice stone for $29: www.jacquagirls. com.
■ SEPHORA'S MINI BEAUTY PARLOR KIT has cherry facial scrub, aloe vera toner, jojoba facial moisturizer, peppermint-scented glimmer polish, and a pumice stone for $28: www.sephora.com or Bloomingdale's, Nordstrom, Sephora, or Henri Bendel.
■ REVLON'S EXPOSE YOUR TOES package comes with a deluxe nail clipper, cushioned shaper, manicure stick, and two toe separator sandals for $4.99: www.revlon.com or 800-473-8566.

FLIP-FLOPS
■ GAP ribbon-strap thongs: www.gap.com or 800-GAP-STYLE.
■ J. CREW classic flip-flop: www.jcrew.com or 800-562-0258.
■ KENNETH COLE REACTION Bedazzled satin thongs: www.ken nethcole.com or 800-KEN-COLE.
■ Mella terry-cloth flip-flops at FLIP FLOP TRUNK SHOW: www.Flip FlopTrunkShow.com.
■ OLD NAVY raffia-strap flip-flops: www.oldnavy.com.

BROWS
■ ANASTASIA, L.A. "star plucker," has a kit with brow stencils, shapers, scissors, tweezers, pre-tweeze gel, and a five-step guide for $125: 310-273-3155 or at Henri Bendel. (Also makes a great gift!)

MASSAGE
■ HAMMACHER SCHLEMMER'S neck and shoulder massager for $59.95: 800-321-1481 or www.hammacher.com.

EDIBLES
■ SMINTS: www.smints.com.
■ ALTOIDS mints: www.altoids.com.
■ Hors d'oeuvre plates for $17.50 at GOODMANS: www.goodmans.net.

BOOKS
■ *The Little Zen Companion,* by David Schiller.

MARK, THE NEW BEAUTY EXPERIENCE FROM AVON, IS MAKEUP YOU CAN BUY AND SELL

Become a Mark representative and treat all the young women you know to a Mark social beauty party where you can be social and beautiful, make friends, and make money. Here's how . . .

Set up your space with aromatherapy candles, comfy floor pillows, and new age music to create a zen-like ambiance. Stock up on supplies like nail files, foot soak tubs, and nail polish remover, and don't forget your favorite Mark-Set-Shine Rapid Action Nail Enamel shades. Then round up some local manicurists from your favorite salon. With sixteen different radiant shades from Mark, they can cre-ate fun, innovative designs for all your guests. When the party is over, give each guest a parting gift—Mark minicure Nail Color Doubles—and tell your guests to go to www.meetmark.com to sign up and become a Mark representative.

INVITATIONS
■ Cards emblazoned with Indian gods ($1.00 each at WWW.WISHY-WASHYCARDS.COM).

AN INDIAN FEAST
FOOD, GLORIOUS FOOD!
■ ROSE OF BOMBAY in the East Village, New York City: 212-982-8848.

DRINKS
■ COFFEE BEAN & TEA LEAF, 800-TEA-LEAF.
■ KINGFISHER BEER ($3.75 for six) at your local liquor store.
■ RED BULL: www.redbull.com or at your local grocer.

DESSERTS
■ CARVEL'S Flying Saucers: www.carvel.com or 860-257-4448.
■ Cases of chicly packaged mints for $2.95 at www.hintmint.com.
■ ETHEL M. orange liqueur, crème de menthe, and almond-butter crisp truffles, and raspberry truffle hearts ($23.50 per box) and gold-foil-wrapped chocolate roses: www.ethelm.com or 800-438-4356.
■ White Rabbit cream candies or ginger candies from GOVINDA'S for $3.75 per bag: 310-204-3263.
■ Reed's Ginger Candies from GOVINDA'S are a great classic candy that is the perfect finishing touch for an Indian dinner: 310-204-3263.

DÉCOR: THIS WAY TO BOMBAY
■ Bangle bracelets as napkin rings, gold incense holders, Plexiglas pictures of Indian gods, and black and gold vases, all at GOVINDA'S, an Indian shop in Los Angeles: 310-204-3263.
■ Gold doilies, gold-rimmed plates, and golden confetti, available at AMSCAN: www.amscan.com or 800-284-4333.

■ Mokuba mesh wrapping paper for place mats at SOOLIP PAPERIE & PRESS ($10.95 per roll): 310-360-0545.
■ Pitchers, punch bowls, and serving platters from CRATE & BARREL: www.crateandbarrel.com or 800-323-6499.

FLOWERS
■ Black and gold vases from GOVINDA'S, $6.99 to $9.99: 310-204-3263.
■ ERIC BUTERBAUGH, L.A. florist to the stars: 310-247-7120.
■ White and pink roses for $1.00 each at 800-FLOWERS or 1800flowers.com.

SERVERS
■ MODEL BARTENDERS: 212-499-0886.
■ ROSE OF BOMBAY in the East Village, New York City: 212-982-8848.

ATTIRE
■ Balinese shoes for $5 to $8 at GOVINDA'S: 310-204-3263.
■ Sarongs for $10 each at GAVINDA'S: 310-204-3262.

LIGHTING
■ 60-watt amber bulbs from TARGET: www.target.com or 800-440-0680.
■ Glass bowl for floating floral-shaped candles from AMSCAN: www.amscan.com or 800-284-4333.
■ Votive candles from AMSCAN for 75 cents each: www.amscan.com or 800-284-4333.

FAVORS
■ Indian gift bags for $5 at GOVINDA'S: 310-204-3263.
■ PARTY ON LA CIENEGA: 310-659-8717.

A HANGOVER BRUNCH
DÉCOR: HOSPITAL CHIC
■ HANGOVER HELPER PILLS to decorate the tables: www.hangover helper.com or 800-838-6228.

■ Aromatherapy has candles made specifically for hangovers. You can find them at RESCUE BEAUTY SPA: www.rescucosmetique.com or www.aromatherapy.com

FOOD, GLORIOUS FOOD!
■ CINN-A-BONS, 888-288-ROLL or www.cinnabon.com.

■ H&H BAGELS, which can be sent anywhere: www.handhbagel.com or 800-49-BAGEL.

■ ZABAR'S in New York City for platters, bagels, cream cheeses, and more: www.zabars.com.

■ BARNEY GREENGRASS in New York City for smoked fish platters and Jewish soul food, which can be sent anywhere: 212-724-4707.

■ Buy granola from EJ'S LUNCHEON-ETTE in New York City, 212-472-0600, or the GREENHOUSE SPA in Arlington, Texas, 214-654-9800. Note: EJ's has yummy lowfat honey granola.

OVER-THE-TOP ADDITIONS
■ WE CARE DETOX PLAN: www.wecare spa.com.

GUYS' NIGHT OUT
INVITATIONS
■ ROBIN MAGUIRE: www.robin maguire.com or 800-998-0323.

DÉCOR: SOMETHING TED TURNER WOULD APPROVE OF
All from AMSCAN: www.amscan.com or 800-284-4333.

■ "First Down" molded candle (twelve for $3.25), a "First Down" sign ($3.75 for a pack of twelve), "First Down" party cups ($.99 for twelve), "First Down" confetti cocktail ($2.00 per package), sparklers, or football candles (twelve packages are $2.50).

■ Bags in every color ($2.25 for twelve packs of twenty-five large and $1.95 for twelve packs of twenty-five small ones).

■ Football cut-outs (30 cents for twelve 5-inchers to 95 cents for twelve 15-inchers).

■ Markers ($2.25 for six).

■ Metallic Curling Ribbon ($8.00 for six rolls), bell weights (25 cents apiece).

■ Metallic football balloons ($2.80 for ten) and latex balloons that say "First Down"($2.00 for twelve).

■ Plastic balloon pump ($5.00 for six pieces).

■ Silly String, $3 per bottle.

■ Toothpicks with footballs ($1.55 for twelve packages of ten).

OVER-THE-TOP ADDITIONS
■ Get DIRTY TAROT CARDS and do readings for your guests: www.dirty tarot.com.

DRINK UP!
Energy supplements for the non-alcoholic road to recovery
■ EMERGEN-C, Alacer Corporation: www.alacer corp.com.

■ GEN BEI, at ELIXIR in Los Angeles, 310-657-9310 or www.elixir.net, and the Stein Ericksen Lodge Spa in Deer Valley, Utah, 435-649-3700.

■ BEROCCA: www.berocca.co.za

■ COUNTRY LIFE VITAMINS: www.country-life.com or 800-645-5768.

■ TRADITIONAL MEDICINAL'S DE-TOX TEA: www.tradi tionalmedicinals.com or 800-543-4372

■ Try MR AND MRS T's for great bloody mary mix, available at www.motts.com.

CHAPTER TEN: RECIPES GALORE

DRINKS

- The Bellini from HARRY CIPRIANI in New York City: 212-343-0999.
- CHATEAU MARMONT Kir Royale: 323-656-1010.
- The Myntini from MYNT in Miami: 768-267-6132.
- NOBU French Martini, in New York: 212-941-1976. (Note: There are also locations in Las Vegas, London, Malibu, and Miami.)
- BOND STREET'S Saketini Martini, locations in Miami, 305-534-3800, and New York, 212-777-2500.
- 60 THOMPSON Thom Martini, in New York City: 212-431-0400.
- METRO Apple Margarita, in Miami: 305-270-4981.
- Planter's Punch from the ISLE DE FRANCE HOTEL RESTAURANT in St. Barth's: 011-59-05-90-27-61-81.
- The Scorpion Bowl, patented by TRADER VIC'S, a Polynesian restaurant in the Beverly Hilton Hotel: 310-276-6345.
- Two great drinks from ASIA DE CUBA: the Tiki Puka Puka and the Mambo King in New York City: 212-726-7755, and California, 323-848-6000.
- The Strawberry Mojito from BUNGA-LOW 8 in New York City: 212-279-3215.
- MATUSALEM Ultimate Mojito: www.spiritofcuba.com.
- SUITE 16 Party Monster, in New York City: 212-627-1680.
- VILLA DOLCE Caramella: 818-781-3534.
- The Sgroppino, a traditional Venetian drink, served at DA SILVANO RESTAUR-ANT in New York City: 212-982-2343.
- TANQUERAY No. TEN Smoothie: www.tanqueray.com.
- Keoki Coffee from the STEIN ERICKSEN LODGE in Dear Valley, Utah: 800-453-1302.
- Iced Tea from LAS VENTANAS, Los Cabos, Mexico: 011-52-624-1440-0300.

FOOD

- Guacamole from ROSA MEXICANO, a famous upscale Mexican restaurant in Manhattan: 212-753-7407.
- CALIFORNIA PIZZA KITCHEN Spinach Artichoke Dip: 310-342-5000 or www.cpk.com.
- Sam and Steven's Cereal Soup from THAT BAR in Brooklyn, New York: 718-260-8900.
- STEIN ERIKSON LODGE Cheese Fondue, in Deer Valley, Utah: 800-453-1302.
- Tuna tartare in an Asian vinaigrette with chili oil and sesame soy emulsion; Thai green curry shrimp with coriander rice and fried basil, both from the CLIFF in Barbados: 246-432-1922.
- Best tomato soup on earth from BARTON G. in Miami: 305-576-8888.
- Mexican grilled-turkey chopped salad from the PINK TACO RESTAURANT at the HARD ROCK HOTEL AND CASINO in Las Vegas: 702-693-5525.
- Watermelon–goat cheese salad from DUNE at the OCEAN CLUB RESORT in the Bahamas: 242-322-2606.
- Eggless tofu salad from WHOLE FOODS: www.wholefoods.com.
- House Salad and Chicken Piccata from TUSCAN STEAK in New York City, 212-977-7777, and Miami, 305-534-2233.

- Calamari salad from ASIA DE CUBA, locations in New York City, 212-726-7755, and Los Angeles, 323-848-6000.
- Salad dressing from the SOUTHAMPTON PRINCESS DINER in Southampton, New York: 631-283-4255.
- BERGDORF GOODMAN'S Thousand Island dressing: 212-753-7300.
- Apricot and currant chicken, courtesy of *THE SILVER PALATE COOKBOOK*.
- Steak au Poivre from RAOUL'S in New York City: 212-966-3518.
- Whitefish from AGO in Los Angeles: 323-655-6333.
- Black Cod with Miso from NOBU in New York City: 212-219-0500.
- Risotto ai Carciofi (poached artichokes) from DA SILVANO RESTAURANT in New York City: 212-982-2343.
- Creamed spinach and hash browns, both from JOE'S STONE CRAB: www.joesstonecrab.com or 800-260-CRAB.
- THE FORGE Haricots Verts: 305-538-8533.

DESSERTS
- Petit fours from LE CIRQUE 2000 in New York City: 212-303-7788.
- New York City's MAGNOLIA BAKERY cupcakes with sweet buttercream icing: 212-462-2572.
- DELANO HOTEL Baked Apple, from Blue Door at the Delano Hotel in Miami: 305-674-6400.
- SERENDIPITY 3's frozen hot chocolate: 800-672-9466 or 212-838-3531.
- Roasted banana from INDOCHINE in New York City: 212-505-5111.
- BEVERLY HILTON HOTEL's baked Alaska: 310-274-7777.

- DELANO HOTEL White Chocolate Yogurt, in Miami: 305-672-2000.
- BUBBIE'S HOMEMADE ICE CREAM AND DESSERTS in Aiea, Hawaii, and elsewhere in Hawaii, for mochi ice cream: 808-487-7218.
- IVY Sticky Toffee Pudding, London, England: 011-44-20-7836-4751.
- KATHLEEN'S Cookies, from her cookbook, *Kathleen's Bakeshop Cookbook*.
- THE COFFEE BEAN & TEA LEAF® Ice Blendeds: 800-TEA-LEAF or www.coffeebean.com.

RECIPES FROM THESE COOKBOOKS
- *The Harry's Bar Cookbook* by Arrigo Cipriani (Doubleday).
- *The Da Silvano Cookbook* by Silvano Marchetto (Bloomsbury).
- *Rosa Mexicano* by Josefina Howard (Viking).
- *The California Pizza Kitchen Cookbook* by Larry Flax and Rick Rosenfeld (Hungry Minds).
- *The Cliff Recipes* by Paul Owens (Miller S. Publishing Company).
- *The Silver Palate Cookbook* by Julee Rosso and Sheila Lukins (Workman Publishing).
- *Nobu: The Cookbook* by Nobu Matsuhisa (Koshanda International).
- *Eat at Joe's* by Joanne Bass and Richard Sax (Bay Books).
- *The Magnolia Bakery Cookbook: Old-Fashioned Recipes from New York's Sweetest Bakery* by Jennifer Appel, Allysa Torey, and Rita Maas (Simon & Schuster).
- *The Ivy: The Restaurant and Its Recipes* by A. J. Gill (Trafalgar Square).
- *Kathleen's Bake Shop Cookbook* by Kathleen King (St. Martin's Press).

RESOURCE GUIDE CAPTIONS

PAGE 250: LEFT: Invitation to the launch of Shoshanna at Scoop uptown. RIGHT: Man-eater book party invitation designed by Creative Intelligence, Inc./LA-NY.

PAGE 251: LEFT: FCUK fragrance launch invitation. Thanks to French Connection United Kingdom for creating and producing the invite. RIGHT: *Playboy*'s 50th anniversary invitation.

PAGE 252: LEFT: Candle centerpiece. © Cesare Bonazza. RIGHT: Jonathan Shriftman spins the night away at Lara & Lara's Old Hollywood Bash. Photo by Jeff Vespa/WireImage.com.

PAGE 253: LEFT: Julia Stiles playing Sony PlayStation 2 at the Hugo House at Sundance. Photo by Jeff Vespa/WireImage.com. RIGHT:

Location is everything, which is why we found this amazing private home. Photo by Amy Graves/WireImage.com.

PAGE 254: LEFT: Drea De Matteo. Photo by Denise Truscello/WireImage.com. RIGHT: Self-service at the Hudson Hotel. Photo by Billy Farrell/PMc.

PAGE 255: LEFT: Bar accoutrements from Crate & Barrel. Photo by Paul Costello. RIGHT: Spice up your bottle service by setting it up with a bevvy of flavors of Rose's Cocktail Infusion. Cosmos, Blue Raspberry Martinis, or Appletinis, anyone? Photo by Jeff Vespa/WireImage.com.

PAGE 256: LEFT: What you need to start your party off right: great appetizers. Photo by Paul Costello. RIGHT: Cheese platters are never cheesy. Place *fro-*

mage neatly on a tray, embellished with fresh fruit and a serving knife. Photo by Paul Costello.

PAGE 257: LEFT: Lara Flynn Boyle with her Cold Stone Creamery cake at Lara & Lara's Old Hollywood Bash. Photo by Jeff Vespa/WireImage.com. RIGHT: Rachel Hunter and her birthday cake at the opening of the Morgan Bar. Photo by Patrick McMullan/PMc.

PAGE 258: LEFT: Lara Shriftman and Chris Heinz and their cake at their Pimps & Ho's birthday party. Photo by Patrick McMullan/PMc. RIGHT: Dessert at the David Bowie after-party at the Hard Rock Hotel & Casino. Photo by Jeff Vespa/WireImage.com.

PAGE 259: LEFT: Elizabeth Harrison, Bonnie Fuller, and Kyra Sedgwick at the American Museum of Natural

History. Photo by Patrick McMullan/PMc. RIGHT: A thank-you note from John Pennoti and Fisher Stevens that came with flowers.

PAGE 260: LEFT: Perfect poses. Photo by Patrick McMullan/PMc. RIGHT: Setting the table is as much a part of etiquette as making guests feel at home. Photo by Sara Jaye.

PAGE 261: LEFT: Clambake inspiration board. Photo by Paul Costello. RIGHT: Barbie themed Krispy Kreme cake. © Cesare Bonazza.

PAGE 262: LEFT: Barbies and Ken go wild. © Cesare Bonazza. RIGHT: Family's Jewels at the Afternoon Tea Party. Photo by Jeff Vespa/WireImage.com.

PAGE 263: LEFT: Tori Spelling shopping at the Juicy Day of Indulgence. Photo by Lester Cohen/

WireImage.com. RIGHT: Nail polishes galore. Photo by Paul Costello.

PAGE 264: LEFT: Rosanna Arquette at the Charles Worthington Golden Globes Suite. Photo by Amy Graves/WireImage.com. RIGHT: Shiva Rose at the Charles Worthington Dream Couture Bungalow at the Beverly Hills Hotel. Photo by Donato Sardella/WireImage.com.

PAGE 265: LEFT: Oranges and an Indian statue—perfect décor for our Indian Dinner. Photo by Paul Costello. RIGHT: The Indian Dinner menu is printed on gold-leaf paper and enhanced with a gold-foil wrapped rose. Photo by Paul Costello.

PAGE 266: LEFT: Everything you'll need for a Hangover Brunch. Photo by Paul Costello. RIGHT: Minis! Comfort food in

bite-sized portions becomes instantly gourmet. Photo by Paul Costello.

PAGE 267: LEFT: Trader Vic's Scorpion Bowl. Photo by Paul Costello. RIGHT: Serve classic, traditional food in a non-traditional way. Here, Ceviche "Vuelve a la Vida" (in highball glasses). Photo by Seth Browarnik/Red Eye Productions.

PAGE 268: LEFT: Popcorn shrimp pops in an old-fashioned popcorn box, turned on its side and overflowing with crispy shrimp and movie theater popcorn. Photo by Cary Songy/Barton G. Restaurant. RIGHT: Chocolate hearts from La Conversation, a great addition to any party or a great gift. Photo by Paul Costello.

INDEX

after-dinner drinks
    Caramella, 214
    Keoki Coffee, 216
    Limoncello, 214
    No. Ten Smoothie, 215
    Sgroppino, 215
    types of, 103
afternoon tea. *See* tea parties
airport runway parties, 34
alcohol. *See also specific types*
    after-dinner drinks, 103
    apéritifs, 102
    beer, 100–101
    champagne, 99–100
    cordials, 102–3
    drinks per bottle, 89
    flaming drinks, 106
    flavoring desserts with, 139
    for home bar, 94
    how much to buy, 89, 94
    mixers for, 94, 95
    most popular cocktails, 88
    pouring method, 93
    at restaurants, 31
    sake, 104
    serving, bartenders for, 93
    serving, buffet-style, 91
    serving, from less-is-more bar, 96
    serving, from minibars, 91–92
    serving, fun ideas for, 104–6
    serving, in shot cooler, 92
    serving, with bottle service, 92

serving, with do-it-yourself bar, 92
    tequila, 101–2
    wine, 96–98
Amaretto di Saronno, 103
antiques store parties, 34
apéritifs, 102
appetizers
    Artichoke Risotto, 235
    Cheese Fondue, 220
    Fruit Ceviche, 164
    Guacamole, 217
    Sam and Steven's Cereal Soup, 219
    Spinach Artichoke Dip, 218
    suggested foods for, 116–18
    Tomato Soup, 222
    Tuna Tartare, 221
apple cider, serving, 105
art gallery parties, 33
arts-and-crafts studio parties, 35
astrology parties, 21, 83
baby zone parties, 19
Bailey's Irish Cream, 103
banana garnishes, 95
bar, at home
    accoutrements for, 91
    beer and wine for, 94
    champagne for, 94
    flavor boosters for, 95
    garnishes for, 95
    liquor for, 94
    location for, 93

mixers for, 94, 95
    resource guide for, 254
    self-serve, 91–92
    setup, for 20–30 guests, 94
    setup, for 50 guests, 94
bar, "cash" and "open," 31, 32
Barbie and Ken party (case study), 166–71
bars and clubs, parties at, 32
bartenders, hiring, 93
bartenders, naked, 81
bathrooms, 25, 85
beach parties, 20
    Hamptons-style clambake (case study), 162–65
    proper attire for, 152
    suggested music for, 75
beauty party (case study), 182–87
beauty salon parties, 33
bedrooms, catching guests in, 147
bedrooms, closing off, 25
beer
    cocktail, preparing, 101
    for home bar, 94
    imported, 100–101
    pouring, 101
    resource guide for, 255
    serving, 101
behavior. *See* manners
beverages. *See* drinks
birthday cakes, 29
birthday party invitations, 55

bitters, 95
boardwalk parties, 33
boat parties, 33
borders, on invitations, 40
bourbon, 94, 103
bowling parties, 20
boxing ring parties, 34
brandy, 103
breadsticks, serving, 115
brownies, serving, 131–32
brunch parties
    glassware for, 89
    "hangover" (case study), 194–99
    proper attire for, 152
    suggested drinks for, 107
    suggested music for, 74
budgets. *See also* expenses
    determining, 14, 21
    template for, 248–49
cakes, birthday, 29
calligraphy, 42
Calvados, 103
cameras, 80
candles, 70–71
candle wax, removing, 24
candy
    with cocktails, 20, 104–5, 138
    for dessert, 136
    resource guide for, 255, 258
candy store parties, 35
canopy, creating, 27
cappuccino machines, 108

car dealership parties, 21
card stock, 40
caricature artists, 81
carpet runners, 169
case studies
   afternoon tea party, 176–81
   Barbie and Ken party, 166–71
   beauty party, 182–87
   guys' night out, 200–203
   Hamptons-style clambake,
    162–65
   hangover brunch, 194–99
   Indian feast, 188–93
   roller-skating party, 172–75
cash bar, 31, 32
caterers, 131
caviar, 116
celery garnishes, 95
centerpieces, 65–66
champagne
   bobbing for apples in, 105
   buying, for brunch, 89
   buying, terms to know, 100
   buying, tip for, 99
   for home bar, 94
   inexpensive, serving, 99
   major brands, 99
   opening, 99
   pouring, 99
   serving ideas, 99–100
   servings per bottle, 89
champagne recipes
   Cipriani's Bellini, 207
   Kir Royale, 207
   Mambo King, 211
cheerleaders, 83
cheese, serving, 115
cherry garnishes, 95
chile peppers, for drinks, 95
chocolate
   resource guide for, 257–58
   serving ideas, 131–33
cinnamon sticks, 95
clambake, Hamptons-style (case
   study), 162–65
classic invitations
   basic formula for, 39
   boxed cards, embellishing, 41
   calligraphy for, 42
   computer-generated, 43
   custom-ordering, 40–41
   fonts and motifs for, 42–44
   resource guide for, 250–51
   with a twist, creating, 45
clothing, for parties, 152
clothing store parties, 34
coat racks, 25
cocktail parties
   at bar or nightclub, 32
   chic tips for, 106
   drinks, for 20–30 guests, 94
   drinks, for 50 guests, 94
   glassware for, 89
   proper attire for, 152
   serving candy at, 20, 104–5,
    138
   serving desserts at, 138
   suggested drinks for, 107
   suggested hors d'oeuvres for,
    116–18
   suggested music for, 74–75

coffee
   adding liquor to, 106
   alternatives to, 109
   creative serving ideas, 108–9
   Keoki Coffee, 216
   serving tips, 109
cognac, 103
color theme parties, 18
computer-generated invitations,
   43
concepts, 13–17. See also theme
   parties
contracts, signing, 32
conversation skills, 145, 154
cookies
   Chocolate Chip Cookies, 247
   creative ideas for, 131–32
   Rugalach, 242
cordials, 102–3
corkage fees, 29
country club parties, 34
craft parties, 20
crazy straws, 105
crudités, 115
cupcakes, serving, 132
custom-ordered invitations, 40–41
daiquiri machines, 105
dancers, professional, 82
décor
   bathroom, 25, 85
   budget template for, 248
   cheap tricks for, 80–83
   details and choices, 14
   flowers, 29, 67–69, 85
   furniture, 25–26, 63–64, 163
   gift bags, 79–80
   lighting, 69–72
   matching with theme, 61–62
   music, 29, 72–79
   resource guide for, 252–53
   at restaurants, 29
   special touches, 14
   tabletop accents, 64–66
dessert recipes
   Baked Apple, 240
   Buttercream Vanilla Icing, 240
   Chocolate Chip Cookies, 247
   Frozen Hot Chocolate, 241
   Griff's Baked Alaska, 244
   Microwave Mochi, 245
   Petit Fours, 238
   Roasted Banana with Coconut
    Sauce, 243
   Rugalach, 242
   Sticky Toffee Pudding, 246
   Vanilla Cupcakes, 239
   Vanilla Ice Blended, 247
   White Chocolate Yogurt, 244
desserts
   for buffet dinner party, 139
   candy, 136
   chocolate, 131–33
   for cocktail party, 20, 104–5,
    138
   cookies and brownies, 131–32
   for dessert and dancing party,
    139
   flavoring, with alcohol, 139
   health-conscious, 137
   homemade, ideas for, 128, 131
   ice cream, 133–35

for luncheons, 138
matching with theme, 130–31
resource guide for, 257–58
for seated dinner party, 129–30
serving, equipment for, 128–29
serving, ideas for, 129–30
store-bought, dressing up, 137
detox day parties, 20
diners, parties at, 33
dinner parties
   glassware for, 89
   invitations for, 55
   limiting length of cocktail hour,
    116
   planning, time line for, 33
   planning food for, 119–20
   proper attire for, 152
   at restaurants, 28–31
   rules for, 120
   seating arrangements for, 142–
    44
   serving meal on time, 147
   several types of wine at, 97
   suggested desserts for, 129–
    30, 139
   suggested drinks for, 107
   suggested music for, 75
   table settings for, 142
   wine amounts for, 89
dips
   Cheese Fondue, 220
   Guacamole, 217
   popular choices for, 116
   Spinach Artichoke Dip, 218
direction cards or maps, 56, 58
doorperson, at restaurant, 30
drink recipes
   Apple Margarita, 209
   Caramella, 214
   Cipriani's Bellini, 207
   French Martini, 208
   Iced Tea, 216
   Jell-O Shots, 213
   Jerry's Planter's Punch, 210
   Keoki Coffee, 216
   Kir Royale, 207
   Limoncello, 214
   Lot 61 Spicy Pineapple Punch,
    193
   Mambo King, 211
   Mediterraneo Iced Tea, 180
   Myntini, 208
   No. Ten Smoothie, 215
   Party Monster, 213
   Saketini, 209
   Scorpion Bowl, 210
   Sgroppino, 215
   Strawberry Mojito, 212
   Thom Martini, 209
   Tiki Puka Puka, 211
   Ultimate Mojito, 212
drinks. See also specific types
   after-dinner, 103
   apéritifs, 102
   bartenders for, 93
   beer, 100–101
   budget template for, 248
   buying alcohol and wine for,
    89, 94
   champagne, 99–100
   champagne servings per

bottle, 89
coffee and tea, 108–9
cordials, 102–3
flamed, 106
flavor boosters for, 95
garnishes for, 95, 105
glassware for, 89–90
for home bar, 94–96
ice supplies for, 89
menu options, 13–14
menus, examples of, 107–8
mixed drinks per bottle, 89
mixers for, 94, 95
most popular cocktails, 88
offering, upon guests' arrival,
   93
pouring method, 93
resource guides for, 254–55,
   267
at restaurants, 31
sake, 104
serving, bartenders for, 93
serving, buffet-style, 91
serving, from less-is-more bar,
   96
serving, from minibars, 91–92
serving, fun ideas for, 104–6
serving, in shot cooler, 92
serving, with bottle service, 92
serving, with do-it-yourself bar,
   92
tequila, 101–2
"white-only," serving, 105
wine, 96–98
wine servings per bottle, 89
edamame, serving, 115
engraved invitations, 40
engraving styles, 44
entrée recipes
   Apricot and Currant Chicken,
    230
   Artichoke Risotto, 235
   Black Cod with Miso, 233
   Chicken Picatta and Angel Hair
    Pasta, 231
   Steak au Poivre, 232
   Thai Curry Shrimp with
    Coriander Rice and Fried
    Basil, 234
   Whitefish, 232
envelopes, for invitations, 52–53
etiquette. See manners
expenses
   budget template for, 248–49
   deejays, 73
   live music, 73, 79
   restaurant, 28–32
   servers, 26–27, 114
   tips, 147–48
face painters, 81
fashion "faux pas" parties, 18
film screenings, 82
fishbowls, serving drinks in, 105
flamed drinks, 106
flowers
   arranging, 68
   in bathroom, 85
   choosing, 67–68
   quick fix ideas, 69
   at restaurant, 29
   where to place, 68–69

font styles and motifs, 42–44, 46
food. *See also* desserts; recipes
  basic rules for, 124
  budget template for, 248
  for classic cocktail party, 116–18
  for dinner party, 119–20
  dips, 116
  for late-night party, 121–22
  for luncheon, 122–24
  matching to theme, 111–12
  menu options, 14
  ordering, at restaurants, 30–31
  ordering in, ideas for, 124
  resource guides for, 256, 267–68
  serving, options for, 14, 114
  serving, tips for, 112–13
fruit juices, 94
fruit purées, 94
fruits, dried, serving, 115
funky and fun invitations
  crafty, tips for, 46–47
  font styles for, 46
  resource guide for, 250–51
  store-bought, embellishing, 46
furniture
  for outdoor parties, 163
  party-proofing, 24–25
  rearranging, 25, 63–64
  renting, 25–26
  resource guide for, 252
furniture store parties, 34
gambling parties, 19
games, party, 84
garnishes, drink, 95, 105
gifts
  bringing to party, 151–52
  guest gift bags, 79–80
  invitations as, ideas for, 48–51
  resource guide for, 259–60
gimmicky invitations, 48–51
  resource guide for, 251
gin, for home bar, 94
ginger, for drinks, 95
girls' night out parties, 20, 55
glassware
  buying, 90
  chilling, for beer, 101
  creative ideas for, 90
  frosting, 93
  numbers needed, 89
  renting, 90
  salt- or sugar-rimmed, 93
  types of, 90
go-cart race track parties, 35
Godiva liqueur, 103
Grand Marnier, 103
grappa, 103
Greek dips, serving, 116
grenadine, 95
guacamole, serving, 116
guest books, 81
guests
  arriving at party, 152
  conversational skills, 145, 154
  deciding number of, 13
  gift bags for, 79–80
  greeting, at party, 145–46
  hostess gifts from, 151–52
  inebriated, handling, 146

introducing, 146
leaving party, 152
no-shows, planning for, 39
over-inviting, benefits of, 38
party attire for, 152
party manners for, 150–59
posing for pictures, 157–59
responding to invitations, 150–51
seating, at tables, 142–44
"surprise," benefits of, 39
table manners, 155
thank-you notes from, 148–50, 154
toasts and speeches by, 156
for two-part parties, 38
unwanted, handling, 146
who to invite, 37–39
guys' night out (case study), 200–203
hangover brunch (case study), 194–99
heaven and hell parties, 19
henna tattoo artists, 81
herb infusions, 94
home-based parties
  benefits of, 23–24
  hiring help for, 26–27
  preparing house for, 24–25
  renting supplies for, 25–26
hotel ballroom parties, 34
hotel suite parties, 34
hummus, serving, 116
ice, for drinks, 89
ice cream
  resource guide for, 258
  serving ideas, 133–35
ice sculptures, 105
Indian feast (case study), 188–93
insurance, liability, 25
introductions, etiquette for, 146
invitations
  boxed, embellishing, 41, 46, 47
  budget template for, 248
  calligraphy for, 42
  classic style, 39–45
  computer-generated, 43
  crafty, tips for, 46–47
  custom-ordering, 40–41
  envelopes for, 52–53
  extra, buying, 40
  fonts and motifs for, 42–44, 46
  funky and fun style, 46–48
  gimmicky and kitschy style, 48–51
  mailing tips, 58–59
  as pre-party gift, 48–51
  resource guide for, 250–51
  responding to, 150–51
  response cards with, 56, 57
  tracking responses to, 59
  wording on, 53–55
Jell-O shots, serving, 106
jukeboxes, 78
karaoke machines, 78
kitschy invitations, 48–51
  resource guide for, 251
lakeside parties, 35
late-night parties
  attire for, 152

planning food for, 121–22
suggested desserts for, 139
suggested drinks for, 107
lemon garnishes, 95
licorice sticks, 105
lighting
  candles, 70–71
  creative ideas for, 70–71
  exterior, 72
  matching with theme, 69
  resource guide for, 252
  rules for, 70
Lillet, 102
lime garnishes, 95
live performers, 73, 78–79
location
  bars or nightclubs, 32
  budget template for, 248
  choosing, 14
  home-based parties, 23–27
  outdoor-based parties, 27
  providing directions to, 56, 58
  resource guide for, 250
  restaurants, 28–31
  unusual ideas for, 33–35
lotto tickets, 83
luncheon recipes
  Calamari Salad, 227
  Eggless Tofu Salad, 225
  Greek Salad Dressing, 228
  House Salad, 226
  Mexican Grilled-Turkey Chopped Salad, 223
  Thousand Island Dressing, 229
  Watermelon–Goat Cheese Salad, 224
luncheons
  planning food for, 122–24
  proper attire for, 152
  sample invitation for, 55
  suggested desserts for, 138
  suggested drinks for, 108
  suggested music for, 74
  suggested salads for, 122–24
  take-out food for, 124
magicians, 81
makeup artists, 81
mani-pedi party (case study), 182–87
manners
  arriving at party, 152
  conversation skills, 154
  greeting guests, 145–46
  for guests, 150–59
  handling inebriated guests, 146
  handling unwanted guests, 146
  for hostess, 141–49, 154–59
  hostess gifts, 151–52
  leaving party early, 152
  making introductions, 146
  paying bills, 147
  picture-taking, 157–59
  proper party attire, 152
  removing stains, 157, 159
  resource guide for, 259–60
  responding to invitations, 150–51
  seating guests, 142–44

setting the table, 142
table manners, 155
thank-you notes, 148–50, 154
tipping hired help, 147–48
toasts and speeches, 156
Maraschino cherry garnishes, 95
margaritas
  Apple Margarita, 209
  serving, ideas for, 102
Marrakesh Express party, 19
martinis
  French Martini, 208
  Myntini, 208
  Saketini, 209
  serving, tip for, 93
  Thom Martini, 209
masked ball parties, 19
menus, drink, 107–8
menus, restaurant, 29–31
miniature golf parties, 35
minimum guarantees, 29
mint garnishes, 95
mints, personalized, 83
mixers, for home bar, 94, 95
monogrammed napkins, 82
monogramming, on invitations, 40
motel parties, 34
motifs, on invitations, 40
mountaintop parties, 34
movie soundtracks, 77
movie theater parties, 34
music
  budget template for, 249
  compilation CDs, 76
  hiring help for, 73
  live performers, 78–79
  mixing, ideas for, 78
  movie soundtracks, 77
  resource guide for, 253
  at restaurants, 29
  sound equipment for, 72
  suggestions for, 74–75
name tags, 81, 82
napkins, monogrammed, 82
nightclubs, 32
office space parties, 35
olive garnishes, 95
olives, serving, 115
open bar, 31, 32
orange garnishes, 95
Oscar-night party invitations, 55
outdoor parties, 20, 27
  clambake (case study), 162–65
  lighting for, 72
  proper attire for, 152
  suggested music for, 75
  warm clothing for, 81
out-of-state parties, 34
pajama parties, 19
parents' houses, parties at, 33
parking lot parties, 35
peppercorns, for drinks, 95
Pernod, 102
pets, at parties, 25
photo booths, 80–81
photo studio parties, 34
picture-taking, 157–59
pineapple garnishes, 95
place cards, 66, 144
place settings, 142

poolside parties, 34
popcorn, 115
port, 103
post office rules, 58–59
production. *See* décor
psychics, 81
recipes (appetizers)
    Artichoke Risotto, 235
    Cheese Fondue, 220
    Fruit Ceviche, 164
    Guacamole, 217
    Sam and Steven's Cereal
      Soup, 219
    Spinach Artichoke Dip, 218
    Tomato Soup, 222
    Tuna Tartare, 221
recipes (desserts)
    Baked Apple, 240
    Buttercream Vanilla Icing, 240
    Chocolate Chip Cookies, 247
    Frozen Hot Chocolate, 241
    Griff's Baked Alaska, 244
    Microwave Mochi, 245
    Petit Fours, 238
    Roasted Banana with Coconut
      Sauce, 243
    Rugalach, 242
    Sticky Toffee Pudding, 246
    Vanilla Cupcakes, 239
    Vanilla Ice Blended, 247
    White Chocolate Yogurt, 244
recipes (drinks)
    Apple Margarita, 209
    Bellini, 207
    Caramella, 214
    French Martini, 208
    Iced Tea, 216
    Jell-O Shots, 213
    Jerry's Planter's Punch, 210
    Keoki Coffee, 216
    Kir Royale, 207
    Limoncello, 214
    Lot 61 Spicy Pineapple Punch,
      193
    Mambo King, 211
    Mediterraneo Iced Tea, 180
    Myntini, 208
    No. Ten Smoothie, 215
    Party Monster, 213
    Saketini, 209
    Scorpion Bowl, 210
    Sgroppino, 215
    Strawberry Mojito, 212
    Thom Martini, 209
    Tiki Puka Puka, 211
    Ultimate Mojito, 212
recipes (entrées)
    Apricot and Currant Chicken,
      230
    Artichoke Risotto, 235
    Black Cod with Miso, 233
    Chicken Picatta and Angel Hair
      Pasta, 231
    Steak au Poivre, 232
    Thai Curry Shrimp with
      Coriander Rice and Fried
      Basil, 234
    Whitefish, 232
recipes (salads and dressings)
    Calamari Salad, 227

Eggless Tofu Salad, 225
Greek Salad Dressing, 228
House Salad, 226
Mexican Grilled-Turkey
  Chopped Salad, 223
Thousand Island Dressing,
  229
Watermelon–Goat Cheese
  Salad, 224
recipes (side dishes)
    Creamed Spinach, 236
    Haricots Verts, 236
    Hash Browns, 237
    Mommer's Fried Matzoh, 199
rental services, 25–26
response cards, 56, 57
restaurant parties
    choosing restaurant, 28
    contract for, 32
    drink choices for, 31
    food choices for, 29–31
    leaving tip at, 148
    venue fees for, 28–30
Ricard, 102
roasting guest of honor parties,
  21
roller-skating parties, 20
roller-skating party (case study),
  172–75
roof deck parties, 35
rugs, carpet runners for, 169
rum
    Caramella, 214
    for home bar, 94
    Jerry's Planter's Punch, 210
    Scorpion Bowl, 210
    Strawberry Mojito, 212
    Tiki Puka Puka, 211
    Ultimate Mojito, 212
sake, 104
    Saketini, 209
salad and dressing recipes
    Calamari Salad, 227
    Eggless Tofu Salad, 225
    Greek Salad Dressing, 228
    House Salad, 226
    Mexican Grilled-Turkey
      Chopped Salad, 223
    Thousand Island Dressing, 229
    Watermelon–Goat Cheese
      Salad, 224
salads, healthy ideas for, 122–24
salsa, serving, 116
salt, for drinks, 95
save-the-date cards, 40, 56
scotch, 94, 103
screwdriver popsicles, 105
seating, assigning, 142–44
seating, mixing up, 83
servers
    for dessert, 129
    dress code for, 26
    feeding, 147
    hiring, 26, 114
    instructions for, 26–27
    resource guide for, 254
    in restaurants, 29
    tips for, 147
sherry, 102
shots, serving, 92, 101, 105, 106

side dish recipes
    Creamed Spinach, 236
    Haricots Verts, 236
    Hash Browns, 237
    Mommer's Fried Matzoh, 199
silverware, placement of, 142
single-barrel bourbon, 103
single-malt scotch, 103
slumber parties, 18
smoke machines, 82
smoking, at parties, 25
snow cones, alcoholic, 105
sodas, 94
soundtracks, movie, 77
spa and beauty party (case
  study), 182–87
spa parties, 20
speeches and toasts, 156
stains, removing, 157, 159
Tabasco sauce, 95
tabbouleh, serving, 116
tablecloths, paper, 83
table manners, 155
tables, seating at, 83, 142–44
table settings, 142
tabletop accents, 64–66
taramosalata, serving, 116
tarot card readers, 81
Tarzan and Jane parties, 19
tattoo artists, 81
tea, serving, 108–9
tea parties
    afternoon (case study), 176–
      81
    proper attire for, 152
    suggested music for, 74
telescopes, 83
tequila
    Apple Margarita, 209
    brand names, 101
    Party Monster, 213
    serving, ideas for, 101, 102
    types of, 101
thank-you notes
    favorite examples of, 149–50
    ordering, 40
    resource guide for, 260
    rules for, 148, 154
theme park parties, 33
theme parties
    afternoon tea (case study),
      176–81
    astrology, 21
    baby zone, 19
    Barbie and Ken (case study),
      166–71
    beach seafood feast, 20
    beauty (case study), 182–87
    bowling extravaganza, 20
    clambake (case study), 162–
      65
    cocktails and candy, 20
    craft-making party, 20
    detox day, 20
    fashion "faux pas-ty," 18
    favorite games, 84
    gambling, 19
    girls' night out, 20
    guy's night out (case study),
      200–203

hangover brunch (case study),
  194–99
heaven and hell, 19
Indian feast (case study), 188–
  93
Marrakesh express, 19
matching décor to, 61–62
matching desserts to, 130–31
matching food to, 111–12
one-color theme, 18
pajamas-required, 19
roasting guest of honor, 21
roller-skating, 20
roller-skating (case study),
  172–75
slumber party, 18
Tarzan and Jane, 19
vehicular madness, 21
Venetian masked ball, 19
thermography, on invitations, 40
tipping, 147–48
toasts and speeches, 156
towels, bathroom, 85
toy store parties, 35
transportation, 83
tzatziki, serving, 116
vegetable juices, 94
Venetian masked ball parties, 19
venue fees, 28–30
video arcade parties, 35
vodka
    French Martini, 208
    for home bar, 94
    Jell-O Shots, 213
    Limoncello, 214
    Mambo King, 211
    Myntini, 208
    Saketini, 209
    Sgroppino, 215
    Thom Martini, 209
waiters. *See* servers
water, serving, 108
whipped cream garnishes, 95
whiskey, 94
wine
    basic information about, 97
    bringing to restaurant, 29
    buying, rules for, 97
    calculating bottles needed, 89
    corkage fees on, 29
    describing, terms for, 96–97
    French, about, 97
    for home bar, 94
    opening, 98
    pouring, 98
    resource guide for, 255
    rosé, about, 97
    sake, about, 104
    servings per bottle, 89
    serving temperatures, 97
    storing, 97
    styles of, 96–97
    tasting parties, 16
    for three-hour party, 89
    tips for, 89
    white, chilling, 97
    wine charms for, 98
yawning, manners for, 147